DIGITAL COMMUNICATION

AUTHORS

Prof. Muralidhar Kulkarni
Professor, Department of ECE,
National Institute of Technology
Karnataka

Prof. K. S. Shivaprakasha
Professor, Department of ECE,
NMAM Institute of Technology, NITTE,
Karnataka

REVIEWER

Prof. Harish Kumar Sahoo
Professor, Department of ECE
Veer Surendra Sai University of Technology,
Burla, Orissa

KHANNA BOOK PUBLISHING CO. (P) Ltd.
4C/4344, Ansari Road, Darya Ganj,
New Delhi, India

All India Council for Technical Education
Nelson Mandela Marg, Vasant Kunj,
New Delhi, India

Dear Readers,

To prevent the piracy, this book is secured with HIGH SECURITY HOLOGRAM on the front title cover. In case you don't find the hologram on the front cover title, please write us to at contact@khannabooks.com or whatsapp us at +91-99109 09320 and avail special gift voucher for yourself.

Specimen of Hologram on front Cover title:

Moreover, there is a SPECIAL DISCOUNT COUPON for you with EVERY HOLOGRAM.

How to avail this SPECIAL DISCOUNT:

Step 1: Scratch the hologram

Step 2: Under the scratch area, your "coupon code" is available

Step 3: Logon to www.khannabooks.com

Step 4: Use your "coupon code" in the shopping cart and get your copy at a special discount

Step 5: Enjoy your reading!

ISBN: 978-93-5538-330-3

Book Code: DIP464EN

Digital Communication

by Prof. Muralidhar Kulkarni,
Prof. K. S. Shivaprakasha

First Edition: 2026

Originally Published by:
All India Council for Technical Education, Ministry of Education, GOI

Exclusively Published & Distributed by:
Khanna Book Publishing Co. (P) Ltd.
4C/4344, Ansari Road, Daryaganj,
New Delhi (INDIA)

Visit us at: **www.khannabooks.com**
Write us at: **contact@khannabooks.com**

To view complete list of books, Please scan the QR Code: KPH

Printed in Bharat.

प्रो. टी. जी. सीताराम
अध्यक्ष
Prof. T. G. Sitharam
Chairman

सत्यमेव जयते

आज़ादी का अमृत महोत्सव

अखिल भारतीय तकनीकी शिक्षा परिषद्
(भारत सरकार का एक सांविधिक निकाय)
(शिक्षा मंत्रालय, भारत सरकार)
नेल्सन मंडेला मार्ग, वसंत कुंज, नई दिल्ली–110070
दूरभाष : 011–26131498
ई–मेल : chairman@aicte-india.org

ALL INDIA COUNCIL FOR TECHNICAL EDUCATION
(A STATUTORY BODY OF THE GOVT. OF INDIA)
(Ministry of Education, Govt. of India)
Nelson Mandela Marg, Vasant Kunj, New Delhi-110070
Phone : 011-26131498
E-mail : chairman@aicte-india.org

FOREWORD

Engineers are the backbone of any modern society. They are the ones responsible for the marvels as well as the improved quality of life across the world. Engineers have driven humanity towards greater heights in a more evolved and unprecedented manner.

The All India Council for Technical Education (AICTE), have spared no efforts towards the strengthening of the technical education in the country. AICTE is always committed towards promoting quality Technical Education to make India a modern developed nation emphasizing on the overall welfare of mankind.

An array of initiatives has been taken by AICTE in last decade which have been accelerated now by the National Education Policy (NEP) 2020. The implementation of NEP under the visionary leadership of Hon'ble Prime Minister of India envisages the provision for education in regional languages to all, thereby ensuring that every graduate becomes competent enough and is in a position to contribute towards the national growth and development through innovation & entrepreneurship.

One of the spheres where AICTE had been relentlessly working since past couple of years is providing high quality original technical contents at Under Graduate & Diploma level prepared and translated by eminent educators in various Indian languages to its aspirants. For students pursuing 2nd year of their Engineering education, AICTE has identified 87 books, which shall be translated into 12 Indian languages - Hindi, Tamil, Gujarati, Odia, Bengali, Kannada, Urdu, Punjabi, Telugu, Marathi, Assamese & Malayalam. In addition to the English medium, books in different Indian Languages are going to support the students to understand the concepts in their respective mother tongue.

On behalf of AICTE, I express sincere gratitude to all distinguished authors, reviewers and translators from the renowned institutions of high repute for their admirable contribution in a record span of time.

AICTE is confident that these outcomes based original contents shall help aspirants to master the subject with comprehension and greater ease.

T. G. Sitharam

(Prof. T. G. Sitharam)

ACKNOWLEDGEMENT

The authors are grateful to the authorities of AICTE, particularly Prof. T. G. Sitharam, Chairman; Prof. M. P. Poonia, Vice-Chairman; Prof. Rajive Kumar, Member-Secretary and Dr Amit Kumar Srivastava, Director, Faculty Development Cell for their planning to publish the books on Digital Communication. We sincerely acknowledge the valuable contributions of the reviewer of the book Prof. Harish Kumar Sahoo, Professor, Department of ECE, Veer Surendra Sai University of Technology, BURLA, Siddhi Vihar, Sambalpur, Orissa for making it students' friendly and giving a technical uplift to the contents of the book by very relevant suggestions for all the units. Special thanks to Mr. Ullas P., Mysuru for his help in preparing the images for the book.

This book is an outcome of various suggestions of AICTE members, experts and authors who shared their opinion and thought to further develop the engineering education in our country. Acknowledgements are due to the contributors and different workers in this field whose published books, review articles, papers, photographs, footnotes, references and other valuable information enriched us at the time of writing the book.

Prof. Muralidhar Kulkarni,

Prof. K. S. Shivaprakasha

PREFACE

The book titled "Digital Communication" is an outcome of the rich experience of our teaching of basic courses on Electronic Communications. The initiation of writing this book is to expose fundamentals of digital communications to the diploma students, the fundamentals of communication engineering and digital communications in particular, as well as enable them to get an insight of the subject. Keeping in mind the purpose of wide coverage as well as to provide essential supplementary information, we have included the topics recommended by AICTE, in a very systematic and orderly manner throughout the book. Efforts have been made to explain the fundamental concepts of the subject in the simplest possible way.

During the process of preparation of the manuscript, we have considered the various standard text books and accordingly we have developed sections like critical questions, solved and supplementary problems etc. While preparing the different sections emphasis has also been laid on definitions and laws and also on comprehensive synopsis of formulae for a quick revision of the basic principles. The book covers all types of medium and advanced level problems and these have been presented in a very logical and systematic manner. The gradations of those problems have been tested over many years of teaching to a wide variety of students.

Apart from illustrations and examples as required, we have enriched the book with numerous solved problems in every unit for proper understanding of the related topics. It is important to note that, we have included the relevant laboratory practical in addition to the theoretical concepts. In addition, besides some essential information for the users under the heading "Know More" we have clarified some essential basic information in the appendix and annexure section.

As far as the present book is concerned, "Digital Communication" is meant to provide a thorough grounding in the broad area of digital communications. This book will prepare diploma engineering students to apply the knowledge of Digital Communications to tackle 21st century and onward engineering challenges such as the 5G and 6G communications and address the related aroused questions. The subject matters are presented in a constructive manner so that a Diploma degree prepares students to work in different sectors or in national laboratories at the very forefront of technology.

We sincerely hope that the book will inspire the students to learn and discuss the ideas behind basic principles of communication engineering and will surely contribute to the development of a solid foundation of the subject. We would be thankful to all beneficial comments and suggestions which will contribute to the improvement of the future editions of the book. It gives us immense pleasure to place this book in the hands of the teachers and students. It was indeed a big pleasure to work on different aspects covered in the book.

Prof. Muralidhar Kulkarni,

Prof. K. S. Shivaprakasha

OUTCOME BASED EDUCATION

For the implementation of an outcome based education the first requirement is to develop an outcome based curriculum and incorporate an outcome based assessment in the education system. By going through outcome-based assessments, evaluators will be able to evaluate whether the students have achieved the outlined standard, specific and measurable outcomes. With the proper incorporation of outcome based education there will be a definite commitment to achieve a minimum standard for all learners without giving up at any level. At the end of the programme running with the aid of outcome based education, a student will be able to arrive at the following outcomes:

Programme Outcomes (POs) are statements that describe what students are expected to know and be able to do upon graduating from the program. These relate to the skills, knowledge, analytical ability attitude and behavior that students acquire through the program. The POs essentially indicate what the students can do from subject-wise knowledge acquired by them during the program. As such, POs define the professional profile of an engineering diploma graduate.

National Board of Accreditation (NBA) has defined the following seven POs for an Engineering diploma graduate:

PO1. **Basic and Discipline specific knowledge:** Apply knowledge of basic mathematics, science and engineering fundamentals and engineering specialization to solve the engineering problems.

PO2. **Problem analysis:** Identify and analyses well-defined engineering problems using codified standard methods.

PO3. **Design/ development of solutions:** Design solutions for well-defined technical problems and assist with the design of systems components or processes to meet specified needs.

PO4. **Engineering Tools, Experimentation and Testing:** Apply modern engineering tools and appropriate technique to conduct standard tests and measurements.

PO5. **Engineering practices for society, sustainability and environment:** Apply appropriate technology in context of society, sustainability, environment and ethical practices.

PO6. **Project Management:** Use engineering management principles individually, as a team member or a leader to manage projects and effectively communicate about well-defined engineering activities.

PO7. **Life-long learning:** Ability to analyze individual needs and engage in updating in the context of technological changes.

COURSE OUTCOMES (CO)

By the end of the course the students are expected to learn:

Describe the different types of baseband and passband modulation schemes and also various line codes

Describe the use of controlled intersymbol interference to achieve maximum data rates & channel equalization.

10. Syllabus

CO-1: Understand the building blocks of digital communication system.

CO-2: Determine the Nyquist sampling rate of a given signal & explain aliasing, number of levels in a quantizer given signal-to-noise ratio and maximum input voltage

CO-3: Understand working of waveform coding techniques and analyze their performance.

CO-4: Analyze the performance of a baseband and pass band digital communication system in terms of error rate and spectral efficiency and various line codes

CO-5: To explore and visualize data by using the applicability of topics learnt with the help of MATLAB.

Mapping of Course Outcomes with Programme Outcomes to be done according to the matrix given below:

Course Outcomes	EXPECTED MAPPING WITH PROGRAMME OUTCOMES (1- Weak Correlation; 2- Medium correlation; 3- Strong Correlation)						
	PO-1	PO-2	PO-3	PO-4	PO-5	PO-6	PO-7
CO-1	3	3	3	3	1	1	3
CO-2	3	2	2	2	1	1	3
CO-3	3	2	2	2	1	1	3
CO-4	3	2	2	3	1	1	3
CO-5	3	2	2	2	1	1	3

GUIDELINES FOR TEACHERS

To implement Outcome Based Education (OBE) knowledge level and skill set of the students should be enhanced. Teachers should take a major responsibility for the proper implementation of OBE. Some of the responsibilities (not limited to) for the teachers in OBE system may be as follows:

- Within reasonable constraint, they should manoeuvre time to the best advantage of all students.
- They should assess the students only upon certain defined criterion without considering any other potential ineligibility to discriminate them.
- They should try to grow the learning abilities of the students to a certain level before they leave the institute.
- They should try to ensure that all the students are equipped with the quality knowledge as well as competence after they finish their education.
- They should always encourage the students to develop their ultimate performance capabilities.
- They should facilitate and encourage group work and team work to consolidate newer approach.
- They should follow Blooms taxonomy in every part of the assessment.

Bloom's Taxonomy

Level	Teacher should Check	Student should be able to	Possible Mode of Assessment
Creating	Students ability to create	Design or Create	Mini project
Evaluating	Students ability to Justify	Argue or Defend	Assignment
Analysing	Students ability to distinguish	Differentiate or Distinguish	Project/Lab Methodology
Applying	Students ability to use information	Operate or Demonstrate	Technical Presentation/ Demonstration
Understanding	Students ability to explain the ideas	Explain or Classify	Presentation/Seminar
Remembering	Students ability to recall (or remember)	Define or Recall	Quiz

GUIDELINES FOR STUDENTS

Students should take equal responsibility for implementing the OBE. Some of the responsibilities (not limited to) for the students in OBE system are as follows:

- Students should be well aware of each UO before the start of a unit in each and every course.
- Students should be well aware of each CO before the start of the course.
- Students should be well aware of each PO before the start of the programme.
- Students should think critically and reasonably with proper reflection and action.
- Learning of the students should be connected and integrated with practical and real life consequences.
- Students should be well aware of their competency at every level of OBE.

ABBREVIATIONS AND SYMBOLS

List of Abbreviations

General Terms			
Abbreviations	**Full form**	**Abbreviations**	**Full form**
ADM	Adaptive Delta Modulation	FM	Frequency Modulation
ADPCM	Adaptive Differential Pulse Code Modulation	FSK	Frequency Shift Keying
AWGN	Additive White Gaussian Noise	ISI	Inter Symbol Interference
APK	Amplitude and Phase Shift Keying	JPM	Joint Probability Matrix
AM	Amplitude Modulation	LPC	Linear Predictive Coding
ASK	Amplitude Shift Keying	MSK	Minimum Shift Keying
ADSL	Asymmetric Digital Subscriber Line	NRZ	Non Return to Zero
BW	Bandwidth	OQPSK	Offset QPSK
BASK	Binary Amplitude Shift Keying	OOK	On Off Keying
BFSK	Binary Frequency Shift Keying	PM	Phase Modulation
BPAM	Binary PAM	PSK	Phase Shift Keying
BPSK	Binary Phase Shift Keying	PSD	Power Spectral Density
BER	Bit Error Rate	PAM	Pulse Amplitude Modulation
CCITT	International Consultative Telegraph and Telephone Committee	PCM	Pulse Code-Modulation
CG	Coding Gain	PPM	Pulse Position Modulation
CP	Continuous Phase	PTM	Pulse Time Modulation
CVSDM	Continuous Variable Slope Delta Modulation	PWM	Pulse Width (or Duration) Modulation
CW	Continuous Wave	QAM	Quadrature Amplitude Modulation
DM	Delta Modulation	QPSK	Quadriphase Shift Keying
DPCM	Differential PCM	QoS	Quality of Service
DPSK	Differential PSK	QPSK	Quaternary PSK

DCS	Digital Communication Systems	RS	Reed Solomon
DSL	Digital Subscriber Line	RZ	Return to Zero
DSLAM	Digital Subscriber Line Access Multiplexer	S/H	Sample and Hold
DSL	Digital Subscriber Loop	SNR	Signal to Noise Ratio
FT	Fourier Transform	TDM	Time-Division Multiplex

List of Units and Symbols

alpha	Α	α	iota	Ι	τ	rho	ρ	ρ
beta	Β	β	kappa	Κ	κ	sigma	Σ	σς
gamma	Γ	γ	lambda	Λ	λ	tau	Τ	τ
delta	Δ	δ	mu	Μ	μ	upsilon	Υ	υ
epsilon	Ε	ε	nu	Ν	ν	phi	Φ	φ
zeta	Ζ	ζ	xi	Ξ	ξ	chi	Χ	χ
eta	Η	η	omicron O	ο		psi	Ψ	ψ
theta	Θ	θ	pi	Π	π	omega	Ω	ω

LIST OF FIGURES

1. Pulse Modulation and Transmission... 1

Fig. 1.1: A typical analog and digital signal representation. 3

Fig. 1.2: Model of a typical digital communication system 4

Fig. 1.3: Baseband transmission systems 6

Fig. 1.4: PAM signal 7

Fig. 1.5: Impulse sampling 9

Fig. 1.6: Spectrum of sampled signal for over sampling and under sampling 10

Fig. 1.7: Natural sampling 11

Fig. 1.8: Flat-topped sampling or S/H circuit 13

Fig. 1.9: Flat-topped sampling 14

Fig. 1.10: Aliasing spectral representation: (a) Signal (b) Sampled signal 15

Fig. 1.11: Prefiltering in frequency domain (a) Signal (b) Sampled signal 15

Fig. 1.12: Post filtering in frequency domain (a) Signal (b) Sampled signal 15

Fig. 1.13: Pulse modulation methods 18

Fig. 1.14: PAM modulator 19

Fig. 1.15: PAM demodulator 19

Fig. 1.16: PCM system 20

Fig. 1.17: Process of quantization 21

Fig. 1.18: Midtread quantization 22

Fig 1.19: Quantization error for a midtread quantizer 22

Fig. 1.20: Midrise quantizer 23

Fig. 1.21: Quantization error for a midrise quantizer 23

Fig. 1.22: (a) NRZ unipolar representation (b) NRZ polar representation 24

Fig. 1.23: Regenerative repeater 25

Fig. 1.24: Decoded signal 25

Fig. 1.25: Decision thresholds in an uniform quantizer 26

Fig. 1.26: Non uniform quantization characteristics 29

Fig. 1.27: Quantization error characteristics 30

Fig. 1.28: Compression characteristic 30

Fig. 1.29: A basic companding model 30

Fig. 1.30: PCM with analog companding 31

Fig. 1.31: Compression characteristics as a function of 31

Fig. 1.32: Manchester coding 34

Fig. 1.33: Differential Manchester encoding 34
Fig. 1.34: Representation of bit sequence 1 1 0 1 0 1 35
Fig. 1.35: Differential Manchester encoding 35
Fig. 1.36: A Digital multiplexer/demultiplexer scheme 37
Fig. 1.37: Multiplexing and demultiplexing in TDM 38
Fig. 1.38: TDM system 39
Fig. 1.39: North American digital hierarchy 40
Fig. 1.40: International (ITU-T) digital telephone hierarchy 41
Fig. 1.41: Line speed of a T1 carrier 42
Fig. 1.42: T1 frame structure 42
Fig. 1.43: E1 frame structure 43

2. Baseband Transmission 53
Fig. 2.1: DPCM transceiver (a) Transmitter (b) Receiver 55
Fig. 2.2: Prediction filter 56
Fig. 2.3: DM system (a) Encoder (b) Decoder 58
Fig. 2.4: Transfer characteristics of DM quantizer 58
Fig. 2.5: DM waveforms 59
Fig. 2.6: DM waveforms showing slope overload and quantising noise 60
Fig. 2.7: Limitations of DM 61
Fig. 2.8: Idling, tracking and slope overload conditions of DM 61
Fig. 2.9: PDF of quantization noise 62
Fig. 2.10: A simple implementation of a DM system 64
Fig. 2.11: ADM transceiver (a) Transmitter (b) Receiver 66
Fig. 2.12: ADM waveforms 66
Fig. 2.13: ADPCM system (a) Encoder (b) Decoder 68
Fig. 2.14: Block diagram of an LPC coder 70
Fig. 2.15: Speech generation model of LPC coder (excitation and vocal tract model) 71
Fig. 2.16: Matched filter 72
Fig. 2.17: Binary baseband communication system 77
Fig. 2.18: Sinc function 80
Fig. 2.19: Frequency response of an ideal low pass filter 81
Fig. 2.20: Response of a practical low pass filter 82
Fig. 2.21: p(t) for $\alpha = 0$ and $\alpha = 1$ 83
Fig. 2.22: Raised cosine spectrum 84
Fig. 2.23: Duobinary encoder 85
Fig. 2.24: Magnitude response of a duobinary filter 87

Fig. 2.25: Phase response of a duobinary filter 87
Fig. 2.26: Impulse response of a duobinary filter 87
Fig. 2.27: Duobinary filter with precoding 88
Fig. 2.28: Detector for precoded duobinary system 89
Fig. 2.29: Adaptive equalization filter 91
Fig. 2.30: Digital subscriber line 92

3. Analysis of Signal Space 98
Fig. 3.1: Synthesizer 100
Fig. 3.2: Analyzer 101
Fig. 3.3: Signal representation for the example 3.2 103
Fig. 3.4: Basis functions for the example 3.3 109
Fig. 3.5: Bank of correlators 111
Fig. 3.6: Illustration of effect of noise on the transmitted signal 112
Fig. 3.7: A typical receiver configuration 114
Fig. 3.8: Correlation receiver 115
Fig.3.9: Binary correlation receiver 116
Fig. 3.10: Integrate and dump correlation receiver 116
Fig. 3.11: (a) Typical MF receiver (b) MF receiver with decision device (c) MF characteristics 118

4. Passband Digital Transmission 125
Fig. 4.1: Modulation types 127
Fig. 4.2: Basic digital waveforms for message data bits '0101101001' 128
Fig. 4.3: Model of a typical passband data transmission system 129
Fig. 4.4: Basic passband modulation schemes 130
Fig. 4.5: Binary OOK and binary ASK waveforms 130
Fig. 4.6: BASK transmitter 131
Fig. 4.7: Signal space diagram of BASK 132
Fig. 4.8: BASK receiver 133
Fig. 4.9: Non-coherent BASK receiver 133
Fig. 4.10: PSD of a BASK signal 134
Fig. 4.11: (a) Generation of BPSK wave (b) Product Modulator 136
Fig. 4.12: BPSK waveform generation 137
Fig. 4.13: Generation of BPSK signal using bipolar NRZ level encoder and balanced modulator 138
Fig. 4.14: Signal space representation of BPSK 138
Fig. 4.15: Detection of BPSK wave 139
Fig. 4.16: BPSK demodulation scheme 139

Fig. 4.17: PSD of a NRZ pulse 140
Fig. 4.18: PSD of a BPSK signal 141
Fig. 4.19: Bandwidth from PSD of BPSK 142
Fig. 4.20: Constellation diagram of BPSK with decision boundary 142
Fig. 4.21: Coherent BPSK receiver 142
Fig. 4.22: BFSK modulator 144
Fig. 4.23: Waveforms for the data 1011001 145
Fig. 4.24: Coherent BFSK receiver 145
Fig. 4.25: Non-coherent BFSK receiver 146
Fig. 4.26: Constellation diagram of BFSK 146
Fig. 4.27: Bandwidth of BFSK 147
Fig. 4.28: QPSK inphase and qudrature streams 148
Fig. 4.29: QPSK waveforms for the data 01101000 149
Fig. 4.30: QPSK waveforms for example 4.1 150
Fig. 4.31: QPSK generator 151
Fig. 4.32: QPSK constellation diagram 151
Fig. 4.33: Non-coherent detection of QPSK 152
Fig. 4.34: DPSK modulator 153
Fig. 4.35: Detector circuit for DPSK 154
Fig. 4.36: DPSK waveforms for example 4.2 154
Fig. 4.37: OQPSK modulator 155
Fig. 4.38: OQPSK demodulator 155
Fig. 4.39: OQPSK waveforms for example 4.3 156
Fig. 4.40: Constellation diagram of 8-PSK 156
Fig. 4.41: 8-PSK waveforms for example 4.4 157
Fig. 4.42: Constellation diagram for 16-ary PSK 159
Fig. 4.43: 16-QAM constellation diagram 159
Fig. 4.44: Decision region for 16-QAM 160
Fig. 4.45: BER performance plot 161
Fig. 4.46: Constellation diagram 162
Fig. 4.47: MSK decoder circuit 163
Fig. 4.48: MSK waveforms for example 4.5 164

5. Information Theory 169
Fig. 5.1: Communication channel 173
Fig. 5.2: Channel diagram representation of the channel 174
Fig. 5.3: Channel diagram for the channel given in example 5.6 176
Fig. 5.4: Binary communication channel 176

Fig. 5.5: Channel diagram 178
Fig. 5.6: Mutual information and channel entropies 180
Fig. 5.7: Communication channel 181

6. Coding Techniques 191
Fig. 6.1: A general block diagram of an linear block code 194
Fig. 6.2: A general block diagram of a concatenated code 207
Fig. 6.3: Convolution encoder 207
Fig. 6.4: Convolution encoder 210
Fig. 6.5: State diagram representation of a encoder given in example 6.3 213
Fig. 6.6: Tree diagram representation of a encoder given in example 6.3 214
Fig. 6.7: Trellis diagram representation of a encoder given in example 6.3 216
Fig. 6.8: Trellis diagram representation 218
Fig. 6.9: Decoding using Viterbi algorithm 219
Fig. 6.10: A rate 1/3 turbo encoder 220
Fig. 6.11: A rate 1/3 turbo decoder 220

CONTENTS

Foreword iii
Acknowledgement v
Preface vii
Outcome Based Education ix
Course Outcomes x
Guidelines for Teachers xi
Guidelines for Students xii
Abbreviations and Symbols xiii
List of Figures xv

1. Pulse Modulation and Transmission 1-52

Unit Specifics 1
Rationale 1
Pre-Requisites 1
Unit Outcomes 1
1.1 Introduction To Communication Systems 2
1.2. Model Of A Typical Digital Communication System 4
1.2.1 Transmitter 4
1.2.2 Channel 5
1.2.3 Receiver 5
1.3 Baseband Transmission Techniques 6
1.4 Sampling 7
1.4.1 Sampling Theorem 7
1.4.2 Uniform Sampling Theorem For Bandlimited Signals 7
1.5 Sampling Techniques 8
1.5.1 Impulse / Ideal Sampling 8
1.5.2 Natural Sampling 10
1.5.3 Flat-Topped Sampling Or Rectangular Pulse Sampling (Sample And Hold) 13
Operation Of The S/H Circuit 13
1.6 Sampling Theorem For Bandpass Signals 16
1.7 Pulse Modulation 18
1.8 Pulse Code Modulation 20
1.8.1 Quantization 21
1.8.2 Encoder 24
1.8.3 Regenerative Repeaters 25
1.8.4. Decoder 25
1.8.5 Reconstruction Circuit 26

1.9	Signal To Quantization Noise Ratio For Uniform Quantizer	26
1.10	Non-Uniform/ Non-Linear Quantizers	29
	1.10.1 M-Law Companding	31
1.11	Line Codes	33
	1.11.1 Unipolar Rz	33
	1.11.2 Polar Rz	34
	1.11.3 Bipolar Nrz	34
	1.11.4 Bipolar Rz	34
	1.11.5 Manchester	34
	1.11.6 Differential Manchester	34
1.12	Bandwidth For Pcm Systems	36
1.13	PCM TDM Hierarchies	37
	1.13.1 Types Of Tdm	38
	1.13.2 Tdm Digital Hierarchy	39
	1.13.2 Frame Structure	41
	1.13.2 Synchronisation And Bit Stuffing Mechanisms	43
	Multiple Choice Questions	46
	Descriptive Type Questions	48
	Objective Questions	48
	State True Or False	49
	Abstract Of The Disclosure	50
	Brief Description Of The Drawing	51
2.	**Baseband Transmission**	**53-97**
	Unit Specifics	53
	Rationale	53
	Unit Outcomes	53
	Mapping Of Unit Outcomes With Course Outcomes	54
2.1	Differential Pcm (Dpcm)	54
	2.1.1 Dpcm Transmitter/Receiver	54
	2.1.2 Processing Gain Of A Dpcm System	56
2.2	Delta Modulation	57
	2.2.1 Limitations Of Dm	60
	2.2.2 Signal To Noise Ratio Of Dm System	62
	2.2.3 Simple Implementation Of A Dm System	64
	2.2.4 Advantages/Disadvantages Of Dm	64
2.3	Adaptive Delta Modulation (Adm)	65
2.4	Adaptive Differential Pulse Code Modulation (Adpcm)	67

2.4.1 Advantages of ADPCM 68
2.4.2 Comparison Between PCM, DPCM, ADPCM, DM and ADM 69
2.5 Low Bit Rate Coding 69
2.6 Baseband Transmission 71
2.7 Matched Filters 71
2.7.1 Properties Of The Matched Filter 75
2.8 Inter Symbol Interference (Isi) 77
2.9 Nyquist Criterion for Zero Isi 79
2.10 Ideal Solution or Nyquist Solution for Zero Isi 80
2.11 Practical Solution For Zero Isi 82
2.11.1 Transmission Bandwidth of a Raised Cosine Filter 84
2.12 Correlative Coding 85
2.12.1 Duobinary Signalling 85
2.13 Equalization 90
2.13.1 Adaptive Equalization 90
2.14 Digital Subscriber Line 91
Numerical Problems 94
Descriptive Type Questions 94
Objective Type Questions 95
John Cioffi 96

3. Analysis of Signal Space 98-124
Unit Specifics 98
Rationale 98
Unit Outcomes 98
Mapping of Unit Outcomes with Course Outcomes 99
3.1 Geometric Representation of Signals 99
3.1.1 Squared Length of a Signal 103
3.1.2 Energy of a Signal 103
3.1.3 Euclidian Distance 104
3.1.4 Gram Schmidt Orthogonalization Procedure 104
3.2 Likelihood Functions 110
3.3 Coherent Detection of Signal in Noise 111
3.3.1 Maximum a Posteriori Probability Decoding 112
3.3.2 Maximum Likelihood Decoding 112

3.3.3 Minimum Mean Square Estimation 114
3.4 Optimum Receivers 114
3.4.1 Optimum Receiver for AWGN Channel 115
3.4.2 The Correlation Receiver 115
3.4.3 Matched Filter Receiver 117
3.5 Equivalence of Correlation Receiver Filter with Matched Filter 118
Numerical Problems 120
Descriptive Type Questions 121
Objective Type Questions 121
The Theory of Optimum Noise Immunity 122

4. Passband Digital Transmission 125-168

Unit Specifics 125
Rationale 125
Unit Outcomes 125
Mapping of Unit Outcomes with Course Outcomes 126
4.1 Introduction 126
4.1.1 Digital Modulation 126
4.1.2 Types of Digital Modulation Techniques 126
4.1.3 Requirements of Passband Modulation Schemes 129
4.1.4 Advantages and Drawbacks of Passband Data Transmission 129
4.1.5 Model of a Typical Passband Data Transmission System 129
4.2 Binary Amplitude Shift Keying (Bask) 130
4.2.1 Generation of BASK/Book 130
4.2.2 Bask Receiver 133
4.2.3 Power Spectral Density (PSD) and Bandwidth (BW) of Bask 133
4.2.4 Probability of Error (PE) of Bask 134
4.3 Binary Phase Shift Keying (BPSK) 136
4.3.1 Generation of BPSK Waves 136
4.3.2 Detection of BPSK Waves 139
4.3.3 Power Spectral Density (PSD) And Bandwidth (BW) of BPSK 140
4.3.4 Probability of Error (PE) of BPSK 142
4.4 Binary Frequency Shift Keying (BFSK) 144
4.4.1 Bfsk Modulator 144
4.4.2 PSD and Bandwidth of FSK 147

4.5 Quadriphase Shift Keying (QPSK) 148
4.5.1 Generation of Coherent QPSK 151
4.5.2 Detection of Coherent QPSK Signals 152
4.5.3 Probability of Error 152
4.6 Differential PSK (DPSK) 153
4.7 Offset QPSK (OQPSK) 155
4.8 M-ARY PSK (MPSK) 156
4.9 Quadrature Amplitude Modulation (QAM) 158
4.10 Minimum Shift Keying (MSK) 162
Numerical Problems 166
Descriptive Type Questions 167
Objective Type Questions 167

5. Information Theory 169-190
Unit Specifics 169
Rationale 169
Pre-Requisites 169
Unit Outcomes 169
Mapping of Unit Outcomes with Course Outcomes 170
5. 1 Introduction 170
5.2 Information Measures 170
5.3 Shannon Entropy 171
5.3.1 Differential Entropy 172
5.3.2 Properties of Entropy 173
5.4 Communication Channels 173
5.4.1 Discrete Communication Channel 174
5.4.2 Binary Communication Channel 176
5.5 Channel Entropies 177
5.6 Mutual Information 179
5.6.1 Properties of Mutual Information 180
5.6.2 Average Rate of Information Transmission 180
5.7 Channel Capacity 182
5.7.1 Channel Capacity Using Muroga's Method 182
5.8 Continuous Channels 183
5.9 Shannon Hartley Law 183

Numerical Problems 186
Descriptive Type Questions 187
Objective Type Questions 187
A Mathematical Theory of Communication 189
By C. E. Shannon 189
Introduction 189

6. Coding Techniques 191-227
Unit Specifics 191
Rationale 191
Pre-Requisites 191
Unit Outcomes 191
6.1 Introduction 192
6.2 Ratioanle for Error Control Coding 192
6.3 Types of Channel Codes 193
6.4 Linear Block Code 194
6.4.1 Generator Matrix 194
6.4.2 Parity Check Matrix (H) 195
6.4.3 Syndrome Calculation 196
6.4.4 Error Detecting And Correcting Capabilities Of A Linear Block Code 199
6.5 Bounds on (N,K) Linear Block Codes 202
6.5.1 Singleton Bound 202
6.5.2 Hamming Bound 203
6.5.3 Gilbert–Varshamov (Gv) Bound 203
6.5.4 Mceliece-Rodemich-Rumsey-Welch (MRRW) Bound 203
6.6 Soft and Hard Decision Decoding 204
6.6.1 Hard Decision Decoding 204
6.6.2 Soft Decision Decoding 205
6.7 Hamming Codes 206
6.8 Reed Solomon (Rs) Codes 206
6.9 Concatenated Codes 206
6.10 Convolution Codes 207
6.10.1 Encoding Using Time Domain Approach 208
6.10.2 Encoding Using Transform Domain Approach 211
6.10.3 Representation Of Convolution Codes 212

6.10.4 Viterbi Decoding 216

6.10.5 BCJR Decoding 219

6.11 Turbo Codes 220

6.12 Low Density Parity Check Codes 221

Numerical Problems 223

Descriptive Type Questions 224

Objective Type Questions 225

Appendix **228-308**

Appendix-I **228**

Appendix-I **283**

References for Further Learning **309**

Index **311-312**

1 Pulse Modulation and Transmission

UNIT SPECIFICS

Through this unit we discuss the following aspects:

- Introduction to Digital Communication Systems.
- Baseband transmission techniques, Sampling techniques, Uniform Sampling theorem
- Principles of pulse modulation techniques.
- Analysis of linear and non-linear quantizers.
- Concept of Line Coding and different line coding techniques.
- Digital hierarchy, frames structures/synchronisation and bit stuffing mechanisms.

RATIONALE

This chapter gives the basics of a digital communication system. The student will be exposed to the concepts of analog to digital conversion. As almost all communication applications use digital domain processing, students will appreciate the concepts of sampling and quantization that are discussed in this unit. The chapter also includes ample number of solved examples. Exercise questions to test the degree of understanding of the concepts will definitely enable students to get better clarity on the topics presented.

PRE-REQUISITES

- Signals and Systems
- Basic Communication Systems
- Stochastic and Random Processes

UNIT OUTCOMES

At the end of this unit the student will be able to

UO 1. Explain the blocks of a digital communication system

UO 2. Demonstrate an ability to define and compare different sampling techniques

UO 3. Appreciate the concepts of Pulse Modulation Techniques : PAM, PWN, PPM

UO 4. Discuss different blocks involved in Pulse Code Modulation system

UO 5. Represent the given binary information using different line coding techniques

UO 6. Explain the concept of digital hierarchy, frame structure and bit stuffing mechanisms

MAPPING OF UNIT OUTCOMES WITH COURSE OUTCOMES

	CO 1	CO 2	CO 3	CO4	CO 5	CO 6
UO 1	3	2	-	-	-	-
UO 2	3	2	-	-	-	-
UO 3	2	2	-	-	-	-
UO 4	3	3	-	-	-	-
UO 5	3	1	-	-	-	-
UO 6	1	1	-	-	-	-

1.1 INTRODUCTION TO COMMUNICATION SYSTEMS

In order to transmit information from a source located at a point to a sink located at a far off place, we need a communication system. For this communication to happen, we require a sender, a recipient, a message and a medium. The message is generally called an information bearing signal or baseband signal and medium is referred to as a channel. Communication systems may be classified as:

- Analog Communication Systems
- Digital Communication Systems (DCS)

An analog communication system is characterised by a message or information signal whose amplitude is a continuous function of time (analog or continuous time signal) as shown in Figure 1.1 (a). The message signal is superimposed upon the high frequency carrier signal. Signals containing information or intelligence to be transmitted are referred to as modulating signals. The information bearing signal is also called as the baseband signal (band of frequencies representing the signal). The amplitude, phase or frequency of the carrier wave is varied with respect to the instantaneous value of the information signal resulting in amplitude, frequency or phase modulation respectively. The carrier frequency is greater than modulating signal frequency. The signal resulting from the process of modulation is known as the modulated signal. When a continuous wave is used for the carrier, the resulting modulation process is called as Continuous Wave (CW) or analog modulation. Human voice, video, temperature, pressure, flow measurements etc., are examples of a baseband modulating signal.

A DCS is characterised by a information signal that is discrete in nature (discrete time signals), which is represented by binary digits (digital signal), like 01111011, as shown in Figure 1.1(b). This binary information is used to modify the amplitude, phase or frequency resulting in digital modulations respectively. In case the information signal is analog in nature, it can be converted to a digital signal by three important processes: sampling, quantizing and encoding. Examples of digital signals are computer data, data stored on cloud, digital watches, mobiles, digital video signals, pen drives, CD's DVD's etc. A typical analog and digital signal representation is shown in figure 1.1.

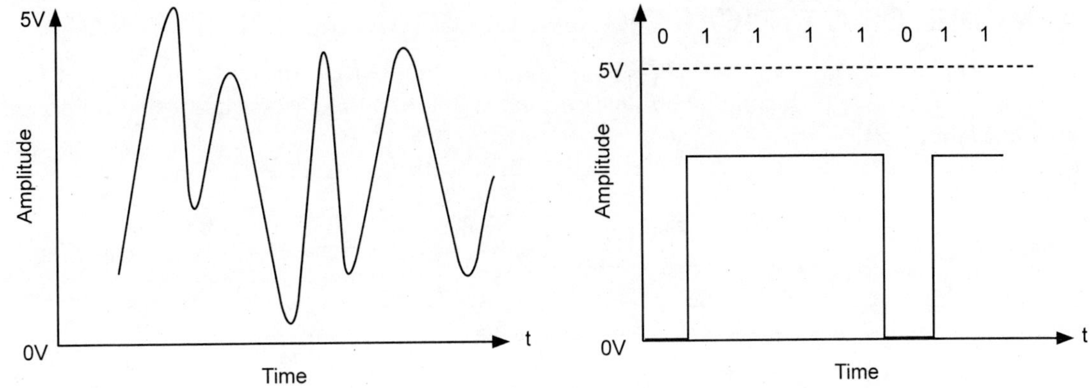

Fig. 1.1 A typical analog and digital signal representation.

DCS have become an integral part of all communication systems today as there is a huge demand for data transmission. Digital communication systems offer several advantages over analog communication.

- Easier and more efficient to multiplex several digital signals.
- Immunity to Noise.
- Reduced cross talk and external interference.
- Ease of storing and retrieval of digital information when necessary. However, it is not possible in analog.
- Possibility of using advanced digital signal processing techniques.
- More flexibility in implementation of hardware as compared to analog communication systems.
- Possibility of coding techniques (compression, error detection/correction, encryption/ decryption) to yield extremely low storage space, low error rates, higher security and fidelity (quality of signal) as well as privacy.
- Developments in digital techniques that have resulted in very powerful and advanced multicore processors, large size memory devices and powerful embedded systems.
- Cheaper and simpler due to advancement of IC technologies.

DCS however, do have few disadvantages which include

- High power consumption.
- Need of precise time synchronization.
- Additional hardware for encoding/decoding.
- Highly signal-processing intensive.
- Incompatible with existing analog facilities.
- More transmission bandwidth requirement due to analog to digital conversion at a high rate.
- Sudden degradation in Quality of Service (QoS).

However, the above disadvantages can be overcome by use of low power VLSI chip design, novel synchronization techniques, efficient advanced signal processing algorithms, robust error detecting/ correcting codes and bandwidth efficient techniques.

1.2. MODEL OF A TYPICAL DIGITAL COMMUNICATION SYSTEM

Figure 1.2 shows the model of a typical DCS, consisting of several blocks. The optional blocks such as encryption/decryption, multiplexing/demultiplexing, spreading, multiple access and equalization are not shown for simplicity.

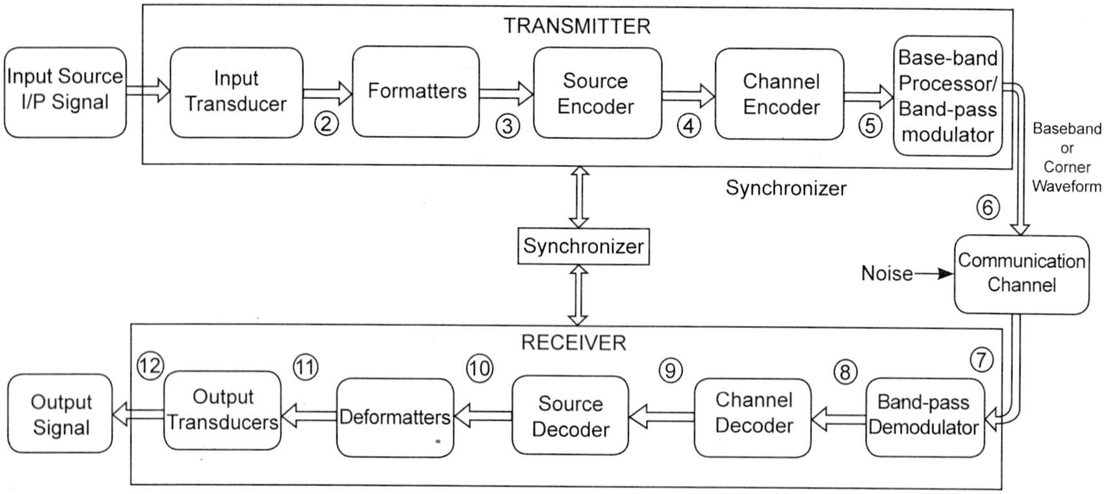

1. Message Signal
2. Message Signal Converted to Electrical Signal
3. Analog to Digital Signal
4. Source Code Word
5. Channel Codeword
6. Baseband or Corner Waveform
7. Received Signal currupted by
8. Estimate of Channel Codeword
9. Estimate of Source Codeword
10. Digital to Analog Connection
11. Analog Signal
12. Estimate of Message Signal

Fig. 1.2 Model of a typical digital communication system

1.2.1 Transmitter

Information source can be categorised as either analog source such as speech or a discrete/digital source such as a computer system.

The transmitter section basically comprises of the input transducer, formatter, source encoder and channel encoder. **Input transducer** converts the physical entity that is to be communicated into an electric signal. The **formatter**, converts an information signal to digital symbols which are then represented by baseband waveforms using line codes and transmitted over a communication channel.

The symbols generated by the source are fed into the source encoder which converts these symbols into digital form. i.e. binary sequence of 1's and 0's. Each binary '1' or '0' is a bit and group of bits is a code word. The source encoder assigns codewords to the symbols. Any redundancy in the signal is removed by the source encoder thus resulting in minimum number of bits (optimised length of the codeword) could be transmitted. This helps reduce the bit rate (the rate at which bits are transmitted per second) at which digital data can be transmitted.

When the signal travels through the channel/medium after **baseband or band pass modulation**, there are chances of some bits going into error as channel adds noise or interference to the signal. To alleviate this problem, the **channel encoder** adds some redundant bits called check bits facilitating error detection or correction. The channel encoder does the coding for error detection and correction. The channel encoder and decoder improve the reliability of the system through error control capability.

The baseband modulator is basically a pulse modulation circuit where each symbol, represented in binary (as a voltage level for logical ones and zeroes) that needs to be transmitted is converted to a baseband waveform. This is known as baseband transmission, generally used for low speed wired transmission. Further these pulse modulated outputs can be quantised and encoded to obtain a binary waveform such as the Pulse Code-Modulation (PCM) waveform (also known as line codes in telephone applications). They are generally denoted as $x_i(t)$ where i= 1, 2.... M.

In computer-to-computer communications, a very high data rate (high speed) transmission will be required. In such situations, binary symbols need to be digitally modulated. Digital modulation maps the input binary symbols 1's and 0's to high frequency analog signal waveforms, which are known as carrier signals. This is known as band pass modulation. Efficient transmission of digital data is achieved by using bandpass or carrier modulation. The baseband and bandpass modulators are mutually exclusive blocks in the sense for low-speed wired transmission, we use baseband modulator and for high-speed wireless data transmission, we use bandpass modulator.

1.2.2 Channel

Communication channel serves as a medium between the transmitter and receiver of a communication system. This communication can take place through a wired or a wireless medium from one or several senders to one or several receivers. Wired transmission channels can be physical media such as open wire transmission lines, TV cable, ethernet cable, coaxial cables, optical fibre cables etc. Wireless transmission channels could be the free space (atmosphere), such as microwave, satellite, an acoustic wave or mobile communication channels. The transmitted signal, when it propagates along the channel, always gets affected by various sources of noise such as thermal noise, shot noise (resulting from electronic devices used in transmitter and receiver chains). Noise sources can be man-made noise like automobile ignition noise, electromagnetic interference (EMI) from other electronic equipment and noise from natural sources (atmospheric noise, electrical lightning discharges during thunderstorms, radiation from space etc).

1.2.3 Receiver

At the receiver, the **bandpass demodulator**, receives the corrupted waveform, processes these signals and converts the input modulated signal into the sequence of binary bits. Actually an estimate of the transmitted data sequence is obtained at the output of the bandpass demodulator. In case of baseband transmission reception, the **decoder**, the line codes are back to the data sequence that was transmitted.

The channel decoder does the reverse function of the channel encoder. Redundant bits added by the channel encoders carry no information but are used for error detection and error correction if any, at the decoder. The performance measures of a channel decoder are the code rate (dependent on the number of check bits introduced at the channel encoder), coding method, P_e, probability of bit error or Bit Error Rate (BER) and coding efficiency (ratio of data rate at the input to that of the output of the encoder). These parameters are dependent on the channel coding characteristics.

The **Source Decoder** performs the reverse operation to that of the source encoder. It estimates the information symbols transmitted from the source, from the bits received from the channel decoder. The difference between the estimated signal and the original transmitted signal gives a measure of distortion that has been introduced by channel and other b locks of the DCS.

The **de-formatter** converts the digital data back to analog form (may be speech signal) or to discrete form (key board characters) in cases where the originating source was not digital.

The **Output Transducer** converts the deformatted signal into their original physical form which can be analog non-electrical signals. In case of computer or data communications, both the input and reconstructed signals are digital in nature and hence an output transducer may not always be required.

The **Output Signal** is what was transmitted at the transmitter that is now received by the recipient.

In addition to the above blocks, DCS also includes a very important block, called the **synchronisation** block. In particular the timing synchronization in which a receiver needs to determine the exact instants of time at which to sample the received signal. It also involves carrier synchronization in which a receiver has to synchronise the phase and frequency of its local carrier oscillator with that of the received signal.

1.3 BASEBAND TRANSMISSION TECHNIQUES

We know that sources can be analog or digital and that a DCS transmits only in digital form. Textual, analog or digital information can be handled by a baseband transmission as shown in Figure 1.3. A formatter is required for converting analog signals into digital form. If data is already in digital format, formatter will not be required. The digital bit stream can then be converted to baseband waveforms using some kind of pulse modulator or line coder.

Analog information requires sampling, quantization and coding. **Sampling** is the first step in formatting, which involves discretization of the analog signal in time. The next step is discretization in amplitude or **quantization** and the final step is **encoding** the quantised values or simply coding. The pulse modulator takes the bit sequence and converts them into pulse waveforms. These are then transmitted using a baseband modulator and pushed into the communication channel. At the receiver, demodulation, de-formatting is done by use of a decoder, de-quantizer and a low pass filter to get back the analog information.

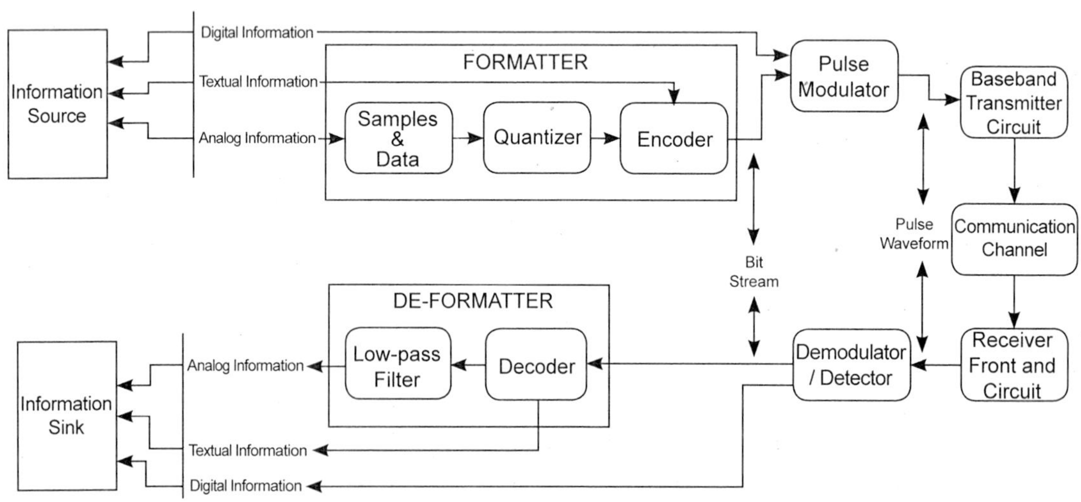

Fig. 1.3 Baseband transmission systems

1.4 SAMPLING

Sampling involves discretization of an analog signal in time domain to get continuous values of the signal at discrete points of time. How closely a sampled waveform can approximate the original continuous signal waveform can be understood by Sampling theorem.

1.4.1 Sampling Theorem

Sampling operation is performed as per the Sampling theorem. Sampling a message signal results in a pulse amplitude modulation (PAM) signal. The message/modulating signal (a continuous waveform) is sampled by a switch (chopper) by a sampling/switching signal as shown in Figure 1.4.

A LPF can be used at the receiver side to reconstruct the message signal.

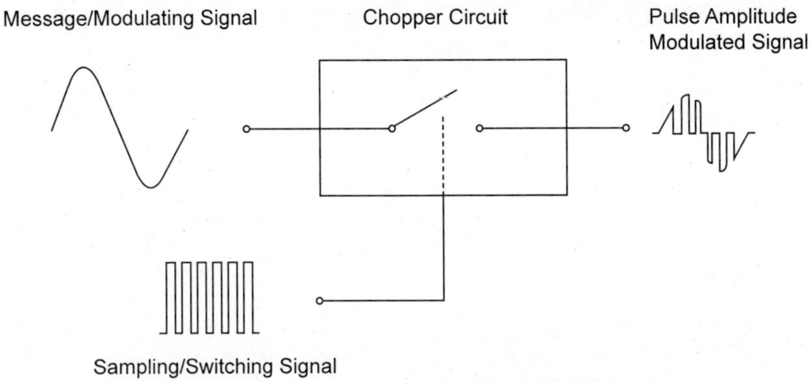

Scan here to know more

Fig. 1.4 PAM signal

1.4.2 Uniform Sampling Theorem for bandlimited signals

Uniform Sampling theorem for a band limited (low pass) signal is stated as follows:

(i) A band limited signal of finite energy, which has no frequency components higher than f_m Hz, can be determined uniquely by values sampled at uniform intervals less than or equal to $½ f_m$ seconds apart. ie. $Ts \leq 1 / 2 f_m$ sec.

(ii) A band limited signal of finite energy, which has no frequency components higher than f_m Hz, may be completely recovered from the knowledge of its samples taken at the rate of $2f_m$ samples per second.

The above two statements can be combined to state the above theorem (also known as the Nyquist Theorem) as follows:

"A continuous-time signal may be completely represented in its samples and recovered back if the sampling frequency is $f_s \geq 2f_m$"

"The sampling frequency (f_s) must be at the rate equal to or greater than twice the highest frequency component (f_m) present in the signal i.e. $fs \geq 2fm$, in order to recover the signal exactly."

(i) The sampling frequency, $f_s = 2f_m$, is known as the Nyquist rate. This is the minimum sampling rate. (1.1)

(ii) Nyquist interval is given by $T_s = 1/2f_m$ seconds where, $fs = 1/ T_s$, (1.2)

(iii) Nyquist criterion requires that $f_s \geq 2f_m$ that ensures correct reconstruction.

In commercial telephone channels, we sample a 4 kHz voice signal at the Nyquist rate of 2 x 4 kHz = 8 kHz.

1.5 SAMPLING TECHNIQUES

There are three types of sampling techniques:

(i) Instantaneous/Impulse/Ideal sampling

(ii) Natural sampling

(iii) Flat topped sampling

1.5.1 Impulse / Ideal sampling

In Impulse sampling, we use a train of impulses as the sampling signal. Here, we sample an analog waveform X(t) by a sequence of unit impulses (Dirac delta functions). x(t) is assumed to be a bandlimited signal. ie. there are no frequency components outside the interval ($-f_m < f < f_m$). We sample x(t) at times t = nTs by a periodic sequence of unit impulses, X_δ (t) known as the sampling function.

$$X_\delta(t) = \sum_{n=-\infty}^{\infty} \delta(t - nT_S) \tag{1.3}$$

Therefore, the sampled signal $X_S(t)$ can be represented as a product of two signals as follows:

$$X_S(t) = X(t).\, X_\delta(t) \tag{1.4}$$

$$X_S(t) = X(t).\, \sum_{n=-\infty}^{\infty} \delta(t - nT_S) \tag{1.5}$$

$$X_S(t) = \sum_{n=-\infty}^{\infty} X(nT_S).\, \delta(t - nT_S) \tag{1.6}$$

Taking Fourier Transform (FT) and using multiplication and convolution property, we have

$$X_s(f) = X(f) * X_\delta(f)$$

$$= X(f) * \left[\frac{1}{T_S} \sum_{n=-\infty}^{\infty} \delta(f - nf_s)\right]$$

$$X_s(f) = \frac{1}{T_S} \sum_{n=-\infty}^{\infty} X(f - nf_s) \tag{1.7}$$

Figure 1.5 which shows process of Impulse Sampling. Figures 1.5 a) to g) show the various waveforms: (a) The message signal: X(t) (b) Fourier transform (FT) of X(t) : X(f), (c) the sampling function: $X_\delta(t)$, (d) FT of Xδ(t): Xδ(f), (e) The sampled signal: Xs(t), (f) FT of $X_s(t)$: $X_s(f)$ (g) Switching circuit/Sampler.

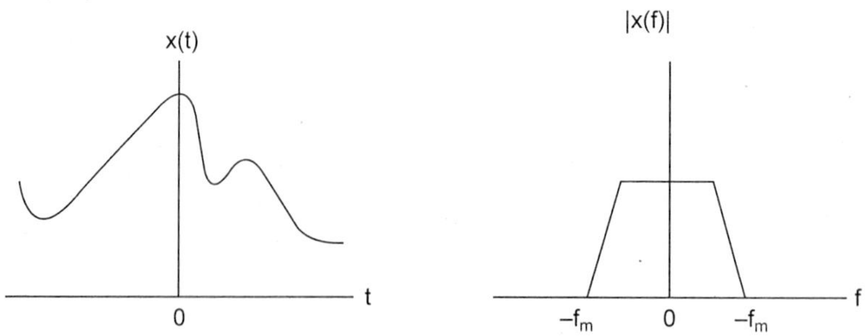

(a) (b)

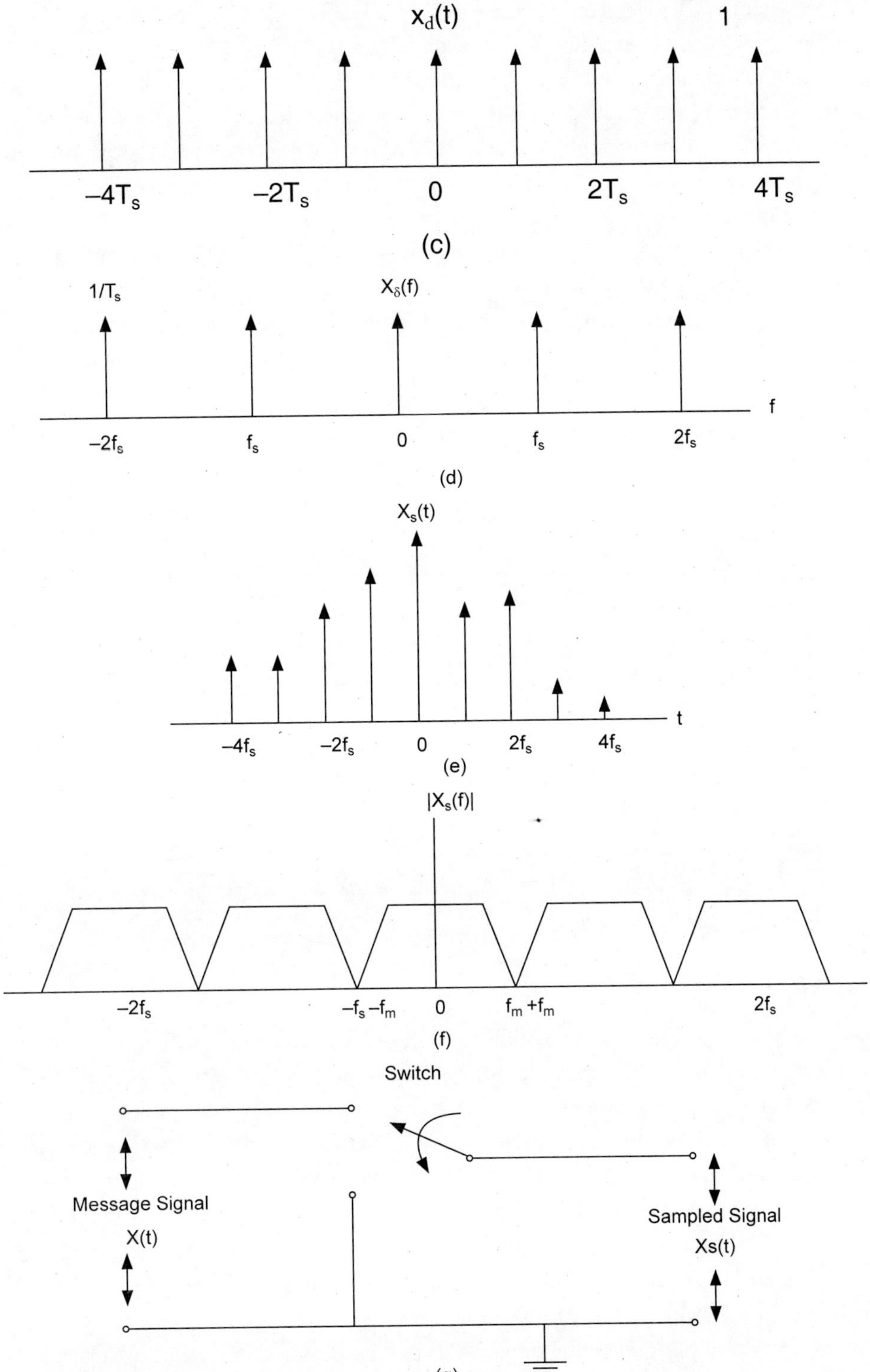

Fig.1.5 Impulse sampling

We can see, that the FT (spectrum) of the input signal repeats itself periodically in frequency every f_s Hz. From Fig. 1.5 (f), we can see that if the sampling rate is chosen just to satisfy the Nyquist rate, it is possible to recover the samples but then we would require filters with steep roll-off, which practically, is impossible. Hence in practice, the sampling rate f_s is always selected such that it is greater than the Nyquist rate. This results in oversampling to allow use of practical filters for reconstructing the original waveform. Figure 1.6 shows the spectrum of sampled signal for $f_s > 2f_m$ and for $f_s < 2f_m$. We observe that for under sampled signal ($f_s < 2f_m$), the spectral replications can be seen to overlap, resulting in loss of information. This is known as "aliasing" that is caused because of under sampling (ie. sampling at less than Nyquist rate). The loss of information due to aliasing (or distortion created by using too low a sampling rate) can be eliminated by use of a pre-alias filter that limits frequency band of the required signal. Therefore, it is required to satisfy the condition, $fs \geq 2fm$, for avoiding aliasing effect.

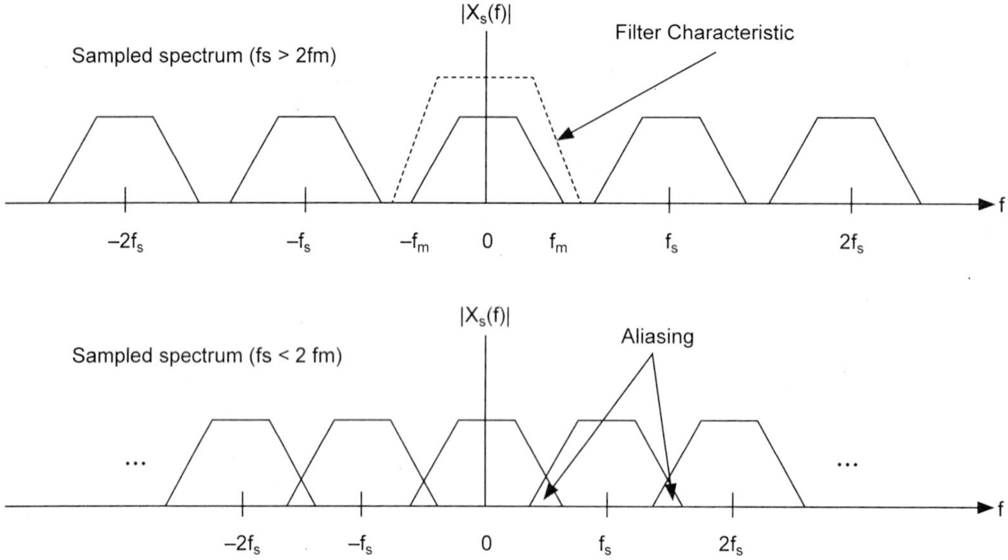

Fig. 1.6 Spectrum of sampled signal for over sampling and under sampling

1.5.2 Natural Sampling

We are aware that it is practically impossible to realise a Kronecker delta function (or an impulse function), however hard we try to reduce its time duration. In practice, a train short pulses is used as a sampling function. This pulse train consists of a flat top rectangular pulse of finite width to sample the message waveform. This sampling process is known as **Natural sampling,** It may be seen from Figure 1.7 (f) that the tops of the naturally sampled pulses are not flat and follow the natural waveform of the signal to be sampled. Hence the name Natural Sampling, which is a practical method that can be implemented.

Figure 1.7 shows the various waveforms of a natural sampler. Fig. 1.7 (g) shows a natural sampler circuit which is a simple switch. The flat top pulse train $X_p(t)$ (a periodic waveform with pulse widths T and amplitude 1/T. Sampling of input signal X(t) can be performed through a switch. When the switch is closed and $X_p(t)$ goes high, $X_s(t)$ is same as the input signal X(t). The switch is open when $X_p(t)$

goes low and in this case $X_s(t) = 0$. This naturally sampled signal, $X_s(t)$, shown in Figure 1.7 (e) can be represented as,

$$X_s(t) = X(t).X_p(t) \tag{1.8}$$

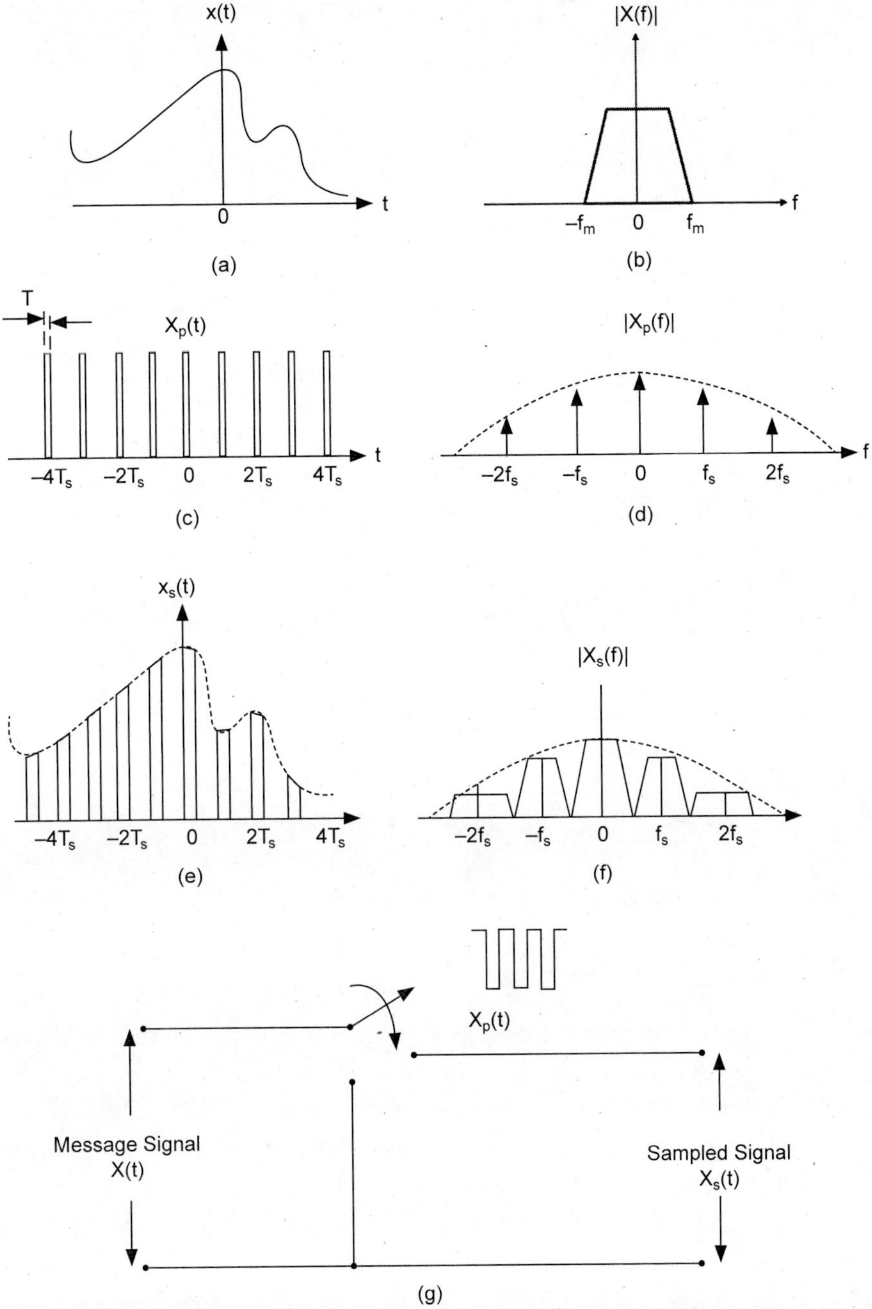

Fig. 1.7 Natural sampling

We know that the exponential Fourier Series (FS) for any periodic waveform such as $X_p(t)$ can be written as,

$$X_p(t) = \sum_{n=-\infty}^{\infty} C_n e^{j2\neq f_s t} \tag{1.9}$$

Where C_n is given by,

$$c_n = \frac{TA}{T_0} \sin c(f_n.T)$$

Note that T is the pulse width = τ and $f_n = nf_s$ (harmonic frequency)

Hence,

$$f_s = \frac{n}{T_0} = nf_0$$

C_n can now be written as,

$$C_n = \frac{\tau A}{T_S} \sin c(f_n.\tau)$$

The FS representation for $X_p(t)$ will be given as,

$$X_p(t) = \sum_{n=-\infty}^{\infty} \frac{\tau A}{T_S} \sin c(fn \cdot \tau) e^{j2\pi f_s nt}$$

Hence, $X_s(t)$ is given by

$$X_s(t) = X_p(t).X(t) = \sum_{n=-\infty}^{\infty} \frac{\tau A}{T_S} \sin c(f_n.\tau) e^{j2\pi f_s nt} . x(t)$$

$$= \frac{\tau A}{T_S} \sum_{n=-\infty}^{\infty} \sin c(f_n.\tau) e^{j2\pi f_s nt} . x(t) \tag{1.10}$$

Taking FT of $X_s(t)$, we get,

$$X_s(f) = \frac{\tau A}{T_S} \sum_{n=-\infty}^{\infty} \sin c(f_n.\tau) FT\,[e^{j2\pi f_s nt} .x(t)] \tag{1.11}$$

Using the frequency-shifting property of FT, we get,

$$X_s(f) = \frac{\tau A}{T_S} \sum_{n=-\infty}^{\infty} \sin c(f_n.\tau) X(f - f_s.n) \tag{1.12}$$

This equation for the spectrum of natural sampled waveform shows that it is periodic in f_s, weighed by the sinc function as shown in Fig. 1.6(f). However, we see can see that there is one difference between Impulse sampled signal and naturally sampled signal. Unlike the spectrum in an ideally sampled signal where it remains constant throughout the frequency range, the naturally sampled signal spectrum is weighted by a sinc function.

Further the sync function in the expression for $X_s(f)$ indicates that it behaves like a LPF and attenuates the upper portion of the message spectrum centred at f = 0, affecting the high frequencies. This is known as *Aperture Effect.* Aperture effect is more when the pulse durations are large. It can however be compensated by employing an equaliser having an amplitude response $1 / |X_s(f)|$ in cascade with a reconstruction filter.

1.5.3 Flat-Topped Sampling or Rectangular Pulse Sampling (Sample and Hold)

Sampler in most practical cases is implemented using a flat-topped sampling technique or rectangular pulse sampling that uses Sample and Hold (S/H) circuit. Sample and hold are a practically possible sampling method. In flat-topped sampling, the top of the samples will be constant and equal to the instantaneous value of the signal at the sampling instant. Thus, the pulses have a constant amplitude within the pulse interval.

1.5.3.1 Practical S/H circuit

Figure 1.8 shows a typical S/H circuit that consists of a series sampling switch, a parallel discharge switch and a capacitor.

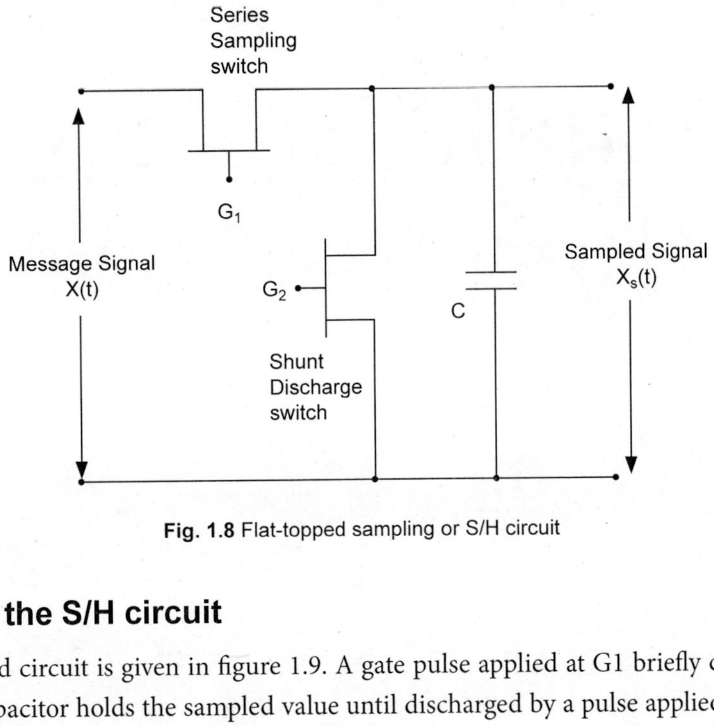

Fig. 1.8 Flat-topped sampling or S/H circuit

Operation of the S/H circuit

A sample and hold circuit is given in figure 1.9. A gate pulse applied at G1 briefly closes the sampling switch and the capacitor holds the sampled value until discharged by a pulse applied to G2. A periodic gating of the S/H circuit generates the sampled signal.

The flat-topped sample signal is obtained by convolution operation of a rectangular pulse P(t) (with unity amplitude and pulse width, Ts) and the sampled impulse train.

$$X_S(t) = P(t) * [x(t)\, x_\delta(t)]$$

$$= P(t) * [x(t)\sum_{n=-\infty}^{\infty} \delta(f - nT_s)] \text{ during the} \quad (1.13)$$

We can express $X_S(f)$ as

$$X_S(f) = P(f)\, F\, \{[x(t)\sum_{n=-\infty}^{\infty} \delta(f - nT_s)]\}$$

$$X_S(f) = P(f)\,F\{[X(f) * \frac{1}{T_s}\sum_{n=-\infty}^{\infty}\delta(f-nf_s)]\}$$

$$= P(f)\,\frac{1}{T_s}\sum_{n=-\infty}^{\infty}X(f-nf_s) \qquad (1.14)$$

The various waveforms explaining the various steps is shown in Figure 1.9.

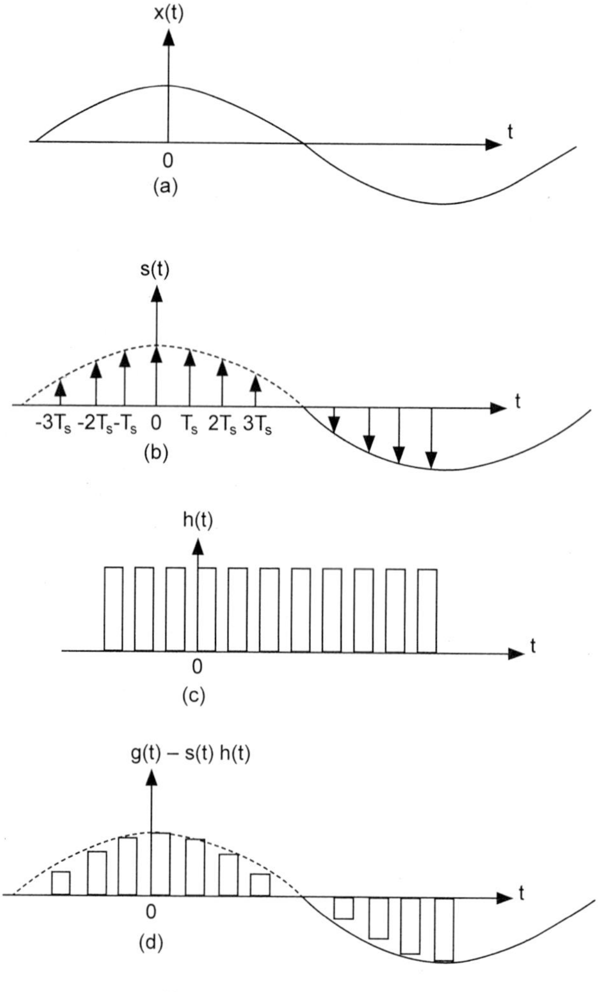

Fig. 1.9 Flat-topped sampling

1.5.3.2 Aliasing

Figure 1.6 (b) and Figure 1.10 shows that the signal x(t) cannot be reconstructed by using an ideal LPF due to the overlapping of adjoining spectral replicates. This means that due to spectral overlapping, the output of the LPF is distorted and this distortion is called aliasing. As the frequency components above fs /2 reappear as frequency components below fs /2 there is some kind of spectral folding or tail inversion, causing aliasing.This occurs due to undersampling (fs < 2fm).

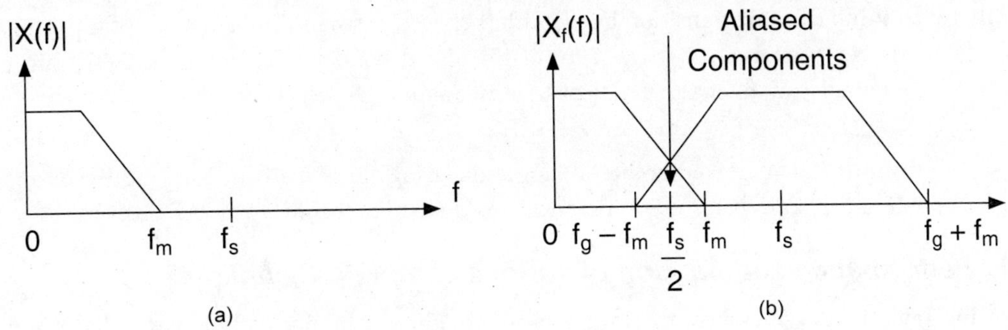

Fig. 1.10 Aliasing spectral representation: (a) Signal (b) Sampled signal

The problem of aliasing can be overcome by using anti-aliasing filters. There are two methods to eliminate aliasing by using

- Prefiltering antialiasing filter.
- Postfiltering antialiasing filter.

A LPF is used in the prefiltering antialiasing filter. The cut off frequency of the filter is chosen such that fc $\leq f_s/2$). The sampled signal spectrum does not show any aliasing components, as shown in Figure 1.11.

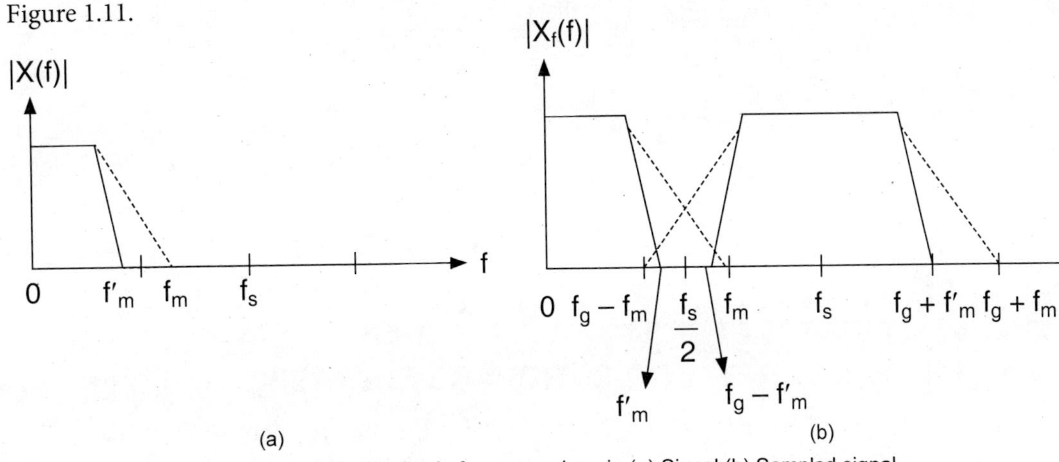

Fig.1.11 Prefiltering in frequency domain (a) Signal (b) Sampled signal

Figure 1.12 shows post filtering in frequency domain and aliased terms can be removed after sampling by using a LPF.

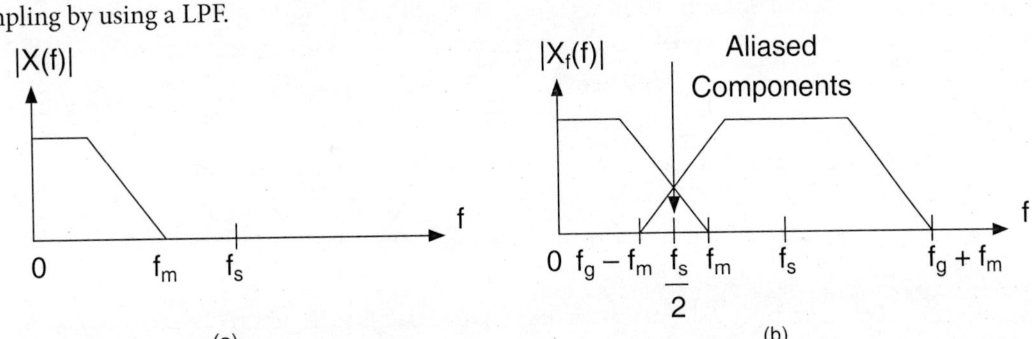

Fig. 1.12 Post filtering in frequency domain (a) Signal (b) Sampled signal

For this as a thumb rule, the transition bandwidth (between passband and stopband) for practically realizable filters, is kept between 10% and 20% of the signal bandwidth. Assuming 20% transition bandwidth for the antialiasing filter, the practical Nyquist Sampling rate is chosen to be

$$f_s \geq 2.2(f_m) \tag{1.15}$$

Further by using digital filters (rather than analog antialiasing filters), we can have a more economical solution for sampling particularly for use in practical analog to digital converters (ADCs).

1.5.3.3 Performance comparison of various sampling techniques

The following Table 1.1 provides a comparison between the three sampling techniques we have studied on the basis of their method, noise interference and spectral properties.

Table 1.1 Performance Comparison of various Sampling Techniques

Parameter	Instantaneous / Ideal Sampling	Natural Sampling	Flat-Topped / SH Sampling
Basic Principle	Multiplication	Chopping	Sample & hold circuit.
Rate of sampling	Almost towards infinite	Nyquist Criteria satisfied	Nyquist Criteria satisfied
Generation Circuit	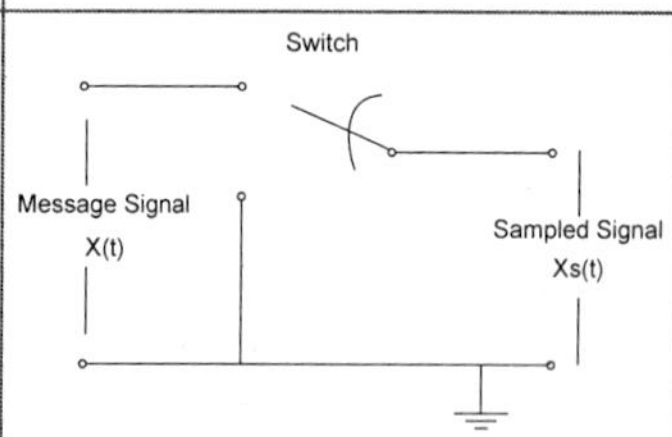	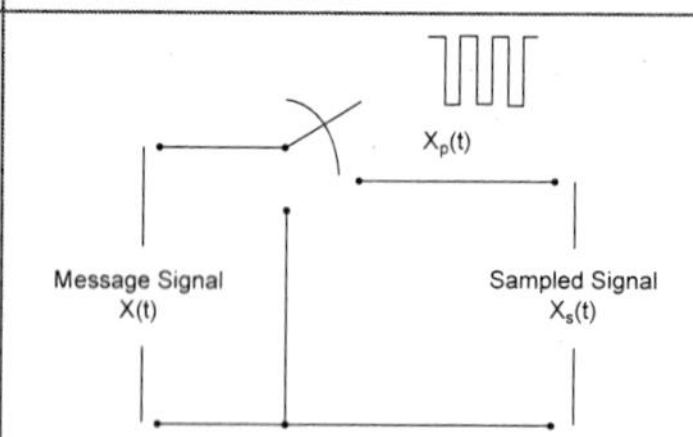	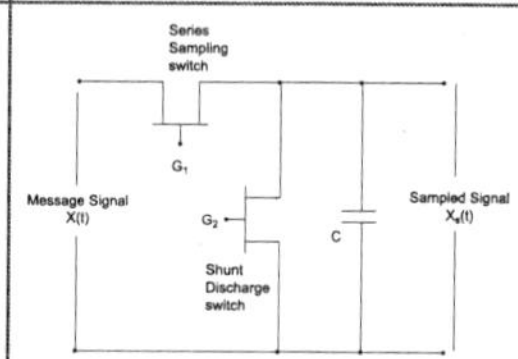
Noise Effects	Maximum	Minimum	Maximum
Feasibility	Practically not feasible	Practically feasible	Practically feasible

1.6 SAMPLING THEOREM FOR BANDPASS SIGNALS

If an analog information signal containing no frequency outside the specified bandwidth B Hz, it may be reconstructed from its samples at a sequence of points spaced 1/(2B) seconds apart with zero-mean squared error. ie. the sampling theorem for bandpass signals can be stated in simple way as follows:

An input signal x(t) can be sampled and recovered back without distortion when we use a sampling frequency $f_s < 2f_H$, where fH is the upper frequency and bandwidth of band pass signal x(t) is $B = f_H - f_L$.

ie. $$f_s = 2f_H / k, \text{ where } k = f_H / B. \tag{1.16}$$

where k is the largest integer $< f_H / B$

It can be inferred from the above expression that a bandpass signal can be sampled at a frequency less the frequency as per the sampling theorem.

Hence, for band pass signals of bandwidth $2f_m$, the minimum sampling rate is given by

$$f_s = 2B = 4f_m \tag{1.17}$$

Example. 1.1: Given an analog signal waveform, x(t) = 5cos (100 πt) + 10 sin (300 πt) – 2cos (400 πt), **Calculate the Nyquist rate.**

Solution: Given: $x(t) = 5\cos(100\pi t) + 10\sin(300\pi t) - 2\cos(400\pi t)$

ie. $2\pi f_1 = 100\pi$ or $f_1 = 50$ Hz

$2\pi f_2 = 300\pi$ or $f_2 = 150$ Hz

$2\pi f_3 = 400\pi$ or $f_3 = 200$ Hz

Maximum signal frequency fm, in x(t) is 200 Hz.

Nyquist Rate is: $f_s = 2fm$

Therefore $f_s = 2x\ 200\ \text{Hz} = 400$ Hz.

Example. 1.2: Calculate the Nyquist rate and Nyquist interval for $x(t) = 10\cos(2000\pi t)\cos(1000\pi t)$.

Solution:

Given: $x(t) = 10\cos(2000\pi t)\cos(1000\pi t)$.

ie. $x(t) = 10\cos(2000\pi t + 1000\pi t) + \cos(2000\pi t - 1000\pi t)$

$= 10\cos(3000\pi t) + \cos(1000\pi t)$

ie. $2\pi f_1 = 3000\pi$ or $f_1 = 1500$ Hz

$2\pi f_2 = 1000\pi$ or $f_2 = 500$ Hz

$f_s = 2f_m = 2 \times 1500 = 3000\ \text{Hz} = 3$ kHz.

$T_s = 1 / f_s = 1 / 3000\ \text{Hz} = 0.333$ msec.

Example. 1.3: The sum of two signals $x_1(t) = 10\sin(4\pi \times 103t)$ and $x_2(t) = 2\pi \times 256t)$ is sampled at 1 k Hz. The sampled signal is give to a LPF with cut off of 2 kHz. Obtain the frequency components contained at the output of the LPF.

Solution:

Here, $2\pi f_1 = 4\pi \times 1000$ or $f_1 = 2000\ \text{Hz} = 2$ kHz

$2\pi f_2 = 2\pi \times 256$ or $f_2 = 256$ Hz

$f_s = 2f_m = 2 \times 2\ \text{kHz} = 4$ kHz.

LPF output will just contain the 256 Hz component as the high frequency component of 2 KHz will be blocked by the LPF.

Example. 1.4: An analog signal has significant spectral components from 2 kHz to 5 kHz. What is the Nyquist sampling rate for this signal?

Solution:

We know that for a bandpass signal,

$fs = 2 \times f_H / k$ where $k = f_H / B$

$k = f_H / B = 5/3 = 1.66 \approx 1$ (to be truncated).

Therefore, $fs = (2\ x\ 5\ \text{kHz}) / 1 = 10$ kHz.

Example 1.5: A bandpass signal extends from 94 -106 Hz. Determine the minimum sampling frequency to avoid aliasing error.

Solution: As per bandpass sampling theorem,

$f_s = 2f_H / k$, where $k = f_H / B$.

Here, $f_L = 94$ Hz and $f_H = 106$ Hz and

$B = f_H - f_L = 106 - 94 = 12$ Hz.

$K = f_H / B = 106 / 12 = 8$

$f_s = 2f_H / k = (2x106) / 8 = 26.5$ Hz

1.7 PULSE MODULATION

As in the case of analog modulation, when we wish to implement pulse modulation, the carrier used is pulse train rather than a continuous waveform. Some parameter of a pulse train is changes with respect to the instantaneous sample values of a message signal to obtain pulse modulation.

We have two types of pulse modulation: Pulse Amplitude Modulation (PAM) and Pulse Time Modulation (PTM).

In PAM, the amplitudes of the pulses of the carrier pulse train are varied in accordance with sample values of a information signal. In PTM, the timing of the pulses of the carrier pulse train is varied.

There are two types of PTM systems:

- Pulse Width (or Duration) Modulation (PWM)
- Pulse Position Modulation (PPM)

In PWM, the width of the pulses of the carrier pulse train is varied in accordance with the message signal whereas in PPM, the position of the pulses of the carrier pulse train is varied. Figure 1.13 shows the three types of pulse modulation methods. In this section, we discuss only the PAM modulator and demodulator.

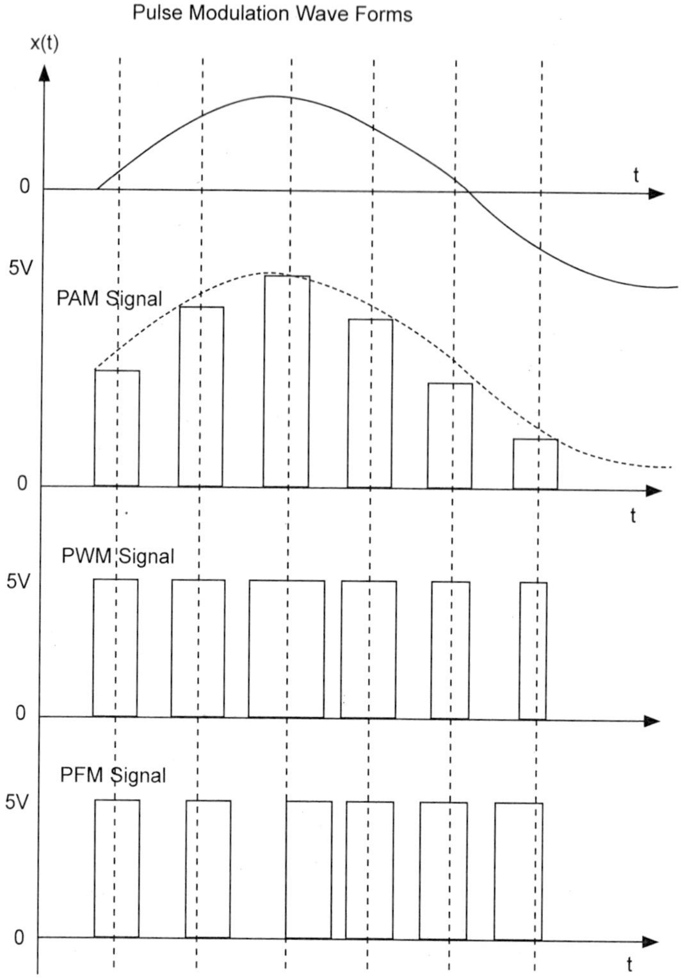

Fig. 1.13 Pulse modulation methods

PAM Modulator/Demodulator

Figure 1.14(a) shows the circuit for generation of PAM signal x(t) from the flat-topped sampler circuit consisting of the sampling switch and discharge switch (already explained in previous section). The flat top samples, sampled at the rising edge of each pulse, are generated with a sampling period of Ts and a pulse width of τ is shown in Figure 1.14(b).

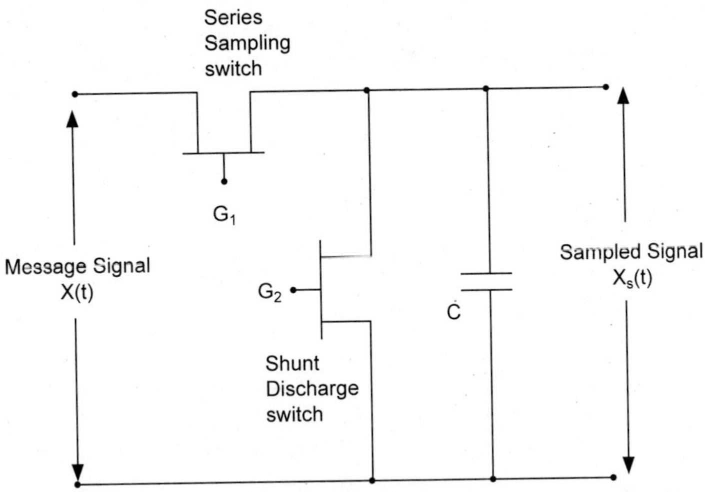

(a)

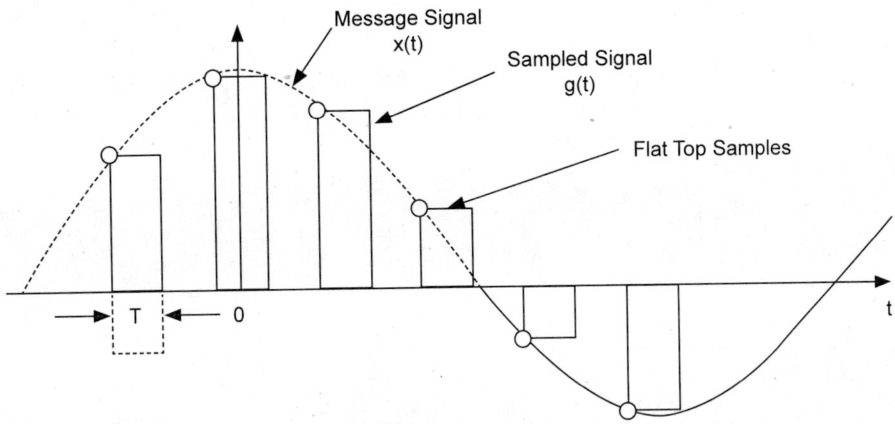

(b)

Fig. 1.14 PAM modulator

The PAM demodulator circuit is shown in Figure 1.15 that consists of a holding circuit and LPF to get the demodulated signal.

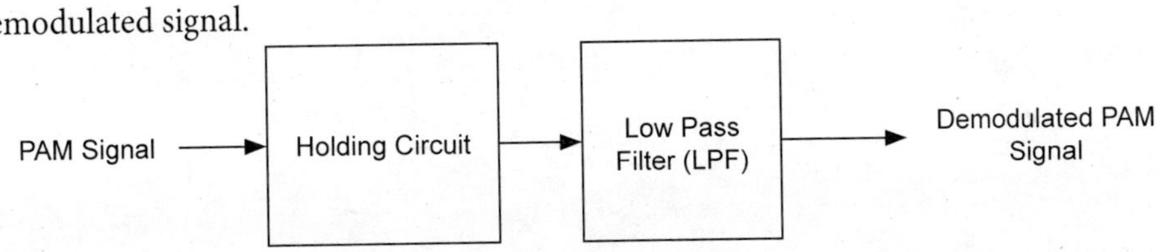

Fig. 1.15 PAM demodulator

The performance comparison of the three pulse modulation schemes is given in Table 1.2.

Table 1.2: Performance Comparison of Pulse Modulation schemes

Parameter	PAM	PWM	PPM
Varying parameter	Amplitude	Width	Position
SNR	Low	Moderate	Comparatively high
Need for synchronization	Not needed	Not needed	Needed
BW requirement	Low	High	High
Transmission Power	Variable	Variable	Constant

1.8 PULSE CODE MODULATION

Pulse-code modulation (PCM) is a technique used to digitally represent sampled analog signals by rounding off the amplitudes of the samples. PCM is basically an analog to digital converter that converts an analog/continuous signal to a digital signal. The analog signal is sampled regularly at uniform intervals, with each sample rounded off to the nearest value by a process called quantization and then encoded. ie. PCM involves three essential steps: Sampling, Quantization and Coding.

We have already studied sampling techniques in section 1.6. In this section, we will focus on Quantization and Coding. The block diagram of a typical PCM system is shown in Figure 1.16.

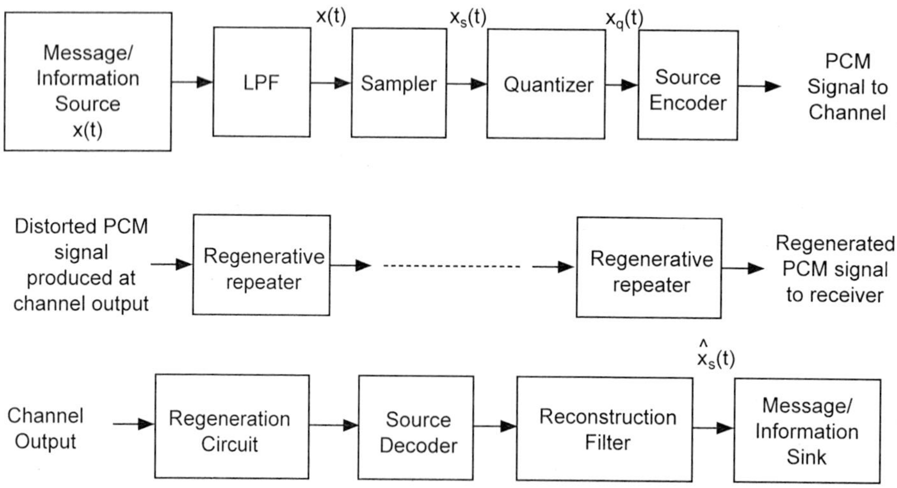

Scan here to know more

Fig.1.16 PCM system

1.8.1 Quantization

Quantization is a process where sample values are rounded off to a discrete value in a set of quantization levels. This process can be accomplished by approximating the amplitude levels of the sampled signals into one of the predefined decision levels. The system performing this task is called as a quantizer. It is denoted in Figure 1.17.

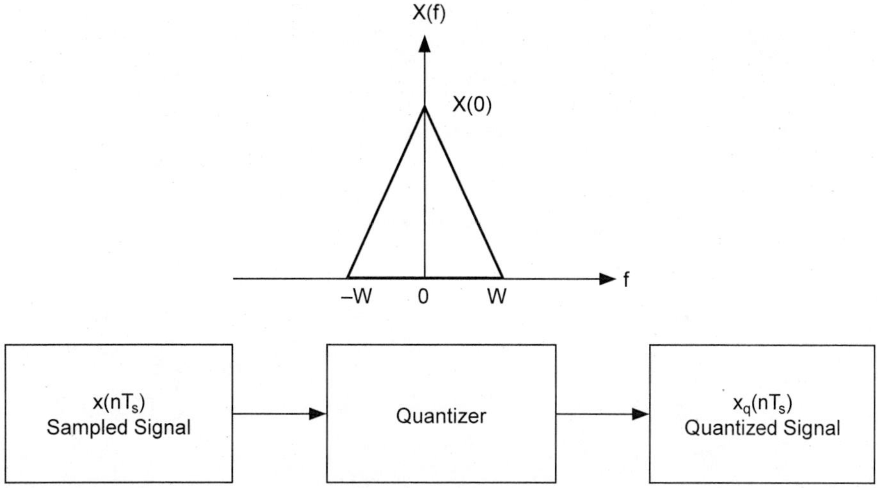

Fig. 1.17 Process of quantization

It can be inferred from the figure that all discrete signals need not be digital but all digital signals are discrete. The number of decision levels is dependent on the number of bits used to represent the levels. For instance, if there are 4 bits to represent the decision levels, then there will be 16 different levels which the amplitude of the signal can be approximated to. In general, for an 'n' bit quantizer the number of decision levels is equal to 2^n.

The peak-to-peak value of the analog signal is divided into number of decision levels dependent on the number of bits used to represent the decision levels. The plot of amplitude levels of the sampled signal $x(nT_s)$ versus quantized levels $x_q(nT_s)$ forms a staircase waveform. Horizontal lines in the staircase waveforms are called as treads and vertical lines are called as risers.

The quantization step size is defined as the difference between the two adjacent decision levels. It is denoted using 'Δ'. If this step size is same for all cases, such quantizers are called as uniform quantizers. In other words uniform quantizers approximate the amplitude level of a sampled signal into one of the decision levels that are equally spaced. On the contrary, in some of the applications like speech processing, we may need finer representation for some part of the signal compared to other. In such cases the quantization steps are not uniform across all levels. Such quantizers are called as non-uniform quantizers.

To understand the concept of uniform quantization, consider the following instance. Let the sampled signal to be quantized has amplitude levels in the range of -4V to +4V and if we use 3 bits to represent the decision levels, then the step size for an uniform quantizer in that case will be 1V. A typical quantization characteristic curve for an uniform quantizer is as shown in Figure 1.18.

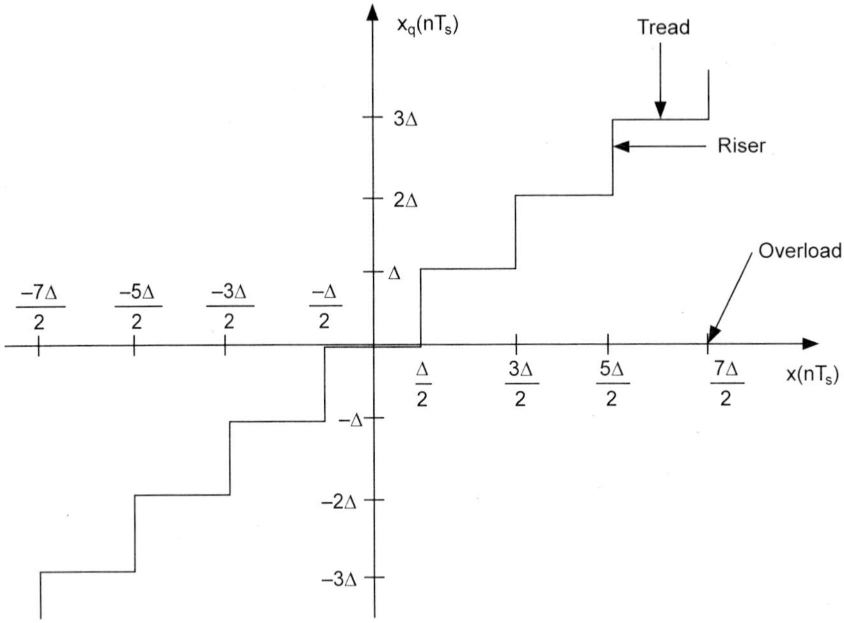

Fig. 1.18 Midtread quantization

The x-axis of the characteristic represents the amplitude levels of the sampled signal and y-axis represents the decision levels. This type of characteristic curve is called as a midtread quantizer as the origin cuts the tread exactly at the centre. Here the sampled threshold values are represented as $\pm\frac{\Delta}{2}, \pm\frac{3\Delta}{2}, \pm\frac{5\Delta}{2}$ and so on. The decision levels or decision thresholds are represented as 0, ±Δ, ±2Δ, ±3Δ and so on. The maximum amplitude level of the sampled signal is known as overload level. It can be seen from the curve that any amplitude of the sampled signal between $\frac{\Delta}{2}$ and $\frac{3\Delta}{2}$ will be quantized to a level Δ and that between $\frac{3\Delta}{2}$ and $\frac{5\Delta}{2}$ will be quantized to a level 2Δ and so on. Therefore, the maximum possible deviation of the quantized level from the actual amplitude level is $\pm\frac{\Delta}{2}$. This deviation in the amplitude is called as quantization error.

The plot of quantization error as a function of the amplitude level of the sampled signal x(nTs) is presented in Figure 1.19.

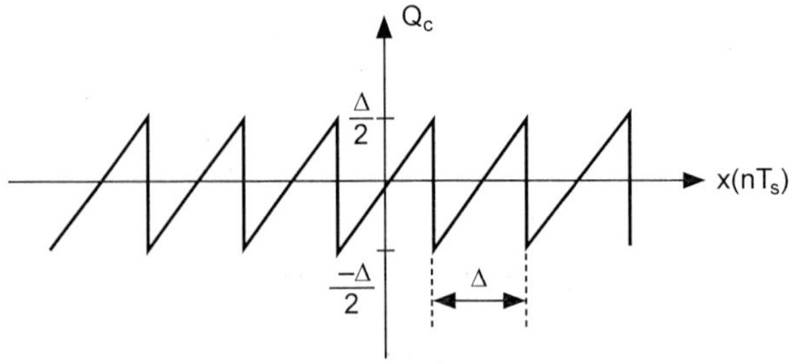

Fig 1.19 Quantization error for a midtread quantizer

There is another way to represent a quantizer characteristic, known as midrise quantizer. The representation is presented in Figure 1.20.

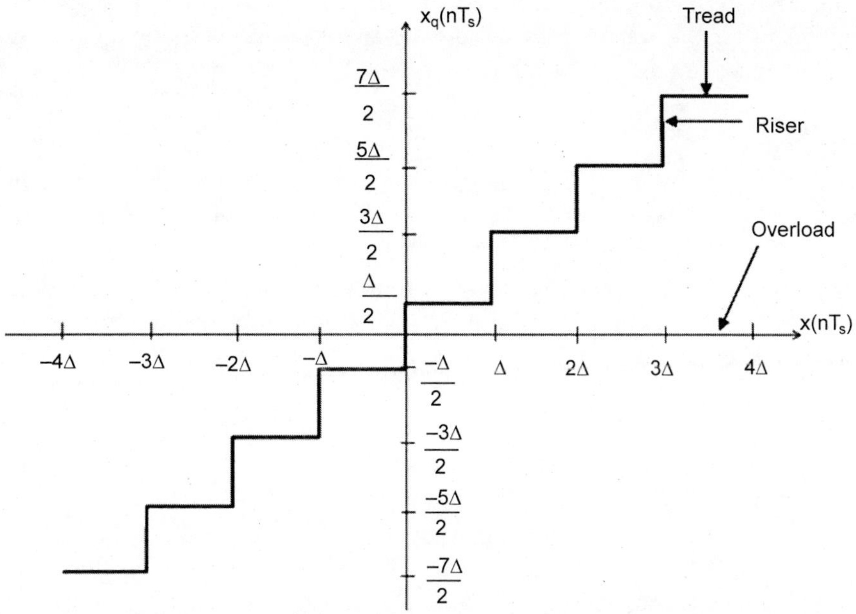

Fig. 1.20 Midrise quantizer

In case of a midrise quantizer, the origin cuts the riser at the middle. In this case, the sampled thresholds on the x-axis are in terms of 0, $\pm\Delta$, $\pm2\Delta$, $\pm3\Delta$ and so on. Decision levels are represented as $\pm\frac{\Delta}{2}, \pm\frac{3\Delta}{2}, \pm\frac{5\Delta}{2}$ and so on. Similar to the previous case, any amplitude between the range 0 and Δ is quantized to a level $\frac{\Delta}{2}$, any amplitude between the range Δ and 2Δ is quantized to a level $\frac{3\Delta}{2}$ and so on. Thus the maximum possible deviation or the quantization error for this case is also $\pm\frac{\Delta}{2}$. Figure 1.21 presents the plot of quantization error as a function of the amplitude of the sampled signal x(nTs).

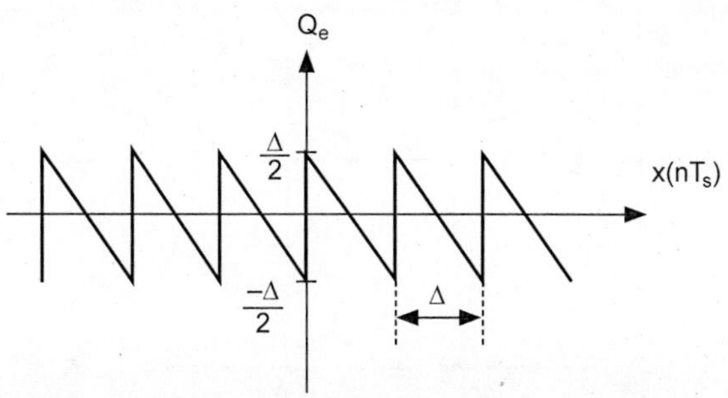

Fig. 1.21 Quantization error for a midrise quantizer

It is very clear from the Figures 1.19 and 1.21 that quantization error is directly proportional to the step size Δ. Thus, we can reduce the error by having decision levels placed at closer intervals. This can be achieved by incorporating more number of bits to represent the levels which in turn increases the bandwidth requirement for the system. Hence there has to be a trade-off between achieving a better representation of the signal and the bandwidth requirement.

1.8.2 Encoder

The block following the quantizer in the PCM block diagram is encoder. Encoder converts the quantized levels into digital code vectors. As discussed in Section 1.8.1, the number of quantization levels is given by

$$N = 2^n$$

where 'n' indicates the total number of bits representing a decision/ quantization level. Here we have assumed that the quantized samples of the analog signal are represented using a binary codeword hence the base used here is 2. Nevertheless, the base can even be non-binary. In general, the number of quantization levels is given by;

$$N = r^n$$

where 'r' the base digits in the codeword. It is 2 for binary, 3 for ternary codes, 4 for quaternary codes and so on. However, at this stage we restrict our discussions to binary case.

It may be noted that the actual transmission of the data over the channel is the transmission of a physical entity like an electric waveform carrying the digital information. A method of representing an analog entity like a voltage, current or a photon so as to carry the digital information through a communication channel is called line coding. There are many such line codes devised for digital communication systems. Two important and widely used methods are nonreturn to zero (NRZ) unipolar waveform and non-return to zero (NRZ) polar waveform. In case of a NRZ unipolar waveform, the bit '1' is represented by an electric pulse of amplitude +A Volts for a duration of Tb and bit '0' is represented by an electric pulse of amplitude 0 Volts for the bit duration. On the contrary in case of NRZ polar representation, bit '1' is represented by an electric pulse of amplitude +A Volts for a duration of Tb and bit '0' is represented by an electric pulse of amplitude -A Volts for the bit duration.

An example for NRZ unipolar and NRZ polar representation for a binary data 1 0 1 0 1 is shown in Figure 1.22.

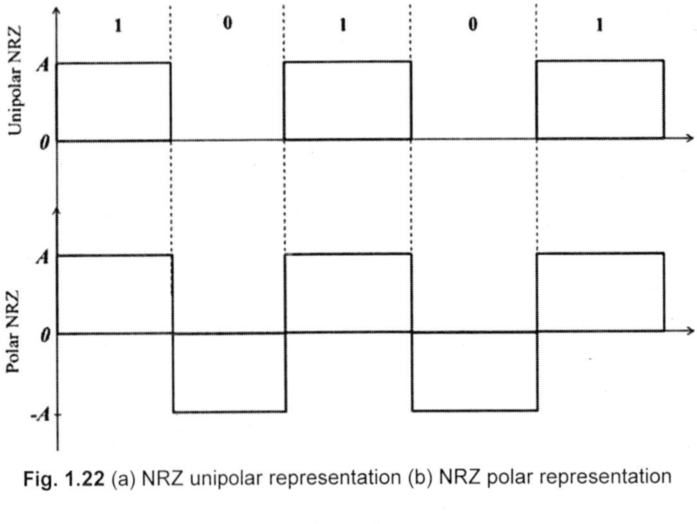

Fig. 1.22 (a) NRZ unipolar representation (b) NRZ polar representation

1.8.3 Regenerative Repeaters

As discussed in Section 1, one of the major advantages of digital communication systems is the ease of reconstructing the signal. In other words, digital signals are more immune to noise compared to analog signals.

The encoded signal at the transmitter side of the PCM will be then communicated to the channel where the signal gets distorted due to the presence of various channel impairments. In order to counter to the effect of noise, regenerative repeaters are placed at sufficiently close distances so that the distorted pulse can be regenerated as the original pulse. The block diagram of a regenerative repeater is as shown in Figure 1.23.

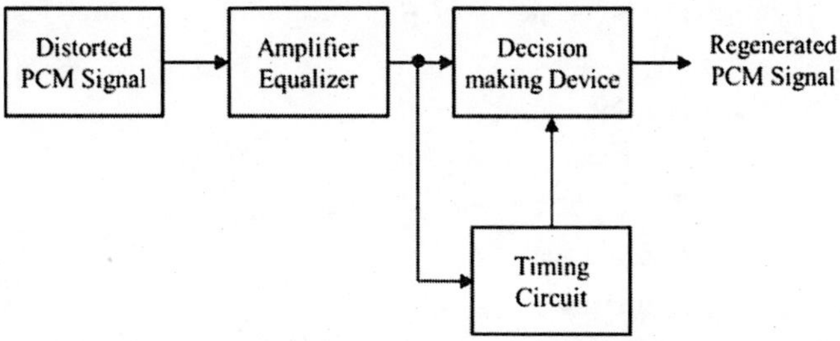

Fig. 1.23 Regenerative repeater

The first part of the regenerative repeater is an amplifier and equalizer circuit. An equalizer is used to compensate the amplitude or phase distortions experienced by the signal during transmission. The output of the equalizer is given to the timing circuit where the train of pulses called sampling waveform is generated. Whenever the sampled value is greater than the set threshold, the decision device takes a decision on whether the pulse is present or not in that particular bit duration. In this manner the entire PCM wave transmitted at the sender side can be regenerated. There are possibilities of a decision-making device committing an incorrect decoding occasionally. This may be due to the severe degradation or jitter introduced in the channel. This will lead bit errors during transmission.

1.8.4 Decoder

Decoder is used at the receiver part of a PCM system to retrieve the information. The output of the decoder is also a staircase waveform which is an approximation of the input signal. The decoded signal for a given message is presented in Figure 1.24.

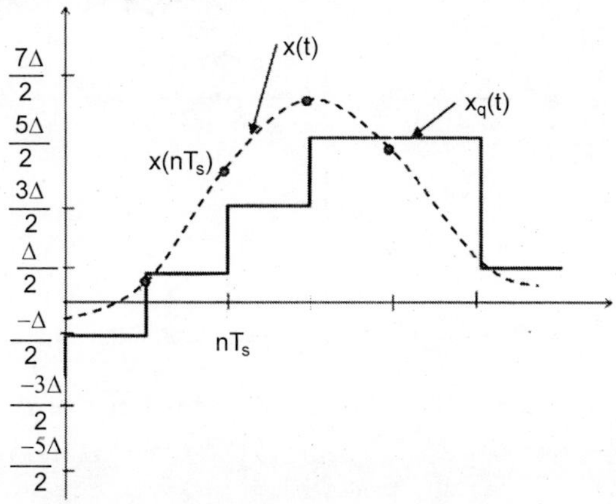

Fig. 1.24 Decoded signal

1.8.5 Reconstruction Circuit

The output of the decoder is given to a reconstruction circuit where the message is extracted from the decoded signal. This is accomplished by passing the signal to a low pass filter whose cut-off frequency is equal to the bandwidth of the signal. It gives a smooth approximation of the is original signal. However, it can be noted that the reconstructed signal differs from the original signal as quantization has resulted in an irreversible deviation in the amplitude levels of the sampled signal.

Example 1.6: How many bits are needed to represent 128 distinct quantization levels?

Solution:

To represent 'N' quantization levels, we need the following number of bits

$$N = 2^n$$

$$n = \log_2 N$$

$N = 128$ in the given problem.

Therefore $n = 8$.

We need atleast 8 bits for representation

Example 1.7: An analog signal has a voltage range of – 5 V to +5 V. If this is quantised to 8 bits, determine the number of levels and the step size required for the quantised signal.

Solution:

No. of levels $=2^n - 1 = 2^8 - 1 = 255$

Step size $= V / 2^n - 1 = [+5 - (-5)] / 255 = 10/255$

1.9 SIGNAL TO QUANTIZATION NOISE RATIO FOR UNIFORM QUANTIZER

As discussed in the section 1.8.1 uniform quantizer is the one in which the difference between the decision levels is uniform or simply the step size Δ is uniform. Uniform quantizers are also called as linear quantizers.

The decision process of an uniform quantizer is presented in Figure 1.25.

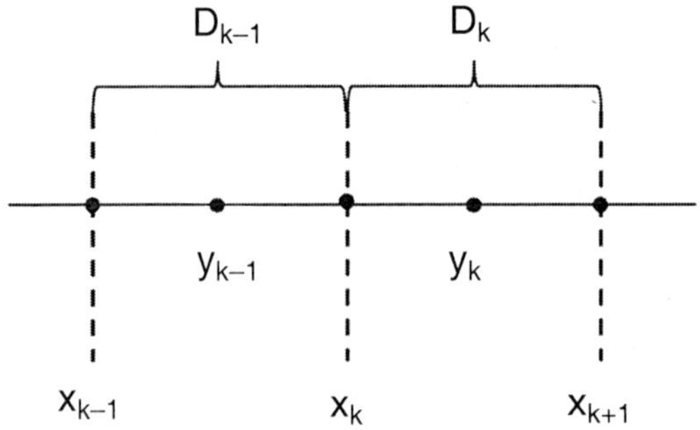

Fig. 1.25 Decision thresholds in an uniform quantizer

If the input amplitude level of the sampled signal lies in the range of x_{k-1} and x_k then the quantized output is y_{k-1} which is the mid-point between x_{k-1} and x_k. Thus the maximum deviation in the amplitude of the sampled signal and quantized signal is $\pm\frac{\Delta}{2}$.

Therefore quantization error Q_e lies in the range of $-\frac{\Delta}{2}$ and $+\frac{\Delta}{2}$.

i.e $$-\frac{\Delta}{2} \leq Q_e \leq +\frac{\Delta}{2} \tag{1.18}$$

Using the equation (1.18) in representing the expression for the output of the quantizer,

$$x_q(nT_s) = x(nT_s) + Q_e \tag{1.19}$$

Assuming that the quantization error is uniformly distributed over the interval Δ, the probability density function of the quantization error Q is given by:

$$f_Q(q) = \begin{cases} \frac{1}{\Delta}, -\Delta/2 \text{ to } \Delta/2 \\ 0, \quad \text{Otherwise} \end{cases} \tag{1.20}$$

where 'q' be the sample value.

The mean of this quantization error can be obtained as follows

Mean $$\{Q_e\} = \int_{-\frac{\Delta}{2}}^{\frac{\Delta}{2}} q\, f_Q(q)\, dq$$

$$= \int_{-\frac{\Delta}{2}}^{\frac{\Delta}{2}} q \frac{1}{\Delta} dq$$

$$= \frac{1}{\Delta}\int_{-\frac{\Delta}{2}}^{\frac{\Delta}{2}} q\, dq$$

Mean $$\{Q_e\} = 0 \tag{1.20}$$

The variance is given by

$$\sigma_Q^2 = \int_{-\frac{\Delta}{2}}^{\frac{\Delta}{2}} q\, f_Q(q)\, dq$$

$$= \int_{-\frac{\Delta}{2}}^{\frac{\Delta}{2}} q^2 \frac{1}{\Delta} dq$$

$$= \frac{1}{\Delta}\int_{-\frac{\Delta}{2}}^{\frac{\Delta}{2}} q^2\, dq$$

$$= \frac{\Delta^2}{12} \tag{1.21}$$

If there are 'n' bits for representation, then the number of decision levels is equal to

$$N = 2^n \tag{1.22}$$

or $$n = \log_2 N \tag{1.23}$$

In uniform quantizer, the step size can be computed as

$$\Delta = \frac{2(\text{maximum amplitude in sampled signal})}{N}$$

$$\Delta = \frac{2 \times \text{Xmax}}{2^n} \tag{1.24}$$

Therefore, the variance of the quantization error is given by

$$\sigma_Q^2 = \frac{x_{max}^2 \times 2^{-2n}}{3} \tag{1.25}$$

Let the average power of the signal be P_x.

Therefore, output signal to quantization noise ratio of an uniform quantizer is given by

$$[\text{SNR}]_q = \frac{P}{\Delta^2/12} \tag{1.26}$$

$$[\text{SNR}]_q = \frac{3 \times P \times 2^{2n}}{x_{max}^2} \tag{1.27}$$

From equation (1.27) it is clear that the signal to quantization noise ratio of an uniform quantizer is inversely proportional to the step size of the quantizer, Δ. The value of the [SNR]q can be improved by increasing the number of decision levels thus necessitating more number of bits to represent the levels.

Consider that a modulating signal with amplitude Vm. Then the average signal power is given by

$$\text{P} = \frac{A_m^2}{2}$$

As the maximum amplitude of the signal x_{max} is A_m, equation (1.25) becomes,

$$\sigma_Q^2 = \frac{A_m^2 \times 2^{-2n}}{3}$$

Using this in (1.27)

$$[\text{SNR}]_q = \frac{3 \times A_m^2 \times 2^{2n}}{A_m^2} \tag{1.28}$$

$$[\text{SNR}]_q = \frac{3}{2} \times 2^{2n} \tag{1.29}$$

Expressing this in dB,

$$[\text{SNR}]_q \text{ dB} = 10 \log_{10}(\frac{3}{2} \times 2^{2n})$$

$$[\text{SNR}]_q \text{ dB} = 10 \log_{10} \frac{3}{2} + 10 \log_{10}(2^{2n})$$

$$[\text{SNR}]_q \text{ dB} = 10 \log_{10} \frac{3}{2} + 20\text{n} \log_{10} 2$$

$$\Rightarrow [\text{SNR}]_q \text{ dB} = 1.76 + 6\text{n} \tag{1.30}$$

The above equation supports the fact that the signal to quantization noise ratio is dependent on the number of bits used to represent the decision levels.

Example 1.8: What is the maximum possible quantization error of the uniform quantizer used to quantize an input of amplitude 10 V peak to peak. Each level uses 2 bits for representation.

Solution: The maximum quantization error is given by

$$Q_{max} = \frac{\Delta}{2}$$

where Δ is the step size.

Number of possible decision levels , $N = 2^n = 2^2 = 4$

Therefore $$\Delta = \frac{10}{4} = 2.5 \text{ V}$$

$$\Rightarrow \qquad Q_{max} = \frac{\Delta}{2} = 1.25 \text{ V}$$

Example. 1.9: Determine how much is contributed by each bit in the codeword of a PCM system under uniform quantization to the (SNR)q.

Solution:

$$[SNR]_q = \frac{3}{2} \times 2^{2n}$$

In dB,

$$[SNR]_q \text{ dB} = 1.76 + 6n \text{ dB}$$

Therefore, each bit in the binary PCM codeword contributes 6 dB to the output $[SNR]_q$ (6 dB thumb rule).

1.10 NON-UNIFORM/ NON-LINEAR QUANTIZERS

For some of the applications, performing uniform quantization may degrade the performance. For instance, in speech processing signals with lower amplitude levels are more significant compared to that of higher amplitude levels. This is because of the fact that our ears exhibit non linear characteristics and hence are less sensitive to higher amplitudes. In such cases it is desirable to have more decision levels for the signals with less amplitude at the cost of increase in the step sizes for higher order signals.

The characteristics of a non uniform quantizer is as shown in Figure 1.26.

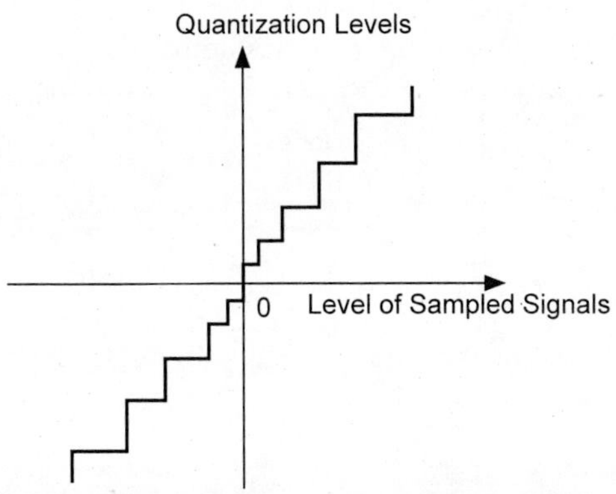

Fig. 1.26 Non uniform quantization characteristics

As the levels of lower order use finer quantization, quantization errors are less for the signal at the lower amplitude values. However, this can be achieved at the cost of higher errors being experienced by the amplitude levels of higher values. Figure 1.27 gives the quantization error characteristics for non uniform quantizers.

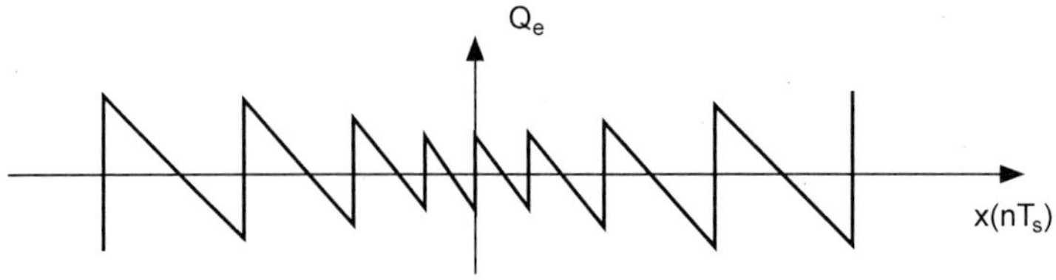

Fig. 1.27 Quantization error characteristics

Non uniform quantization can be achieved through uniform quantization by performing compression on the message signal at the sender end. This is because of the fact that in the compression characteristic, slope of the characteristic is more at the smaller amplitude levels compared to that of higher order amplitudes. This assures smaller order amplitudes getting quantized using more number of levels and hence assuring better precision. The effect can be reversed by performing the expansion operation at the receiver side. The compression can be achieved through a logarithmic operator. The relationship curve between the input and output for a compressor is shown in Figure 1.28.

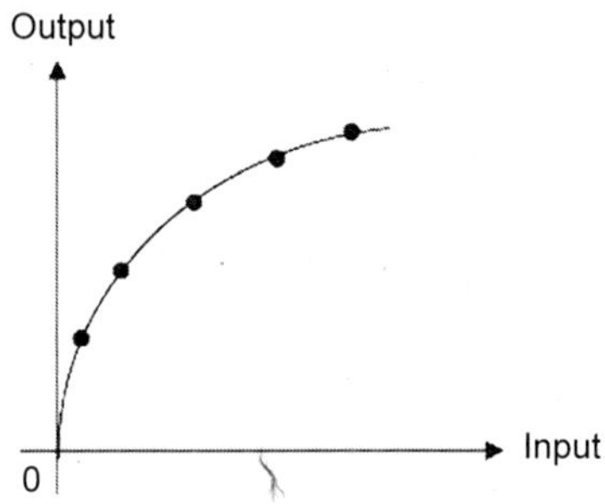

Fig. 1.28 Compression characteristic

Non uniform quantization can be achieved through uniform quantizer by adding a compressor block at the transmitter side and an expander block at the receiver side. The process of compression and expansion are collectively called as companding. A basic companding model is shown in Figure 1.29.

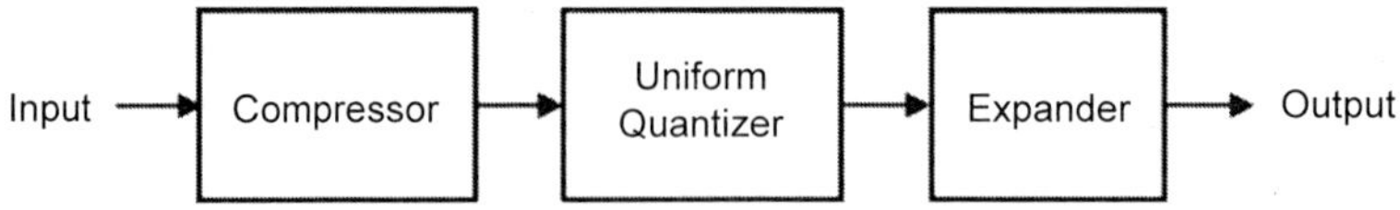

Fig. 1.29 A basic companding model

A PCM incorporating analog companding is presented in Figure 1.30.

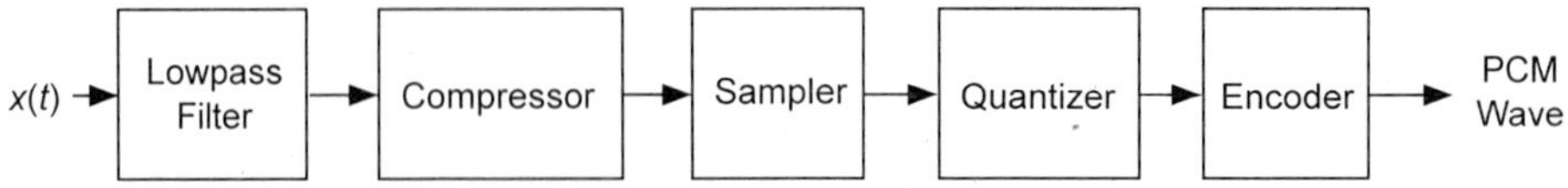

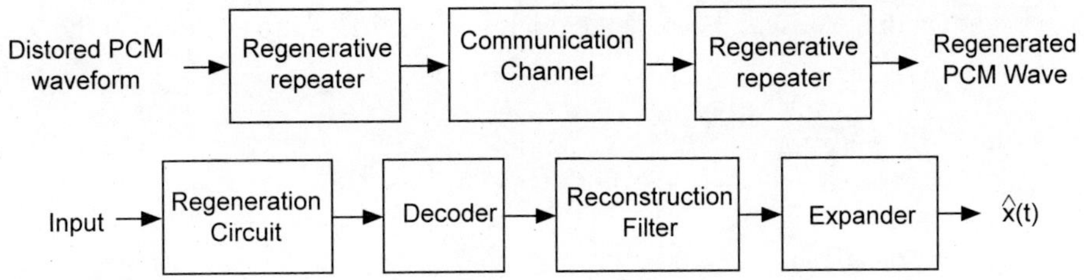

Fig. 1.30 PCM with analog companding

There are two popular ways of performing companding, namely μ- law companding and A- law companding. We will discuss about these in the next subsections.

1.10.1 μ-law Companding

The compression characteristic for a μ- law companding is governed by the following equation.

$$\frac{|Y|}{X_{\max}} = \frac{\ln[1+\mu\left(\frac{|X|}{X_{\max}}\right)]}{\ln[1+\mu]} \tag{1.31}$$

where

Y is the amplitude of the output

X is the amplitude of the sampled input

Xmax is the maximum value of the uncompressed signal X

μ is the design parameter.

The design parameter 'μ' defines the amount of compression achieved. No compression is achieved when its value is 0. The effect of degree of compression achieved as a function of μ is as shown in Figure 1.31.

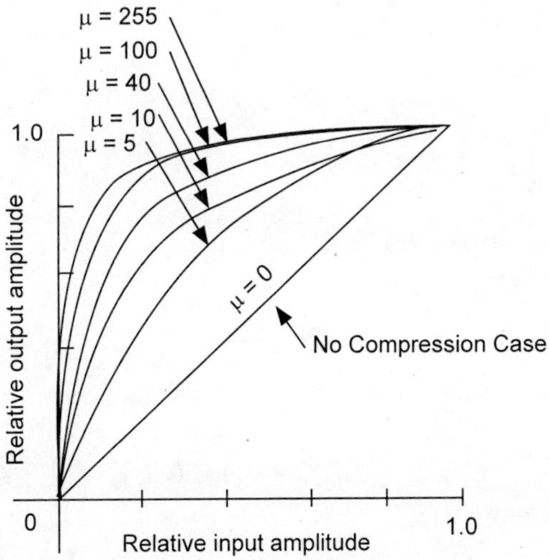

Fig. 1.31 Compression characteristics as a function of

When μ law companding is used, the signal to quantization noise ratio achieved at the output of the PCM system is given by,

$$[\text{SNR}]_o = \frac{3 \times N^2}{[\ln(1+\mu)]^2} \tag{1.32}$$

1.10.2 A- law Companding

The equation governing A - law companding is as given below:

$$\frac{|Y|}{X_{max}} = \begin{cases} \dfrac{A|X|X_{max}}{1+\ln A}, & 0 \le \dfrac{|X|}{X_{max}} \le \dfrac{1}{A} \\ \dfrac{1+\ln[A|X|/X_{max}]}{1+\ln A}, & \dfrac{1}{A} \le \dfrac{|X|}{X_{max}} \le 1 \end{cases} \tag{1.33}$$

To find the signal quantization noise ratio for an A- law companding, we need to define the term Companding Gain (CG). The companding is be defined as

$$\text{CG} = \lim_{x \to 0} \frac{dy}{dx} \tag{1.34}$$

The compression characteristics of a μ law companding is

$$\frac{|Y|}{X_{max}} = \frac{\ln[1+\mu\left(\dfrac{|X|}{X_{max}}\right)]}{\ln[1+\mu]}$$

Let $\quad a = \left(\dfrac{|X|}{X_{max}}\right)$ and $b = \left(\dfrac{|Y|}{X_{max}}\right)$

Then the μ law becomes

$$b = \frac{\ln[1+\mu a]}{\ln[1+\mu]} \tag{1.35}$$

Hence Coding Gain (CG) can be computed as

$$\text{CG} = \lim_{a \to 0} \frac{db}{da}$$

$$= \lim_{a \to 0} \frac{1}{\ln(1+\mu)}\left[\frac{1}{1+\mu a} \times \mu\right]$$

$$= \frac{\mu}{\ln(1+\mu)} \tag{1.36}$$

For small signals the signal to quantization noise ratio using A- Law companding can be related to the signal to quantization noise ratio achieved by the uniform quantizer by the following relation:

$$10 \log [\text{SNR}]_{\text{A- Law}} = 10 \log [\text{SNR}]_q + 20 \log(\text{CG}) \tag{1.37}$$

Where CG is the Companding Gain.

It is evident from the above equation that the A-Law compander achieves an improvement in the SNR as compared to uniform quantizer, however at the cost of increased complexity.

Example. 1.20: Determine the companding gain improvement that is obtained in the companding process by using a μ law compander assuming μ =255.

Solution:

The companding gain for a μ law compander is given by

$$CG = \mu / \ln(1+\mu) = 255 / \ln(1+255) = 45.98$$

$$CG(dB) = 20 \log_{10} CG = 20 \log_{10}(45.98) = 33.3 \text{ dB.}$$

1.11 LINE CODES

In digital communication although the binary information is to be transmitted through the channel, actual communication involves the transmission of analog signals like electric or optic pulses representing the binary information. Thus, appropriate coding scheme is to devised to represent bits '0' and '1' in the form of pulses. This technique is called as line coding.

Line coding is a process of representing binary information in the form of digital pulses.

Basically, there are three types of representing the pulses namely,

- Unipolar representation
- Polar representation
- Bipolar representation

In unipolar representation the amplitude level can be either zero or a positive value. Whereas in case of polar and bipolar representations both positive and negative amplitude levels are used.

Note: Signal levels are the different amplitude levels the pulse can take on and data levels are the different data types represented by the pulses. For binary case, number of data levels is 2.

There are two ways of representing the pulses within a bit duration, namely Return to Zero (RZ) and Non Return to Zero (NRZ). In case of RZ representation, the bit duration is divided into two exact halves for every pulse. The first half represents the voltage depending on the coding scheme used. The second half of the bit duration of the pulse takes an amplitude of '0'V irrespective of the type of the data it is representing. On the contrary in case of NRZ, the amplitude levels of the pulses are same throughout the pulse width and are not forced to zero within the pulse duration.

Two of the important line coding techniques namely unipolar NRZ and bipolar NRZ have been discussed in Section 1.9. In this section we discuss a few more types of line coding methods that are widely used in digital communication systems.

Example 1.21: State True or False

For a given code, pulse with NRZ representation contains more energy compared to that of RZ representation.

Solution: TRUE

As the amplitude of the pulse is zero for half of the pulse duration, RZ representations contain lower energy compared to NRZ representations.

1.11.1 Unipolar RZ

In this representation a bit '1' is represented by +A V for first half of the bit duration and to 0V for the next half. However, a bit '0' is represented by 0V.

1.11.2 Polar RZ

In this representation a bit '1' is represented by +A V for first half of the bit duration and to 0V for the next half. Similarly, a bit '0' is represented by -AV for the first half of the bit duration and 0V for the next half.

1.11.3 Bipolar NRZ

In this representation there are three signal levels, namely +A, -A and 0. A bit '1' is represented by +A and -A alternatively and bit '0' is represented by 0V. As the representation is NRZ, the same amplitude levels continue for the complete bit duration.

1.11.4 Bipolar RZ

The only difference between this with respect to bipolar NRZ is that the amplitude level of the pulse is forced to 0V for the second half of the bit width.

1.11.5 Manchester

A bit '0' is represented by a pulse with high-to-low combination and a bit '1' is represented by a pulse with low-to-high combination within a bit duration. The pulses representing bits '0' and '1' are given in Figure 1.32.

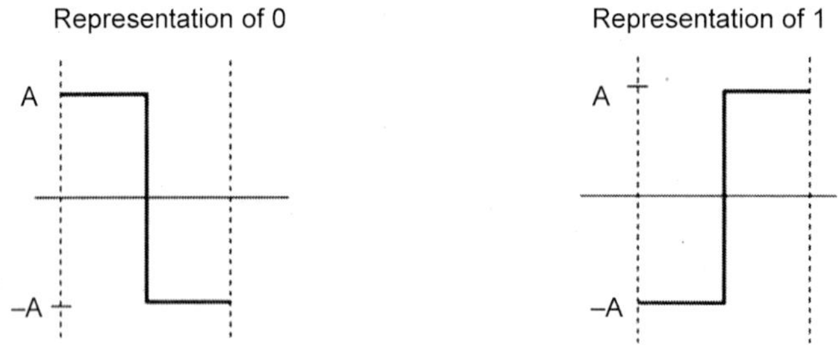

Fig. 1.32 Manchester coding

1.11.6 Differential Manchester

In this representation, there is a change in the signal level at the beginning of the pulse whenever a bit '0' is to be represented. On the other hand, bit '1' represents no shift in the amplitude at the beginning of the pulse. Figure 1.33 details the representation format used for differential manchester coding.

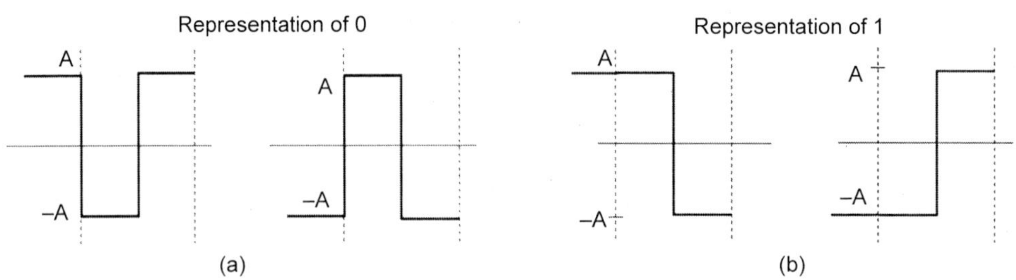

Fig. 1.33 Differential Manchester encoding

Figure 1.33 (a) presents the cases of representing bit '0' when the signal level of the previous pulse at the beginning of the current pulse is high and the signal level of the previous pulse at the beginning of the current pulse is low respectively. Figure 1.33 (b) denotes the same two cases for representing a bit '1'. To summarize, let us consider the bit sequence 1 1 0 1 0 1. The representation of this bit sequence using the line coding techniques discussed in this section are as shown in Figure 1.34.

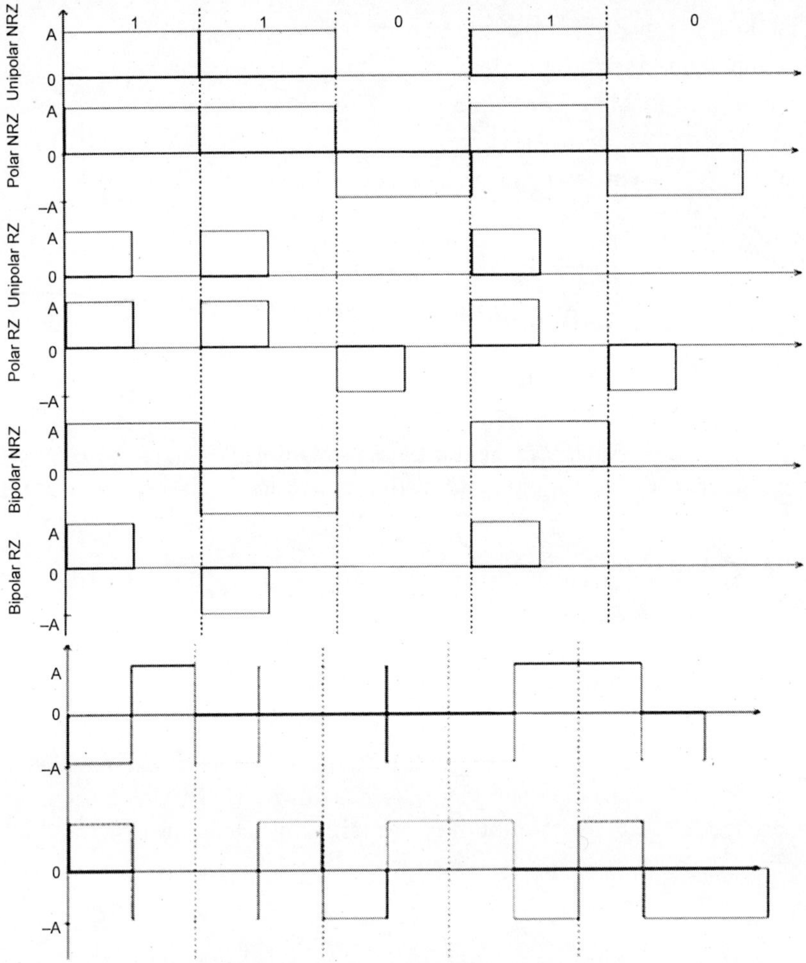

Scan here to know more

Fig. 1.34 Representation of bit sequence 1 1 0 1 0 1

Example 1.22: Represent the following bitstream in the form of differential manchester encoding: 1 1 0 1 1 0 1

Solution:

The Differential Manchester encoding for the given bit sequence is as shown in Figure 1.35

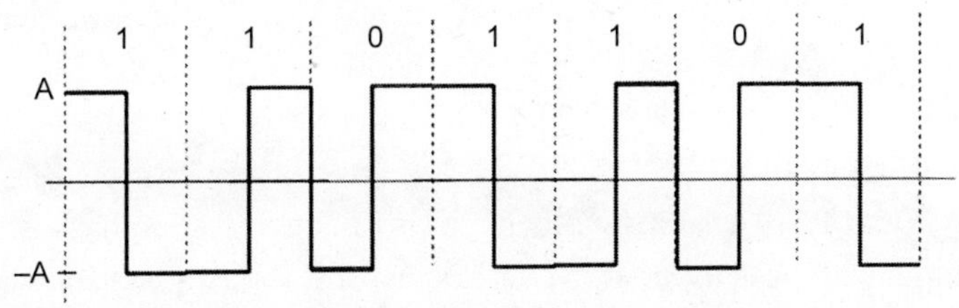

Fig. 1.35 Differential Manchester encoding

1.12 BANDWIDTH FOR PCM SYSTEMS

Let 'n' bits are used to represent a quantization level. In other words each quantization level is represented using 'n' bits.

Consider that the f_s number of samples are transmitted every second.

Therefore, we can define a term signalling rate which denotes the number of bits per seconds.

Signalling rate in PCM $= R_s$ = Number of bits/samples × Number of samples/secs

$$= n \times f_s \quad (1.38)$$

Bandwidth of a PCM system should be at least equal to half of the Signalling rate R_S.

$$B_{PCM} \geq \frac{1}{2} R_S$$

$$\Rightarrow \quad B_{PCM} \geq \frac{1}{2} n \times f_s \quad (1.39)$$

But $\quad f_s \geq 2 \times f_m$

Therefore $\quad B_{PCM} \geq n \times f_m \quad (1.40)$

Example 1.23: In a PCM system, an analog signal is sampled at a rate of 1000 samples/sec and encoded with 6 bits. What is the minimum bandwidth required for faithful reconstruction?

Solution:

The minimum bandwidth required is given by,

$$B_{PCM} \geq \frac{1}{2} n \times f_s$$

$$B_{PCM} \geq \frac{1}{2} \times 6 \times 1000 = 3000 \text{ Hz}$$

Example. 1.24: Five signals are to be multiplexed and transmitted. The first, second and fourth signals have a bandwidth of 4 kHz and the rest two have bandwidths of 10 kHz. Each sample requires 8 bits for PCM encoding. Calculate the minimum transmission bit rate of the system?

Solution: $\quad f_s = 2f_m$

Transmission rate, R = No. of bits × No. of signals × Sampling frequency

$= 8 \times 5 \times 2 \times 10{,}000 = 800$ Kbps.

Example. 1.25: A TV signal having a bandwidth of 5 MHz is transmitted using binary PCM.

If the number of quantization levels used in this PCM system is 512, determine the codeword length, transmission bandwidth, output bit rate and (SNR)q.

Solution:

Given $\quad f_m = 5$ MHz, L = No. of quantization levels= 512.

$L = 2^n = 512$, Therefore, n = 9 bits. (Code word length)

$BW \geq n\, f_m = 9 \times 5 \text{ MHz} = 45$ MHz.

$R = nfs = n \times 2\, f_m = 9 \times 2 \times 5 \text{ MHz} = 90$ MHz

$[SNR]q = 1.76 + 6n \text{ dB} = 1.76 + (6 \times 9) = 55.76 \approx 56$ dB.

Example. 1.26: A 10-bit PCM system employing uniform quantization has a bit rate of 64 kbps.

For a sinusoidal input with peak input of 5 volts, calculate the (SNR)q. Also determine the maximum frequency that this system can handle?

Solution:

$$(SNR)q = (1.76 + 6n)\text{ dB} = 1.76 + 6 \times 10 = 61.76\text{ dB}.$$

Also, $R = nf_s$

Hence, $f_s = R/n = 64 \times 103/\,10 = 6.4\text{ kHz}$

We know that $f_s \geq 2f_m$ or $f_m \leq 0.5 \times f_s \leq 0.5 \times 6.4\text{ kHz} \leq 3.2\text{ kHz}$.

This is the maximum frequency that the system can handle.

1.13 PCM TDM HIERARCHIES

We have seen in the previous section that sampling process basically is a process of conservation of-time, meaning that the communication channel is used only at the sampling time instances. Therefore, it makes sense to insert the samples of other message in between the adjacent samples of this message on a time-shared basis. This actually is the basis of a time-division multiplex (TDM) system. That is, the communication channel can be used by more than one independent message sources. In general, N users can be multiplexed digitally that facilitates us to combine digital signals of difference types (say computer data, digital voice etc.) of different bandwidths (low data rates) on to a single higher bandwidth (high speed) transmission line (or Communication channel). The reverse process happens at the demultiplexer a shown in Figure 1.36.

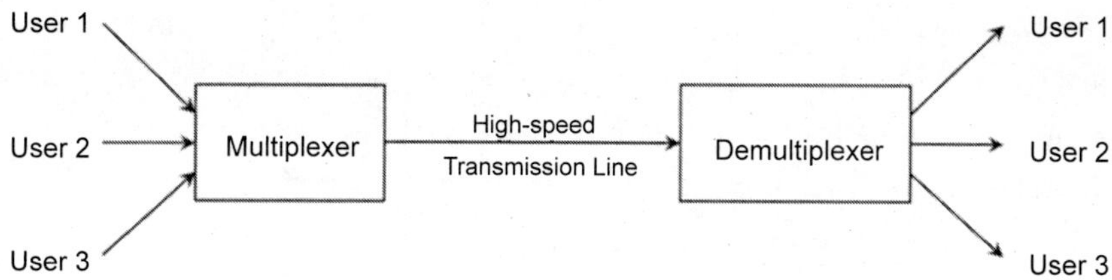

Fig. 1.36 A Digital multiplexer/demultiplexer scheme

PAM and PCM transmission systems normally use this time division multiplexing by allocating time slots to each of the signals (from various users) to be multiplexed. These users get serviced at least once in a TDM frame. Each TDM frame is splitted into time slots and every user is assigned with a unique time slot. However more than one slot can also be assigned to a user. That means a frame structure must exist so that several low data rate signals can be time-multiplexed to form composite signals of much greater bandwidth. This composite signal further can be time-multiplexed with other wideband signals to form the main multiplexed signal. Framing and synchronisation signals also will be required to locate the beginning of each frame, time slot, and symbol. We will discuss the frame structure and synchronisation in the next section.

The multiplexing and demultiplexing at the transmitter and receiver can be explained by allocating time slots for each user as shown in Figure 1.37. Four timeslots for users A, B, C and D arriving at their own pace in each of the timeslots. If each time slot is pre-assigned to a constant source, then we call this as ***Synchronous TDM.*** The time slots are sent irrespective of whether the sources have anything to transmit or not. As shown, 1st four time slots have symbols A, B, C, D, 2nd A, B, C only (4th time slot no symbol from user C) and 3rd four slots have symbols A & B in first two time slots (and nothing from users C & D in the next two slots).

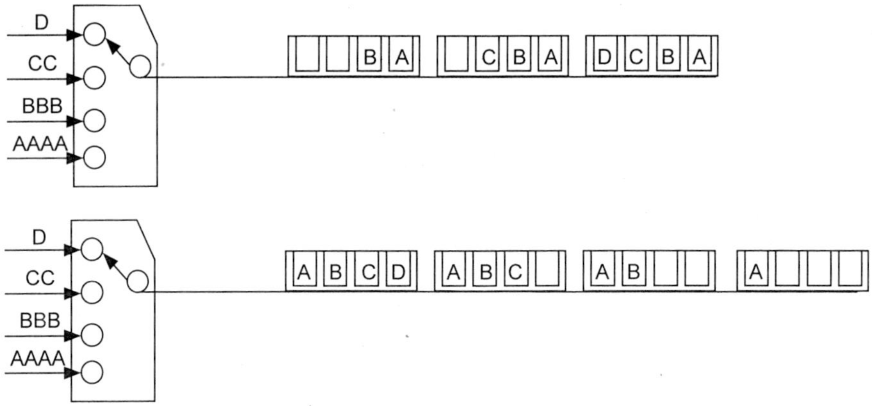

Fig. 1.37 Multiplexing and demultiplexing in TDM

1.13.1 Types of TDM

As discussed in previous section, in a TDM system, each user is given the access to the complete bandwidth of the channel for a fixed duration of time (time slot). The control over the channel will be then moved to the next user on a round-robin basis. Therefore, there will be no interference between the users. This is the greatest advantage over frequency division multiplexing (FDM). An example TDM can be employed for television broadcast. Suppose while broadcasting a television serial of say 30 minutes, for every 10 minutes serial time, a 2 minutes advertisement is generally incorporated. The time in which the serial is being broadcasted, the total bandwidth is dedicated to the serial.

TDM can be of two types:

1. Synchronous TDM &
2. Asynchronous (or Statistical) TDM.

Synchronous TDM is (what we have studied so far) where each time slot is pre-assigned to a particular user. The time slots are sent irrespective of whether the users have a few records to share or not. In such a scheme, the TDM devices can manage the users of various data rates. This is completed by authorising fewer slots per cycle to the slower, passive input devices than the faster, rapid devices as explained in Figure 1.37. One disadvantage of the synchronous TDM scheme is that some of the time slots in the frame are wasted.

Asynchronous (or Statistical) TDM is a technique in which the data is transmitted asynchronously. ie. dynamic allocation of bandwidth to each channel is adopted here, on an as-needed basis. This overcomes the disadvantage of synchronous TDM, in which quiet devices use up a portion of the multiplexed data stream, filling it with empty packets (which is a waste of bandwidth). This means that there is a dynamic allocation of bandwidth only to channels that are currently transmitting, resulting in efficient usage of the available bandwidth. It normally uses a FIFO (first in, first out) basis, but can also allocate extra bandwidth to specific input channels if they need.

Table 1.3: Comparison between Asynchronous and synchronous transmissions

Parameter	Synchronous	Asynchronous
Information transmitted at once	Multiple bytes	One byte (in general)
Start and stop bits	Not needed	Needed
Gap between message blocks	Absent	Present
Synchronisation	Requires perfect synchronization	Not required. Synchronization is achieved through start and stop bits
Data transmission speed	Fast. Suitable for high-speed communication between computers.	Slow
System complexity	Complex	Simple
Efficiency	Offer higher efficiency as start and stop bits are not needed	Efficiency is relatively less due to the presence of additional bits
Cost	High	Low

A typical TDM system is shown in Figure 1.38. As shown, the TDM system consists of N users (message inputs) being multiplexed on to a single composite PCM signal on a common channel. The commutator at the transmitter side, takes a narrow sample of each of the N input messages at a rate fs slightly higher than $2f_m$ (where f_m is the cut-off frequency of the anti-aliasing filter), and then interleaves these N samples inside the sampling interval Ts. TDM is immune to nonlinearities in the channel as a source of crosstalk. The reason is that different message signals are not simultaneously applied to the channel. The only disadvantage of the TDM scheme is that N samples need to be squeezed in a time slot of duration Ts.

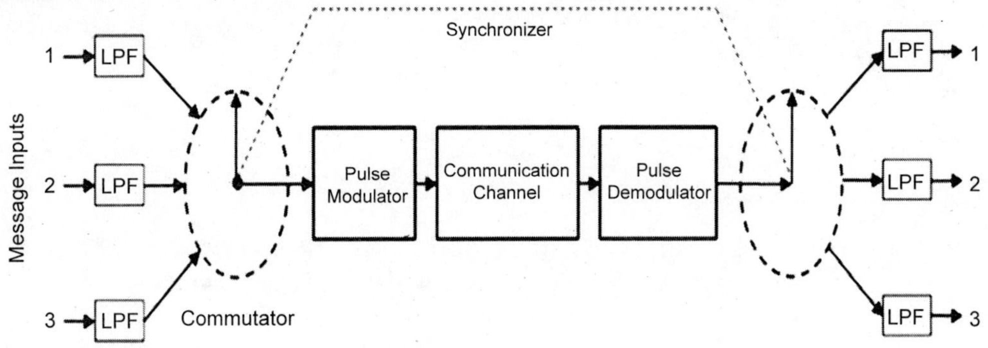

Fig. 1.38 TDM system

1.13.2 TDM Digital Hierarchy

Digital TDM hierarchy is identified differently by different countries. North America and Canada identify them as "T," where as Japan identifies it as "J,". International identification of the digital TDM hierarchy is "E,". It is detailed in Table 1.4.

Table 1.4 TDM hierarchy levels.

North America (Canada, Japan)			International (ITU-T)	
Designation	Number of Channels (DS0s)	Data Rate (Mbps)	Number of Channels (DS0s)	Data Rate (Mbps)
DS-1	24 (T1)	1.544	30 (E1)	2.048
DS-1C	48 (T1c)	3.152	120 (E2)	8.448
DS-2	96 (T2)	6.312	480 (E3)	34.368
DS-3	672 (T3)	44.736	1920 (E4)	139.264

North American Digital Telephone Hierarchy is shown in Figure 1.39. A T1 carrier systems was designed to combine PCM and TDM Techniques for the transmission of 24, 4Kbps voice channels, with each channel capable of carrying voice band telephone signals or data at 64 kbps data rate. The transmission bit rate (line speed) for a T1 carrier is 1.544 Mbps. All 24 DS-0 channels are then multiplexed to get a data rate of 1.544 Mbps, this digital signal level is also called DS-1. Therefore, T1 lines are referred as DS-1 lines.

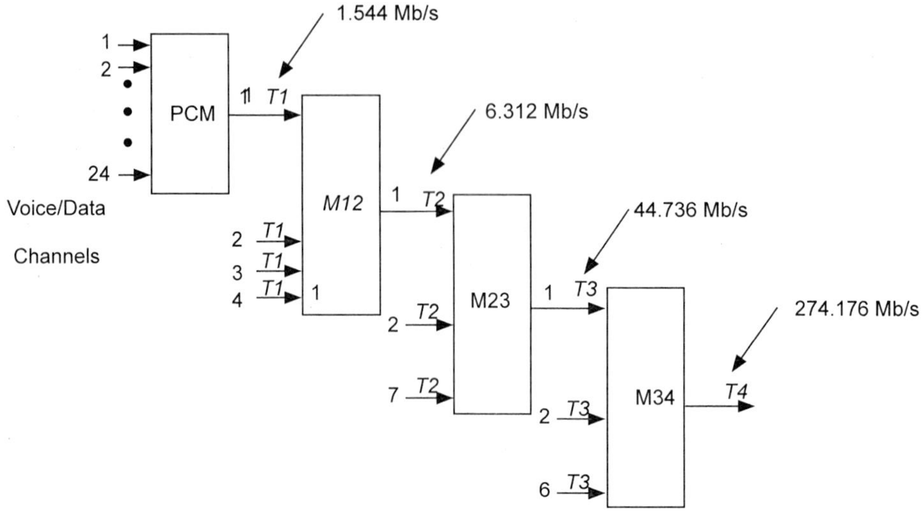

Fig. 1.39 North American digital hierarchy

T2 carriers multiplex 4, T1 signals (96, 64-Kbps voice or data channels) into a single 6.312 Mbps data signal transmission, T3 carriers multiplex 7, T2 signals (672, 64-kbps voice or data channels) at a data rate of 44.736 Mbps. T4 carriers multiplex 6, T3 signals (4032, 64-kbps voice or data channels) for transmitting at a data rate of 274.16 Mbps.

International (ITU-T) Digital Telephone Hierarchy is shown in Figure 1.40. The E1 carrier format carries data at a rate of 2.048 Mbps and can carry 30 channels of 64 Kbps each. E1 carries at a somewhat higher data rate than T1 (which carries 1.544 Mbps). E2 is a line that carries four multiplexed E1 signals with a data rate of 8.448 Mbps. E3 carries 16 E1 signals with a data rate of 34.368 Mbps. E4 carries four E3 channels with a data rate of 139.264 Mbps. E5 carries four E4 channels with a data rate of 565.148 Mbps.

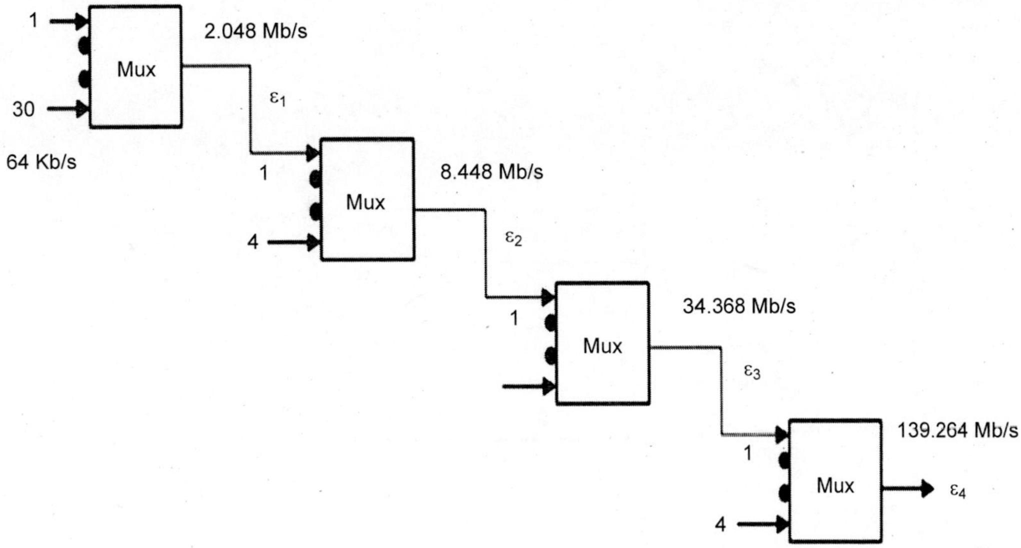

E1 - 2048 Mbps Channel

E2 - 8448 Mbps Channel

E3 - 34368 Mbps Channel

E4 - 139264 Mbps Channel

Fig. 1.40 International (ITU-T) digital telephone hierarchy

1.13.3 Frame Structure

The basic building block in digital transmission, we know that, 24 voice signals are sampled uniformly in a T1 carrier system employing TDM. If the highest frequency component in each voice signal is 4 kHz, we can calculate the bit rate of theT1 carrier as follows.

The multiplexer basically combines 24 voice channels sampled at the Nyquist rate of 2×4 kHz = 8 kHz (8000 samples per second) . Further, if each of the 24 voice channels is encoded with an 8-bit PCM code, and is sampled 8000 times a second resulting in a T1 frame, the line speed for a T1 carrier can be calculated (shown in Figure 1.41) as follows:

24 channels/frame × 8 bits/channel = 192 bits/frame

+ 1 bit (additional bit added, called the framing bit to each frame) = 193 bits/frame.

i.e. 8000 × 193 bps = **1.544 Mbps.**

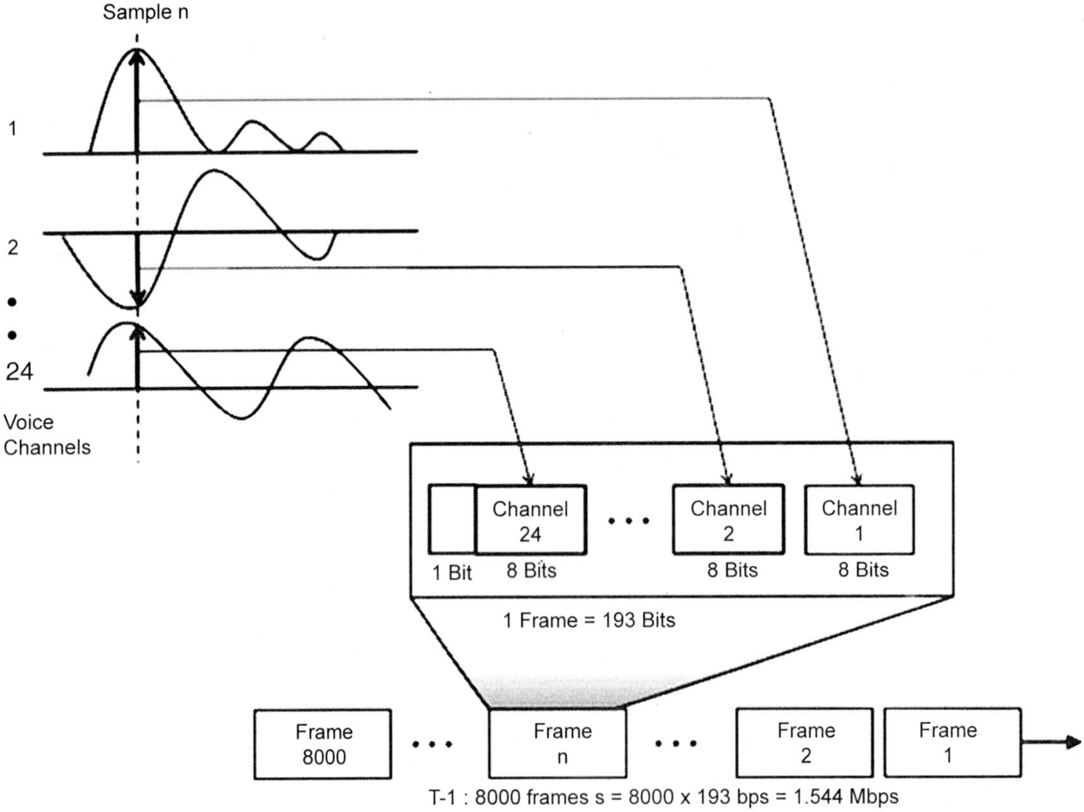

Fig. 1.41 Line speed of a T1 carrier

It may be noted that framing bit once per frame and is recovered at the receiver. The framing bit is used to maintain frame and sample synchronisation between TDM Transmitter and Receiver(Tranceiver). It is observed that 8000 frames /second translates to 125 μsec. ie. 1 frame occupies 125 μsec. The PCM frame for a T1 carrier is shown in Figure 1.42.

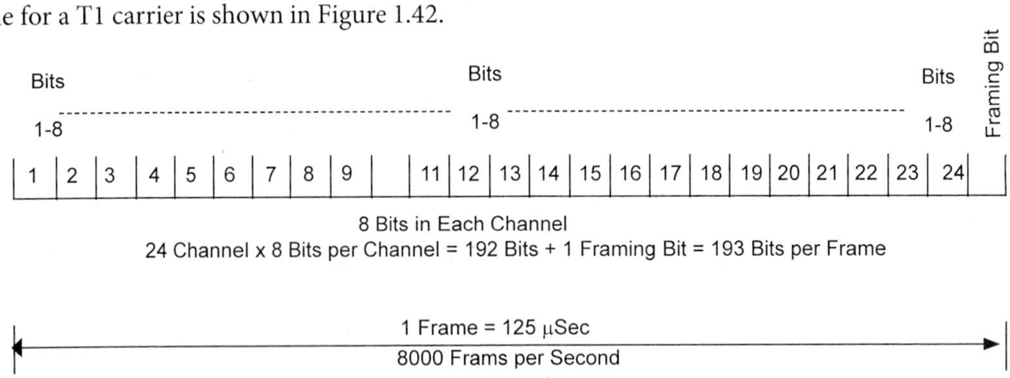

Fig. 1.42 T1 frame structure

Similarly, as per International (ITU-T) Digital Telephone Hierarchy, we have E1, E2... lines with corresponding bit rates as discussed earlier. In a basic E1 system (European TDM 30 + 2 Channels), a 125 μsec frame is divided into 32 equal time slots. The E1 frame format is shown in Figure 1.45. Channel 0 is used for framing(synchronising) and signalling. Channels 1-15 and 17- 31 are used for voice transmission. Channel 16 is reserved for future as a signalling channel and timeslot 17 is used for common signalling channel (CSC). E1 frame structure is as shown in Figure 1.43.

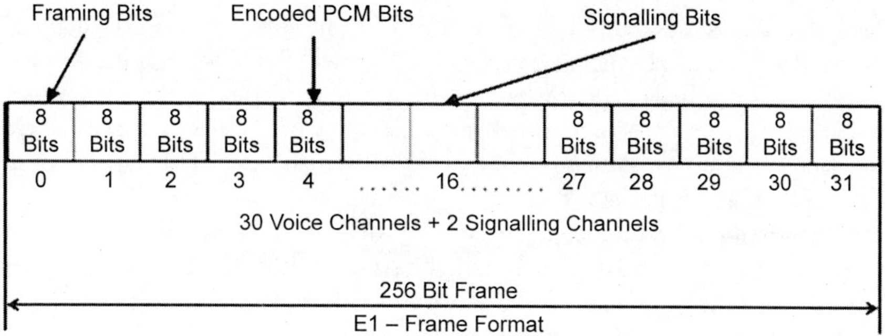

Fig. 1.43 E1 frame structure

The signalling rate for E1 line is 2.048 Mbps (64 kbps × 32) with 8bits/timeslot × 32 timeslots/frame resulting in 256 bits / frame and the line speed for E1 carrier is given by

256 bits/frame × 8000 frames / sec = **2.048 Mbps.**

1.13.4 Synchronisation and Bit Stuffing Mechanisms

We have seen that the first level(order) hierarchy combines 24 DS0(voice channels) to get a primary rate DS1 (T1) at 1.544 Mb/s. The second-level multiplexer combines 4 DS1(T1) so as to achieve a DS2(T2) with rate 6.312 Mb/s. The third-level multiplexer combines 7 DS2(T2) to get a DS3(T3) at 44.736 Mb/s and fourth-level combines 6 DS3(T3) so as to achieve a DS4(T4) at 274.176 Mb/s. Continuing, the fifth-level multiplexer combines 2 DS4(T4) to obtain a DS5(T5) at 560.160 Mb/s. The combined bit rate is more than the multiple of the incoming bit rates due to the presence of bit stuffing and control signals.

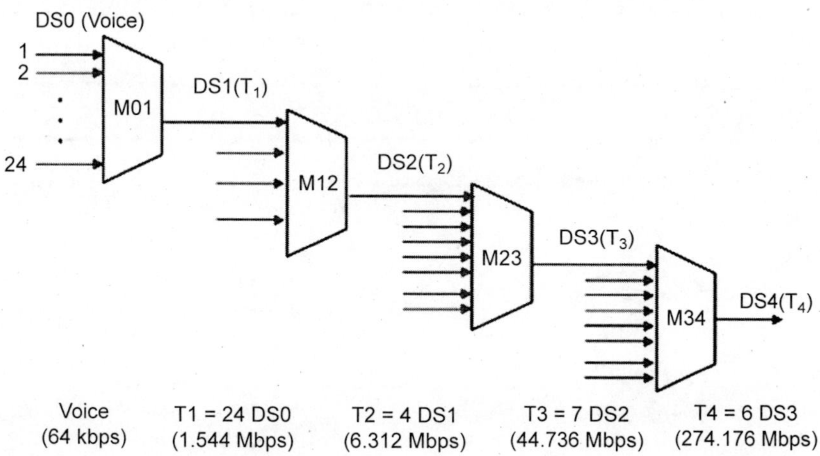

Some of the major issues encountered in the design of multiplexing system are Synchronization (so as to facilitate proper recovery of the interleaved digital signals), Framing (so as to identify individual at the Rx) and also variation in the bit rates of incoming signals (should be considered in the design). The Synchronization and rate variation problems can be resolved by what is called as Pulse stuffing or bit stuffing.

In the first order multiplexing, there is just a single clock to contend with, ie. the clock that drives the commutator at the M01 multiplexer. However, there will be a problem that might occur in connection with the higher orders of multiplexing.

Nevertheless, the 4 DS1 (T1) input lines in the Ml2 multiplexer come from physically widely separated locations. It employs four separate unsynchronized clocks. Although these clocks are chosen to be very stable crystal-controlled oscillators and are designed to operate at the same nominal frequency as nearly as possible. If this happens, clocks can be assumed to be perfectly synchronised. However, these clocks might experience a relative frequency/phase drift. That is, they won't be in synchronism. This will result in a situation, where the faster clock will have generated one more time slot than the slower clock in the course of transmission of even a few frames. For proper interleaving of bits at the second level of multiplexing ie. Ml2 level, it is necessary that all input bit streams (here the 4, T1 carriers) must somehow be made to appear to have the same rate. Bit rates can be made equal by adding extra bits to the slower bit stream through a process called pulse stuffing.

Pulse stuffing, generally referred to as bit stuffing, is the mechanism of adding one or more non-information bits into a message to be transmitted. It is also used to break up the message and often used as a means of controlling synchronization in systems that require both Tx (transmitter) and Rx(receiver) to transmit at the same bit rate.

The Ml2 multiplexer in the North American Digital Hierarchy, inserts nominally 17 bits for frame synchronization and pulse stuffing. Hence the number of bits per frame for a T2 carrier is

$$193 \times 4 + 17 = 789 \text{ bits/frame}$$

The T2 carrier bit rate is therefore = 789 bits/frame x 8000 frames/s = 6.312 Mb/s

Similarly, the M23 multiplexer adds nominally 69 bits for synchronization and pulse stuffing. Therefore, the number of bits per frame for a T3 carrier is

$$789 \times 7 + 69 = 5592 \text{ bits/frame}$$

The T3 carrier bit rate is therefore = 5592 bits/frame × 8000 frames/sec = 44. 736 Mb/s

Further the M34 multiplexer adds nominally 720 bits for synchronization and pulse stuffing. Therefore, the T4 system has a bit rate as {(5592 x 6) + 720} × 8000 = 274.176 Mb/s and so on for further multiplexing levels.

UNIT SUMMARY

- Functional blocks in a Digital Communication System
- Information Source
- Source Coder/ Decoder
- Channel Coder/ Decoder
- Modulator/Demodulator
- Communication Channel
- Sink
- Sampling - Transform analog waveform to discrete-time continuous wave
- Nyquist rate: $f_s = 2f_m$

- Quantization – Transform discrete-time continuous wave to discrete data.
- Human can only detect finite intensity difference.
- Pulse Modulation Techniques
- Pulse Amplitude Modulation (PAM)
- Pulse Width Modulation (PWM)
- Pulse Position Modulation (PPM)
- PCM is a process of representing analog signals in the digital form.
- PCM systems however have some limitations as well
- Complexity of hardware
- Large Bandwidth requirement
- But with the advance of VLSI technology, and with the availability of wideband communication channels (such as fiber) and compression technique (to reduce the bandwidth demand), the above two limitations could be overcome.
- Number of Decision levels, $N = 2^n$
- Quantization error Q_e lies in the range of $-\frac{\Delta}{2}$ and $+\frac{\Delta}{2}$.
- Signal to Quntization Noise Ratio for uniform quantization
  $[SNR]_q\ dB = 1.76 + 6n$
- Companding - Non uniform quantization can be achieved through uniform quantizer by adding a compressor block at the transmitter side and an expander block at the receiver side. The process of compression and expansion are collectively called as companding
- μ- law Companding

$$\frac{|Y|}{X_{max}} = \frac{\ln[1+\mu\left(\frac{|X|}{X_{max}}\right)]}{\ln[1+\mu]}$$

- A- law Companding

$$\frac{|Y|}{X_{max}} = \begin{cases} \frac{A|X|X_{max}}{1+\ln A}, & 0 \le \frac{|X|}{X_{max}} \le \frac{1}{A} \\ \frac{1+\ln[A|X|/X_{max}]}{1+\ln A}, & \frac{1}{A} \le \frac{|X|}{X_{max}} \le 1 \end{cases}$$

- Companding Gain $CG = \frac{\mu}{\ln(1+\mu)}$
- Line coding is a process of representing binary information in the form of digital pulses.
- Unipolar representation
- Polar representation
- Bipolar representation
- Bandwidth of PCM Systems
  $B_{PCM} \ge n \times f_m$
- Time Division Multiplexing
- Synchronous TDM &
- Asynchronous (or Statistical) TDM.

EXERCISE

Multiple Choice Questions

1. A signal $x(t) = 2\cos 400\pi t + 6\cos 640\pi t$ is sampled at 500 Hz using instantaneous sampling. If the signal is passed through an ideal filter with a cut off frequency of 400 Hz, determine the spectrum of the signal, spectrum of the sampled signal and the components that will appear at the output of the filter.

2. Obtain the Nyquist rates for the following signals
   (i) $X(t) = \text{Sinc}(400t)$
   (ii) $X(t) = \text{Sinc}^2(400t)$
   (iii) $X(t) = \text{Sinc}(400t) + \text{Sinc}^2(400t)$

3. The signals $x_1(t) = 10\cos 100\pi t$ and $x_2(t) = 10\cos 50\pi t$ are both sampled at nTs at a sampling rate of $Fs = 1/Ts = 75$ samples/sec. Show that the sequence of samples obtained are identical in both time and frequency domain.

4. A signal $X_1(t)$ is bandlimited to 3.6 kHz and three other signals $X_2(t)$, $X_3(t)$ and $X_4(t)$ are bandlimited to 1.2 kHz each. These are transmitted by means of TDM. Set up a commutator scheme to realize multiplexing with each signal sampled at Nyquist rate and also find the speed of the commutator in samples /sec and minimum bandwidth of the channel.

5. What is the theoretical minimum system bandwidth needed for a 10 Mb/s signal using 16-level PAM without ISI? How large can the filter roll-off factor (r) be if the applicable system bandwidth is 1.375 MHz?

6. A speech signal in the range 300 to 3400 Hz is sampled at 8000 samples/s. We may transmit these samples directly as PAM pulses or we may first convert each sample to a PCM format and use binary (PCM) waveform for transmission.
   (i) What is the minimum system bandwidth required for the detection of PAM with no ISI and with a filter roll-off factor of 1.
   (ii) Using the same roll-off, what is the minimum bandwidth required for the detection of binary PCM waveform if the samples are quantized to 8-levels.
   (iii) Repeat part (ii) using 128 quantization levels.

7. Consider a PCM system employing a sampling rate of 2000 samples/ sec. Samples are encoded using 8 bits. Determine the minimum bandwidth required for faithful reconstruction?

8. Consider a Uniform quantizer using 3 bits to represent the decision levels. Determine the maximum possible quantization error when a signal with peak to peak to amplitude of 12V is fed into this uniform quantizer.

9. The bandwidth of the signal given to a PCM system employing uniform quantization is limited to 10kHz. The amplitude of the input signal ranges from -4V to 4V and its power is 50mW. If a signal to noise ratio of 25dB is needed, calculate the number of bits required to represent a sample. If 25 such signals are to be multiplexed, find the minimum required bandwidth for the multiplexed signal.

10. Represent the information "1 0 1 1 0 1 1 1" using following line coding schemes

(i) Unipolar NRZ

(ii) Polar NRZ

(iii) Bipolar NRZ

(iv) Unipolar RZ

(v) Polar RZ

(vi) Bipolar RZ

(vii) Manchester

(viii) Differential Manchester

11. Consider a signal represented by $x(t) = 30 \cos(750\pi t)$ given as an input to a 10-bit PCM system.

(i) Find the signal to quantization noise ratio, if uniform quantization is used.

(ii) If a minimum signal to quantization noise of 50dB is needed, how many bits are needed to represent the quantization levels?

[HINT: Use the result obtained in Example 1.9]

12. Consider a signal bandlimited to 5MHz, is given a 512-bit PCM. Determine the number of bits/secs generated by the PCM. Assume that sampling is performed at a rate of 50% above the Nyquist rate.

13. An analog signal with maximum frequency of 4 kHz, is to be transmitted using a PCM system, where the number of pulse levels is M=64. The quantization error is specified not to exceed (+/-)1% of the peak-to-peak amplitude of the analog signal.

(a) What is the PCM word size that must be used?

(b) What is the minimum required sampling rate, and bit rate?

(c) If the transmission bandwidth is 16 kHz, determine the bandwidth efficiency for this PCM system.

14. The spectrum of bandpass signal x(t) has a bandwidth of 0.8 kHz cantered around +/- 10 kHz. Write the equation for x(t) in terms of quadrature components. Determine the Nyquist rate and Nyquist interval.

15. Given the binary sequence 10011011 draw the following line codes

(a) Unipolar NRZ and Unipolar RZ

(b) Polar NRZ and Polar RZ

(c) Bipolar NRZ and Bipolar RZ

(d) Manchester format

16. A low pass signal has a spectrum X(f) given by

$X(f) = 1 - |f|/200$ for $|f| < 200$

$= 0$ elsewhere

(a) Sketch the spectrum $X_\delta(f)$ for $|f| < 200$ if x(t) is ideally sampled at fs = 300 Hz.

(b) Repeat part a) for fs = 400 Hz.

Descriptive Type Questions

1. Explain briefly the various blocks of a digital communication system.
2. Mention some of the advantages and disadvantages of digital communication.
3. State Uniform Sampling Theorem for a low pass signal and bandpass signal.
4. What is Nyquist rate? Define the Nyquist Theorem.
5. What is meant by sampling? Explain the concepts of the various methods of sampling.
6. What is sample and hold operation? Explain by means of a circuit.
7. Distinguish between ideal, natural and flat-topped sampling in terms of their performance parameters.
8. What is meant by Aliasing? How can it be reduced?
9. What is aperture effect?
10. What is pulse modulation? Explain how a PAM signal can be generated and recovered at the receiver.
11. Why is Formatting necessary in digital communication systems?
12. Compare the performance parameters of PAM, PWM and PPM.
13. With the help of a neat block diagram, explain the transmitter and receiver sections of a PCM system.
14. Define quantization error. Derive an expression for signal to quantization noise ratio for a PCM system using uniform quantization.
15. Explain the concept of companding.
16. What is line coding? Explain with an example, the following line coding techniques:
    (i) Unipolar NRZ
    (ii) Polar NRZ
    (iii) Bipolar NRZ
    (iv) Unipolar RZ
    (v) Polar RZ
    (vi) Bipolar RZ
    (vii) Manchester
    (viii) Differential Manchester
17. Deduce the expressions for signaling rate and bandwidth of a PCM system.
18. Compare the performance parameters of synchronous and asynchronous transmission.
19. Distinguish between synchronous and asynchronous TDM.

Objective Questions

1. Aperture effect is a result of
    (A) Ideal sampling (B) Flat topped sampling
    (C) Natural sampling. (D) Quantizing.

2. The T4 system is generated when 6 T3 lines are multiplexed in an M3-4 multiplexer. The transmission rate in T4 system is

   (A) 1.544 Mbps (B) 6.132 Mbps

   (C) 12.624 Mbps (D) 274.176 Mbps

3. Four signals each bandlimited to 5 kHz are sampled at twice the Nyquist rate. The resulting PAM samples are transmitted over a single channel after TDM. The theoretical minimum transmission BW of the channel should be equal to

   (A) 5 kHz (B) 20 KHz

   (C) 40 kHz (D) 80 KHz

4. Thc use of non-uniform quantization leads to

   (A) Reduction in transmission BW (B) Increase in maximum SNR

   (C) Increase in SNR for low level signals (D) Simplification of sampling process

5. A modulated signal y(t) = m(t) Cos(4000πt), where base band signal m(t) has frequency components less than 5 Khz only. The minimum required rate at which y(t) should be sampled to recover m(t) is = --------

   (A) 10 kHz (B) 25 KHz

   (C) 20 kHz (D) 15 KHz

6. In PCM, number of bits are changed from 10 to 12. The Signal to Quantization Noise Ratio (SNRQ) is increased by a factor of

   (A) 12 (B) 15

   (C) 8 (D) 16

7. Manchester encoding is principally designed to,

   (A) Ensure that transition occurs in the center of each bit period.

   (B) Ensures that the line remains unbalanced.

   (C) Have more than one symbol per bit period.

   (D) Increase the bandwidth of a signal transmitted on the medium.

8. In a communication system, noise is most likely to affect the signal

   (A) at the transmitter (B) in the channel

   (C) in the information source (D) at the receiver

State True or False

1. All discrete signals are digital signals
2. Quantization process leads to loss in the original signal.
3. Non uniform quantization can be realized using uniform quantization.
4. Number of signal levels in unipolar line codes is three.

KNOW MORE

Harry Nyquist was born in 1889. Although he hails Swedan, his family has then shifted to America. Nyquist completed his B.S and M.S degrees in Electrical Engineering from the University of North Dakota. He obtained his Ph.D from Yale University in 1917. He worked for Bell Laboratories in the department of R&D. He made remarkable contributions in the field of communication. There are 138 US patents to his credit witnessing his tremendous contribution in the field of communication. Shannon in his remarkable paper, "The Mathematical Theory of Communications" quotes the works of Nyquist as his major references. He has He died in the year 1976.

HARRY NYQUIST MEMORIAL

UNITED STATES PATENT OFFICE

1. Pulse Code Modulation and Differential Pulse Code Modulation Encoders

   Henry S. McDonald, Murray Hill, N.J., assignor to Bell Telephone Laboratories, Incorporated, Murray Hill, Filed Mar. 18, 1968, Ser. No. 713,891

   Int. Cl. H03h 13/22

   U.S. Cl. 332 - 11 8 Claims

ABSTRACT OF THE DISCLOSURE

Differential pulse code modulation (DPCM) signals are produced by first subjecting an analog input signal to a delta modulator which is operated at many times the Nyquist rate of the signal. The modulator output is applied to an accumulator, which, in turn transfers its output to a storage register. The accumulator is strobed so that its contents are transferred at a rate at least equal to the Nyquist rate. The register is similarly strobed to produce its contents as DPCM Signals.

Pulse code modulated (PCM) signals are produced by accumulating the DPCM signals in a second accumulator at a rate many times the Nyquist rate of the signal. The binary delta modulation code elements are then summed during intervals occurring at least at the Nyquist rate of the analog signal. The sums thus produced are DPCM representations of the analog signal. PCM representations of the analog signal are produced by summing the DPCM representations.

A feature of the invention is the use of delta modulation. This operation immediately converts the analog signal to a digital form which permits all subsequent processing to be performed by digital circuits. These circuits, along with the delta modulator, are all relatively simple, inexpensive and easy to maintain, thus producing an over all combination having the same characteristics.

Other objects and features of the invention will become apparent from a study of the following detailed description of a specific embodiment.

BRIEF DESCRIPTION OF THE DRAWING

In the drawings :

Fig. 1 shows a block diagram of an embodiment of the invention; and Fig. 2 shows typical waveforms appearing at identified locations within the embodiment of Fig. 1.

NUGGEHALLY SAMPATH JAYANT

Bell Labs

Other affiliations: Alcatel-Lucent, AT&T

Bio: Nuggehally Sampath Jayant is an academic researcher from Bell Labs. The author has contributed to research in topic(s): Speech coding & Quantization (signal processing). The author has an h-index of 32, co-authored 68 publication(s) receiving 5695 citation(s).

Education: Bachelor of Science, National College, Bangalore, 1962. Bachelor of Engineering, Indian Institute of Science, Bangalore, 1965. Doctor of Philosophy, Indian Institute of Science, Bangalore, 1970.

His most cited work include:

Digital Coding of Waveforms: Principles and Applications to Speech and Video (832 citations)

Signal compression based on models of human perception (769 citations)

Three-dimensional sub band coding of video (240 citations)

2020 - Fellow, National Academy of Inventors

1996 - Member of the National Academy of Engineering for contributions to coding and compression of speech, audio, and image signals.

1982 - IEEE Fellow For contributions to adaptive quantization and digital speech communication.

Topics: Speech coding, Quantization (signal processing), Signal, Vector quantization, Adaptive Multi-Rate audio codec

FURTHER READING

[1] Haykin, Simon. "Digital Communications", John Wiley, New York, 2001.

[2] Sklar, Bernad. "Digital Communication: Functions and Applications", Prenice Hall., 1988.

[3] K. Sam Shanmugam , « Digital and Analog Communication Systems», John Wiley, New York, 2006.

[4] M. Kulkarni and Farooq Husain, "Analog and Digital Communication Systems", Umesh Publications,

New Delhi, 2005.

[5] K. N. Hari Bhat and D. Ganesh Rao, "Digital Communications", Third Edition, Pearson, 2012.

2 Baseband Transmission

UNIT SPECIFICS

Through this unit, we have discussed the following aspects:

- Analog to digital conversion methods and generation of baseband digital data (DPCM, DM, ADM & ADPCM).
- Analyze the performance of baseband modulations.
- Distinguish between waveform coding and parametric coding.
- Explore Low bit rate coding of speech and video signals such as vocoders.
- Compute the output SNR of the matched filter
- Performance of baseband transmission systems in presence of additive Gaussian noise
- Effect of Inter-symbol interference (ISI), its causes, mitigation mechanisms including Ideal solution or Nyquist criterion for zero ISI and Practical solution
- Appreciate the concepts of transmission bandwidth requirement (sinusoidal roll-off filtering, Raised Cosine Filter) Correlative coding, design of equalizers and adaptive equalizers, Digital subscriber lines.

RATIONALE

Study and analysis of baseband transmission systems are critical when we have to transmit digital data on wired channels. As in carrier modulation schemes, the baseband signal frequencies need not be shifted to higher frequency bands. This allows the entire bandwidth of the system to be available for the baseband signal. However, the remaining bandwidth may not be utilized. But by employing TDM, multiple baseband signals can share the bandwidth. All of us are aware of the most popular Ethernet-based local area networks (LANs) that use baseband transmission. Hence, the study and analysis of baseband data transmission permit us to understand and explore the various practical applications of networking.

UNIT OUTCOMES

List of outcomes of this unit is as follows:

U2-O1: Describe the basic baseband modulation techniques

U2-O2: Analyse the quantization noise performance of the baseband modulations schemes.

U2-O3: Distinguish between waveform and parametric coding techniques (Low bit rate Coding).

U2-O4: Analyse ISI, its and mitigation mechanisms.

U2-O5: Evaluate the performance of matched filters, correlative coders, equalizers

MAPPING OF UNIT OUTCOMES WITH COURSE OUTCOMES

Unit-2 Outcomes	EXPECTED MAPPING WITH COURSE OUTCOMES (1- Weak Correlation; 2- Medium correlation; 3- Strong Correlation)					
	CO-1	CO-2	CO-3	CO-4	CO-5	CO-6
U2-O1	3	3	3	-	3	1
U2-O2	2	1	2	2	1	-
U2-O3	2	1	2	1	2	1
U2-O4	1	-	2	1	2	1
U2-O5	1	-	-	-	2	1

2.1 DIFFERENTIAL PCM (DPCM)

While discussing PCM system, in Unit-1, we have seen that, adjacent samples of the sampled signal will have high correlation when a signal is over sampled (higher than Nyquist rate to avoid aliasing). That is, in a typical PCM system, we have successive samples where there is very little difference between the amplitudes of two samples. We can think of a Differential PCM(DPCM) system, that can be designed to take advantage of the redundancies between consecutive samples, typically observed in speech waveforms. Due to redundancy, a high degree of correlation exists between samples. Thus the future sample values can be predicted from the information of previous sample values. Instead of assigning a fixed number of bits (say 8 bits) to every sample as was done in PCM, we take the difference between samples (which will have a small value than the samples themselves) that can be coded by fewer number of bits. This process of quantising and subsequent coding of the difference between the samples (rather than coding each of the samples) is known as **DPCM** technique. This results in lesser number of bits for encoding and thus removing redundancy between the samples and low bit rate coding.

2.1.1 DPCM Transmitter/Receiver

Figure 2.1 shows a DPCM Tx/Rx system. The transmitter (Tx) part in Figure 2.1 (a), has a sampled PAM signal $X(nT_S)$ applied to a summer followed by a quantizer and a predictor in the feedback circuit and an encoder. Figure 2.1 (b) shows the DPCM Receiver (Rx).

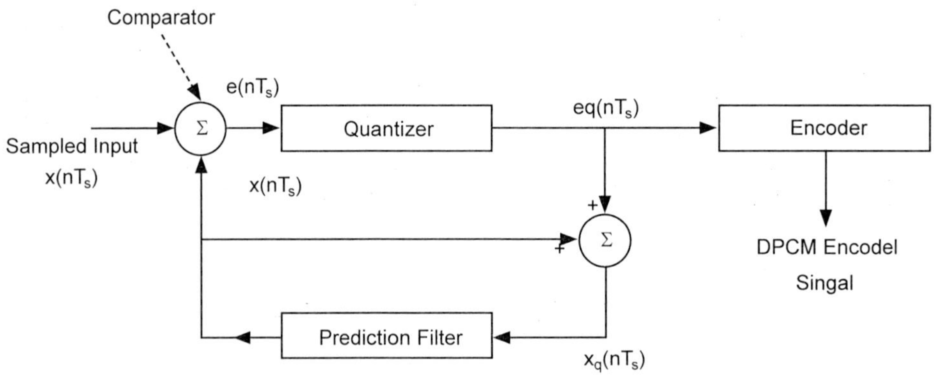

(a)

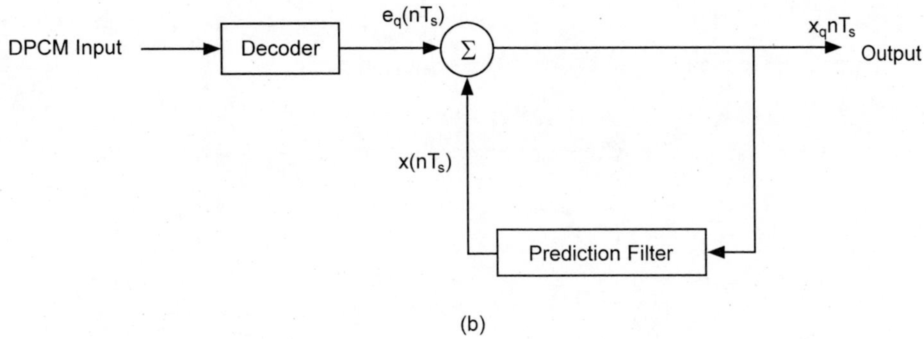

Fig. 2.1 DPCM transceiver (a) Transmitter (b) Receiver

In Figure 2.1 (a), X(nTs) is the sampled version of the analog signal x(t) with Ts being the sampling period (which is the sampled PAM signal). $X(nT_S)$ is given to a summer that produces a signal e(nTs), known as prediction error, given by

$$e(nTs) = X(nT_S) - \hat{X}(nT_s) \tag{2.1}$$

where $\hat{X}$ (nTs) : prediction of $x(nT_S)$.

The prediction error e(nTS) is then quantised to produce $e_q(nTS)$. This quantized signal is then encoded to produce a DPCM signal. That is, the DPCM signal to be transmitted is the result of coding the difference in the amplitude of a sample and its predicted value rather than the coding of the actual sample. This difference in sample values being very small, fewer bits would be required for DPCM transmitted signal than the conventional PCM.

Referring to Figure 2.1 (a),

$$e_q(nT_S) = e(nTs) + q_e(nTs) \tag{2.2}$$

Here, $q_e(nTs)$: quantisation error.

$X_q(nTs)$ is the predictor input can be written as

$$\begin{aligned} X_q(nTs) &= \hat{X}(nT_s) + e_q(nT_s) = \hat{X}(nT_s) + e(nT_s) + q_e(nT_s) \\ &= \hat{X}(nT_s) + X(nT_s) - \hat{X}(nT_s) + q_e(nT_s) \end{aligned}$$

ie.

$$X_q(nT_s) = X(nT_s) + q_e(nT_s) \tag{2.3}$$

This shows that, $X_q(nT_s)$ has a quantization error term $q_e(nT_s)$. We can observe that this expression is true irrespective of the predictor. The predictor is basically a filter that predicts a signal (nT_s) with a value very close to $x(nT_s)$ from the previous outputs of the quantizer.

The predictor filter used at the transmitter is made use of at the receiver, to recover the quantized version of the original signal. The output of the decoder will be similar to the encoded signal assuming that there is no channel noise. "$q_e[nT_s]$" is the quantization error and these quantization errors do not accumulate in the receiver.

We can use a tapped-delay-line filter to implement a prediction filter required for the DPCM system as shown in Figure 2. Here, delay is set equal to the sampling period Ts. The output of the prediction filter is obtained by looking at the previous 'samples and predicting the present value using a linear combination of these past samples, in which case the order of the prediction filter is 'j'.

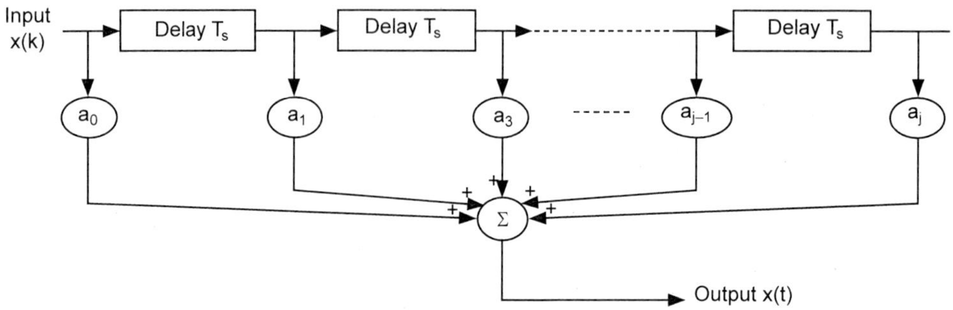

Fig. 2.2 Prediction filter

2.1.2 Processing Gain of a DPCM System

The output SNR of a DPCM system can be defined as,

$$[\text{SNR}]_o = \frac{\delta_x^2}{\delta_Q^2}$$

$$= \frac{\delta_x^2/\delta_E^2}{\delta_Q^2/\delta_E^2}$$

$$= G_p \times [SNR]_Q \tag{2.4}$$

where, $\delta_X{}^2$: Variance of the input signal x(t) with zero mean,

$\delta_Q{}^{2:}$ Quantization error variance,

$\delta_E{}^2$: Prediction error variance,

$[\text{SNR}]_Q$: Signal to quantization noise ratio and

$G_p = \delta_X{}^2/\ \delta_E{}^2$ is known as the processing (or prediction gain) of the DPCM system.

Equation (2.4) shows that the output SNR can be increased by maximizing G_p.

The processing gain can also be defined as,

$$G_P = 1 / (1 - \rho_1{}^2) \quad \text{and} \quad \delta_E{}^2 = \delta_X{}^2(1 - \rho_1{}^2) \tag{2.5}$$

where ρ_1 – Autocorrelation function of the information signal.

The 6 dB rule of PCM system is also applicable to a DPCM system and is given by

$$(S / N)\ dB = 6.02n + \alpha \tag{2.6}$$

where $-3 < \alpha < 15$ for DPCM speech (300 to 3,400 Hz, telephone-quality).

Typically, DPCM uses 4-6 bits/sample with a bit rate of 32 to 48 Kbps (as compared to 7-8 bits/ sample and 56 to 64 Kbps bit rate in PCM). DPCM can be used to efficiently code speech and video signals and the bandwidth required is lower than PCM.

2.2 DELTA MODULATION

DPCM has a particular case known as delta modulation. Delta modulation (DM) is exactly such a scheme, where the baseband signal is sampled at a rate much higher than the Nyquist rate with the intention of increasing the correlation between adjacent samples of the signal. This will enable the use of a straightforward quantizing strategy to construct the encoded signal. The one-bit (or two-level) form of DPCM is called delta modulation.

DM can be viewed as a simplified form of DPCM where the predictor of DPCM [Fig. 2.1 (a)] is replaced by only a delay element. The block diagram of a DM encoder and decoder are shown in Figure 2.3 (a) and (b).

Here we can see that,

$$\begin{aligned} e(nT_s) &= x(nT_s) - \hat{x}(nT_s) \\ &= x(nT_s) - u(nT_s - T_s) \\ b(nT_s) &= \delta\ sgn[e(nT_s)] \\ u(nT_s) &= u(nT_s - T_s) + b(nT_s) \end{aligned} \tag{2.7}$$

where, T_s : Sampling period,

$e(nT_s)$: prediction error (difference between present sample $x(nT_s)$ of the input signal and the estimated(predicted) value $\hat{x}(nT_s) = u(nT_s - T_s)$

$b(nT_s)$: 1- bit word transmitted by DM system.

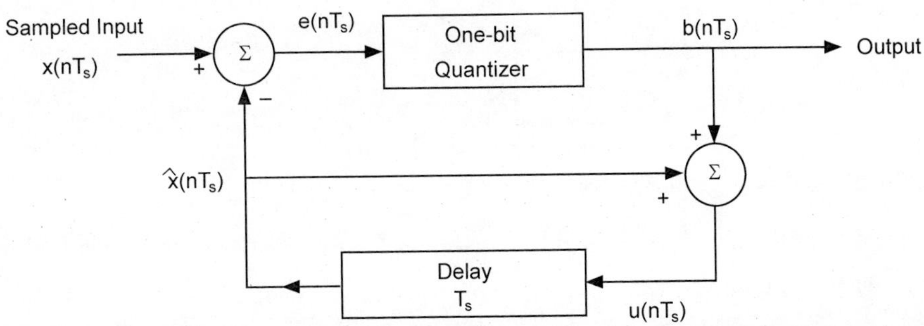

(a)

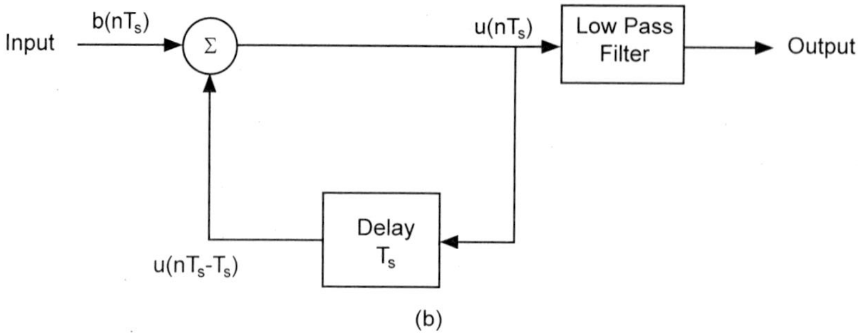

Fig. 2.3 DM system (a) Encoder (b) Decoder

It may be clearly seen that, the estimated or predicted value of $\hat{x}$(nTs) is really the previous sample x(nTs-1) modified by the quantisation noise e(nTs). A summer, a two-level quantizer, and an accumulator are the main components of the DM encoder depicted in Fig. 2.3 (a). Depending on the modulator's binary output, the accumulator increases the approximate value of the input signal by ±δ at each sampling instant.

From Eq. (2.7), we have

$$u(nT_S) = \delta\sum_{i=1}^{n}\text{sgn}[e(iT_S)] = \sum_{i=1}^{n} b(iT_S) \tag{2.8}$$

For an input signal that has been over sampled, DM offers a staircase approximation. There are only two quantization levels for the difference, ±δ (between the input and the approximation), which correspond to positive and negative differences, respectively. As a result, the approximation is increased by δ, if it is below the signal at any sample period. We find that the stair case approximation stays within ±δ of the input signal as long as the signal does not fluctuate dramatically from sample to sample. The symbol δ indicates the absolute value of the two level representation of the 1-bit quantizer used in DM. These two levels are shown as the transfer characteristics as shown in Fig. 3.14. The step size Δ of the quantizer is related to δ by the relation,

$$\Delta = 2\delta \tag{2.9}$$

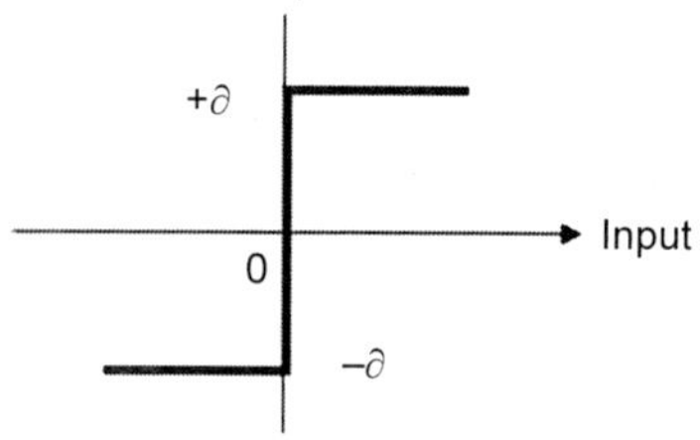

Fig. 2.4 Transfer characteristics of DM quantizer

The operation of DM can be explained by looking at Figure 2.5 which shows the DM waveforms. The initial values of x(t) and $\hat{x}$(t) are assumed to have arbitrary values. At the time t_1 of the first pulse in x(nT_s) or $P_i(t)$ is such that δ (t) is positive as the amplitude of x(t) > amplitude of $\hat{x}$(t). Hence the first pulse in b(nT_s) or output pulse, $P_o(t)$ is positive.

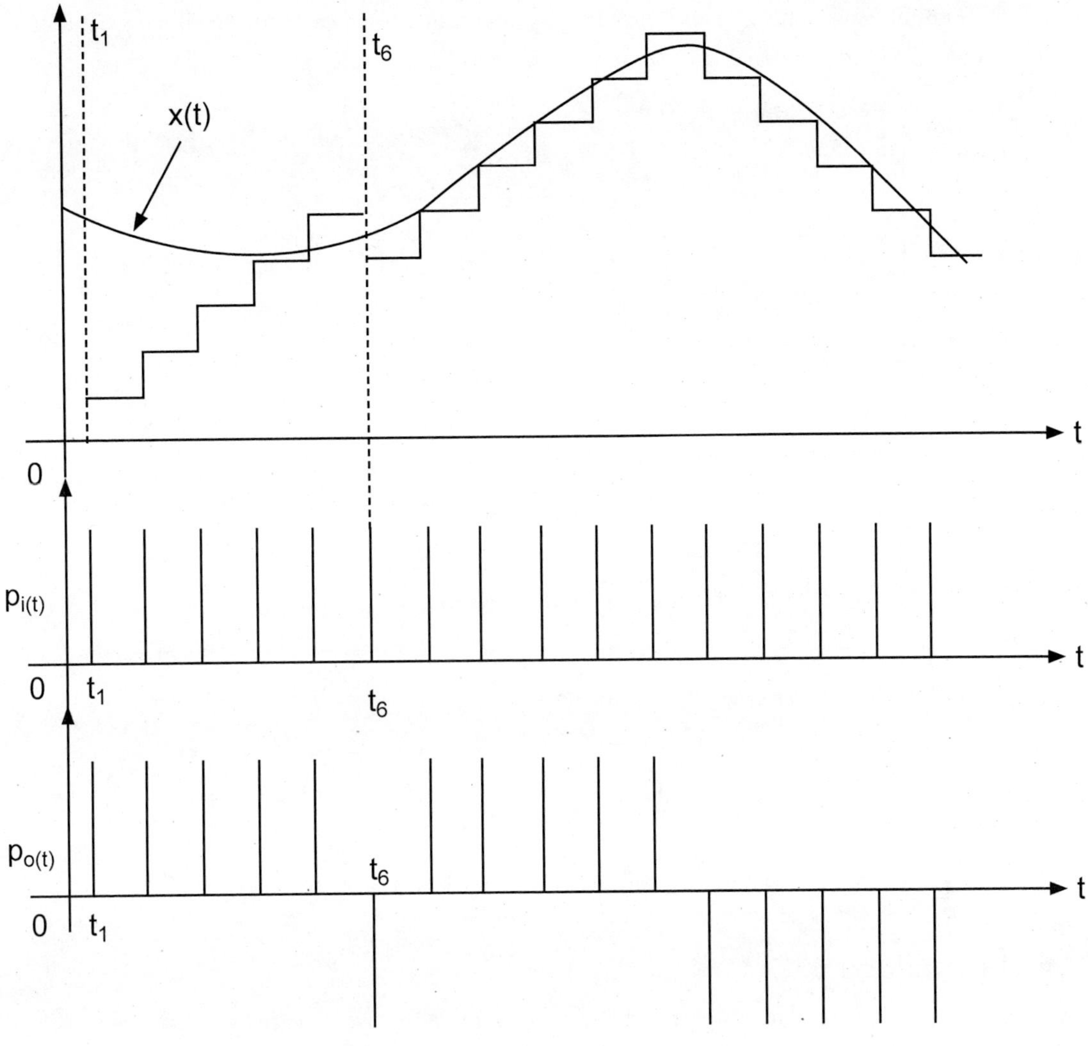

Fig. 2.5 DM waveforms

Similarly, the pulses in Po(t) are either positive or negative depending upon whether $\Delta(t)$ is positive or negative. For example, at time t6, δ (t) is negative and hence Po(t) is a negative pulse. The input signal x(t) approaches $\hat{x}(t)$ in the form of a staircase and then, closely follows it. Thus $\hat{x}(t)$ is an approximation to the input signal x(t). The output waveform Po(t) is transmitted over the communication channel. At the receiver side, the quantizer takes a decision on whether the received pulse is positive or negative. Hence assuming no error, the output of the quantizer is the same as the waveform Po(t) and is fed to an integrator, whose output takes the form of the waveform, $\hat{x}(t)$. The LPF smoothens the output voltage of the integrator and gives a waveform similar to the signal x(t). As the information is transmitted as a difference signal $\delta(t) = x(t) - \hat{x}(t)$, this scheme is known as Delta modulation.

The DM output waveforms x(t) and the staircase approximation along with the binary data output of DM is shown in Figure 2.6 along with slope overload and granular noise.

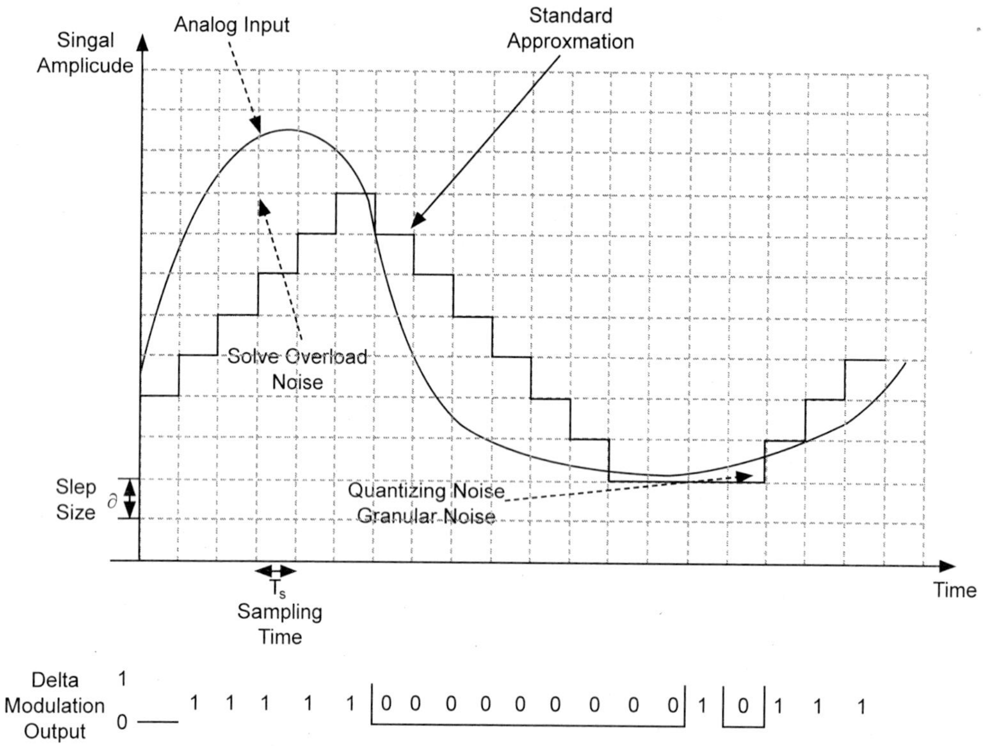

Fig. 2.6 DM waveforms showing slope overload and quantising noise

2.2.1 Limitations of DM

The waveform $\hat{x}(t)$ is supposed to closely follow the waveform m(t) in which case the recovered waveform (t) resembles x(t). However, as we can see in Figure 2.7 (a), the staircase waveform, $\hat{x}(t)$ is unable to follow the input analog signal x(t) because the slope of x(t) is greater than the slope of (t). Same is true with Figure 2.7 (b), where slope of x(t) is more negative than the slope of $\hat{x}(t)$. In both the cases, the recovered waveform will be distorted. The DM system is then said to be slope overloaded resulting in slope overload distortion or noise. Figure 2.7 (c) further shows that the fluctuations in x(t) are such that they are inside the step size, resulting in a waveform that resembles a square wave. The signal x(t) is strictly not a dc signal, whereas this can be recovered as dc. Hence in this case as well, we have distortion known as granular distortion or granular noise.

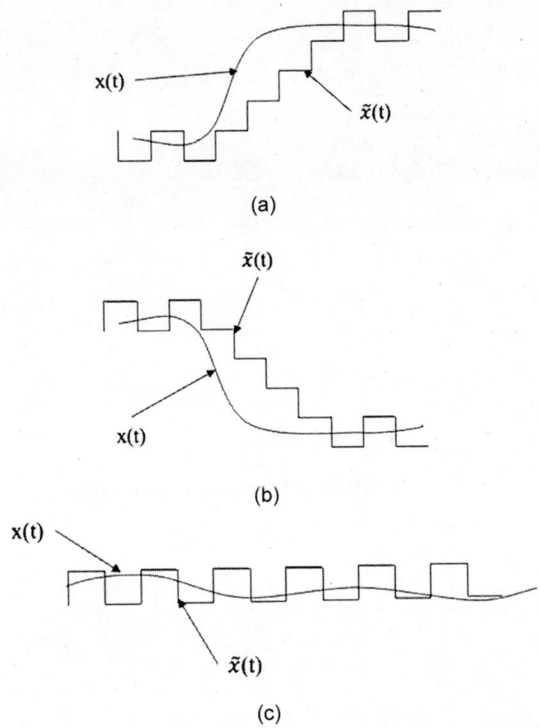

(a) Slope overload(+ve) (b) Slope overload(-ve) (c) Slow varying signal (almost dc)

Fig. 2.7 Limitations of DM

The three conditions and associated DM output are shown in Figure 2.8.

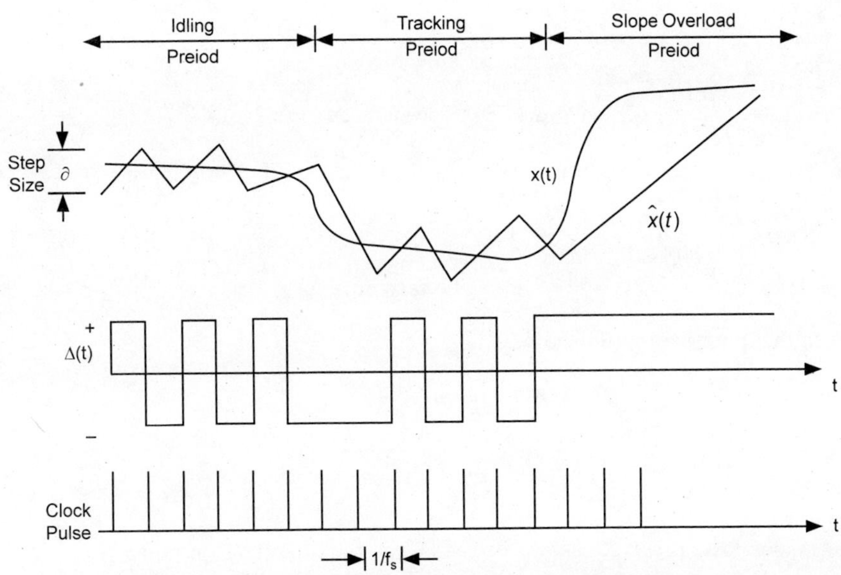

Fig. 2.8 Idling, tracking and slope overload conditions of DM

It is desirable to have 'Δ' as small as possible to minimise granular distortion. In summary, a large step size is required to minimise slope overload noise whereas smaller step sizes are required to reduce granular noise.

2.2.2 Signal to Noise Ratio of DM system

We have seen that the quantization error(noise) 'q_e' is the difference between the message signal, x(t) and the quantized signal, $X_q(t)$. Let a random variable 'Q' be the quantisation error and 'q_e' its sample value.

In that case, $Q = x(t) - X_q(t)$.

Assumptions:

(i) The sampling rate be fs and step size be δ.

(ii) The magnitude of q_e is $\leq \delta$

(iii) All signal amplitudes are equally likely

(iv) Quantisation error is uniformly distributed between $+\delta$ and $-\delta$.

(v) The probability density function (pdf) of quantization noise is shown in Figure 2.9.

$$\int_{-\partial}^{\partial} f_\Phi(g_e)dg_e = 1$$

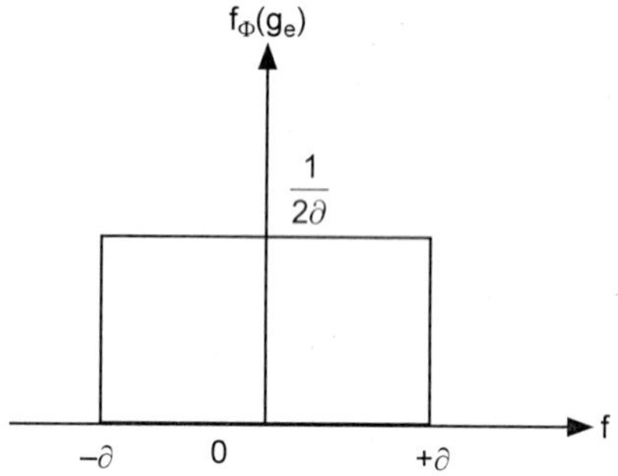

Fig. 2.9 PDF of quantization noise

Assume quantizing error 'q_e' as uniformly distributed as in Fig.2.9, the pdf $f_Q(q_e)$ is

$$f_Q(q_e) = \begin{cases} \frac{1}{2\delta} & \text{for } -\delta \leq qe \leq +\delta \\ 0 & Otherwise \end{cases}$$

The mean of the quantization noise is

$$\mu = \int_{-\delta}^{\delta} q_e f_Q(q_e)dq_e$$

$$= \int_{-\delta}^{\delta} q_e \frac{1}{2\delta} dq_e = 0 \tag{2.10}$$

and the variance or the mean square value (MSV) of the quantization noise is

$$\sigma_Q^2 = P_q = \int_{-\delta}^{\delta} (q_e - \mu)^2 f_Q(q_e)dq_e$$

$$\Rightarrow \qquad P_q = \int_{-\delta}^{\delta} q_e^2 f_Q(q_e) dq_e$$

$$= \int_{-\delta}^{\delta} q_e^2 \frac{1}{2\delta} dq_e$$

$$= \frac{\delta^2}{3} \tag{2.11}$$

Further assuming the quantization noise power P_q is uniformly distributed over the frequency say up to f_s, the output quantizing noise power within the bandwidth f_m of the low pass filter at the DM receiver can be obtained as,

$$N_q = \frac{P_q}{f_s} f_m = \frac{\delta^2}{3}\left(\frac{f_m}{f_s}\right) \tag{2.12}$$

$(SNR)_o$ of the DM system is therefore

$$(SNR)_o = \frac{P}{N_q} = \frac{3Pf_s}{\delta^2 f_m} \tag{2.13}$$

We can now calculate output SNR for sinusoidal modulation assuming no slope overload distortion.

Let $\qquad x(t) = A\cos(2\pi f_o t)$

$$\max\left|\frac{dx(t)}{dt}\right| = 2\pi f_0 A$$

To avoid slope overload distortion,

$$\frac{\delta}{T_s} \geq \max\left|\frac{dx(t)}{dt}\right| = 2\pi f_0 A$$

$$A \leq \frac{\delta}{2\pi f_0 T_s}$$

$$\delta \geq 2\pi\, f_0 A\, T_s$$

Maximum output signal power is given by,

$$P_{max} = \frac{A^2}{2} = \frac{\delta^2}{8\pi^2 f_0^2 T_s^2}$$

The Rx is a LPF with message bandwidth, W. Further, assuming that the average power of 'q_e' is uniformly distributed over -fs to +n fs, average noise power at the output is,

$$N_0 = \left(\frac{f_c}{f_s}\right)\frac{\delta^2}{3} = WT_s\left(\frac{\delta^2}{3}\right)$$

The output SNR of DM system is then given by,

$$(SNR)_o = \frac{P_{max}}{N_0} = \frac{3}{8\neq^2 W f_0^2 T_s^3} \tag{2.14}$$

2.2.3 Simple Implementation of a DM system

Figure 2.10 shows a simple, low-cost implementation of a DM system by use of a comparator, an integrator and a D Flip flop along with a clock signal.

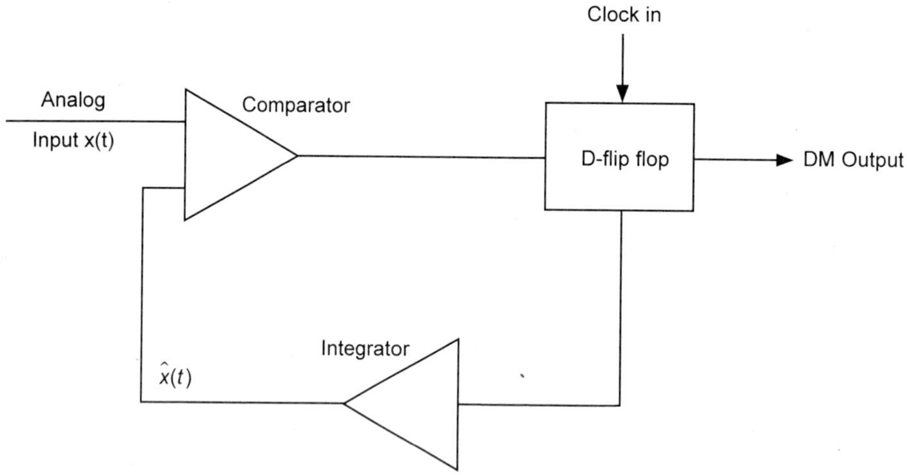

Fig. 2.10 A simple implementation of a DM system

2.2.4 Advantages/Disadvantages of DM

- DM needs a simple circuit as compared to PCM (As there is no need of ADC or DAC in a DM system. In fact, the predictor can be replaced by a simple RC integrator (LPF), to reduce the cost).
- DM is preferred when the bandwidth conservation is desirable at the cost of quality of transmission.
- (SNR)q of DM is less than PCM.
- For a good quality transmission, the bandwidth needed by DM is more than PCM.

Example 2.1: Determine the step size for a DM system to take care of distortion due to slope overload, assuming a sinusoidal signal with frequency f_m and amplitude A_m.

Solution:

Let the sinusoidal signal be given by $x(t) = A_m \text{Sin}(2\pi f_m t)$

The slope of a DM system is

$$= \text{Step Size / Sampling Period}$$

$$= \frac{\delta}{T_s}, \text{ where } \delta \text{ is the step size and Ts is the sampling period.}$$

Slope overload distortion takes place when slope of the sinusoidal signal is greater than the slope of DM.

ie.

$$\max \left| \frac{dx(t)}{dt} \right| > \frac{\delta}{T_s}$$

$$\max\left|\frac{d}{dt}[A_m \sin(2\neq f_m t)]\right| > \frac{\delta}{T_s}$$

$$\max|A_m 2\pi f_m \cos(2\pi f_m t| > \frac{\delta}{T_s}$$

$$\Rightarrow \quad A_m 2\pi f_m > \frac{\delta}{T_s}$$

or $$A_m > \delta / 2\pi f_m Ts$$

Hence to avoid slope overload distortion, the step size 'δ' is chosen such that

$$\delta > 2\pi f_m A_m / fs \text{ where } f_s = 1 / T_s.$$

However, the step size should not be made too large else the granular noise will increase.

Example 2.2: A delta modulator operates at 3 times the Nyquist rate for a message signal of 4 kHz bandwidth. If the step size of the quantiser is 500 mV, Determine

(i) The maximum amplitude of a 2 kHz input sinusoid for which the DM does not show slope overload.

(ii) The postfiltered $(SNR)_o$.

Solution:

$$W = 4 \text{ kHz}, f_o = 2 \text{ kHz}$$

$$f_s = 2, f_o = 4 \text{ kHz, Sampling frequency} = 3 \times \text{Nyquist rate} = 3 \times 4 \text{ kHz} = 12 \text{ kHz}$$

$$\text{Step size} = 500 \text{ mV}, T_s = \frac{1}{f_s} = \frac{1}{12000} = 0.00083$$

(i) Slope overload does not occur if

$$A \leq \frac{\delta}{2\pi f_0 T_s}$$

i.e. $A \leq (500 \times 10^{-3}) / 2\pi \times 2000 \times 0.00083 \leq 0.4774 \text{ V} \leq 477.4 \text{ mV}$.

(ii) $$(SNR)_o = \frac{P_{Max}}{N_0} = \frac{3}{8\neq^2 W f_0^2 T_s^3}$$

$$(SNR)_o = 3 / (8\pi^2 \times 4000 \times (2000)^2 \times 0.00083) = 2.86 = 4.56 \text{ dB}$$

2.3 ADAPTIVE DELTA MODULATION (ADM)

The limitations discussed in section 1.2.1 can be overcome by suitably changing the step size. ADM is employed to reduce slope overload and granular noise. Slope overload can be minimized if the step size is increased in such a way that the magnitude of the slope of $\hat{X}(t)$ becomes greater than the magnitude of the slope of x(t). When the signal variations are less than the step size, the step size may be reduced to care of the situation. A DM system that adjusts its step size is known as an Adaptive Delta Modulation (ADM) system.

We also observe that the SNR response of the DM system is a function of signal power. To achieve a constant SNR, we need to vary the step size as per the variations in the amplitude of the message signal. Lower amplitude message signals should result in a smaller step size and larger amplitude signals in a larger step size. This helps maintain a constant SNR over a large dynamic range of the input signal. The Adaptive delta modulators can take continuous or discrete changes in step sizes.

A typical ADM Transceiver is shown in Figure 2.11.

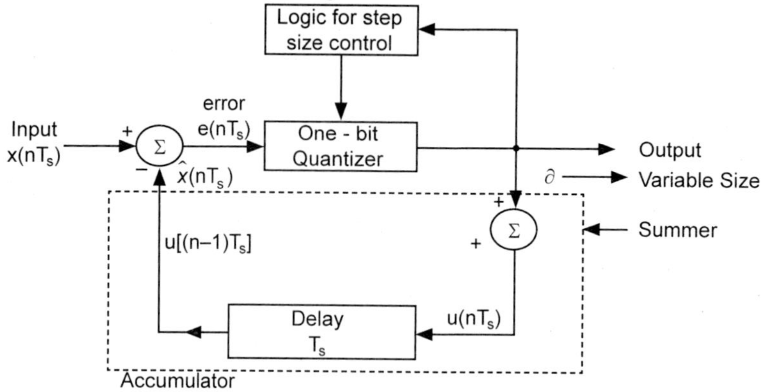

(a)

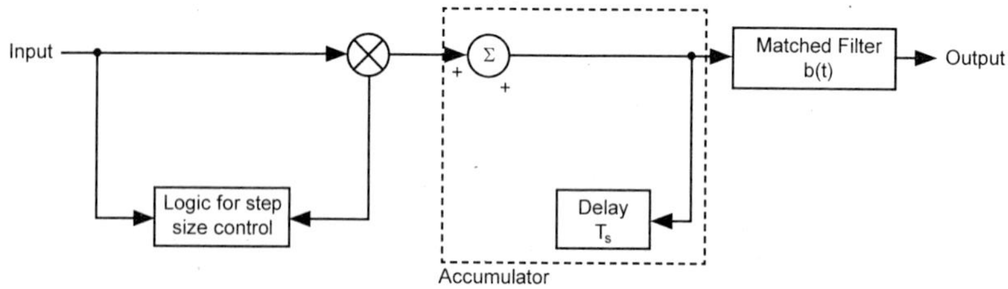

(b)

Fig. 2.11 ADM transceiver (a) Transmitter (b) Receiver

The logic for step size control is added in the ADM system (as compared to the DM system discussed in the previous section). The step size is increased or decreased according to a certain rule depending on the output of the one-bit quantizer. Figure 2.12 shows the waveforms of ADM and the sequence of bits transmitted. If the output of the one-bit quantizer is high (a logical '1'), step size is doubled for the next sample. If the output of the one-bit quantizer is low (a logical '0'), the step size is reduced by one step. In the ADM receiver, the first part generates the step size from each incoming bit. The same process as in transmitter, is followed in the receiver. The present and the previous input decides the step size and it is then given to an accumulator which builds up the staircase waveform. The LPF then smoothens out the staircase waveform to reconstruct the smooth signal.

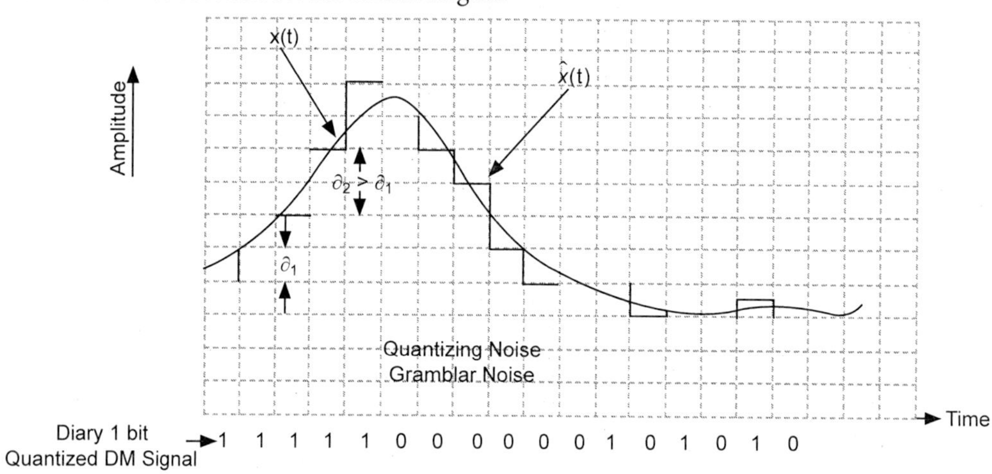

Fig. 2.12 ADM waveforms

A simple algorithm of an ADM system is shown in Table 2.1. In the data sequence, if we have the number of successive binaries 1's and 0's are 1 or 2 the step size is δ. However, if three successive binary 1's or three successive 0's occurs, the step size is increased to 2δ. For four successive 1's and 0's, the step size is increased to 4δ.

Table 2.1: Simple Step Size Algorithm for an ADM System

Data Sequence				Number of Successive Binary 1's or 0's	Step Size Algorithm f(d)
X	X	0	1	1	δ
X	0	1	1	2	δ
0	1	1	1	3	2δ
1	1	1	1	4	4δ

X - Don't care

ADM is preferred over DM, since it provides better SNRs, a larger dynamic range (because of the variable step size), and better bandwidth utilisation.

Example 2.3: A 10 kHz sinusoid with an amplitude 1 V peak has an SNR of about 45 dB. Determine bit rate and bandwidth of the system given that the sampling frequency is twice the Nyquist rate.

Solution:

$$\text{Signal power } P = (1/\sqrt{2})^2 = 0.5 \text{ W.}$$

$$\text{Noise power} = \delta_Q^2 = \Delta^2/12 \text{ where } \Delta = (2 \times 1)/2^n$$

$$(SNR)_o = 10 \log \{P/\delta_Q^2\} = 10 \log (\Delta^2/\delta) = 10 \log (2^{2n}/1.5) = 45 \text{ dB.}$$

Since δ dB of $(SNR)_o$ corresponds to 1 bit, we get, n = 8 bits.

With fs = 10 kHz x 2 = 20 kHz,

Bit rate = nf_s = 8 x 20 kHz = 160 kHz.

2.4 ADAPTIVE DIFFERENTIAL PULSE CODE MODULATION (ADPCM)

ADPCM (also known as Delta Pulse Code Modulation), was developed by Bell Labs in the 1970s for efficient coding of speech signals and now for Voice over IP (VoIP) communications. ADPCM is currently the most widely used technique for designing audio and video systems with high-quality audio, images, and video signals. ADPCM also is used for computer storage of digital speech, and modern cellular communication systems.

ADPCM encodes the differences between samples. ADPCM employs just 4 bits per sample (rather than 8 bits per sample used in commercial PCM). This enables a voice signal to be transmitted at a bit rate of 32 kbps or even at lower sampling rates of 8 or 16 kbps, however these result in voice communications of lesser quality. ADPCM uses the previous sample to predict the current sample. It then computes the difference between the current sample and its predictions and quantizes the difference.

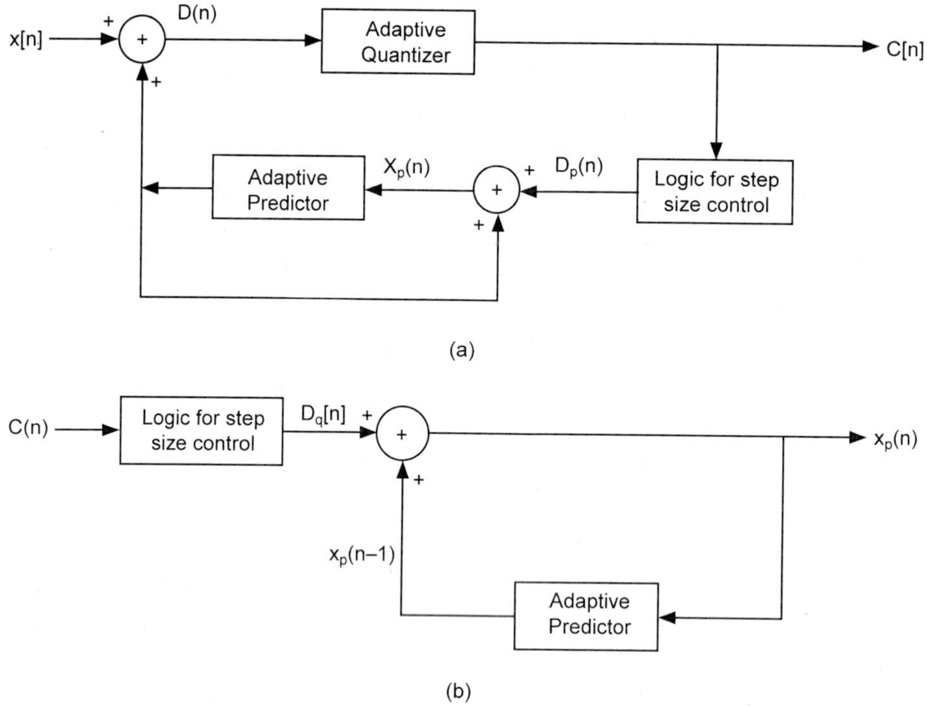

Fig. 2.13 ADPCM system (a) Encoder (b) Decoder

ADPCM has been developed to overcome the disadvantages of the DM system (slope over load and granular noise). It uses an adaptive quantizer and an adaptive predictor as shown in the simplified block diagram of an ADPCM encoder and decoder (Figure 2.13). The adaptive quantizer is provided with the difference D(n) between the current input sample, x(n), and predicted signal, X_p(n-1). The quantizer calculates the quantized code C(n) of x(n) and outputs it. The same code c(n) is sent to adaptive dequantizer, which produces the next quantized difference value D_P(n). This value is added to previous predictor value X_p(n−1) and sum X_p(n) is sent to the predictors to the used in next step. In the ADPCM decoder, the input ADPCM code c(n) is given to an adaptive dequantizer producing a difference D_q(n), which is added to preceding predictor output X_p(n−1) to form next output X_p(n). The next output is also fed into predictor to be used in next step.

In general, the term "adaptive quantization" refers to a variable step size, $\Delta(nTs)$, where Ts is the sampling period. The step size $\Delta(nTs)$ is varied so as to follow the variations in the input signal x(nTs).

2.4.1 Advantages of ADPCM

- Overcomes the drawback of slope overload and granular noise resulting in higher output SNRs.
- Provides lower bit rates of 16-32 kbps as compared to 64 kbps companded PCM system.
- Requires lesser powers to transmit bits.
- No synchronization issues (no need of start and stop bits).
- ADPCM is simple to implement.

However, there will be quantization noise that will still be present, and CVSDM (Continuous Variable Slope Delta Modulation) can be a better alternative.

2.4.2 Comparison between PCM, DPCM, ADPCM, DM and ADM

Sl. No	Performance Parameters	PCM	DM	ADM	DPCM
1.	Bits/sample	4/8/16	1	1	> 1 but <PCM
2.	Step Size/No. of levels	Depends on no. of levels	Fixed/2 levels	Adaptive	Fixed
3.	Quantisation noise/distortion	Decided by number of levels	Both Slope overload & Granular noises are present	Quantisation noise still are present	Both Slope overload & Granular noises are present
4.	BW of transmission channel	Highest	Lowest	Lowest	BW<PCM
5.	Feedback	No	Feedback in Tx	Exists	Exists
6.	System Complexity	Complex	Simple	Simple	Simple
7.	SNR	Good	Poor	Better than DM	Fair
8.	Applications	Audio & Video telephony	Speech & Images	Speech & Images	Speech & Video

2.5 LOW BIT RATE CODING

Digital Speech Coding basically involves conversion of analog speech to digital form in more compressed form and transmit using minimum number of bits (low bit rate coding) with fairly good quality of reception. The major issues include

- Compression of speech to lower bit rate per user so that a greater number of users can efficiently use the bandwidth available.
- Requirement of toll grade or better quality in a specific transmission environment: Quality: BW trade off
- Acceptable BER, packet loss, packet out of order delivery, delay, etc.
- Hardware complexity.
- Speed (coding/decoding delay)
- Computation requirement and power consumption.

Speech coding essentially is used to analyse the speech signal in order to extract its important parameters at the transmitter and using these parameters, synthesize the speech at the receiver for reconstruction. This is known as *Parametric coding*. This is in contrast to *waveform coding* techniques (which we have studied in previous sections), where the waveform of the message signal is sampled quantized and then encoded. Examples of waveform coding are PCM, DPCM, DM, ADM, ADPCM etc. which use sample by sample coding scheme and preserve its output related to the input.

Parametric coding however is a lossy type of coding and hence the output signal does not exactly sound like the input resulting in synthetic quality. The most prevailing, worthy quality, low bit rate parametric coding scheme is the Linear Predictive Coding (LPC). Parametric Coders (or Voice Coders: Vocoders) basically model the vocalisation of speech. Speech samples are broken into small frames (typically 25 seconds frame). Instead of transmitting digitized speech, they transmit parameters of model and synthesize approximation of speech.

An LPC vocoder models the vocal tract as a filter and filter excitation is done by a periodic pulse (for voiced speech) or noise (for unvoiced speech). The parameters in an LPC Vocoder include voiced / unvoiced (Voiced for quasiperiodic speech frames like vowels and unvoiced for noisy consonants) decision, Gain, pitch for a voiced frame and the LPC predictor filter coefficients representing the speech producing source filter model.

The block diagram of an LPC encoder and decoder is shown in Figure 2.14 and the speech generation model in Figure 2.15. For example, we can code these parameters as follows:

- V/UV decision: 1 bit
- Pitch: 8 bits
- LPC filter coefficients: 8 bits
- Gain: 5 bits

Total of just 22 bits would be required for a 25 msec LPC frame.

These parameters can be synthesized at the receiver, resulting in bit rates as low as 1.2 to 4.8 kbps (as compared to 64 kbps for an 8-bit PCM system).

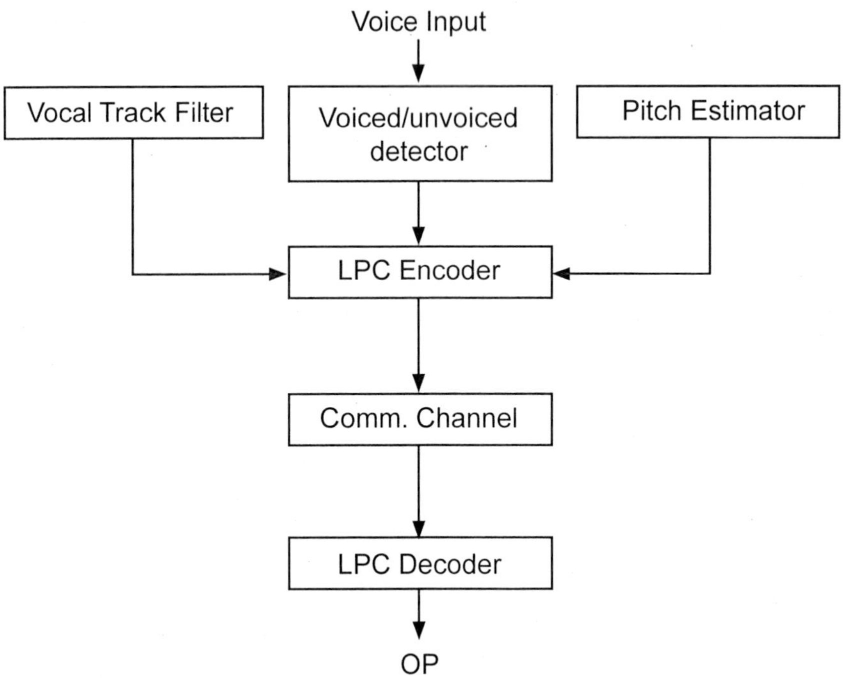

Fig. 2.14 Block diagram of an LPC coder

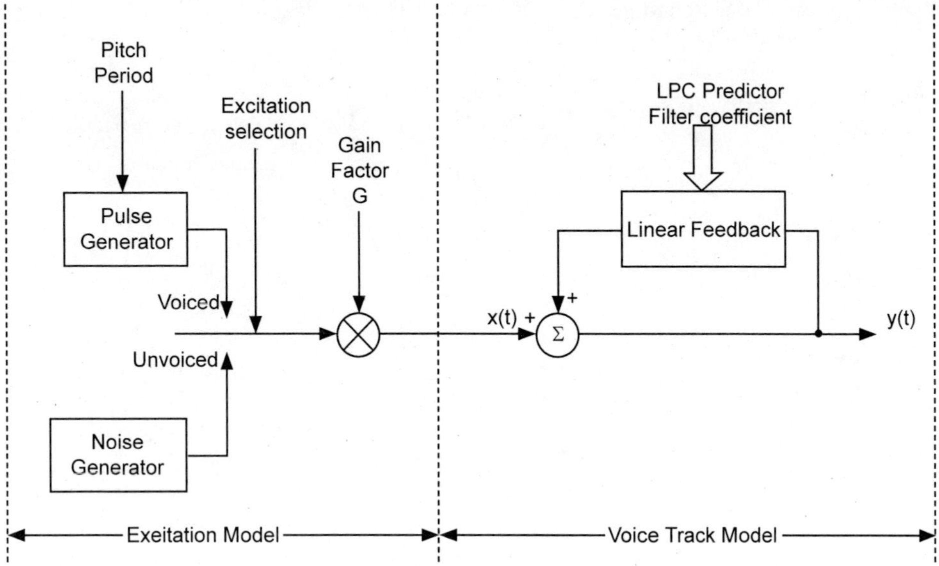

Fig. 2.15 Speech generation model of LPC coder (excitation and vocal tract model)

However, LPC systems are characterised by low quality (synthetic), moderate complexity, moderate delays and are less robust. The quality of pure LPC vocoder is quite low for cellular telephony although by using hybrid coders, quality can be improved.

2.6 BASEBAND TRANSMISSION

Baseband transmission is a method of transmitting the information over a communication channel using a single frequency electric pulse. They are bidirectional communication where transmission and reception can happen simultaneously. Repeaters can be used to regenerate the weakened signals during transmission.

The major sources for bit errors in baseband transmission are channel noise and Inter Symbol Interference (ISI). The effect of Additive White Gaussian Noise (AWGN) and the method of recovering the signal in the presence of noise using a matched filter will be discussed in the next section and the causes for ISI and the methods to overcome the same will be discussed in the later sections of the chapter.

2.7 MATCHED FILTERS

As discussed in the previous section, the transmitted signal over a baseband channel experiences degradation due to the addition of AWGN in the channel. Inorder to have a satisfactory estimation of the transmitted signal, designing of an appropriate filter at the receiver becomes a necessity. This requires the calculation of the impulse response of the filter matching to the baseband pulses transmitted over the channel. Such filters are called matched filters. Matched filters strive to minimizes the effect of channel noise on the received signal and thus improving the signal to noise ratio at the output of the receiver.

The block diagram of a Matched filter is as shown in Figure 2.16.

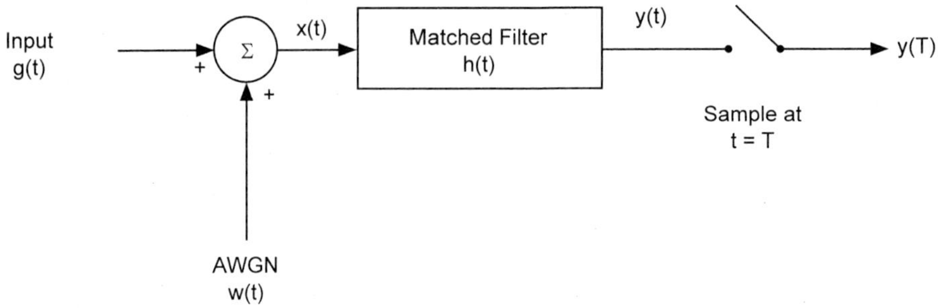

Fig. 2.16 Matched filter

Let us consider that g(t) is the transmitted signal and x(t) is the received signal which is an input to the matched filter.

Clearly,

$$x(t) = g(t) + w(t) \tag{2.15}$$

where w(t) is the AWGN with zero mean and a power spectral density of $\frac{N_0}{2}$, added during transmission.

Let the impulse response of the matched filter is denoted by h(t).

The output of the matched filter can be denoted as:

$$\begin{aligned} y(t) &= x(t) * h(t) \\ &= [g(t) + w(t)] * h(t) \\ &= [g(t) * h(t)] + [w(t) * h(t)] \\ y(t) &= g_0(t) + n(t) \end{aligned} \tag{2.16}$$

Where

$g_0(t)$ is the response of the filter due to the input g(t) and

n(t) is the filtered noise

Let us now derive the expression for output SNR of a matched filter. The output SNR of a matched filter can be defined as

$$(SNR)_o = \frac{|g_0(t)|^2}{E[n^2(t)]} \tag{2.17}$$

Where

$|g_0(t)|^2$ is the instantaneous power of g(t)

$E[n^2(t)]$ is the average output noise power

We have

$$g_0(t) = g(t) * h(t)$$

Taking FT both sides

$$G_0(f) = G(f)\,H(f) \tag{2.18}$$

We can now find the time domain sequence $g_0(t)$ by taking the inverse FT of equation (2.18)

$$g_0(t) = \int_{-\infty}^{\infty} G(f)H(f)e^{j2\pi ft}\,df \tag{2.19}$$

To find the instantaneous power of the output signal, consider the sample at t = T

$$|g_0(t)|^2 = \left|\int_{-\infty}^{\infty} G(f)H(f)e^{j2\neq fT}\,df\right|^2 \tag{2.20}$$

Equation (2.20) gives the expression for the numerator of the expression for $(SNR)_o$.

To get the expression for the noise power, consider the fact that the noise is an AWGN with zero mean and a power spectral density of $\frac{N_0}{2}$. Therefore, the power spectral density of the filtered noise can be given as

$$S_N(f) = \frac{N_0}{2}|H(f)|^2 \tag{2.21}$$

Average power of the noise is given by,

$$E[n^2(t)] = \int_{-\infty}^{\infty} S_N(f)\,df$$

$$= \int_{-\infty}^{\infty} \frac{N_0}{2}|H(f)|^2\,df$$

$$E[n^2(t)] = \frac{N_0}{2}\int_{-\infty}^{\infty}|H(f)|^2\,df \tag{2.22}$$

Using equations (2.20) and (2.22) we can now write the expression for the output SNR of a matched filter given by,

$$(SNR)_o = \frac{\left|\int_{-\infty}^{\infty} G(f)H(f)e^{j2\neq fT}\,df\right|^2}{\frac{N_0}{2}\int_{-\infty}^{\infty}|H(f)|^2\,df} \tag{2.23}$$

The solution for the expression (2.23) can be obtained by considering the Schwarz's inequality.

Schwarz's inequality states that, if there are two complex functions $f_1(x)$ and $f_2(x)$ satisfying the following conditions

$$\int_{-\infty}^{\infty}|f_1(x)|^2\,dx < \infty$$

and

$$\int_{-\infty}^{\infty}|f_2(x)|^2\,dx < \infty$$

Then

$$\left|\int_{-\infty}^{\infty} f_1(x)\,f_2(x)dx\right|^2 \le \int_{-\infty}^{\infty}|f_1(x)|^2\,dx\int_{-\infty}^{\infty}|f_2(x)|^2\,dx \tag{2.24}$$

If and only if

$$f_1(x) = K\,f_2^*(x) \tag{2.25}$$

Suppose that

$$f_1(x) = H(f)$$

$$f_2(x) = G(f)e^{j2\pi fT}$$

Substituting this in (2.24)

$$\left|\int_{-\infty}^{\infty} H(f)G(f)e^{j2\neq fT}df\right|^2 \leq \int_{-\infty}^{\infty}|H(f)|^2\,df \int_{-\infty}^{\infty}|G(f)e^{j2\neq fT}|^2\,df$$

But

$|e^{j2\neq fT}| = 1$

Therefore

$$\left|\int_{-\infty}^{\infty} H(f)G(f)e^{j2\neq fT}dt\right|^2 \leq \int_{-\infty}^{\infty}|H(f)|^2\,df \int_{-\infty}^{\infty}|G(f)|^2\,df \tag{2.26}$$

Using (2.26) in (2.23)

$$(\text{SNR})_o = \frac{\left|\int_{-\infty}^{\infty} G(f)H(f)e^{j2\neq fT}df\right|^2}{\frac{N_0}{2}\int_{-\infty}^{\infty}|H(f)|^2\,df}$$

$$(\text{SNR})_o \leq \frac{\int_{-\infty}^{\infty}|H(f)|^2\,df \int_{-\infty}^{\infty}|G(f)|^2\,df}{\frac{N_0}{2}\int_{-\infty}^{\infty}|H(f)|^2\,df}$$

$$(\text{SNR})_o \leq \frac{\int_{-\infty}^{\infty}|G(f)|^2\,df}{\frac{N_0}{2}}$$

$$(\text{SNR})_o \leq \frac{2}{N_0}\int_{-\infty}^{\infty}|G(f)|^2\,df \tag{2.27}$$

It is clear from (2.27) that the $(\text{SNR})_o$ is not dependent only of the input signal and the $(\text{SNR})_o$ attains it maxima when the inequality is converted into an equation, i.e

$$(\text{SNR})_{o,\,\text{Max}} = \frac{2}{N_0}\int_{-\infty}^{\infty}|G(f)|^2\,df \tag{2.28}$$

as per the definition of Schwarz's inequality, this is possible if and only if

$f_1(x) = K\, f_2^*(x)$

i.e.

$H_{opt}(f) = KG^*(f)e^{-j2\neq fT}$

For simplicity we can assume K =1

Therefore

$$H_{opt}(f) = G^*(f)e^{-j2\neq fT} \tag{2.29}$$

Equation (2.29) represents the expression for the optimum transfer function of the matched filter so as to maximize the output SNR at t = T and G*(f) is the complex conjugate of G(f).

Finally, we can find the optimum impulse response of the matched filter, $h_{opt}(t)$ by taking the IFT of H(f).

$$h_{opt}(t) = \int_{-\infty}^{\infty} G^*(f)e^{-j2\pi fT}e^{j2\pi ft}\,df$$

$$h_{opt}(t) = \int_{-\infty}^{\infty} G^*(f)e^{-j2\pi f(T-t)}df \tag{2.30}$$

For real valued signal,

$G^*(f) = G(-f)$

Using this in (2.30)

$$h_{opt}(t) = \int_{-\infty}^{\infty} G(-f)e^{-j2\pi f(T-t)}df$$

Using the properties of the FT,

$$h_{opt}(t) = g(T-t) \tag{2.31}$$

It is clear from (2.31) that the impulse response of a matched filter is the time reversed and delayed version of the transmitted signal g(t). Thus, the name matched filter as the impulse response is matched with the input sequence.

2.7.1 Properties of the Matched Filter

For a Matched Filter,

$$h_{opt}(t) = S(T - t)$$
$$H_{opt}(f) = KS^*(f)e^{-j2\pi fT}$$

where K is a constant

1. The output signal-to-noise ratio (SNR)o is maximised by the impulse response,

$$h(t) = S(T - t)$$

$$SNR_{max} = \frac{\varepsilon_s}{N_0/2} = \frac{2\varepsilon_s}{N_0} \text{ for an AWGN with zero mean}$$

and spectral density

$$\Phi_{nn}(\omega) = \frac{N_0}{2} \text{ W/ Hz}$$

and ε_s is the energy of the signal $S(t)$

$$\varepsilon_s = \int_0^T S^2(t)\,dt$$

We can see that the maximum SNR only depends on the waveform's energy, and not on any other aspects of $S(t)$.

2. The FT of the MF output is proportional to the energy spectral density of the input signal. From equation (2.26)

$H(f) = G^*(f)\, e^{-j2\pi fT}$

$Y(f) = |S(f)|^2\, e^{-j2\pi fT}$

and

$$y_s(t) = \int_{-\infty}^{\infty} Y(f)e^{j2\pi fT}df = \int_{-\infty}^{\infty} |S(f)|^2 = \int_0^T S^2(t)dt$$

The power spectral density of the output is given by

$$\Phi_0(f) = \frac{1}{2}N_0 \,|H(f)|^2 = \frac{1}{2}N_0\varepsilon_s$$

Signal to Noise Ratio $SNR_{max} = \frac{2\varepsilon_s}{N_0}$

3. A shifted version of the ACF of the input signal determines the output of the matching filter.

$R(f) = |G(f)|^2$

$S_0(f) = |S(f)|^2 \, e^{-2\pi fT} = R(f)e^{-2\pi fT}$

i.e.

$S_0(t) = R(t - T)$ (Shifted version of the ACF of the input signal).

Example 2.4: Consider a finite energy signal x(t) defined as

$$x(t) = \begin{cases} 5, & 0 \leq t < 10 \\ 0, & Otherwise \end{cases}$$

Find the spectrum of the output of the matched filter to x(t).

Solution:

Let y(t) be the output of the matched filter to which the input is x(t) and let $h_{opt}(t)$ be the impulse response.

$$y(t) = x(t) * h_{opt}(t)$$

Taking FT both sides

$$Y(f) = X(f)\, H_{opt}(f)$$

But

$$H_{opt}(f) = X^*(f)e^{-j2\pi fT}$$

Therefore

$$Y(f) = X(f)\, X^*(f)e^{-j2\pi fT}$$

$$= |X(f)|^2 \, e^{-j2\pi fT}$$

By the definition of FT

$$X(f) = \int_{-\infty}^{\infty} x(t)e^{-j2\neq ft}\,dt$$

$$= \int_{0}^{10} 5e^{-j2\neq ft}\,dt$$

$$X(f) = \frac{5}{\neq f}\sin(10\pi f)\, e^{-j10\pi f}$$

Therefore,

$$|X(f)|^2 = \left(\frac{50}{10\neq f}\sin(10\neq f)\right)^2$$

The spectrum of the output signal is given by

$$Y(f) = \left(\frac{50}{10\neq f}\sin(10\neq f)\right)^2 e^{-j2\neq fT}$$

2.8 INTER SYMBOL INTERFERENCE (ISI)

A binary baseband communication system as shown in Figure 2.17.

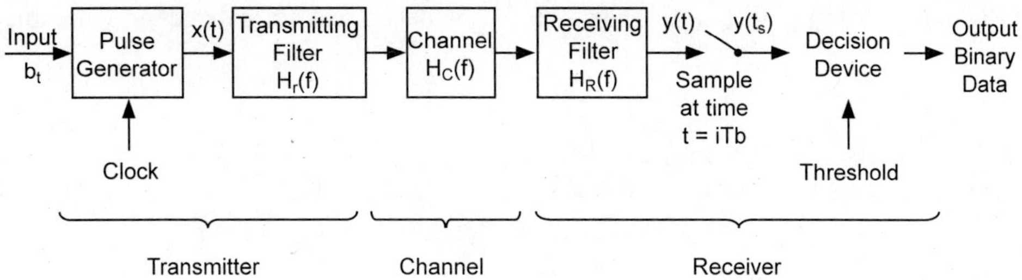

Fig. 2.17 Binary baseband communication system

The binary data that is to be transmitted is applied to a pulse generator. The pulse generator block generates a PAM signal x(t) given by,

$$x(t) = \sum_{k=-\infty}^{\infty} c_k g(t - kT_b) \tag{2.32}$$

where g(t) is a basic pulse shaping function, whose value is normalized to 1.

In other words g(0) = 1V.

C_k depicts the amplitude of the kth input pulse. The value of C_k is dependent on the line coding technique used at the transmitter side. For instance, if the polar representation is used, then its value is +A if the bit '1' is received and '-A' if bit '0' is received.

The frequency domain representation of equation (2.32) can be obtained by taking Fourier Transformation both sides

$$X(f) = \sum_{k=-\infty}^{\infty} c_k G(f) e^{-2\neq fkT_b} \tag{2.33}$$

The electric pulse thus generated by the pulse generator is then applied to a transmitting filter with a transfer function of $H_T(f)$. The output of the transmitting filter is given to the channel. The channel characteristics is denoted by the function $H_C(f)$. The signal is subjected to variations in accordance with the channel characteristics. One of the major parameters affecting the signal during transmission over the channel is dispersion. Signal transmitted by the sender suffers multiple reflections due to obstacles and hence multiple copies of the same signal reach the destination. Nevertheless, different copies of the signal reach destination at different instances of time. This would lead to the spreading or expansion of the signal in time domain, which is termed as channel dispersion. This would result in the interference to the subsequent symbols, if this delay incurred due to multipath transmissions exceed the symbol period of the transmitted symbols.

At the receiver part of the system, the received signal is first applied to the receiving filter, whose transfer function is given by $H_R(f)$. The output of the receiving filter is then sampled at a rate synchronous to that of the transmitter. The sampled signals are given to the decision device. The decision device compares the amplitude of the incoming sample with the threshold and it decodes the sample value as '1' if the received sample amplitude is higher than the threshold, else it decodes the sample value as '0'.

The output of the receiving filter can be mathematically represented as

$$y(t) = \propto\sum_{k=-\infty}^{\infty} c_k p(t - kT_b) \quad (2.34)$$

where μ is the scaling factor

p (t) is the pulse shaping function for the output y(t) which is also normalized to 1V. In other words p(0) = 1.

Taking Fourier Transformation for both sides of equation (2.34)

$$Y(f) = \sum_{k=-\infty}^{\infty} \mu c_k P(f) e^{-2\pi f k T_b} \quad (2.35)$$

From the Figure 2.17, the output of the receiving filter can be obtained in frequency domain as,

$$Y(f) = X(f)\, H_T(f)\, H_C(f)\, H_R(f) \quad (2.36)$$

Using Equation (2.35) and (2.33) in equation (2.36)

$$\sum_{k=-\infty}^{\infty} \mu c_k P(f) e^{-2\pi f k T_b} = \sum_{k=-\infty}^{\infty} c_k G(f) e^{-2\neq f k T_b}\ H_T(f)\, H_C(f)\, H_R(f) \quad (2.37)$$

$$\Rightarrow \quad \mu\, P(f) = G(f)\, H_T(f)\, H_C(f)\, H_R(f) \quad (2.38)$$

It can be inferred from equation (2.38), that the pulse shaping signal p(t) can be obtained by taking inverse Fourier Transformation on both sides.

From Figure 2.17, it can be seen that the output of the receiving filter y(t) is applied to a sampler which samples the signal y(t) at a rate equal to iT_b, where T_b is the bit duration. Thus the sampled signal can be obtained by considering equation (2.34) and replacing 't' with 'iT_b'.

The sampled form of the output of the received filter becomes,

$$y(iT_b) = \propto\sum_{k=-\infty}^{\infty} c_k p(iT_b - kT_b)$$

$$= \propto\sum_{k=-\infty}^{\infty} c_k [p(i - k)T_b]$$

When k = i,

$$y(iT_b) = \mu C_i\, p(0) + \propto\sum_{k=-\infty}^{\infty} c_k p(iT_b - kT_b)$$

As p(0) = 1

$$\Rightarrow \quad y(iT_b) = \mu C_i + \propto\sum_{k=-\infty, k\neq i}^{\infty} c_k p(iT_b - kT_b) \quad (2.39)$$

The equation (2.39) has two terms. The first term of the RHS of (2.39) represents the contribution of the ith transmitted symbol, which is the desired symbol. However, the second term denotes the contributions of all symbols on the reconstruction of the output at instance 'i', except the one transmitted at the instance 'i'. Thus, the second part of the LHS of equation (2.39) denotes unwanted components contributing towards the reconstruction at the receiver. This term denotes the interference by all unwanted signals experienced during the reconstruction of the ith input bit. This term is thus denoted as ISI. As already discussed, the ISI is a result of dispersion experienced by the signal during the transmission in the channel. If the spread due to dispersion exceeds the symbol duration, interference between symbols is induced. This would result in tending the decision device to make incorrect decisions.

From the equation (2.39), it is clear that the condition for zero ISI is that the second part of the RHS should be 0. That is,

$$\propto\sum_{k=-\infty, k\neq i}^{\infty} c_k p(iT_b - kT_b) = 0$$

$$\Rightarrow \quad \propto\sum_{k=-\infty, k\neq i}^{\infty} c_k p(iT_b - kT_b) = 0 \quad (2.40)$$

This is possible if p(iTb-kTb) = 0 for all values of k such that k ≠ i.

Nyquist has given a condition to achieve zero ISI which we will be discussing in the next section.

2.9 NYQUIST CRITERION FOR ZERO ISI

The Nyquist criterion for Zero ISI can be stated as follows:

The Fourier Transformation of the pulse shaping signal p(t) satisfying the condition,

$$\sum_{n=-\infty}^{\infty} P(f - nR_b) = T_b \tag{2.41}$$

would result in the zero ISI denoted by

$$p(iT_b - kT_b) = \begin{cases} 1, & i = k \\ 0, & i \neq k \end{cases}$$

The above condition can be proved as follows:

Let us assume that the signal p(t) is sampled and the sampled signal is represented by $P_s(t)$.

In Unit I, using the expression for ideal sampling for the signal X(t), as denoted in equation (1.6),

$$X_s(t) = \sum_{n=-\infty}^{\infty} X(nT_s).\delta(t - nT_s)$$

Where T_s is the sampling period.

The expression in frequency domain is given by,

$$X_s(f) = \frac{1}{T_S}\sum_{n=-\infty}^{\infty} X(f - nf_S)$$

Let $\quad T_s = T_b$

Replacing X(f) with P(f) and using $f_s = \frac{1}{T_b} = R_b$ in the above expression,

$$P_s(f) = \frac{1}{T_S}\sum_{n=-\infty}^{\infty} P(f - nf_s)$$

$$P_s(f) = R_b \sum_{n=-\infty}^{\infty} P(f - nR_b) \tag{2.42}$$

The signal $P_s(f)$ can also be obtained by considering the Fourier Transformation of the signal $P_s(t)$ which is given by,

$$P_s(f) = \int_{-\infty}^{\infty} p_S(t)\, e^{-j2\neq ft}\, dt \tag{2.43}$$

Where

$$P_s(t) = \sum_{n=-\infty}^{\infty} P(nT_b).\,\delta(t - nT_b) \tag{2.44}$$

using (2.41) in (2.40)

$$P_s(f) = \int_{-\infty}^{\infty}\sum_{n=-\infty}^{\infty} P(nT_b).\,\delta(t - nT_b)e^{-j2\pi ft}\, dt \tag{2.45}$$

Let n = (i - k), when i= k, n =0 and p(0) = 1, and when i ≠ k, p[(i - k)T_b] = 0 as discussed earlier.

Therefore, recalling the condition

$$p(iT_b - kT_b) = \begin{cases} 1, & i = k \\ 0, & i \neq k \end{cases}$$

The summation in the RHS of (2.45) therefore exists only when n = 0.

$$\Rightarrow \qquad P_s(f) = \int_{-\infty}^{\infty} \sum_{n=-\infty}^{\infty} P(nT_b).\,\delta(t-nT_b)e^{-j2\pi ft}\,dt = \int_{-\infty}^{\infty} p(0)\,\delta(t)\,e^{-j2\pi ft}\,dt$$

$$\Rightarrow \qquad P_s(f) = p(0) = 1 \tag{2.46}$$

Using the result obtained in (2.46) in (2.45)

$$P_s(f) = R_b \sum_{n=-\infty}^{\infty} P(f-nR_b) = 1$$

Therefore

$$\sum_{n=-\infty}^{\infty} P(f-nR_b) = \frac{1}{R_b} = T_b \tag{2.47}$$

Hence the criterion is proved.

2.10 IDEAL SOLUTION OR NYQUIST SOLUTION FOR ZERO ISI

As discussed in the previous section, the ISI can be minimized by having control over the signal p(t) in time domain and P(f) in frequency domain. One possible signal that fulfills the condition of Nyquist criterion for zero ISI is a sinc function which is denoted by the following mathematical equation:

$$p(t) = \text{sinc}\,(2B_0t) \tag{2.48}$$

Where B_0 is is called as the Nyquist bandwidth. It is also defined as the minimum bandwidth required for zero ISI.

We have

$$B_0 = \frac{1}{2T_b} \tag{2.49}$$

Where T_b is the duration of symbol.

Using (2.49) in (2.48) sinc function can also be represented as

$$p(t) = \text{sinc}\,(\frac{t}{T_b}) \tag{2.50}$$

The sinc signal or the impulse response of an ideal low pass filter is shown in Figure 2.18.

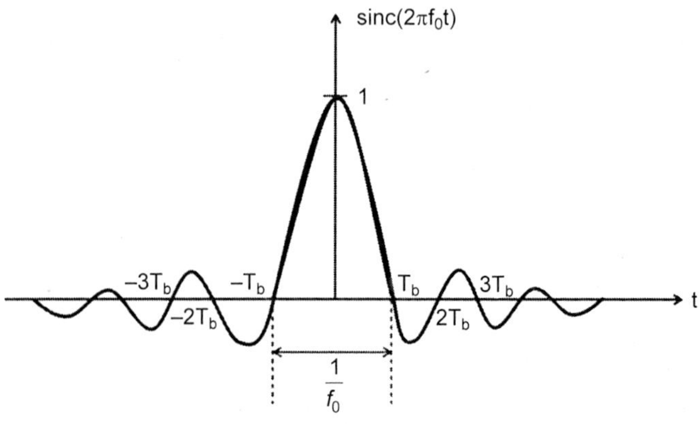

Fig. 2.18 Sinc function

Taking the Fourier Transformation of the signal p(t), we will get

$$P(f) = \begin{cases} \frac{1}{2B_0}, & |f|<0 \\ 0, & |f|>0 \end{cases} \tag{2.51}$$

Therefore, the frequency response of an ideal low pass filter is as shown in Figure 2.18.

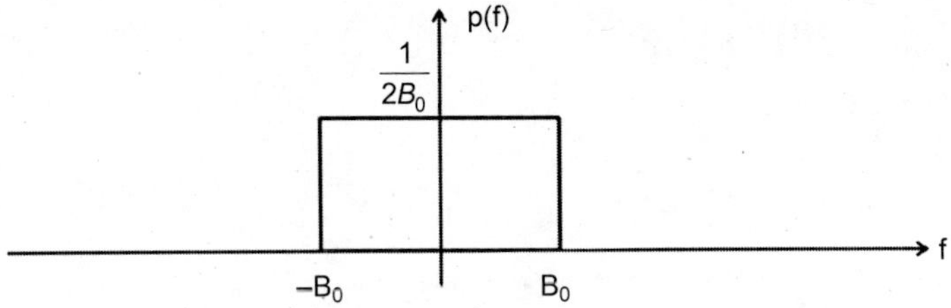

Fig. 2.19 Frequency response of an ideal low pass filter

The realization of the ideal low pass filter as discussed above poses two practical problems:

- The frequency response of the filter P(f) has to be flat for the range $-B_0 < f < B_0$ and has to be zero elsewhere. Realizing filters with such sharp edges is practically infeasible.
- The clock at the receiver should be in perfect synchronization with the clock at the sender. A small difference in the timing pulses would lead to the introduction of ISI.

The possibility of error being induced due to inaccurate synchronization amongst the clocks can be explained through the following mathematical analysis.

From equation (2.50) we can write,

$$p(t - kT_b) = \text{sinc}\,[2B_0(t-kT_b)] \tag{2.52}$$

From equation (2.31)

$$y(t) = \propto\sum_{k=-\infty}^{\infty} c_k p(t - kT_b)$$

Using Equation (2.52) in equation (2.34)

$$y(t) = \propto\sum_{k=-\infty}^{\infty} c_k Sinc\,[2B_0(t - kT_b)]$$

$$= \propto\sum_{k=-\infty}^{\infty} c_k Sinc\,[2B_0 t - 2B_0 kT_b] \tag{2.53}$$

Since $\qquad B_0 = \frac{1}{2T_b}$

$$2B_0T_b = 1$$

using this in equation (2.53),

$$y(t) = \propto\sum_{k=-\infty}^{\infty} c_k Sinc\,[2B_0 t - k] \tag{2.54}$$

Consider a timing error at the receiver due to inaccuracy in the synchronization denoted by Δt.

Evaluating the expression (2.51) at $t = \Delta t$

$$y(\Delta t) = \mu\sum_{k=-\infty}^{\infty} c_k Sinc\,[2B_0 \Delta t - k] \tag{2.55}$$

By the definition of the sinc function

$$\text{sinc x} = \frac{\sin \pi x}{\pi x}$$

Using this in equation (2.55)

$$y(\Delta t) = \mu \sum_{k=-\infty}^{\infty} c_k \frac{\sin [2\pi B_0 \Delta t - \pi k]}{[2\pi B_0 \Delta t - \pi k]} \tag{2.56}$$

We have Sin (A - B) = (Sin A × Cos B) - (Cos A × Sin B)

Equation (2.56) becomes

$$y(\Delta t) = \mu \sum_{k=-\infty}^{\infty} \frac{c_k}{\pi(2B_0 \Delta t - k)} [\sin(2B_0 \pi \Delta t] \cos \pi k - \cos(2B_0 \pi \Delta t) \sin \pi k]$$

We have

$$\sin \pi k = 0$$

and $\cos \pi k = (-1)^k$

Therefore equation (2.56) becomes

$$y(\Delta t) = \mu \sum_{k=-\infty}^{\infty} \frac{c_k}{\pi(2B_0 \Delta t - k)} (-1^k) \sin(2B_0 \pi \Delta t)$$

$$= \mu \frac{c_0}{2\pi B_0 \Delta t} \sin(2B_0 \pi \Delta t) + \mu \sum_{k=-\infty \text{ and } k \neq 0}^{\infty} \frac{c_k}{\pi(2B_0 \Delta t - k)} (-1^k) \sin(2B_0 \pi \Delta t)$$

$$\Rightarrow y(\Delta t) = \mu c_0 \sin c\,(2B_0 \pi \Delta t) + \frac{\mu}{\pi} \sum_{k=-\infty \text{ and } k \neq 0}^{\infty} \frac{c_k}{(2B_0 \Delta t - k)} (-1^k) \sin(2B_0 \pi \Delta t) \tag{2.57}$$

The first term in the RHS of the above equation represents the desired component and the second terms gives the ISI component introduced due to the inaccuracy in the synchronization.

2.11 PRACTICAL SOLUTION FOR ZERO ISI

As already discussed in the previous section, realization of filter with a frequency response shown in Figure 2.16 is practically infeasible as it exhibits sharp edges at -B_0 and B_0. In other words, the frequency response of the filter should exhibit flat portion followed by the roll-off portion. This modified response P(f) is therefore should take a form of raised cosine spectrum as shown in Figure 2.20.

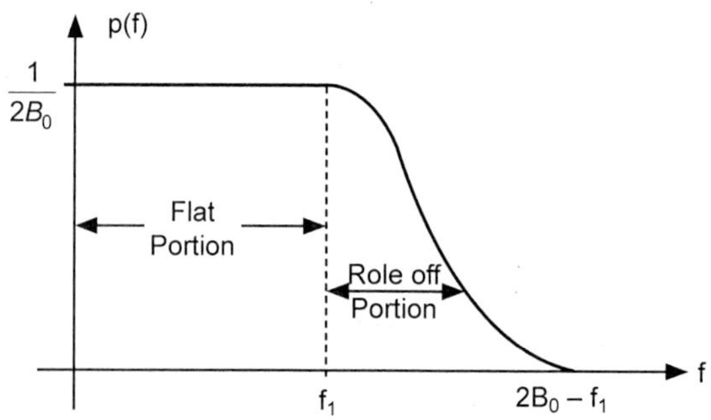

Fig. 2.20 Response of a practical low pass filter

Raised Cosine spectrum can be mathematically represented as follows:

$$P(f) = \begin{cases} \dfrac{1}{2B_0}, & |f| < f_1 \\ \dfrac{1}{4B_0}\left[1+\cos\left(\dfrac{\pi(|f|-f_1)}{2B_0-2f_1}\right)\right], & f_1 \le |f| < 2B_0 - f_1 \\ 0, & |f| \ge 2B_0 - f_1 \end{cases} \quad (2.58)$$

The first part of the expression denotes the flat portion of the response and the second part of the expression gives the roll-off portion.

The roll-off factor can be defined as follows:

$$\alpha = 1 - \frac{f_1}{B_0} \quad (2.59)$$

We will consider two special cases of α

Case 1: $\alpha = 0$, in this case $f_1 = B_0$. This corresponds to the ideal case.

Case 2: $\alpha = 1$, in this case $f_1 = 2B_0$. This corresponds to full roll-off characteristics where the required bandwidth is two times the minimum bandwidth needed for zero ISI.

Let us now consider the time domain representation of P(f) as represented in (2.55). This can be done by considering the Inverse Fourier Transformation of the equation leading to the following expression:

$$p(t) = \text{sinc}\,(2B_0t)\,\frac{\cos(2\pi\alpha B_0 t)}{1-16\alpha^2 B_0^2 t^2} \quad (2.60)$$

The expression (2.60) has two parts. The first part is sinc $(2B_0t)$ which is the desired component and the second term is a function of $\dfrac{1}{t^2}$ which decreases for larger values of t.

The response p(t) for $\alpha = 0$ and $\alpha = 1$ are as shown in Figure 2.21.

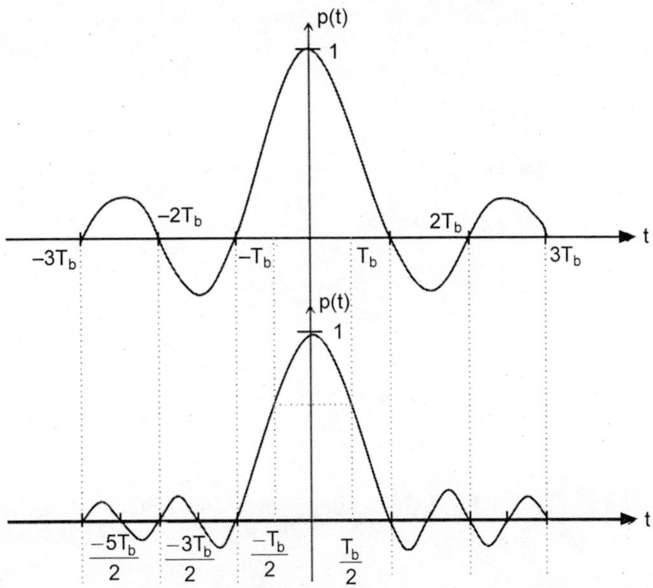

Fig. 2.21 p(t) for α = 0 and α = 1

For the case α = 1, we can make the following observations:

- The amplitude of the signal is $\frac{1}{2}$ at t = $\frac{T_b}{2}$ and $\frac{-T_b}{2}$
- There are zero crossings at t = $\pm\frac{3T_b}{2}, \pm\frac{5T_b}{2}, \pm\frac{7T_b}{2}$ and so on along with the usual crossings at $\pm T_b$, $\pm 2T_b$, $\pm 3T_b$ and so on.
- The amplitudes of the side lobes have reduced compared to the case when α=0.

The above desired features of raised cosine filter are achieved at the cost of increased bandwidth.

2.11.1 Transmission Bandwidth of a Raised Cosine Filter

Consider the raised cosine spectrum as shown in Figure 2.22.

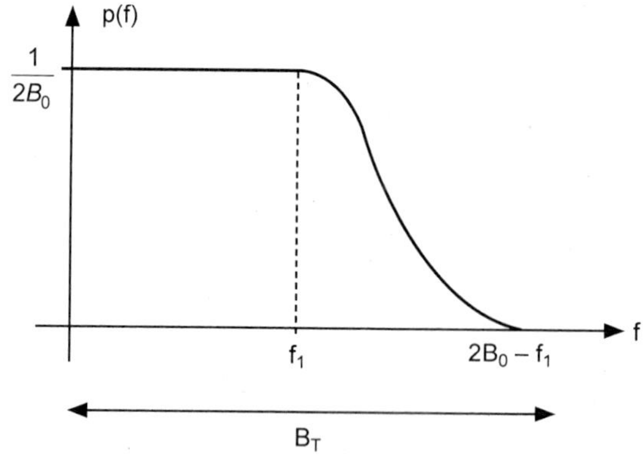

Fig. 2.22 Raised cosine spectrum

The transmission bandwidth is given by:

$$B_T = 2B_0 - f_1 \tag{2.61}$$

But

$$\alpha = 1 - \frac{f_1}{B_0}$$

⇒

$$f_1 = B_0 (1 - \alpha) \tag{2.62}$$

Using (2.62) in (2.61),

$$B_T = 2B_0 - B_0 (1 - \alpha)$$

$$B_T = B_0 (1 + \alpha) \tag{2.63}$$

Following inferences can be drawn from equation (2.63)

- When α = 0, the transmission bandwidth will be equal to the Nyquist Bandwidth which is the minimum bandwidth required for zero ISI.
- When α = 1, the transmission bandwidth will be equal to twice the Nyquist Bandwidth.

Example 2.5: A binary PAM is to transmitted over a low pass channel of transmission bandwidth of 50kHz. The bit duration is 15μsec. Find the value of the roll of factor α of the raised cosine pulse spectrum to fulfill these requirements.

Solution:

$$B_T = 50\text{kHz}$$
$$T_b = 15\ \mu\text{sec}$$
$$B_T = B_0(1+\alpha)$$
$$B_0 = \frac{1}{2T_b} = 33333.333$$
$$\Rightarrow \quad \alpha = 0.5$$

2.12 CORRELATIVE CODING

In the previous sections, we have discussed ISI in the negative context. Nevertheless, adding ISI in a controlled manner would enhance the bit rate to $2B_0$ in a channel of bandwidth B_0. This technique is called as correlative coding or partial response signalling schemes. In other words, correlative coding is a method of adding ISI in a controlled manner so as to enhance the rate of transmission. As the ISI introduced is known, an appropriate receiver can be designed to mitigate the effect of ISI.

The concept of correlative coding can be better explained using the concept of Duobinary signalling.

2.12.1 Duobinary Signalling

The term 'duo' has come from the fact that the transmission capacity of the system is double the bandwidth. The block diagram of a duobinary encoder is shown in Figure 2.23.

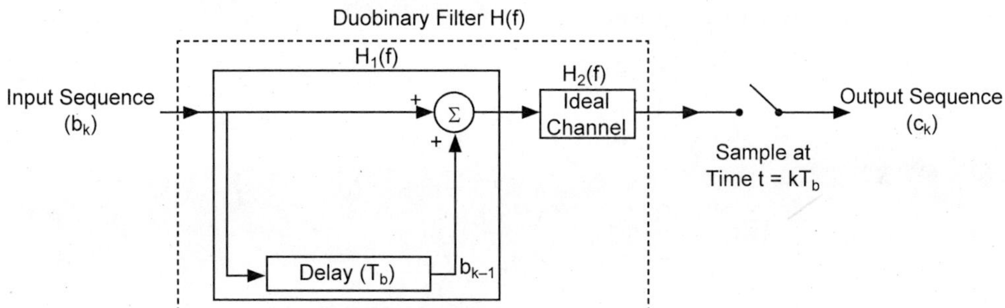

Fig. 2.23 Duobinary encoder

Consider an input stream consisting of binary sequence of uncorrelated bits. Let us assume the duration of each bit is T_b seconds. Let us suppose that a polar representation is used for coding. That is a bit '1' is represented by an electric pulse of 'A' Volts and bit '0' is represented by an electric pulse of '-A' Volts. Let the amplitude A be 1 Volts.

From the Figure 2.23, it is clear that the sequence c_k is dependent on the input bit b_k and its delayed version b_{k-1}. In other words, the bit c_k at the instance 'k' is dependent on the input bit at the instances 'k' and 'k-1'. Mathematically the sequence c_k can be written a,

$$c_k = b_k + b_{k-1} \tag{2.64}$$

From the equation (2.61), it is clear that the ISI is introduced. But it can also be noted that the interference is only between two consecutive bits. It is therefore evident that the sequence c_k is a correlated sequence although b_k was not. As the values b_k can take on are +1 or -1 depending on the input bit being 0 or 1, the sequence c_k can take on any of the following values:

- If both b_k and b_{k-1} are same and is equal to bit 1, then c_k takes a value of 2V.
- If both b_k and b_{k-1} are same and is equal to bit 0, then c_k takes a value of -2V.
- If both b_k and b_{k-1} are different, then c_k takes a value of 0V.

Therefore, depending on the amplitude level of the signal c_k, we can infer the following:

Amplitude Level of c_k	Bit b_k	Bit b_{k-1}
Positive	1	1
Negative	0	0
Zero	Compliment to one another.	

Let us now find the expression for the overall frequency response of a Duobinary filter H(f) which is the cascade connection $H_1(f)$ and $H_2(f)$.

Therefore $$H(f) = H_1(f)\, H_2(f) \tag{2.65}$$

$H_1(f)$ has two parts: one is a direct connection to summer whose transfer function is unity and the second is a delay element introducing a delay of T_b, whose transfer function is given by .

Therefore $$H_1(f) = 1 + e^{-j2\neq fT_b} \tag{2.66}$$

Let us assume that the channel is ideal and the bandwidth of the channel be B_0.

$$H_2(f) = \begin{cases} 1, & |f| \le B_0 \\ 0, & |f| > B_0 \end{cases} \tag{2.67}$$

Using (2.66) and (2.67) in (2.65)

$$H(f) = \begin{cases} 1 + e^{-j2\pi fT_b}, & |f| \le B_0 \\ 0, & |f| > B_0 \end{cases}$$

But

$$1 + e^{-j2\pi fT_b} = e^{-j\pi fT_b}[e^{j\pi fT_b} + e^{-j\pi fT_b}] = e^{-j\pi fT_b} \times 2\cos(\pi fT_b)$$

Therefore $$H(f) = \begin{cases} 2e^{-j\pi fT_b}\cos(\pi fT_b), & |f| \le B_0 \\ 0, & |f| > B_0 \end{cases} \tag{2.68}$$

The magnitude and phase responses of the duobinary filter is therefore given by,

$$|H(f)| = \begin{cases} 2|\cos(\pi fT_b)|, & |f| \le B_0 \\ 0, & |f| > B_0 \end{cases} \tag{2.69}$$

$$\theta(f) = \begin{cases} -\pi fT_b, & |f| \le B_0 \\ 0, & |f| > B_0 \end{cases} \tag{2.70}$$

The magnitude and phase responses of a duobinary filter are given in Figures 2.24 and 2.25 respectively.

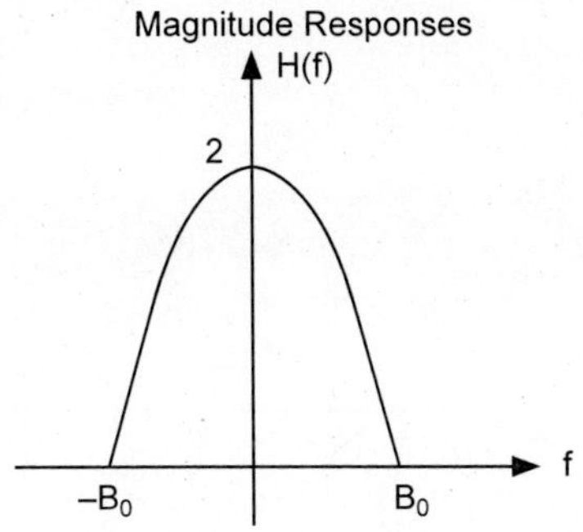

Fig. 2.24 Magnitude response of a duobinary filter

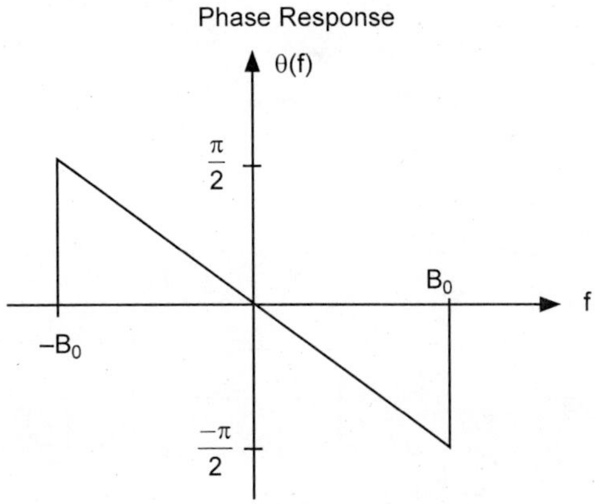

Fig. 2.25 Phase response of a duobinary filter

The impulse response of the duobinary filter can be obtained by taking the inverse Fourier transformation of its transfer function.

$$h(t) = \int_{-\infty}^{\infty} H(f)e^{j2\pi ft}df \Rightarrow h(t) = \text{sinc}\left(\frac{1}{T_b}\right) + \text{sinc}\left(\frac{1-T_b}{T_b}\right) \tag{2.71}$$

The plot of impulse response of a duobinary filter is as shown in Figure 2.26. It can be seen from the figure that the amplitude level of h(t) at the instances t = 0 and t = T_b are equal to 1. This is because of the fact that the input bit at two adjacent instances are considered in duobinary filter.

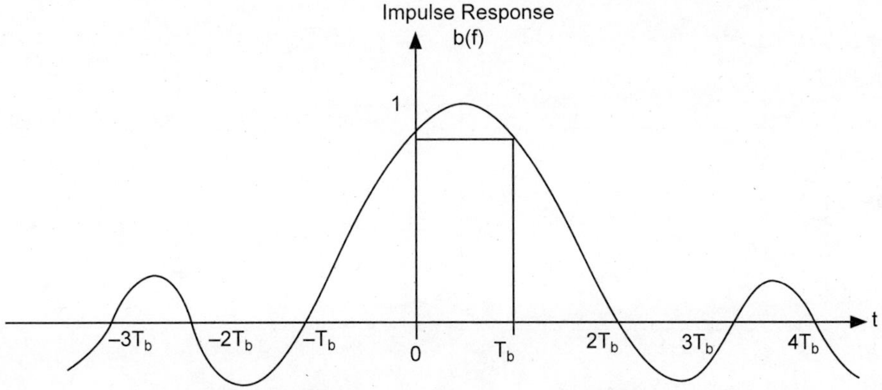

Fig. 2.26 Impulse response of a duobinary filter

The decoding process of a duobinary filter can be explained through the following mathematical expression:

$$\hat{b}_k = c_k - \hat{b}_{k-1} \tag{2.72}$$

Example 2.6: A binary sequence 0110110011 is applied to a duobinary encoder. Find the duobinary coded sequence and the corresponding receiver output. Assume that no precoder is used.

Solution:

Input b_k	0	1	1	0	1	1	0	0	1	1
Polar representation of b_k	-1	1	1	-1	1	1	-1	-1	1	1
Polar representation of c_k		0	+2	0	0	+2	0	-2	0	+2
Estimated b_k	-1	+1	+1	-1	+1	+1	-1	-1	+1	+1
Output	0	1	1	0	1	1	0	0	1	1

Example 2.7: In the example 2.6, consider that the voltage level of the third digit is made 0. Demonstrate how error is propagated in this case.

Solution:

Input b_k	0	1	1	0	1	1	0	0	1	1
Polar representation of b_k	-1	1	1	-1	1	1	-1	-1	1	1
Polar representation of c_k		0	~~+2~~ 0	0	0	+2	0	-2	0	+2
Estimated b_k	-1	+1	-1	+1	-1	+3	-3	+1	-1	+3
Output	0	1	0	1	0	1	0	1	0	1
			Error	Error	Error			Error	Error	

From the above example it is clear that the error is propagated in this case as precoder is not used.

It is clear from the equation (2.72) that the estimation at the present instance 'k' is dependent on the estimation at the previous instant 'k-1'. Thus, if an error is incurred during the estimation of a symbol, it gets propagated in the upcoming bits as well. This is a biggest disadvantage in the duobinary filter. Nevertheless, we can overcome this shortcoming by introducing a precoding block ahead of the normal duobinary encoding system.

This system is presented in Figure 2.27.

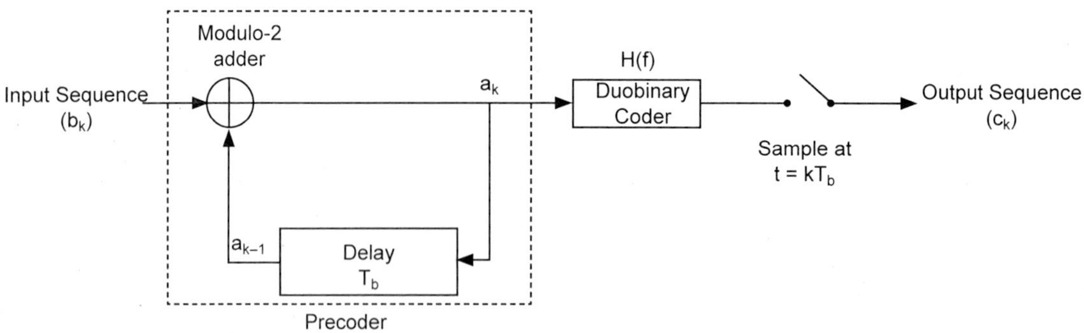

Fig. 2.27 Duobinary filter with precoding

It can be noted that the block Duobinary filter in Figure 2.26 represents the complete system shown in Figure 2.22. It is clear from the Figure 2.26 that the input b_k is first applied to a precoder whose output a_k is then applied to the normal duobinary filter. The mathematical expressions governing the sequences a_k and c_k are given by:

$$a_k = b_k \oplus a_{k-1} \tag{2.73}$$

$$c_k = a_k + a_{k-1} \tag{2.74}$$

Using (2.73) in (2.74)

$$c_k = [b_k \oplus a_{k-1}] + a_{k-1}$$

Using the property of EXOR operation, if $b_k = 0$, bk $\oplus$ $a_{k-1} = a_{k-1}$ and if $b_k = 1$, $b_k \oplus a_{k-1}$ = complement of a_{k-1}

Therefore $c_k = 2a_{k-1}$ if $b_k = 0$ and $c_k = 0$ if $b_k = 1$

If the polar form is used to represent a_k,

$$c_k = \begin{cases} \pm 2, b_k = 0 \\ 0, \quad b_k = 1 \end{cases} \tag{2.75}$$

The block diagram of the detector used to estimate the input sequence is as shown in Figure 2.28.

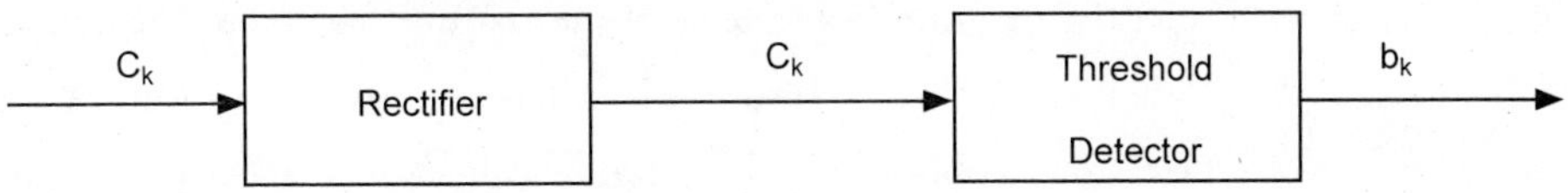

Fig. 2.28 Detector for precoded duobinary system

The first block of the detector shown in Figure 2.28, considers the magnitude of the sequence c_k. We can then decode the sequence by applying the following decision rule.

$$\hat{b}_k = \begin{cases} 1, |c_k| \le 1 \\ 0, |c_k| > 1 \end{cases} \tag{2.76}$$

Example 2.8: A binary sequence 0110110011 is applied to a duobinary encoder with precoder. Find the duobinary coded sequence and the corresponding receiver output.

Solution:

Input b_k		0	1	1	0	1	1	0	0	1	1
Precoded Sequence $a_k = b_k \oplus a_{k-1}$	0	0	1	0	0	1	0	0	0	1	0
Polar representation of a_k	-1	-1	+1	-1	-1	+1	-1	-1	-1	+1	-1
Duobinary encoder output $c_k = a_k \oplus a_{k-1}$		-2	0	0	-2	0	0	-2	-2	0	0
Recovered output		0	1	1	0	1	1	0	0	1	1

Example 2.9: In the example 2.8, consider that the voltage level of the fourth digit is made 0. Demonstrate how error is localised in this case.

Solution:

Input b_k		0	1	1	0	1	1	0	0	1	1
Precoded Sequence $a_k = b_k \oplus a_{k-1}$	0	0	1	0	0	1	0	0	0	1	0

Polar representation of a_k	-1	-1	+1	-1	-1	+1	-1	-1	-1	+1	-1
Duobinary encoder output $c_k = a_k \oplus a_{k-1}$		-2	0	0	~~-20~~	0	0	-2	-2	0	0
Recovered output		0	1	1	1	1	1	0	0	1	1
					Error						

It can be seen from the above table that the error is confined only to one bit due to the presence of the precoder.

2.13 EQUALIZATION

A communication channel is characterized by the following mathematical expression:

$$H_c(f) = |H_c(f)| \tag{2.77}$$

Scan here to know more

where, $H_c(f)$ is the transfer function of the channel

$|H_c(f)|$ is the magnitude response of the channel

$\theta_c(f)$ is the phase response of the channel.

For distortion-less reception, the magnitude response of the channel has to be constant within the channel bandwidth and the phase response has to be a linear function of frequency. On the contrary, if the magnitude response is not constant within the channel bandwidth, the signal experiences amplitude distortion and if the phase response exhibits non linear characteristics, then the signal transmitted experiences phase distortion. Generally a transmitted signal experiences both amplitude and phase distortions leading to dispersions and ISI. Equalization is a process of countering such channel distortions.

There are basically two types of equalization techniques:

1. Maximum Likelihood Sequence Estimation: In this technique the channel's impulse response is estimated and the receiver is adjusted to the transmission environment.
2. Equalization with Filters: In this method, filters are used to compensate the distortions induced during transmission. In this section, we will restrict our discussions to equalizers with filters.

Ideally, the frequency response of the equalizer should be an inverse of the frequency response of the channel. The equalizers can also be categorised as preset equalizers or adaptive equalizers. In preset equalizers the channel is assumed to be time invariant. Thus the filter coefficients once designed remain same. On the other hand, adaptive equalization is a more realistic approach where the time varying nature channel is also taken into account. Thus the coefficients of the adaptive filter change/ and get updated in accordance with the channel characteristics.

2.13.1 Adaptive Equalization

In most of the practical scenario, it is desirable to have equalization filters to get their coefficients updated in accordance with the behaviour of the channel. Such equalization filters are said to be adaptive equalization filters or simply adaptive filters.

The block diagram of an adaptive filter is shown in Figure 2.29.

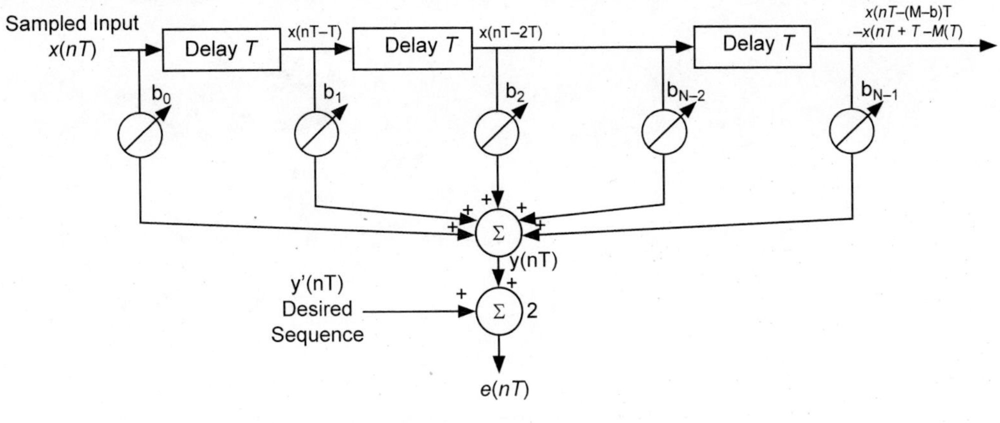

Fig. 2.29 Adaptive equalization filter

The sampled sequence x(nT) is the input t the filter and y(nT) is the filter output. The coefficients of the filter are denoted by b_0, b_1, b_2 and so on. The order of the filter is assumed to be N and hence there are N filter coefficients. These coefficients are adaptive in nature. That is the values of the filter coefficients change in accordance with the channel behaviour. An adaptive algorithm computes the filter coefficients in a continuous manner.

The expression for the filter output y(nT) can be written as

$$y(nT) = \sum_{k=0}^{N-1} b_k x(nT - kT) \tag{2.78}$$

Where b_k is the filter coefficient of the kth tap.

The error signal can be determined by

$$e(nT) = y'(nT) - y(nT) \text{ for all n} \tag{2.79}$$

Where y'(nT) is the desired response. The filter coefficients are adjusted such that the total energy of the error sequence is to be minimized. There are sophisticated algorithms like LMS or RLS using which the filter coefficients can be updated. These algorithms run in iterations and the filter coefficients are updated till the system is said to have reached the equilibrium. The details of these algorithms is out of the scope of this book.

2.14 DIGITAL SUBSCRIBER LINE

Digital Subscriber Line (DSL) or Digital Subscriber Loop (DSL) is a technology of transmitting digital data over a telephone line. This enables to send internet data along with the normal voice information over the copper wires. The voice and data traffic make use of different frequency spectrum so that there will not be any interference between the two. A typical DSL setup used for Internet access through telephone lines is shown in Figure 2.30.

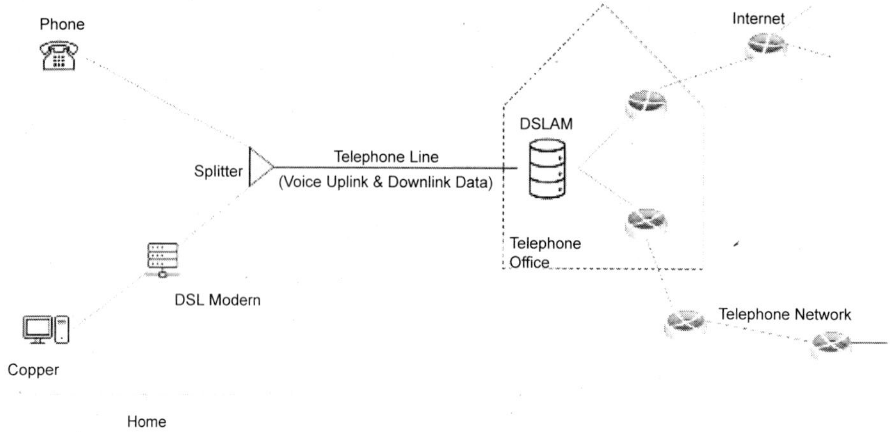

Fig. 2.30 Digital subscriber line

A DSL modem takes the digital information from the computer and converts it into high frequency tones to be transmitted over the telephone line. Splitter at the customer side separates voice and internet data and routes the internet data towards modem and voice traffic to the telephone. Digital Subscriber Line Access Multiplexer (DSLAM) located at the telephone office, separates data and voice and routes the data appropriately to corresponding networks. A single DSLAM can support thousands of customers.

Different frequency bands are used for uplink and downlink. Thus, along with the voice traffic both uplink and downlink can happen simultaneously over the single line.

Generally, uplink and downlink traffic use different data rates. Such systems where the uplink and downlink transmissions are not symmetric are termed as Asymmetric Digital Subscriber Line (ADSL).

UNIT SUMMARY

- Differential PCM(DPCM) system, that can be designed to take advantage of the redundancies between consecutive samples, typically observed in speech waveforms
- Delta Modulation (DM) is a baseband modulation technique, which can be considered a special case of DPCM, by exploiting sample correlation by oversampling (by at least 4 times).
- The output SNR of DM system is given by,

$$(\text{SNR})_o = \frac{P_{Max}}{N_0} = \frac{3}{8\neq^2 W f_0^2 T_s^3}$$

- Adaptive Delta Modulation is employed to reduce slope overload and granular noise. A DM system that adjusts its step size is known as an ADM system.
- Adaptive Differential Pulse Code Modulation (ADPCM), was developed by Bell Labs in the 1970s for efficient coding of speech signals and now for Voice over IP (VoIP) communications.
- Speech coding essentially is used to analyse the speech signal in order to extract its important parameters at the transmitter and using these parameters, synthesize the speech at the receiver for reconstruction - Parametric coding.
- Baseband transmission is a method of transmitting the information over a communication channel using a single frequency electric pulses.

- Maximum output SNR of a matched filter

  $(SNR)_{o,\,Max} = \frac{2}{N_0}\int_{-\infty}^{\infty} |G(f)^2|\, df$

- Optimum impulse response of a matched filter is the time reversed and delayed version of the transmitted signal g(t)

  $h_{opt}(t) = g(T-t)$
- ISI is a result of dispersion experienced by the signal during the transmission in the channel.
- The Nyquist criterion for Zero ISI can be stated as follows:
- The Fourier Transformation of the pulse shaping signal p(t) satisfying the condition,

  $\sum_{n=-\infty}^{\infty} P(f - nR_b) = T_b$

  would result in the zero ISI denoted by

  $p(iT_b - kT_b) = \begin{cases} 1, & i = k \\ 0, & i \neq k \end{cases}$

- Minimum bandwidth required for zero ISI.

  $B_0 = \frac{1}{2T_b}$

- Raised Cosine spectrum can be mathematically represented as follows:

  $$P(f) = \begin{cases} \frac{1}{2B_0}, & |f| < f_1 \\ \frac{1}{4B_0}\left[1 + \cos\left(\frac{\pi(|f| - f_1)}{2B_0 - 2f_1}\right)\right], & f_1 \leq |f| < 2B_0 - f_1 \\ 0, & |f| \geq 2B_0 - f_1 \end{cases}$$

- The roll-off factor can be defined as follows:

  $\alpha = 1 - \frac{f_1}{B_0}$

- The transmission bandwidth is given by:

  $B_T = B_0\,(1 + \alpha)$
- Correlative coding is a method of adding ISI in a controlled manner so as to enhance the rate of transmission
- Generally a transmitted signal experiences both amplitude and phase distortions leading to dispersions and ISI. Equalization is a process of countering such channel distortions.
- Adaptive Equalization Filters - equalization filters with their coefficients updated in accordance with the behaviour of the channel.
- Digital Subscriber Line (DSL) or Digital Subscriber Loop (DSL) is a technology of transmitting digital data over a telephone line.

EXERCISE

Numerical Problems

1. A voice signal has an rms bandwidth of 1.4 kHz and prefiltered with a cut off frequency of to 4. Determine the SNR of this system assumong a bandwidth expansion factor of 8.
2. The sampling frequency in a DM system is 10 times the Nyquist rate. What is the maximum permissible amplitude of the message signal if slope overload is to be avoided? Assume the step size as 0.5 volts.
3. Find the Nyquist sampling rate for the signal x (t) = sin 200t sinc2 1000t
4. The input is sampled at 5 times the Nyquist rate in a DM system. The input signal frequency is varied from 300 Hz to 3400 Hz with a peak amplitude of 1 Volt.
   (a) Determine the value of the step size in order to avoid slope overload when the input signal frequency is 1 kHz.
   (b) What is the peak amplitude of the input signal to just overload the modulator, when the input signal frequency is 300 Hz.
   (c) Is the modulator overloaded when the input signal frequency is 3.4 kHz
5. Consider a finite energy signal g(t) defined as

$$g(t)=\begin{cases} V_m, & 0 \leq t < T \\ 0, & Otherwise \end{cases}$$

   Determine the impulse response of the matched filter. Find the spectrum of the output of the matched filter to g(t).
6. A baseband signal is to transmitted over a channel with a transmission bandwidth of 40kHz. The bit duration is 10μsec. Find the value of the roll of factor α of the raised cosine pulse spectrum that satisfy these requirements.
7. A binary sequence 11010011101 is applied to a duobinary encoder.
   (a) Find the duobinary coded sequence
   (b) Determine the decoded binary sequence at the receiver.

   Assume that no precoder is used.
8. A binary sequence 1011010111 is applied to a duobinary encoder with precoder. Find the duobinary coded sequence and the corresponding receiver output. Assume the initial bit as '0'.

Descriptive Type Questions

1. Distinguish between PCM, DPCM, ADPCM, DM and ADM systems.
1. What is slope overload noise and granular noise in DM systems?
2. How does ADM over come slope overload noise and granular noise?
3. Adaptive quantization and adaptive prediction are necessary in ADPCM system.Justify the statement.

4. ADM is better than DM. How? What are the advantages of ADM over DM?
5. How does a tapped delay line filter acts as a prediction filter ?
6. Compare and contrast DPCM and ADPCM.
7. Explain noise in DM systems.
8. Define Processing Gain of a DPCM system.
9. With transmitter and receiver block diagram, explain an ADPCM system.
10. How are step sizes decided in a ADPCM system? Explain a simple alogorothm to achieve this.
11. Derive an expression foe output SNR of a DM system.
12. Distinguish between Waveform Coding and Parametric Coding.
13. LPC Vocoders give synthetic quality. Explain Why?
14. Which are the LPC parameters that are transmitted? Write the speech generation model for an LPC Vocoder.
15. What are matched filters? Derive the expression for the output SNR for a matched filter.
16. With the help of a neat block diagram, explain baseband communication system.
17. State and prove the Nyquist criterion for zero ISI.
18. Explain the effect of roll factor on the bandwidth of a raised cosine filter.
19. Derive the expression for the transmission bandwidth of a raised cosine filter.
20. Explain the concept of adaptive equalization in detail.

Objective Type Questions

1. The distortion arises due to signal dispersion exceeding the symbol duration is called as
   a. Inter Symbol Interference
   b. Quantization error
   c. Channel attenuation
2. Which of the following signal satisfies the Nyquist criterion for zero ISI?
   a. Sine function
   b. Cosine function
   c. Sinc function
3. The Nyquist bandwidth required for zero ISI is
   a. $B_0 = \frac{1}{T_b}$
   b. $B_0 = \frac{1}{2T_b}$
   c. $B_0 = \frac{2}{T_b}$

4. The value of the roll off factor for which the raised cosine filter turns to be an ideal filter is
   a. $\alpha = 0$
   b. $\alpha = 1$
   c. $\alpha = 0.5$
5. Which of the following system is used to reduce distortion
   a. Sampler
   b. Multiplexer
   c. Equalizer

KNOW MORE

The National Digital Communications Policy, 2018

The National Digitial Communications Policy, 2018 seeks to unlock the transformative power of digital communications networks - to achieve the goal of digital empowerment and improved well being of the people of India; and towards this end, attempts to outline a set of goals, initiatives, strategies and intended policy outcomes.

The National Communication Policy aims to accomplish the following Strategic Objectives by 2022:

1. Provisioning of Broadband for All
2. Creating 4 Million additional jobs in the Digital Communications sector
3. Enhancing the contribution of the Digital Communications sector to 8% of India's GDP from ~6% in 2017
4. Propelling India to the Top 50 Nations in the ICT Development Index of ITU from 134 in 2017
5. Enhancing India's contribution to Global Value Claims
6. Ensuring Digital Sovereignty

Scan here to know more

JOHN CIOFFI

Image Courtesy: https://en.wikipedia.org/wiki/File:John_Cioffi_2006.jpg

John Cioffi is an engineer from American origin who is popularly known as "Father of DSL". His contributions in the area of information theory and coding is remarkable. His innovation in making the practical realization of Digital Subscriber Lines (DSL) is one of his pioneer works. He has more than 100 publications to his credit. He has been the recipient of numerous awards and recognitions.

FURTHER READING

[1] Haykin, Simon. "Digital Communications", John Wiley, New York, 2001.

[2] Sklar, Bernad. "Digital Communication: Functions and Applications", Prenicc Hall., 1988.

[3] K. Sam Shanmugam , « Digital and Analog Communication Systems», John Wiley, New York, 2006.

[4] M. Kulkarni and Farooq Husain, "Analog and Digital Communication Systems", Umesh Publications, New Delhi, 2005.

[5] K. N. Hari Bhat and D. Ganesh Rao, "Digital Communications", Third Edition, Pearson, 2012.

3 Analysis of Signal Space

UNIT SPECIFICS

Through this unit, we have discussed the following aspects:

- Introduction to Signal Space representation and Geometrical Interpretation of signals.
- Detection of signals, estimation concepts and criteria:
    - Minimum Mean Square Error (MMSE)
    - Maximum A Posteriori (MAP)
    - Maximum Likelihood (ML) Estimation
    - Maximum Likelihood Detector.
- Detection of binary signals in presence of noise.
- Optimum Receivers: Analysis of correlation receiver and matched filter receivers.
- Equivalence of Correlation receiver filter with Matched Filter.

RATIONALE

Geometrical representation of signals can serve as a powerful tool in the study of data transmission. The message symbols are encoded into signal vectors that can be represented as a linear combination of vectors. The receiver, after receiving the signal should estimate the message based on decoding principles. One of the popular decoding techniques is maximum likelihood decoding. This unit gives an insight into geometric representation of signals and the concept of decoding and optimum filters.

UNIT OUTCOMES

U3-O1: Illustrate the process of geometric representation of signals.

U3-O2: Define likelihood functions

U3-O3: Estimate the message over an AWGN channel using maximum likelihood decoding

U2-O4: Explain the concepts of optimum receivers

U3-O5: Establish equivalence of receiver filter with matched filter

MAPPING OF UNIT OUTCOMES WITH COURSE OUTCOMES

Unit-3 Outcomes	EXPECTED MAPPING WITH COURSE OUTCOMES (1- Weak Correlation; 2- Medium correlation; 3- Strong Correlation)					
	CO-1	CO-2	CO-3	CO-4	CO-5	CO-6
U3-O1	2	-	-	-	-	-
U3-O2	2	-	-	-	-	-
U3-O3	2	1	-	-	-	-
U3-O4	1	1	-	1	-	-
U3-O5	1	1	-	-	-	-

3.1 GEOMETRIC REPRESENTATION OF SIGNALS

Representing signals geometrically proves to be an efficient way of denoting any signal as a linear combination of basis signals. These basis signals are to be orthonormal functions. The advantage of representing signals in geometric domain is the ease of analysis of their performance as modulation signals.

More formally we can define the geometric representation of signals as a process of representing number of signals with finite energy in terms of linear combination of N number of basis functions. It is to be noted that these basis functions are to be orthonormal to one another. Clearly N has to be less than or equal to M.

The number of functions in the basis set also indicates the dimension of the signal space.

Let us consider M energy signals represented as

$$s_i\,(t) = [s_1\,(t), s_2\,(t),\ldots, s_M(t)] \tag{3.1}$$

Let the orthonormal basis functions are represented as

$$\phi_i(t) = [\phi_1(t), \phi_2(t), \ldots, \phi_N(t)] \tag{3.2}$$

We can now represent the signal $s_i(t)$ as a linear combination of the signals in the basis set. The governing equation is represented by (3.3)

$$s_i(t) = s_{i1}(t)\,\phi_1(t) + s_{i2}(t)\,\phi_2(t) + \ldots s_{iN}(t)\,\phi_N(t)$$
$$1 \le i \le M \tag{3.3}$$

Equation (3.3) can be rewritten as

$$s_i(t) = \sum_{j=1}^{N} s_{ij}(t)\,\phi_j(t)$$
$$1 \le i \le M \tag{3.4}$$

The terms s_{ij} are the coefficients.

Equation (3.4) is called as synthesis equation as it is used to find the signal $s_i(t)$ from the basis functions and coefficients.

A synthesizer used to generate signal $s_i(t)$ is as shown in Figure 3.1.

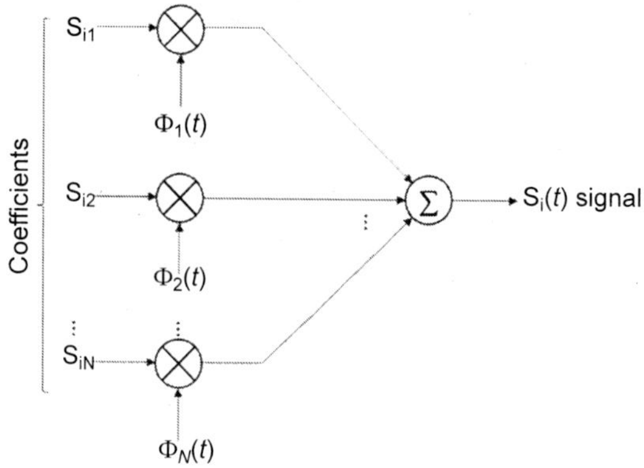

Fig. 3.1 Synthesizer

It can be seen from Figure 3.1 that the synthesizer consists of a N multipliers where the coefficients are multiplied with the basis functions. All these products are then added to get the signal $s_i(t)$.

As the basis functions are to be orthonormal, they have to satisfy the following condition:

$$\int_0^T \phi_i\ (t)\ \phi_j\ (t)dt = \delta_{ij} = \begin{cases} 1, & if\ i = j \\ 0, & if\ i \neq j \end{cases} \tag{3.5}$$

Using $i = j$ in equation (3.5)

$$\int_0^T \phi_i\ (t)\ \phi_j\ (t)dt = \int_0^T \phi_i\ (t)\ \phi_i\ (t)\ dt$$

$$\int_0^T \phi_i{}^2\ dt = 1 \tag{3.6}$$

It is clear from equation (3.6) that the energy of the basis function is normalized to unity.

Also, from equation (3.5)

$$\int_0^T \phi_i\ (t)\ \phi_j\ (t)\ dt = 0 = \text{when } i \neq j \tag{3.7}$$

From equation (3.7) it can be seen that the basis signals are orthogonal to one another.

The process of finding the coefficients in the RHS of equation (3.4) is called as analysis. To get the expression to find the coefficients, consider equation (3.3)

$$s_i\ (t) = s_{i1}\ (t)\ \phi_1\ (t) + s_{i2}\ (t)\ \phi_2\ (t) + \ldots\ s_{iN}\ (t)\ \phi_N\ (t)$$

$$1 = \leq i \leq M$$

Taking $i = 1$

$$s_1\ (t) = s_{11}\ (t)\ \phi_1\ (t) + s_{12}\ (t)\ \phi_2\ (t) + \ldots\ s_{1N}\ (t)\ \phi_N\ (t)$$

Multiplying both sides by $\phi_1(t)$

$$s_1\ (t)\ \phi_1\ (t) = s_{i1}\ (t)\ \phi_1\ (t)\ \phi_1\ (t) + s_{i2}\ (t)\ \phi_2\ (t)\ \phi_1\ (t) + \ldots..\ s_{iN}\ (t)\ \phi_N\ (t)\ \phi_1\ (t)$$

Integrating both sides

$$\int_0^T s_1\ (t)\ \phi_1\ (t)\ dt = \int_0^T s_{11}\ \phi_1\ (t)\ \phi_1\ (t)\ dt + \int_0^T s_{12}\ \ \phi_1\ (t)\ \phi_2\ (t)\ dt + \ldots$$

$$+ \int_0^T S_{1N}\ \phi_1(t)\ \phi_N\ (t)\ dt \tag{3.8}$$

From (3.7)

$$\int_0^T \phi_i(t)\phi_j(t)\,dt = 0 \text{ when } i \neq j$$

Therefore equation (3.8) becomes,

$$\int_0^T s_1(t)\phi_1(t)dt = \int_0^T s_{11}\phi_1(t)\phi_1(t)dt$$

$$\int_0^T s_1(t)\phi_1(t)dt = s_{11}\int_0^T \phi_1(t)\phi_1(t)dt \tag{3.9}$$

But

$$\int_0^T \phi_i^2 dt = 1$$

Therefore equation (3.9) becomes

$$\int_0^T s_1(t)\phi_1(t)dt = s_{11}$$

or $$s_{11} = \int_0^T s_1(t)\phi_1(t)dt$$

Similarly $$s_{12} = \int_0^T s_1(t)\phi_2(t)dt$$

And so on.

In general $$s_{ij} = \int_0^T s_i(t)\phi_j(t)dt \tag{3.10}$$

Equation (3.10) represents the analyzer equation. Figure 3.2 presents the block diagram representation of an analyzer.

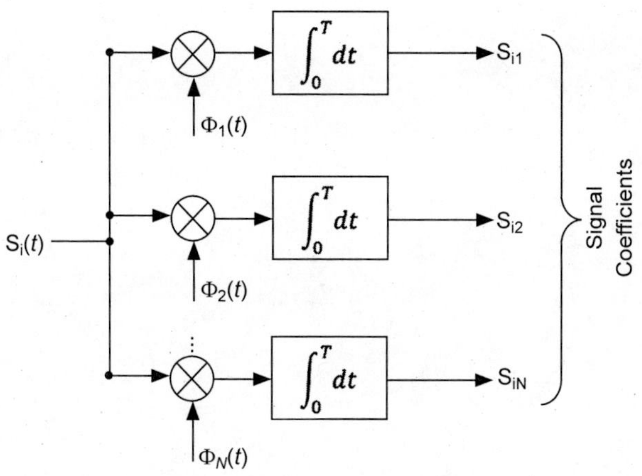

Fig. 3.2 Analyzer

An analyzer consists of N multipliers and N integrators. All coefficients for a particular value of i can be derived using the signal $s_i(t)$ and N basis functions. It is to be noted that the orthonormality property of basis functions has been explored to derive the expression for the coefficients.

Example 3.1: Write synthesizer and analyzer equations for three signals defined in a two dimensional signal space.

Solution:

Given $N = 2$ and $M = 3$

Synthesizer equations are given by

$$s_i(t) = \sum_{j=1}^{N} s_{ij}(t)\phi_j(t) \qquad 1 \le i \le M$$

Substituting $N = 2$ and $M = 3$

$$s_i(t) = \sum_{j=1}^{2} s_{ij}(t)\phi_j(t) \qquad i = 1, 2, 3$$

$$s_1(t) = s_{11}(t)\,\phi_1(t) + s_{12}(t)\phi_2(t)$$

$$s_2(t) = s_{21}(t)\,\phi_1(t) + s_{22}(t)\,\phi_2(t)$$

$$s_3(t) = s_{31}(t)\,\phi_1(1) + s_{32}(t)\,\phi_2(1)$$

Analyzer equations are given by

$$s_{ij} = \int_0^T s_i(t)\phi_j(t)\,dt$$

$$s_{11} = \int_0^T s_1(t)\phi_1(t)\,dt$$

$$s_{12} = \int_0^T s_1(t)\phi_2(t)\,dt$$

$$s_{21} = \int_0^T s_2(t)\phi_1(t)\,dt$$

$$s_{22} = \int_0^T s_2(t)\phi_2(t)\,dt$$

$$s_{31} = \int_0^T s_3(t)\phi_1(t)\,dt$$

$$s_{32} = \int_0^T s_3(t)\phi_2(t)\,dt$$

Example 3.2: Represent a signal with the coefficient vector [3, 2, 4] in a three dimensional signal space.

Solution:

Given

$M = 1$ and $N = 3$

Coefficient Vector = [3, 2, 4]

The signal is as shown in Figure 3.3.

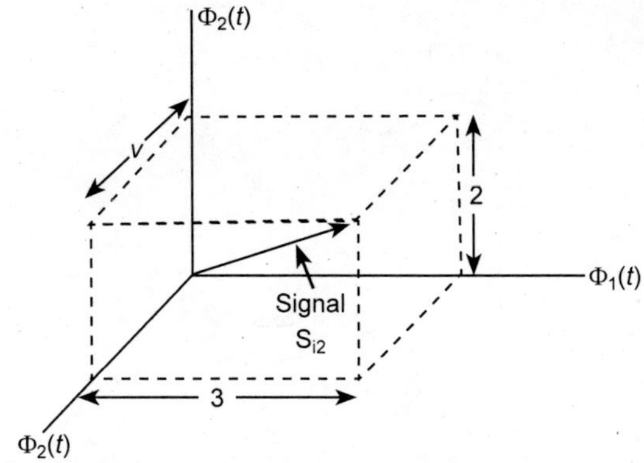

Fig. 3.3 Signal representation for the example 3.2

3.1.1 Squared Length of a Signal

Using the synthesizer equation as denoted by equation (3.3), The signal $s_i(t)$ can be denoted by its coefficients as follows:

$$s_i = \begin{bmatrix} s_{i1} \\ s_{i2} \\ \vdots \\ s_{iN} \end{bmatrix} \quad (3.11)$$

Where s_i is called as the signal vector.

These M signal vectors can be represented as points on an N dimensional Euclidean space called signal space. Please note that the N basis functions represent N mutually orthogonal axes of the N - dimensional space.

Another important parameter is squared length of a signal vector. It is defined as the inner product of the signal vector with itself. It can be derived as follows:

$$||s_i||^2 = s_i^T s_i \quad (3.12)$$

Where s_{ij} indicates the jth element of the signal vector s_i.

3.1.2 Energy of a Signal

We can define energy of a signal as,

$$E\{s_i(t)\} = E_i = \int_0^T s_i^2(t)\,dt \qquad 1 \le i \le M \quad (3.13)$$

Using (3.4) in (3.13)

$$E_i = \int_0^T \left[\sum_{j=1}^{2} s_{ij}\phi_j(t)\right]\left[\sum_{k=1}^{2} s_{ik}\phi_k(t)\right]dt$$

We can now interchange the positions of integration and summation,

$$E_i = \sum_{j=1}^{N}\sum_{k=1}^{N} s_{ij}s_{ik}\int_0^T \phi_i(t)\phi_k(t)dt \quad (3.14)$$

From (3.5)

$$\int_0^T \phi_i(t)\phi_j(t)dt = \delta_{ij} = \begin{cases} 1, \text{ if } i = j \\ 0, \text{ if } i \neq j \end{cases}$$

Using this in (3.14)

$$E_i = \begin{cases} \sum_{j=1}^{N}\sum_{k=1}^{N} s_{ij}s_{ik}, & \text{if } j = k \\ 0, & \text{if } j \neq k \end{cases}$$

Therefore when $j = k$,

$$E_i = \sum_{j=1}^{N}\sum_{k=1}^{N} s_{ij}s_{ik}$$

As $j = k$, double summation can be reduced to a single summation

$$= \sum_{j=1}^{N} s_{ij}^2 \qquad 1 \leq i \leq M$$

But the RHS of the above equation represents the squared length of a signal vector.

Therefore energy of the signal can be represented as

$$E_i = \|s_i\|^2 \tag{3.15}$$

From equation (3.15) it is clear that the energy of a signal is same as the squared length of a signal vector.

3.1.3 Euclidian Distance

The Euclidian distance between two points represented by the signal vectors and can be defined as

$$d_{ij} = \|s_i - s_j\| \tag{3.16}$$

From (3.12) we have

$$\|s_i - s_j\|^2 = \sum_{k=1}^{N} (s_{ik} - s_{jk})^2 \tag{3.17}$$

Also from (3.13) and (3.15)

$$E_i = \int_0^T s_i^2(t)dt = \|s_i\|^2 \tag{3.18}$$

Using (3.18) in (3.17)

$$\|s_i - s_j\|^2 = \int_0^T (s_i(t) - s_j(t))^2 dt \tag{3.19}$$

Equation (3.19) represents the squared Euclidian distance.

The angle between the two signal vectors s_i and s_j can be defined as follows:

$$\cos(\theta_{ij}) = \frac{s_i^T s_j}{||s_i||||s_j||} \tag{3.20}$$

Two signals are said to be orthogonal if the value of $\theta_{ij} = 90°$, this is possible when $s_i^T s_j = 0$. In other words two signals are said to be orthogonal, if their inner product is zero.

3.1.4 Gram Schmidt Orthogonalization Procedure

In the previous section we have discussed about the procedure to represent a signal as a combination of orthonormal basis functions. In this section we will look into the procedure for orthonormalizing a set of vectors. In other words, Gram Schmidt Orthogonalization Procedure is a method of getting orthonormal basis functions $\phi_i(t)$ that are used to represent signals geometrically.

Let us consider the following M signals with finite energy

$$s_i(t) = [s_1(t), s_2(t),...., s_M(t)]$$

Let the orthonormal basis functions used to represent these signals are

$$\phi_j(t) = [\phi_1(t), \phi_2(t),...., \phi_N(t)]$$

The Gram Schmidt Orthogonalization Procedure can be illustrated as follows:

Step 1: To find $\phi_1(t)$

A signal $s_1(t)$ is arbitrarily chosen from the signal set and the first basis function be defined as follows:

$$\phi_1(t) = \frac{s_1(t)}{\sqrt{E_1}} \tag{3.21}$$

Where E_1 is the energy of the signal $s_1(t)$

From (3.21)

$$s_1(t) = \sqrt{E_1}\,\phi_1(t) = s_{11}\phi_1(t)$$

where the coefficient $s_{11} = \sqrt{E_1}$

Step 2: To find

Let us consider the signal $s_2(t)$ the coefficient s_{21} can be defined as

$$s_{21} = \int_0^T s_2(t)\,\phi_1(t)\,dt \tag{3.22}$$

Let us define an intermediate function $f_2(t)$ as follows:

$$\phi_2(t) = s_2(t) - s_{21}\,\phi_1(t) \tag{3.23}$$

The function $f_2(t)$ is orthogonal to $\phi_1(t)$ for the interval $0 \le t \le T$. This can be showed from the equation (3.22) and considering $\int_0^T \phi_1^2(t)dt = 1$.

Considering this into account, we can now define the second basis function as follows:

$$\phi_2(t) = \frac{f_2(t)}{\sqrt{\int_0^T f_2^2(t)\,dt}} \tag{3.24}$$

$$\phi_2(t) = \frac{s_2(t) - s_{21}\phi_1(t)}{\sqrt{\int_0^T (s_2(t) - s_{21}\phi_1(t))^2\,dt}} \tag{3.25}$$

Consider the term inside the square root of the denominator of the equation (3.25)

$$\int_0^T (s_2(t) - s_{21}\phi_1(t))^2 dt = \int_0^T (s_2(t))^2 dt + \int_0^T (s_{21}\phi_1(t))^2 dt - 2\int_0^T s_2(t)s_{21}\phi_1(t)dt$$

$$\int_0^T (s_2(t) - s_{21}\phi_1(t))^2 dt = \int_0^T (s_2(t))^2 dt + \int_0^T (s_{21}\phi_1(t))^2 dt - 2\,s_{21}\int_0^T s_2(t)\phi_1(t)dt \tag{3.26}$$

But from (3.23)

$$s_{21} = \int_0^T s_2(t)\phi_1(t)dt$$

Using this in (3.26)

$$\int_0^T (s_2(t) - s_{21}\phi_1(t))^2 dt = \int_0^T (s_2(t))^2 dt + \int_0^T (s_{21}\phi_1(t))^2 dt - 2(s_{21})^2 \tag{3.27}$$

The first term of the above equation represents the energy of the signal $s_2(t)$, given by E_2.

$$E_2 = \int_0^T (s_2(t))^2 dt \tag{3.28}$$

The second term of the equation (3.27) can be simplified as

$$\int_0^T (s_{21}\phi_1(t))^2 dt = (s_{21})^2 \int_0^T (\phi_1(t))^2 dt$$

But

$$\int_0^T \phi_1^2(t)dt = 1.$$

Therefore

$$\int_0^T (s_2(t) - s_{21}\phi_1(t))^2 dt = E_2 + (s_{21})^2 - 2\times(s_{21})^2 = E_2 - (s_{21})^2 \tag{3.29}$$

Therefore equation (3.27) becomes

$$\int_0^T (s_2(t) - s_{21}\phi_1(t))^2 dt = E_2 + (s_{21})^2 - 2\times(s_{21})^2 = E_2 - (s_{21})^2 \tag{3.30}$$

Equation (3.25) now becomes,

$$\phi_2(t) = \frac{s_2(t) - s_{21}\phi_1(t)}{\sqrt{E_2 - (s_{21})^2}} \tag{3.31}$$

To show that the function $\phi_2(t)$ has unit energy:
Consider equation (3.24)

$$\phi_2(t) = \frac{f_2(t)}{\sqrt{\int_0^T f_2^2(t)dt}}$$

The energy of the signal $\phi_2(t)$ is given by,

$$\int_0^T \phi_2^2(t)dt = \int_0^T \frac{f_2^2(t)}{\int_0^T f_2^2(t)\,dt}\,\mathrm{dt}$$

$$\int_0^T \phi_2^2(t)dt = \int_0^T \frac{f_2^2(t)}{E_{f2}}dt \tag{3.32}$$

Where E_{f2} is the energy of the signal $f_2(t)$

$$E_{f2} = \int_0^T f_2^2(t)dt \tag{3.33}$$

Therefore equation (3.32) becomes

$$\int_0^T \phi_2^2(t)dt = \frac{1}{E_{f2}} \int_0^T f_2^2(t)\,dt$$

$$\int_0^T \phi_2^2(t)dt = \frac{1}{E_{f2}} \times E_{f2} = 1$$

Hence it is showed that the second basis function has unit energy.

To show that the functions $\phi_1(t)$ and $\phi_2(t)$ are orthogonal:

Consider equation (3.31)

$$\phi_2(t) = \frac{s_2(t) - s_{21}\phi_1(t)}{\sqrt{E_2 - (s_{21})^2}}$$

Multiplying the above equation by $\phi_1(t)$ and taking the integration

$$\int_0^T \phi_1(t)\phi_2(t)dt = \int_0^T \phi_1(t)\left[\frac{s_2(t) - s_{21}\phi_1(t)}{\sqrt{E_2 - (s_{21})^2}}\right]dt$$

$$\int_0^T \phi_1(t)\phi_2(t)dt = \frac{1}{\sqrt{E_2 - (s_{21})^2}}\left[\int_0^T \phi_1(t)s_2(t)dt - \int_0^T \phi_1(t)\, s_{21}\phi_1(t)dt\right] \tag{3.34}$$

Consider the RHS of equation (3.34). The first term inside the brackets can be simplified using equation (3.22)

$$\int_0^T \phi_1(t)s_2(t)dt = s_{21}$$

Also, the second term inside the brackets of the RHS of equation (3.34) can be written as

$$\int_0^T \phi_1(t) \times s_{21} \times \phi_1(t)dt = s_{21}\int_0^T \phi_1(t)\phi_1(t)dt = s_{21}\int_0^T \phi_1^2(t)\,dt = s_{21}$$

Therefore equation (3.34) becomes

$$\int_0^T \phi_1(t)\,\phi_2(t)\,dt = \frac{1}{\sqrt{E_2 - (s_{21})^2}}[s_{21} - s_{21}] = 0$$

Therefore, the basis functions $\phi_1(t)$ and $\phi_2(t)$ are orthogonal to one another.

Step 3: Generalized equation for orthonormal basis functions

We can define the function $f_i(t)$ as

$$f_i(t) = s_i(t) - \sum_{j=1}^{i=1} s_{ij}\phi_j(t) \tag{3.35}$$

It can be noted that the equation (3.23) is a special case of (3.35) with $i = 2$.

Coefficients s_{ij} can be obtained from the equation (3.10),

$$s_{ij} = \int_0^T s_i(t)\phi_j(t)dt$$

The orthonormal basis functions can be now defined in terms of the function $f_i(t)$ as follows:

$$\phi_i(t) = \frac{f_i(t)}{\sqrt{\int_0^T f_i^2(t)dt}} \qquad 0 \le i \le N \qquad (3.36)$$

The number of orthonormal basis functions N has to be less than or equal to M. The value of N is equal to M, if the M energy signals are linearly independent. Else the value of N is less than M and the intermediate function $f_i(t)$ takes 0 value for the values of $i > N$.

Example 3.3: Consider the signals

$S_1(t) = 3\,u(t) - 3\,u\,(t-4)$

$S_2(t) = 3\,u(t) - 3\,u\,(t-2)$

$S_3(t) = 3\,u(t-2) - 3\,u\,(t-4)$

Determine the basis function using Gram Schmidt procedure.

Solution:

It is clear that $S_3(t) = S_1(t) - S_2(t)$

Therefore $N < M$. We need to find $\phi_1(t)$ and $\phi_2(t)$.

To find $\phi_1(t)$:

$$\phi_1(t) = \frac{s_1(t)}{\sqrt{E_1}}$$

Where E_1 is the energy of the signal $s_1(t)$

$$E_1 = \int_0^T (s_1(t))^2\,dt$$

$$E_1 = \int_0^4 (3)^2\,dt = 36$$

$$\phi_1(t) = \frac{s_1(t)}{\sqrt{36}} = \frac{s_1(t)}{6}$$

$$\phi_1(t) = \begin{cases} 0.5, & 0 \le t \le 4 \\ 0, & t \ge 4 \end{cases}$$

To find $\phi_2(t)$

$$s_{21} = \int_0^T s_2(t)\,\phi_1(t)dt$$

$$s_{21} = \int_0^T 3 \times 0.5\,dt$$

$$s_{21} = 3$$

Let us define an intermediate function $f_2(t)$ as follows:

$$f_2(t) = s_2(t) - s_{21}\,\phi_1(t)$$

$$s_2(t) = \begin{cases} 3, & 0 \le t \le 2 \\ 0, & t \ge 2 \end{cases}$$

$$3 \times \phi_1(t) = \begin{cases} 1.5, & 0 \le t \le 4 \\ 0, & t \ge 4 \end{cases}$$

$$f_2(t) = s_2(t) - s_{21}\,\phi_1(t) = \begin{cases} 1.5, & 0 \le t \le 2 \\ -1.5, & 2 \le t \le 4 \end{cases}$$

$$\int_0^T f_2^2(t)dt = \int_0^4 f_2^2(t)dt = \int_0^2 \left(\frac{3}{2}\right)^2 dt + \int_2^4 \left(-\frac{3}{2}\right)^2 dt = 9$$

The second basis function can be written as:

$$\phi_2(t) = \frac{f_2(t)}{\sqrt{\int_0^T f_2^2(t)dt}}$$

$$\phi_2(t) = \frac{f_2(t)}{\sqrt{9}} = \frac{f_2(t)}{3}$$

$$\phi_2(t) = \begin{cases} 0.5, & 0 \le t \le 2 \\ -0.5, & 2 \le t \le 4 \end{cases}$$

The basis function can be represented as follows:

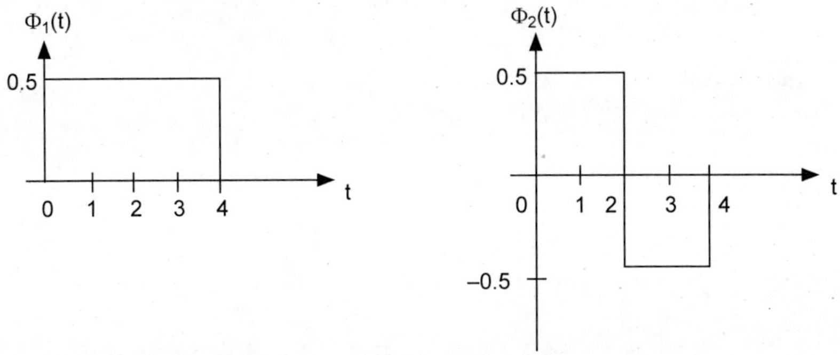

Fig. 3.4 Basis functions for the example 3.3

Example 3.4: In the example 3.3, represent the signals $S_1(t)$, $S_2(t)$ and $S_2(t)$ in terms of the basis functions.

Solution:

$$\phi_1(t) = \begin{cases} 0.5, & 0 \le t \le 4 \\ 0, & t \ge 4 \end{cases}$$

$$\phi_2(t) = \begin{cases} 0.5, & 0 \le t \le 2 \\ -0.5, & 2 \le t \ge 4 \end{cases}$$

We have

$$s_{ij} = \int_0^T s_i(t)\,\phi_j(t)dt$$

$$s_{11} = \int_0^T s_1(t)\,\phi_1(t)dt$$

$$s_{11} = \int_0^4 3\times 0.5\, dt = 6$$

$$s_{12} = \int_0^T s_1(t)\, \phi_2(t) dt$$

$$s_{12} = \int_0^2 3\times 0.5\, dt + \int_2^4 3\times(-0.5)\, dt = 0$$

Similarly

$$s_{21} = \int_0^T s_2(t)\, \phi_1(t)\, dt$$

$$s_{21} = \int_0^2 3\times 0.5\, dt = 3$$

$$s_{22} = \int_0^T s_2(t)\, \phi_2(t) dt$$

$$s_{22} = \int_0^2 3\times 0.5 dt + \int_2^4 0\times(-0.5)\, dt = 3$$

Similarly, we can show that

$$s_{31} = 3$$

$$s_{31} = -3$$

Therefore, the signals can be represented as

$$S_1(t) = 6\phi_1(t)$$

$$S_2(t) = 3\phi_1(t) + 3\phi_2(t)$$

$$S_3(t) = 3\phi_1(t) - 3\phi_2(t)$$

3.2 LIKELIHOOD FUNCTIONS

The function $f_X(X|m_i)$ is defined as the conditional probability density function of the observed signal X given the transmitted signal being $s_i(t)$ or simply the message m_i. This function gives the functional dependency of X given the transmitted message m_i. Nevertheless, in the real time scenario, we need to perform an estimate of the transmitted message $\hat{m}$ from the observation vector X.

Let us define a likelihood function $L(m_i)$ as follows:

$$L(m_i) = f_X(X|m_i) \qquad 1 \le i \le M \tag{3.37}$$

In general, it is advantageous to deal with the $\log_e$ of the likelihood function. The log likelihood function can be thus defined as

$$l(m_i) = \log_e (L(m_i)) \qquad 1 \le i \le M \tag{3.38}$$

It is to be noted that the log likelihood function maintains one to one relationship with the likelihood function.

The $f_X(X|m_i)$ can be represented as

$$f_X(X|m_i) = (\neq N_0)^{-N/2} \exp\left[-\frac{1}{N_0}\sum_{j=1}^{N}(x_i - s_{ij})^2\right] \qquad 1 \le i \le M \tag{3.39}$$

Derivation for the equation (3.39) is out of the scope of this book.

Using (3.39) in (3.38)

$$l(m_i) = \log_e (f_X (X|m_i)) \qquad 1 \le i \le M$$

$$= \log_e \left[(\neq N_0)^{-N/2} \exp\left[-\frac{1}{N_0} \sum_{j=1}^{N} (x_i - s_{ij})^2 \right] \right]$$

$$= \log_e \left[(\neq N_0)^{-N/2} \right] + \log_e \left[\exp\left[-\frac{1}{N_0} \sum_{j=1}^{N} (x_i - s_{ij})^2 \right] \right]$$

$$l(m_i) = \frac{-N}{2} \log_e (\neq N_0) + \left[-\frac{1}{N_0} \sum_{j=1}^{N} (x_i - s_{ij})^2 \right] \tag{3.40}$$

The first term of (3.40) can be ignored as it does not contain the message m_i.

Therefore
$$l(m_i) = \left[-\frac{1}{N_0} \sum_{j=1}^{N} (x_i - s_{ij})^2 \right] \tag{3.41}$$

We can recall that s_{ij} for $1 \le j \le N$ denotes the coefficients of the signal vector used to represent the message m_i.

3.3 COHERENT DETECTION OF SIGNAL IN NOISE

Consider there are signals in the signal space, namely $s_1(t), s_2(t), \ldots, s_M(t)$. These signals are transmitted with equal probability given by $p = \frac{1}{M}$. Since the information on the signal vector s_i is sufficient to determine the signal $s_i(t)$, we can consider representing any signal $s_i(t)$ as a point s_i in the Euclidean signal space. As mentioned before, the dimension N has to be clearly less than or equal to M. The point s_i on the Euclidean space is called as the message point m_i. The set of these message points for all M possible signals forms the constellation of the signal.

Received signal consists of the transmitted signal $s_i(t)$ and the noise $w(t)$. Thus the received vector can be defined as

$$X = s_i + W \qquad 1 \le i \le M \tag{3.42}$$

Consider a bank of correlators shown in Figure 3.5. When the received signal $x(t)$ is applied, the observation vector X is obtained as the output of the correlator.

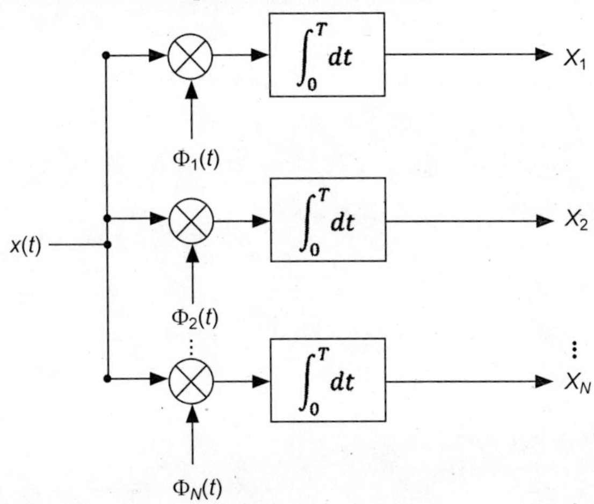

Fig. 3.5 Bank of correlators

It is clear from the equation (3.42) that the observation vector X is different compared to the actual signal vector s_i by an amount specified by the noise vector W. It is to be noted that the noise vector W denotes the part of the noise $w(t)$ that contributes towards the deviation of the observation vector from the transmitted signal vector.

The observation vector can similarly be represented as a point on the Euclidean plane. This point can be termed as received signal point. The received signal point can be deviated from the transmitted signal point in a random fashion. Consider the signal representation shown in Figure 3.6. The message transmitted is m_i and the received vector is X. It is clear from the figure that there is a deviation in the actual data point, and the received signal point. This deviation can be termed as the noise vector W.

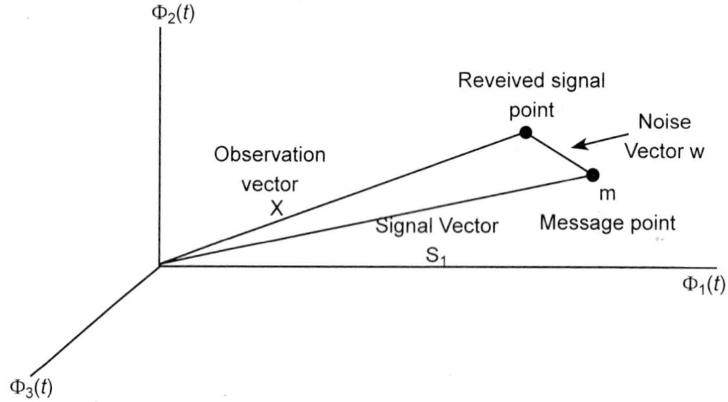

Fig. 3.6 Illustration of effect of noise on the transmitted signal

Scan here to know more

The signal representation shown in Figure 3.6 represents a 3D diagram. The job of the detector is to estimate the signal $\hat{m}$ such that the probability of symbol error is minimized.

3.3.1 Maximum a Posteriori Probability Decoding

Considering a transmitted message m_i and the received vector X and the estimate of the message be $\hat{m}$. Then the probability of symbol error is defined as

$$P_e\,(m_i \text{ not sent} \mid X \text{ received}) = P\,(m_i \text{ not sent} \mid X \text{ received})$$

$$= 1 - \mathrm{P}\,(m_i \text{ sent} \mid X \text{ received}) \qquad (3.43)$$

In order to minimize the symbol error in decoding, the estimate at the decoder can be set to m_i if and only if

$$P(m_i \text{ sent} \mid X \text{ received}) \geq P(m_k \text{ sent} \mid X \text{ received}) \;\; \forall k \text{ and } k \neq i \qquad (3.44)$$

The equation defined in (3.44) is termed as maximum a posteriori probability (MAP) rule. It is called as a posteriori as we are trying to estimate the transmitted signal provided the received vector is known to us.

3.3.2 Maximum Likelihood Decoding

The equation (3.44) can be better represented considering the a priori probabilities and the likelihood function using Bayes' rule as follows:

Set

$$\hat{m} = m_i$$

$$\text{if } \frac{p_k f_X(X|m_k)}{f_X(X)} \text{ is maximum for } k = i \tag{3.45}$$

Where p_k is the probability of the transmission of the message m_k

$f_X(X|m_k)$ is the conditional probability density function of the received vector X provided m_k is transmitted

$f_X(X)$ is the probability density function of X

It is clear from the above condition that the term $f_X(X)$ is not dependent on the message m_k and the term p_k is same for all messages m_k as per our assumption of equal probability. Therefore Baye's rule can be rewritten as

Set

$$\hat{m} = m_i$$

$$\text{if } f_X(X|m_k) \text{ is maximum for } k = i \tag{3.46}$$

But the likelihood function $f_X(X|m_k)$ has one to one relationship with the log likelihood function. Therefore, the decoding condition can be rewritten by considering the log likelihood function, as

Set

$$\hat{m} = m_i$$

$$\text{if } l_i(m_k) \text{ is maximum for } k = i \tag{3.47}$$

This rule is called maximum likelihood rule and the corresponding detector that uses this rule is called as maximum likelihood detector. Thus, in maximum likelihood decoding, the detector computes the likelihood functions for all possible M messages and the decoding is done in favour of the message with the maximum value of the likelihood function.

We can also explain the process of maximum likelihood decoding geometrically. Let $\Re$ denotes a space of dimensions containing all possible observation vectors X. The region $\Re$ is partitioned into M sub-regions $\Re_1, \Re_2, \Re_3, \ldots \Re_M$. The decision rule can now be defined as

The vector X lies in the region $\Re_i$ if $l_i(m_k)$ is maximum when $k = i$.

The log likelihood function for an AWGN channel can be represented as,

The vector X lies in the region $\Re_i$ if

$\sum_{j=1}^{N}(x_i - s_{kj})^2$ is minimum when $k = i$.

From equation (3.17) we have

$$\sum_{j=1}^{N}(x_i - s_{kj})^2 = (||X - s_k||)^2$$

Where $||x - m_k||$ is the Euclidian distance between the received signal point and the message point. Thus, in this rule the decoding is done in favour of the message point that is nearest to the received signal point.

3.3.3 Minimum Mean Square Estimation

To understand the concept of decoding, consider a transmitted message m_i and the received vector X. Let the estimate of the message be $\widehat{m}$. The term Mean Square Error (MSE) can be defined as

$$\text{MSE} = \left\| m_i - \widehat{m} \right\|^2 = (m_i - \widehat{m})^T (m_i - \widehat{m}) \tag{3.48}$$

The estimation of $\widehat{m}$ is made so as to minimize the MSE denoted in equation (3.48).

3.4 OPTIMUM RECEIVERS

The main purpose of any digital communication receiver is to demodulate and detect the symbols that were transmitted, based on observations of the received signal. Uncertainties caused by noise in the communication system chain (transmitter, channel, and receiver) may not ensure that the receiver can accurately identify the actual transmitted symbol. We may recollect that the major sources of errors due to noise are

- Thermal Noise (modelled as AWGN)
- Intersymbol interference (ISI due to filtering effects of transmitters, channels and receivers where symbols interfere with each other).
- A receiver, if it has to be an optimum receiver, it needs to be designed in such a way so as to minimize the probability of error. The demodulator/detector (which filters and tests the incoming signal) and the decision maker (which uses patterns to make decisions) are the main components of an ideal receiver. A typical receiver configuration is shown in Figure 3.7.

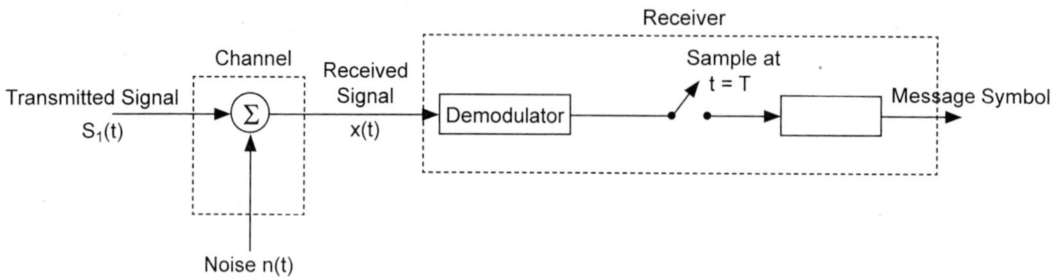

Fig. 3.7 A typical receiver configuration

Optimum receivers can be of two types:

- Correlation Receiver
- Matched filter Receiver

Correlation receivers use a probabilistic approach and consider the correlation of a received signal with a stored copy of a given signal. A matched filter receiver is an optimum receiver in the sense that it maximises the output SNR. Matched filter is essentially a filter that is matched to the signal component of the received signal. Here the fidelity of the pulses may not be preserved but SNR is maximised.

If there is no noise on the channel, the two approaches mentioned above can successfully recover the modulating signal's original components. In reality, noise has contaminated the received signal at the demodulator's input. In this scenario, the channel noise is AWGN.

3.4.1 Optimum Receiver for AWGN Channel

The performance of a communication system depends primarily on two main considerations:

(i) Error probability when the received signal is tainted by noise.

(ii) The channel bandwidth transmitting an information signal.

The receiver of a binary communication system has to distinguish between the two transmitted binary signals $S_1(t)$ and $S_2(t)$ in the presence of noise. If we assume that this noise is AWGN, say, $W(t)$ with a PSD of $\frac{N_0}{2}$ and zero mean.

$$x(t) = S(t) + n(t) \qquad 0 \le t \le T \tag{3.49}$$

where,

$x(t)$ is the received signal,

$S(t)$ is the transmitted signal [$S_1(t)$ and $S_2(t)$ denoting the two binary symbols],

$n(t)$ is the noise signal, (an AWGN process with power spectral density,

$$\Phi_{nn}(\omega) = \frac{N_0}{2} \text{ W/ Hz} \tag{3.50}$$

An ideal or optimal receiver should be designed that minimizes the probability of error based on observations of $x(t)$ in the signal range $0 \le t \le T$. Signal demodulation (converting the received waveform into an N-dimensional vector) and detection (selecting one of M possible signal waveforms based on the X vector) are two steps in the receiving process, as shown in Figure 3.6. The N-dimensional vector X can be written as,

$$x = [x_1, x_1, \dots, x_N] \tag{3.51}$$

3.4.2 The Correlation receiver

The Correlation Receiver decomposes $x(t)$ into N-dimensional vectors $[x_1, x_1, \dots x_N]$ as in Eq.3.11 by use of N correlators as shown in Figure 3.8.

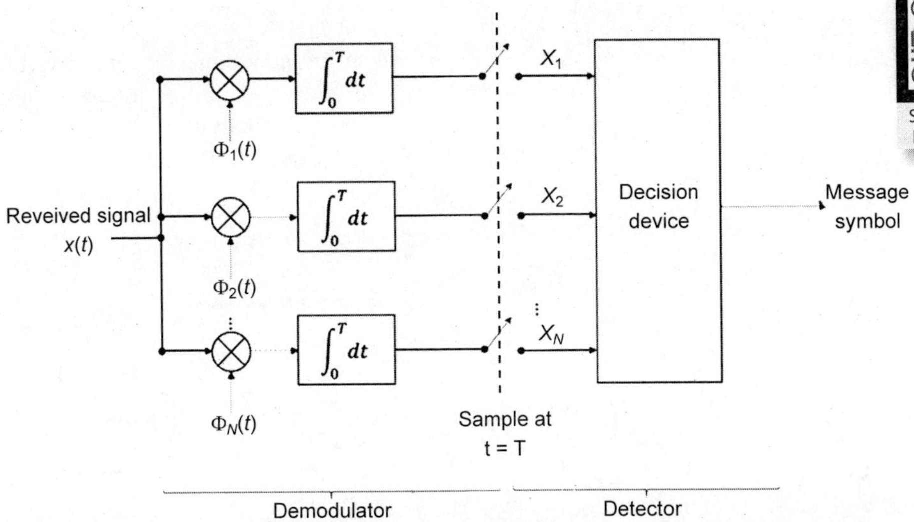

Fig. 3.8 Correlation receiver

Here the demodulator uses a combination of multiplier and integrator. The output of the demodulator is sampled at $t = T$, to obtain the vectors $x = [x_1, x_1, \dots x_N]$.

Decision-making devices are used as detectors. The function of the detector is to determine the actual transmitted symbol. The decision rule for the detector is to select a symbol based on the position of the received vector X in a specific decision region of the signal space.

In order to represent all members of the signal set $\{S_1(t), 1 \le i \le N\}$, the signal and noise are expanded into a set of linearly weighted orthonormal basis functions called $\Phi_i(t)$.

The correlation receiver assuming binary transmission will have only two symbols '0' and '1'.

$$x(t) = S_1(t) + n(t)\ S_2(t) + n(t) \tag{3.52}$$

where $S_1(t)$ and $S_2(t)$ are finite energy signals transmitted to represent symbols '1' and '0'.

The output of the correlation receiver at $t = T$, where T is the bit interval.

$$y_j(T) = \int_{-\infty}^{\infty} x(\tau)\,\phi_j(\tau)d\tau \tag{3.53}$$

Figure 3.9 shows a binary correlation receiver. Here the integration is ideal with zero initial conditions with $T = T_b$.

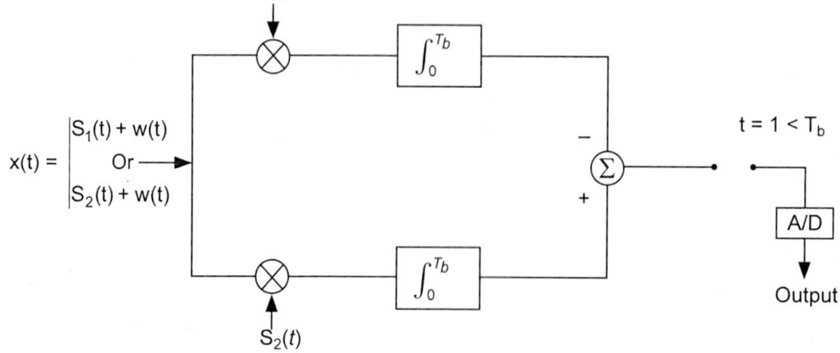

Fig.3.9 Binary correlation receiver

In practice, the correlation receiver is implemented as an integrate and dump receiver as shown in Figure 3.10. Here the integrator has to be reset at the end of each signalling interval. To avoid ISI, $RC >> T_b$ which would approximate an ideal integrator. The sampling and discharging of capacitor are to be synchronised and also the reference signal $S_2(t) - S_1(t)$ must also be in phase with receiver signal input, $x(t)$.

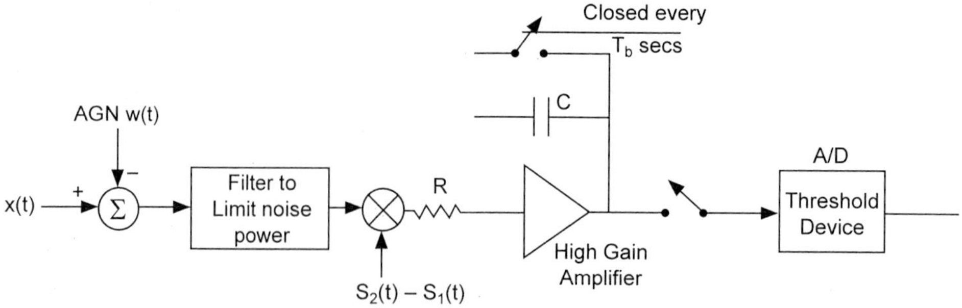

Fig. 3.10 Integrate and dump correlation receiver

3.4.3 Matched Filter Receiver

As stated earlier a matched filter receiver maximises the SNR of the received signal and it does not preserve the input signal waveshape. It generates the output $Y(t)$ using a series of N linear filters instead of N correlators as in a matched filter (MF) receiver. In fact, the signal waveshape is distorted in a matched filter and it filters the noise such that at the sampling instant, the output signal will be as large as possible with respect to the noise level.

Consider the best-fit linear filter in Figure 3.11 (a), which has an impulse response $h(t)$ to the input signal $S(t)$ and white noise $n(t)$. As seen in Section 2.7, the output SNR is a function of only the signal energy and noise PSD and not a function of the transfer function of the filter.

From equation (2.25),

$$(\text{SNR})_{\text{o Max}} = \frac{2}{N_0}\int_{-\infty}^{\infty} |S(f)|^2 \, df \tag{3.54}$$

And

Thus $(\text{SNR})_o$ will be maximum when

$$H_{opt}(f) = KS^*(f)\, e^{-j2\pi fT} \tag{3.55}$$

Using the equation (2.28)

$$H_{opt}(t) = S(T-t) \tag{3.56}$$

It follows that the input signal $S(t)$, which is time-reversed and delayed, is what the matched filter's impulse response represents. Therefore, a filter name that is appropriate as a filter characteristic matches the received input signal.

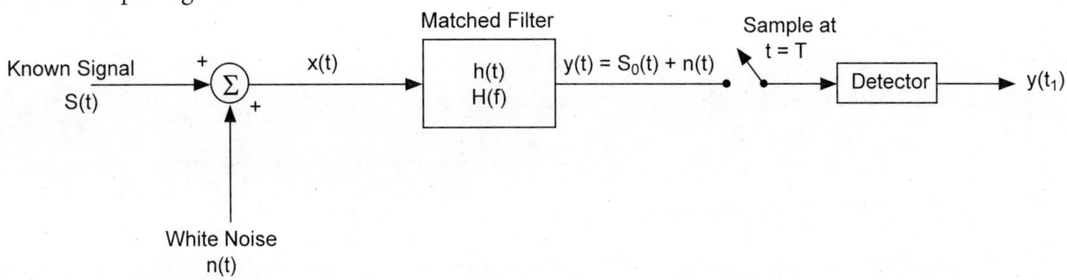

(a)

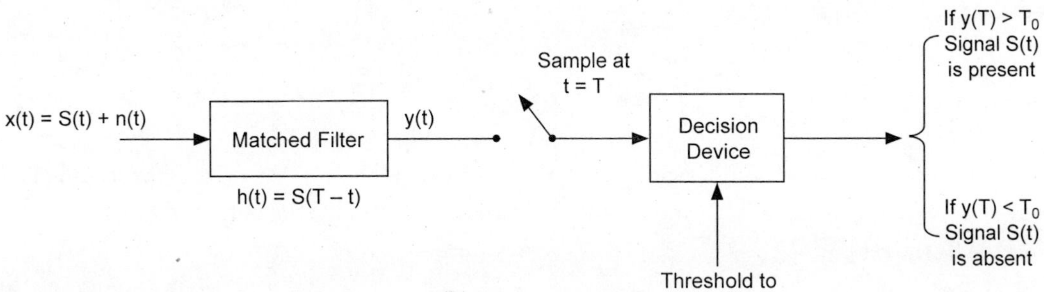

(b)

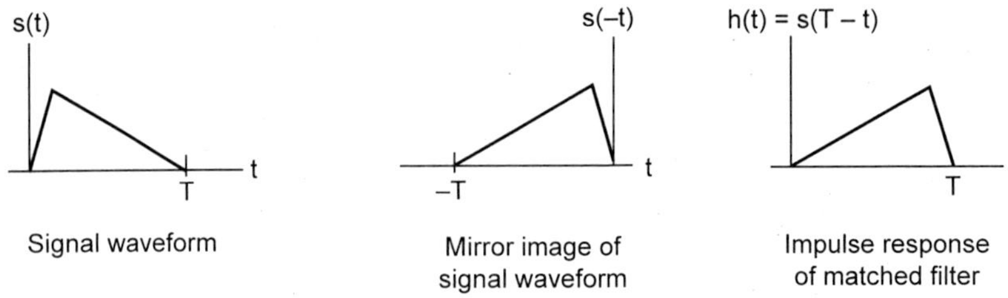

(c)

Fig. 3.11 (a) Typical MF receiver (b) MF receiver with decision device (c) MF characteristics

A typical MF receiver has a sampler, decision device and matched filter as shown in Figure 3.11 (b). At time $t = T$, the matched filter output $y(t)$, is sampled and compared to the a threshold T_0. If $y(t) > T_0$, the signal $S(t)$ is present and if it is less than T_0, signal $S(t)$ is absent.

Causality needs to be satisfied for the matched filter to be physically realisable.

i. e.

$$h_{opt}(t) = 0 \quad \text{for} \quad t < 0 \tag{3.57}$$

This is possible if

$$h_{opt}(t) = 0 \quad \text{for} \quad t < 0 \tag{3.58}$$

and

For $\quad t \geq 0$

$$h_{opt}(t) = S(T - t) \tag{3.59}$$

i.e

$$S(t) = 0 \quad \text{for} \quad t > T \tag{3.60}$$

This means that all the input signal $S(t)$ must have entered the filter by the time $t = T$ at which $y(t)$ is sampled with maximum SNR. MF characteristics are best described in Figure 3.11 (c).

3.5 EQUIVALENCE OF CORRELATION RECEIVER FILTER WITH MATCHED FILTER

A correlator correlates the received signal with a stored replica of the known signal. Here an input noisy signal $\{x(t)+ n(t)\}$ is multiplied with a locally generated signal $x(t)$, integrated over a 0 to T and then sampled at $t = T$ to give $Y(T)$.

i. e.

$$Y(T) = \int_0^T \{x(t) + n(t)\} \cdot x(t)dt \tag{3.61}$$

A matched filter however does not need a locally generated replica of the input signal $x(t)$. Convolution of the input signal $x(t)$ and its impulse response $h(t)$ yields the output of the MF.

For a MF, the output

$$Y(T) = \frac{2k}{N_0} \int_0^T \{x(t) + n(t)\} \cdot x(t)dt \tag{3.62}$$

It is observed that output of the correlator and matched filter are identical except the constant $\frac{2k}{N_0}$, which can be normalised to 1. This means that the MF and correlator provides the same output.

For example, a matched filter can be made utilising the correlation concept. However, when we refer to a receiver design as a correlator, we mean one that resets itself after each symbol. This causes the matching filter and the correlator, when running at M samples/symbol, to generate different results for the following $M - 1$ samples but the same result for the Mth sample.

UNIT SUMMARY

- Geometric representation of signals as a process of representing M number of signals with finite energy in terms of linear combination of N number of basis functions.
- We can represent the signal $s_i(t)$ as a linear combination of the signals in the basis set. The governing equation is

  $$s_i(t) = s_{i1}(t)\,\phi_1(t) + s_{i2}(t)\,\phi_2(t) + \dots s_{iN}(t)\,\phi_N(t) \qquad 1 \le i \le M$$

  $$\text{or } s_i(t) = \sum_{j=1}^{N} s_{ij}(t)\phi_j(t) \qquad 1 \le i \le M$$

  The terms s_{ij} are the coefficients.
- Basis functions are to be orthonormal, they have to satisfy the following condition:

  $$\int_0^T \phi_i(t)\phi_j(t)dt = \delta_{ij} = \begin{cases} 1, & if\ i = j \\ 0, & if\ i \ne j \end{cases}$$

- Coefficients can be obtained using

  $$s_{ij} = \int_0^T s_i(t)\phi_j(t)dt$$

- Squared length of a signal vector is defined as the inner product of the signal vector s_i with itself.

  $$\|s_i\|^2 = s_i^T s_i = \sum_{j=1}^{N} s_{ij}^2 \qquad 1 \le i \le M$$

- Relationship between energy of the signal and the squared length is

  $E_i = \| s_i \|^2$
- The Euclidian distance between two points represented by the signal vectors s_i and s_j can be defined as

  $d_{ij} = \|s_i - s_j\|$
- The angle between the two signal vectors si and sj can be defined as follows:

  $$\cos(\theta_{ij}) = \frac{s_i^T s_j}{\|s_i\|\|s_j\|}$$

- A likelihood function $L(m_i)$ can be defined as follows:

  $$L(m_i) = f_X(X|m_i) \qquad 1 \le i \le M$$

- The log likelihood function can be thus defined as

  $l(m_i) = \log_e (L(m_i)) \qquad 1 \le i \le M$

- Maximum A Posteriori Probability Decoding

  $P(m_i \text{ sent} \mid X \text{ received}) \ge P(m_k \text{ sent} \mid X \text{ received}) \quad \forall k \text{ and } k \ne i$

- Maximum Likelihood Decoding

  Set

  $m = m_i$

  if

  $l_i\,(m_k)$ is maximum for $k = i$

- Optimum receivers can be of two types: Correlation Receiver or Matched filter Receiver
- The Correlation Receiver decomposes $x(t)$ into N-dimensional vectors $[x_1, x_1, \ldots\ x_N]$ by use of N correlators
- A matched filter receiver maximizes the SNR of the received signal and it does not preserve the input signal waveshape. It generates the output $Y(t)$ using a series of N linear filters instead of N correlators as in a matched filter (MF) receiver.

EXERCISES

Numerical Problems

1. Write synthesizer and analyser equations for four signals defined in a three-dimensional signal space.
2. Represent a signal with the coefficient vector [–4, 5, 6] in a three-dimensional signal space.
3. Consider the signals

   $S_1(t) = 3u(t) - 3u(t-1)$

   $S_2(t) = 6u(t) + 6u(t-2)$

   $S_3(t) = 4u(t) - 4u(t-3)$

   Determine the basis function using Gram Schmidt procedure.
4. In the Problem 3.3, represent the signals $S_1(t)$, $S_2(t)$ and $S_2(t)$ in terms of the basis functions.
5. Consider the following signals

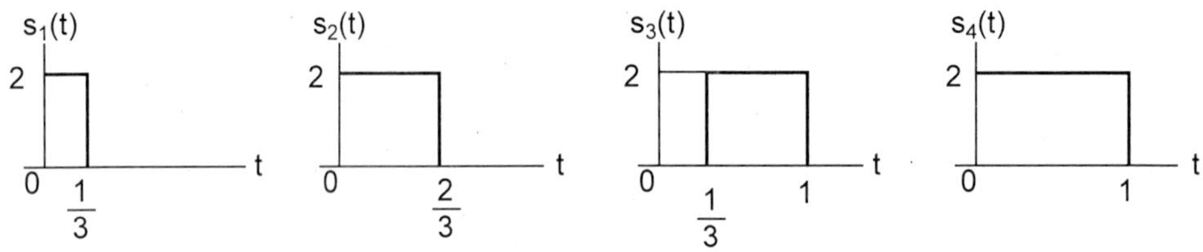

   Determine the basis function using Gram Schmidt procedure.
6. In the Problem 3.5, represent the signals $S_1(t)$, $S_2(t)$ and $S_2(t)$ in terms of the basis functions.

Descriptive Type Questions

21. What is geometrical representation of a signal?
22. Define basis functions.
23. Explain the properties of basis function set used to represent a signal.
24. With the help of a neat block diagrams explain synthesizer and Analyzer.
25. What is squared length of a signal? Explain.
26. Establish the relationship between the energy and squared length of a signal.
27. Define Euclidean distance between the two points represented by signal vectors.
28. Explain in detail the procedure to generate orthonormal basis set using Gram Schmidt orthogonalization procedure.
29. Define likelihood function.
30. What is Maximum A Posteriori Decoding? Explain.
31. Explain the concept of Maximum Likelihood Decoding.
32. What are optimum receivers?
33. With the help of a neat block diagram explain, binary correlation receiver.
34. List the properties of Matched Filters.
35. Maximum SNR of a Matched filter depends only on the waveform's energy, and not on any other aspects of $S(t)$. Justify the statement.
36. Establish the equivalence between the correlation filters and Matched filer receivers.

Objective Type Questions

6. The number of basis functions needed to a set of 3 linearly independent signals is
   a. 3
   b. 2
   c. 1
7. State TRUE or FALSE: The two signals are said to be orthogonal, if their inner product is zero
   a. True
   b. False
8. Consider a scenario where the set of 5 signals are represented using 3 basis functions. The dimension of the signal space is
   a. 5 b. 3
   c. 2 d. 4
9. The basis functions are to be
   a. Orthogonal to one another b. Normalized to have unit energy
   c. Both (a) and (b)
10. Which of the following statements for a matched filter are true?
    1. SNR of a matched filter depends only on the ratio of the signal energy to the PSD of white noise at the filter output

2. SNR of a matched filter depends only on the ratio of the PSD of white noise to the signal energy at the filter output
3. Impulse response of a matched filter depends on the signal shape
4. Matched filter produces ISI.
5. Matched filter measures the correlation between received information signal and its impulse response.

The correct options are

a. 1, 2, 3 b. 1, 3, 5

c. 2, 3, 4 d. 3, 4, 5

KNOW MORE

THE THEORY OF OPTIMUM NOISE IMMUNITY

In 1947 V. A. Koteľnikov, a comuni cations engineer already well known for his work on sampling theorems for band-limited functions, published a doctoral dissertation that has proved to be one of the most important Soviet contributions to the statistical communications art. Because this work was virtually unknown outside the U. S. S. R. until quite recently, few Western scientists were aware that Dr. Koteľnikov had developed a statistical analysis of communication problems (using what we now call decision theory techniques), which anticipated by several years much of the work by Western communication experts

This book is a verbatim translation of THE THEORY OF POTENTIAL NOISE IMMUNITY, published in Moscow in 1956, and is essentially iden tical with the 1947 dissertation. Kotel-nikov's paper extensively analyzes the effects of additive gaussian noise on communication systems and determines what can be done at the receiving end to minimize them.

the The author's approach is always that of a practical engineer. He invokes only the most elementary notions of probability theory, the steps in his analysis are easy to follow, and his primary intention is to establish behavior of communications systems at a level that is of practical use to the engineer. The development is also notable for its lack of dependence on advanced mathematics. The reader who is passingly familiar with Fourier series, discrete and continuous probabilities and probability densities (simple, joint, and conditional), and the notion of statistical independence will have no trouble with the material.

Dr. Koteľnikov made extensive use of geometric models of the signalling and detection process as operations on vec-tors in multi-dimensional space, an arti fice that Shannon introduced later. The reader will find these geometric inter-pretations very helpful. The subject matter of almost every chapter is re-viewed in terms of the geometric model at the end of the chapter.

(Coummed from front flag

When Dr. Koteľnikov's paper first re-ceived limited circulation in Russia, the approach was startlingly new. Since that time, most of the major concepts in his work have been obtained independently in the West, although many of his results have yet to be worked out. Much of the material has appeared in the professional literature, but has not previously been published in book form.

Both as an historical document and as a reference work. THE THEORY OF OP TIMUM NOISE IMMUNITY should prove extremely helpful to students and research workers involved in commi cation theory or the mathematical anal ysis of communication systems.

V. A. KOTEL NIKOV

Photograph courtesy of ELECTRONIC DAILY, Hose Publik Company Publication

Vladimir Aleksandrovich KoteFnikov was born in 1908 in Kazan and received his education in electrical engineering at the Molotov Power Engineering Institute in Moscow. He has been on the research and teaching staff of that institution since his graduation in 1931, and since 1947 has headed the Chair of Radio Engineering

He has received two Stalin prizes and in 1953 was elected Academician, the highest rank in the U. S. S. R. Academy of Sciences. He is one of the three or four Soviet electronics engineers ever to have received this honor. He is a member of the Presidium of the Popov Society, the radioenginering and electronics professional society of the Soviet Union. Since 1954 Academician Kotelnikov has been Director of the Institute of Radio Engineering and Electronics, a large tesearch center

FURTHER READING

[1] Haykin, Simon. "Digital Communications", John Wiley, New York, 2001.

[2] Sklar, Bernad. "Digital Communication: Functions and Applications", Prentice Hall., 1988.

[3] K. Sam Shanmugam , « Digital and Analog Communication Systems», John Wiley, New York, 2006.

[4] M. Kulkarni and Farooq Husain, "Analog and Digital Communication Systems", Umesh Publications, New Delhi, 2005.

[5] K. N. Hari Bhat and D. Ganesh Rao, "Digital Communications", Third Edition, Pearson, 2012.

[6] Alan S. Willsky, Gregory W. Wornell, and Jeffrey H. Shapiro, " Stochastic Processes, Detection and Estimation", Department of Electrical Engineering and Computer Science Massachusetts Institute of Technology, Cambridge, MA 02139.

4 Passband Digital Transmission

The unsung HERO: Jagadish Chandra Bose is known as the father of wireless telecommunication. He had invented the Mercury Coherer, a radio wave receiver that was used by Guglielmo Marconi to build an operational two-way radio. The science behind capturing radio waves was first demonstrated by Bose. Jagdish Chandra was acknowledged by IEEE, USA as one of the pioneers in the discovery of radio.

UNIT SPECIFICS

Through this unit, we have discussed the following aspects:

- Distinguish between baseband and passband modulation techniques.
- Discuss the various types of passband modulation schemes.
- Describe the transmitter and receivers of basic passband modulations.
- Analyse and evaluate the performance of passband transmission systems in presence of additive Gaussian noise.
- Compare the various passband modulation techniques in terms of BER, bandwidth, spectral efficiency of BASK, BFSK, BPSK and QPSK modulation methods.

RATIONALE

When digital data needs to be transmitted through wireless channels, passband transmission techniques will be required. The baseband signal frequencies must be moved to higher frequency bands for passband or carrier modulation methods. Because it would require impractically large antennas, we can not send baseband signals over radio or satellites. This necessitated the need for moving to higher frequency spectrum. This is accomplished by using a higher frequency carrier to modulate a baseband digital signal. Bandpass channels are used for communication, like a satellite channel, microwave radio connection, optical fiber link, etc. Digital passband communication or digital carrier modulation are two terms used to describe this method.

UNIT OUTCOMES

List of outcomes of this unit is as follows:

U4-O1: Distinguish between baseband and passband modulation techniques.

U4-O2: Discuss the various types, requirements, advantages and drawbacks of basic passband modulation techniques.

U4-O3: Analyse the noise performance of the passband modulation schemes.

U4-O4: Derive expressions for BER and bandwidths of BASK, BFSK, BPSK and QPSK passband modulation systems.

U4-O5: Compare the performance parameters of passband modulation schemes.

MAPPING OF UNIT OUTCOMES WITH COURSE OUTCOMES

Unit-4 Outcomes	EXPECTED MAPPING WITH COURSE OUTCOMES (1- Weak Correlation; 2- Medium correlation; 3- Strong Correlation)					
	CO-1	CO-2	CO-3	CO-4	CO-5	CO-6
U4-O1	3	3	3	-	3	1
U4-O2	2	1	2	2	1	-
U4-O3	2	1	2	1	2	1
U4-O4	1	-	2	1	2	1
U4-O5	1	-	-	-	2	1

4.1 INTRODUCTION

Baseband pulse transmission has been covered in Unit II. In today's world, information signals or messages in the form of speech/video or data signals are generally coded as digital signals. The input data for baseband pulse transmission can be in the form of discrete PAM signal (the various line codes that we studied in the previous unit). Baseband signal cannot be transmitted using radio links as they require impractically large antennas. This necessitated the need for moving to higher frequency spectrum. This is accomplished by using a higher frequency carrier to modulate a baseband digital signal. Bandpass channels are used for communication, like a satellite channel, microwave radio connection, optical fiber link, etc.

4.1.1 Digital Modulation

The data in digital domain is generally transmitted by varying the parameters of the carrier signal in accordance with the data to be transmitted. The carrier frequency is often chosen higher than the highest frequency of the modulating signals, similar to analog modulation systems. To create digital passband modulation, the amplitude, phase, frequency, or combination of these parameters of the sinusoidal carrier are changed. Pass-band modulation is the process of modifying an RF carrier's amplitude, frequency, and phase, individually or in combination, to match the content that will be wirelessly transmitted or broadcast.

In this unit we discuss a few digital modulation techniques in detail.

4.1.2 Types of Digital Modulation Techniques

We know that modulation can be done by the use of an analog or digital carrier. Further, as shown in Fig.4.1, analog data varies the amplitude, frequency, or phase of the analog carrier resulting in Amplitude Modulation (AM), Frequency Modulation (FM), or Phase Modulation (PM) and if digital data varies the amplitude, frequency and phase will result in ASK or OOK, Frequency Shift Keying (FSK) or PSK. If the digital data varies both amplitude and phase of the analog carrier, it would result in Quadrature

Amplitude Modulation (QAM). (You may recall that if the analog data varies the pulse amplitude, width, and position, that would result in PAM, PWM, and PPM. If digital data is used to encode the digital carrier, it would result in PCM).

In this unit, we will be looking at digital data, modulating an analog carrier.

Digital modulation schemes can be categorised based on the following:

(A) Detection method,

(B) Mapping technology

(C) Performance of the modulation scheme and the characteristics of the modulating signal.

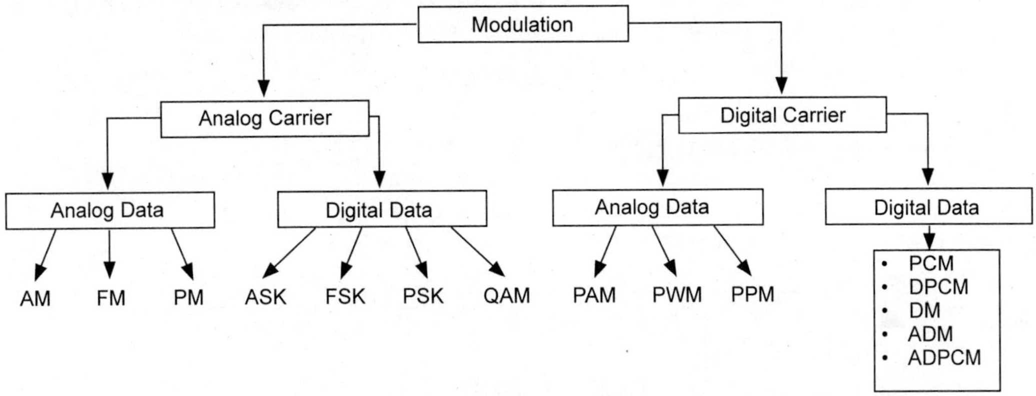

Fig. 4.1 Modulation types

(A) Based on the method of detection we have two digital modulation methods:

➢ Coherent (Synchronous) detection

➢ Non-coherent (Envelope) detection.

In order to account for the phase shifts caused by the channel, a *coherent detection* requires a reference signal at the receiver that is in phase coherence with the carrier of the transmitted signal. Such a reference signal is not necessary for *noncoherent detection* schemes, although this comes at the cost of poor power efficiency. The greater complexity of the reference acquisition circuit is the cost to be paid for the enhanced performance of coherent systems.

(B) *Based on the mapping techniques we have four different schemes:*

➢ Binary Scheme: Binary ASK(BASK)/ OOK, Binary FSK (BFSK), Binary PSK(BPSK)

➢ Quaternary Scheme: Quaternary PSK (QPSK), Minimum Shift Keying (MSK)

➢ M-ary Scheme: M-ary ASK, M-ary FSK, M-ary PSK

➢ Hybrid Scheme: Quadrature Amplitude Modulation (QAM), Amplitude and Phase Shift Keying (APK)

The waveforms of the digital modulation techniques BASK(OOK), BFSK, BPSK are shown in figure 4.2 for a binary information signal (bits) '0101101001'.

In ASK, the carrier amplitude is varied to obtain the modulated signal. However, the frequency and phase components remain same. In ASK, we can see that the sinusoidal carrier representing the modulated signal, has two amplitude levels for a logical '0' input and logical '1' input. However, for OOK there is absence of carrier for a logical '0' input and presence of carrier for a logical '1'input.

In FSK, the frequency of the carrier signal is varied to represent data as '0' and '1'. The frequency of the modulated signal is constant for the duration of one signal bit and it depends upon bits '0' and '1', but changes for the next signal bit if the data bit changes. However, the peak amplitude and phase remain same for all data bits. In binary FSK, two frequencies say f_1 for a data bit '0' and f_2 for a data bit '1'.

In PSK, the phase of the carrier is varied in accordance with the information bits. However peak amplitude remains the same. Also, within each bit duration, the phase of the signal is constant and depends on the input. In BPSK, we have used only two message bits, one with a phase of 0°, and the other with a phase of 180°. BPSK performs superior to ASK as it is less susceptible to noise.

In ASK, the criterion for bit detection is the amplitude of the signal, in FSK it's the frequency change and in PSK, it is the change of phase from one bit to the next. It may be noted that the noise can easily modify amplitude than phase and hence we can safely say that PSK is less susceptible to noise than ASK. Also, PSK is superior to FSK because we do not need two carrier signals.

C.*Based on the performance of the modulation scheme and the characteristics of the modulating signal.*

In this category, the digital modulation techniques look at some important performance parameters (Power efficiency & Bandwidth efficiency) or type of modulations (Continuous phase (CP) / In phase Quadrature phase (I-Q)/Constant envelope/non-Constant envelope, Linear/ Non-linear/ Modulation scheme with memory or without memory).

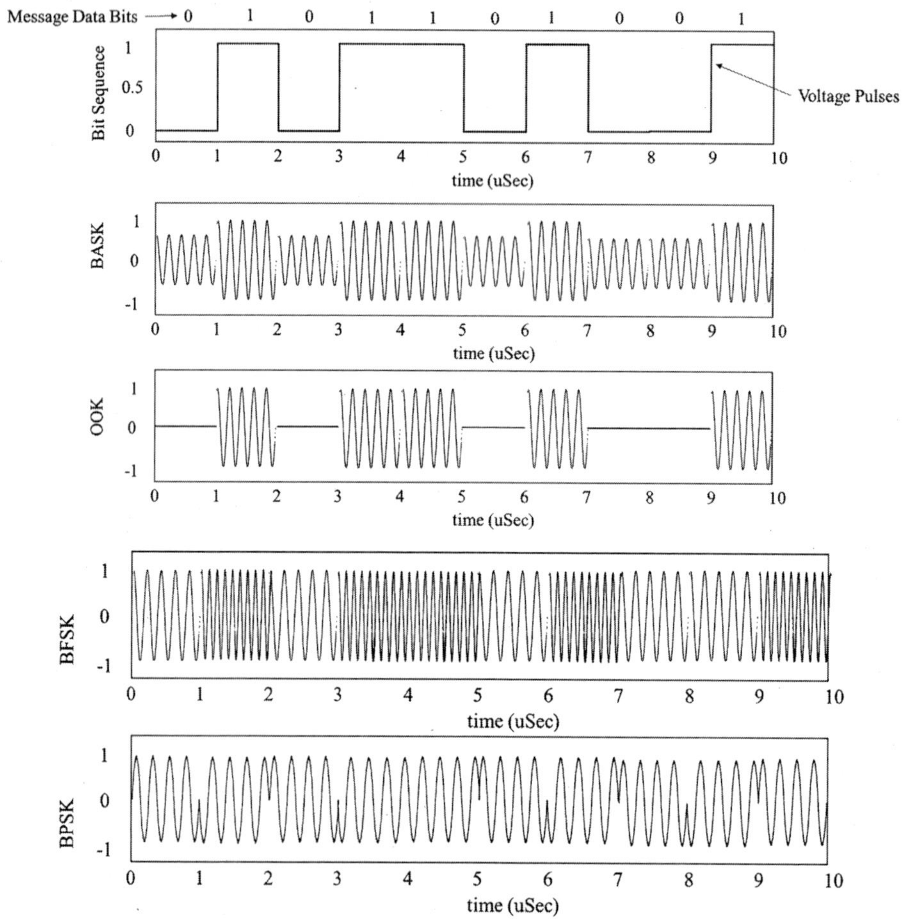

Fig. 4.2 Basic digital waveforms for message data bits '0101101001'

4.1.3 Requirements of Passband Modulation Schemes

The following parameters are the major requirements of passband or carrier modulation schemes:

- Minimum
  - Probability of symbol errors
  - Transmitted power
  - Channel BW and
  - Circuit complexity
- Maximum
  - Data transmission rate
  - Resistance to interfering signals

4.1.4 Advantages and Drawbacks of Passband Data Transmission

Passband data transmission has several advantages over baseband data transmission as follows:

- Long distance transmission.
- ISI and cross talks can be minimized.
- Bandwidth conservation by way of various multiplexing possibilities.
- Suitable for wireless transmission.
- Availability of a large number of modulation techniques.

There are however some drawbacks of using passband data transmission in that they are not suitable for short distance communications and also system complexity due to complexities of modulator/ demodulator circuits, transmit/ receive antennas and interference issues due to wireless environments.

4.1.5 Model of a typical Passband Data Transmission System

In Figure 4.3, message $m_i(t)$ from a source is fed to an encoder which generates the signal vector. The modulator generates the modulated signal with the help of a high frequency carrier giving out a modulated signal $S_i(t)$ that is transmitted through the channel. This signal passes through the transmission channel producing a received signal $x(t)$. The receiver has a detector (either synchronous or envelope detector) and a decoder producing an estimate of the transmitted message $\widehat{m_i}(t)$.

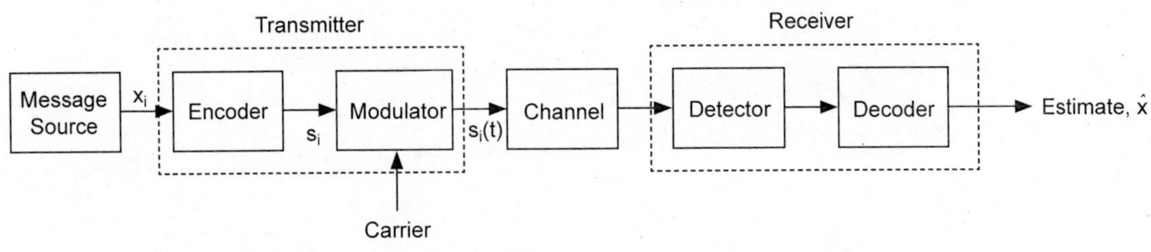

Fig. 4.3 Model of a typical passband data transmission system

In this section, we will look at BASK, BFSK and BPSK the basic digital modulation schemes and also understand how these can be generated and detected along with probability of error and bandwidth calculations.

4.2 BINARY AMPLITUDE SHIFT KEYING (BASK)

This method is also called as On Off Keying (OOK). The basic passband modulation techniques, BASK, BFSK and BPSK are shown in figure 4.4, which are basically obtained as amplitude/frequency/phase modulation of the carrier signal, $\cos(2\pi f_c t)$.

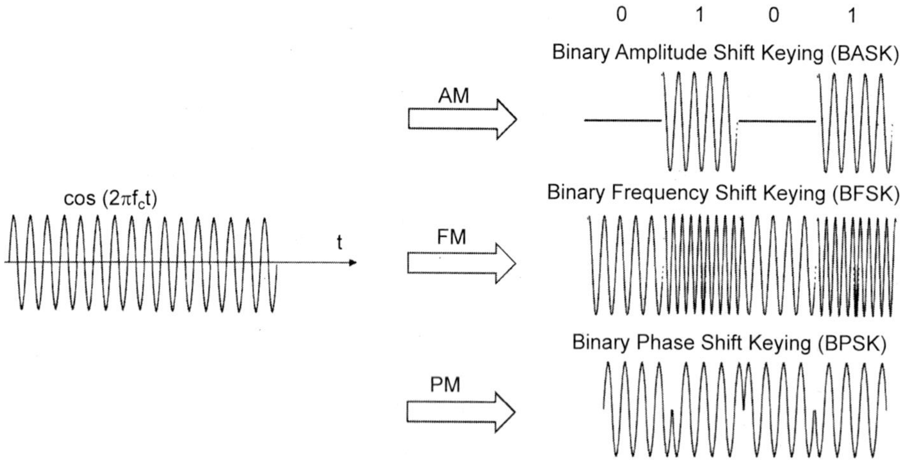

Fig. 4.4 Basic passband modulation schemes

4.2.1 Generation of BASK/BOOK

A binary ASK signal is generated by sending a carrier signal $A_c\cos(2\pi f_c t)$, whenever the information bit is '1' and by sending a '0' if the information bit is '0' as shown in figure 4.5.

$$S_{BASK}(t) = S_{BASK}(t) \times A_c \cos(2\pi f_c t) \tag{4.1}$$

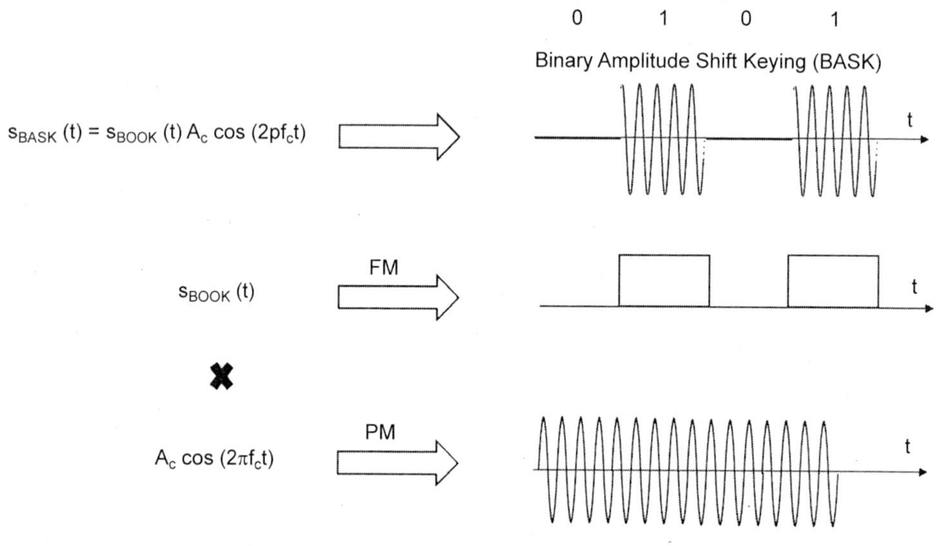

Fig. 4.5 Binary OOK and binary ASK waveforms

A BASK transmitter essentially consists of a product modulator as shown in figure 4.6 with a binary wave in unipolar form $x(t)$ as input to the product modulator multiplied by a carrier wave $A_c \cos(2\pi f_c t)$, producing a binary ASK wave $s(t)$.

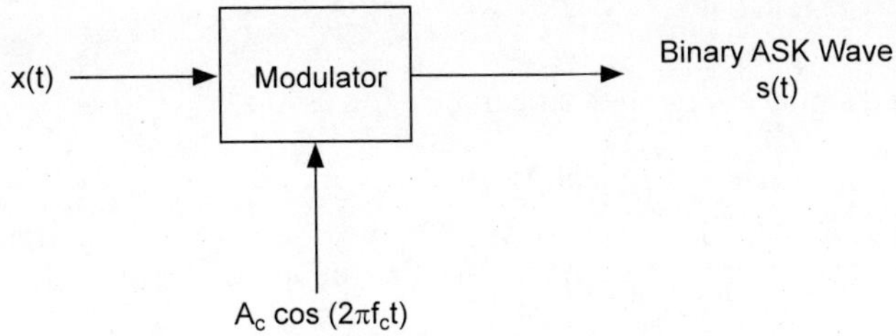

Fig. 4.6 BASK transmitter

The product modulator acts as a switch, controlled by the carrier wave $A_c\cos(2\pi f_c t)$. For an input '1' the switch is closed and the output of the product modulator will be the carrier wave itself. On the other hand, a '0' the switch is off and product modulator generates no output. The product modulator behaves like an on-off switch producing BASK, because of which BASK is also known as Binary On Off Keying (BOOK) modulator.

Let us consider that the symbol '1' be represented by $s_1(t)$ and symbol '0' by $s_2(t)$.

Also let us assume a coherent BASK system. In general, the carrier has unit energy measured over one symbol duration.

$$A_c = \sqrt{\frac{2}{T_b}} \tag{4.2}$$

Where T_b is the bit duration. Hence, we can express the carrier as,

$$c(t) = \sqrt{\frac{2}{T_b}} \cdot \cos(2\pi f_c t) \tag{4.3}$$

Hence, we can write a BASK signal as,

$$s(t) = c(t)\, b(t) \tag{4.4}$$

Where

$c(t)$ is the carrier wave, and $b(t)$ denotes an incoming binary wave.

We can then express the modulated wave as

$$s(t) = \int_0^{Tb} |s(t)|^2\, dt \tag{4.5}$$

Transmitted signal energy per bit can also be written as,

$$E_b = \int_0^{Tb} |s(t)|^2\, dt \tag{4.6}$$

$$= \frac{2}{T_b}\int_0^{Tb} |b(t)|^2 \cos^2(2\pi f_c t)\, dt$$

$$= \frac{1}{T_b}\int_0^{Tb} |b(t)|^2\, dt + \frac{1}{T_b}\int_0^{Tb} |b(t)|^2 \cos(4\pi f_c t)dt \tag{4.6}$$

$|b(t)|^2$ can be assumed to be essentially constant over one complete cycle of the carrier wave $\cos(4\pi f_c t)$ and hence

$$\frac{1}{T_b}\int_0^{T_b} |b(t)|^2 \cos(4\pi f_c t)dt \approx 0$$

Hence the transmitted signal energy per bit can be expressed as,

$$E_b \approx \frac{1}{T_b}\int_0^{T_b} |b(t)|^2 \, dt \tag{4.7}$$

For a BASK system, we can consider a binary data stream $b(t)$ that can be defined by,

$$b(t) = \begin{cases} \sqrt{E_b}, & \textit{for binary symbol } 1 \\ 0, & \textit{for binary symbol } 0 \end{cases} \tag{4.8}$$

We now multiply $b(t)$ by the carrier wave of equation 4.3, to get the BASK wave

$$s(t) = \begin{cases} \sqrt{\dfrac{2E_b}{T_b}} \cdot \cos(2\pi f_c t) & \textit{for binary symbol } 1 \\ 0, & \textit{for binary symbol } 0 \end{cases} \tag{4.9}$$

In other words,

$$s_1(t) = \sqrt{\frac{2E_b}{T_b}} \cdot \cos(2\pi f_c t) = \sqrt{2P_S} \cdot \cos(2\pi f_c t) \text{ for symbol 1} \tag{4.10}$$

$$s_1(t) = 0 \text{ for symbol 0} \tag{4.11}$$

ie. We would then require only one basis function $\phi_1(t)$ given by

$$\phi_1(t) = \sqrt{\frac{2}{T_b}} \cdot \cos(2\pi f_c t) \tag{4.12}$$

The ASK waveform of equation (4.10) for symbol '1' can be represented as,

$$s_1(t) = \sqrt{P_S T_b} \cdot \sqrt{\frac{2}{T_b}} \cos(2\pi f_c t) = \sqrt{P_S T_b} \cdot \phi_1(t) \tag{4.13}$$

The signal space diagram for BASK will have two points on $\phi_1(t)$. One will be at zero and other will be at $\sqrt{P_S T_B}$ as shown in figure 4.7.

The distance between the two signal points is,

$$d = \sqrt{P_S T_B} = \sqrt{E_b} \tag{4.14}$$

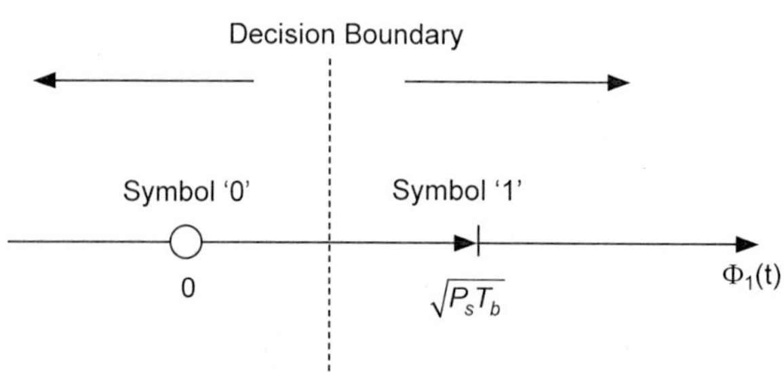

Fig. 4.7 Signal space diagram of BASK

4.2.2 BASK Receiver

The BASK receiver performs the coherent demodulation function by use of a coherent detector as shown in figure 4.8. It basically consists of a product modulator, an integrator and a decision device. The binary ASK signal is applied to one input of the product modulator and the other is supplied with a local carrier $A_c \cos(2\pi f_c t)$. The integrator essentially performs a low-pass filtering operation, whose output is fed to a decision device.

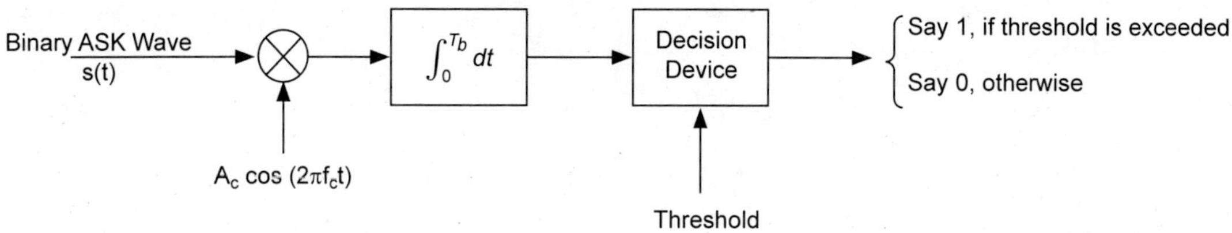

Fig. 4.8 BASK receiver

The decision device compares the output of the integrator with the threshold value. If the output value is more than the threshold, a is decoded, else it decodes the bit as . However, an assumption of perfect synchronization between local oscillator and the carrier used in the transmitter has been made here. This essentially means that the frequency and phase of the local oscillator are the same as those of the carrier used in the transmitter. Hence in a coherent detector, both phase synchronization (local carrier wave locked in phase with respect to carrier at transmitter) and timing synchronization are required.

A non-coherent BASK receiver is also possible by using an envelope detector wherein we do not require a phase-coherent local oscillator. Such a non- coherent receiver for BASK receiver is shown in figure 4.9.

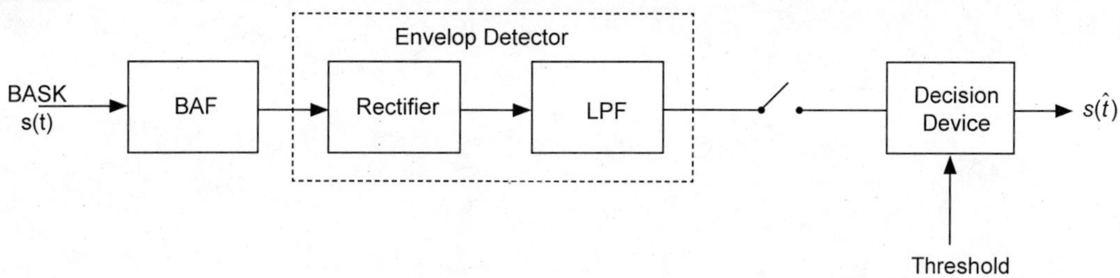

Fig. 4.9 Non-coherent BASK receiver

It may be noted that the greatest advantage of using BASK is its simplicity. It is easy to generate and demodulate a BASK signal (simple circuitry). However, BASK is very sensitive to noise, and can only be used at very low data rates, (only up to 100 bps).

4.2.3 Power Spectral Density (PSD) and Bandwidth (BW) of BASK

The ASK signal $[s(t) = c(t)b(t)]$ has a PSD same as that of the baseband on-off signal but shifted in the frequency domain by $\pm f_c$ as shown in figure 4.10. We can see that two impulses occur at $\pm f_c$.

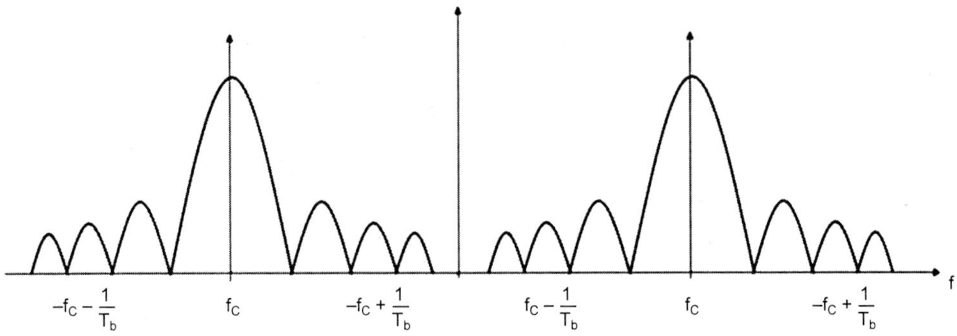

Fig. 4.10 PSD of a BASK signal

The spectrum of the ASK signal as shown above, looks like it has infinite BW. However, the BW, practically, is defined as the BW of an ideal BPF centred at f_c which has around 95% of the average power of ASK signal contained in the output.

4.2.4 Probability of Error (P_e) of BASK

Binary '1'

$$x_1(t) = \sqrt{2P_s}\cos(2\pi f_0 t) \tag{4.15}$$

and

Binary '1'

$$x_2(t) = 0 \text{ (no signal)} \tag{4.16}$$

In earlier chapter, we have shown that for a matched filter, the probability of error is given by the expression,

$$P_e = \frac{1}{2} erfc\left\{\frac{x_{01}(T) - x_{02}(T)}{2\sqrt{2}\sigma}\right\} \tag{4.17}$$

We also know that,

$$\left\{\frac{x_{01}(T) - x_{02}(T)}{\sigma}\right\}^2_{\max} = \int_{-\infty}^{\infty} \frac{|X(f)|^2}{S_{ni}(f)} df \tag{4.18}$$

$$S_{ni}(f) = \frac{N_0}{2} \tag{4.19}$$

Therefore

$$\left\{\frac{x_{01}(T) - x_{02}(T)}{\sigma}\right\}^2_{\max} = \int_{-\infty}^{\infty} \frac{|X(f)|^2}{\frac{N_0}{2}} df$$

$$\left\{\frac{x_{01}(T) - x_{02}(T)}{\sigma}\right\}^2_{\max} = \frac{2}{N_0}\int_{-\infty}^{\infty} |X(f)|^2\, df \tag{4.20}$$

As per Parseval's Theorem,

$$\int_{-\infty}^{\infty} |X(f)|^2\, df = \int_{-\infty}^{\infty} x^2(t)dt \tag{4.21}$$

$$\Rightarrow \quad \left\{\frac{x_{01}(T)-x_{02}(T)}{\sigma}\right\}^2_{max} = \frac{2}{N_0}\int_{-\infty}^{\infty} x^2(t)\,dt$$

$$\left\{\frac{x_{01}(T)-x_{02}(T)}{\sigma}\right\}^2_{max} = \frac{2}{N_0}\int_{-\infty}^{T} x^2(t)\,dt \tag{4.22}$$

$$\left\{\frac{x_{01}(T)-x_{02}(T)}{\sigma}\right\}^2_{max} = \frac{2}{N_0}\int_{0}^{T} x_1^2(t)\,dt$$

$$= \frac{2}{N_0}\int_0^T \left[\sqrt{2P_S}\cos(2\pi f_0 t)\right]^2 dt$$

$$= \frac{4P_S}{N_0}\int_0^T \cos^2(2\pi f_0 t)\,dt$$

$$= \frac{4P_S}{N_0}\int_0^T \frac{1+\cos(4\pi f_0 t)}{2}\,dt$$

$$= \frac{4P_S}{N_0}\cdot\frac{1}{2}\left[\int_0^T t\,dt + \int_0^T \cos(4\pi f_0 t)\,dt\right]$$

$$= \frac{4P_S}{N_0}\cdot\frac{1}{2}\left[T + \frac{\sin(4\pi f_0 T)}{4\pi f_0}\right] \tag{4.23}$$

One bit period,

$$T = \frac{1}{f_0} + \frac{1}{f_0} \tag{4.24}$$

$\therefore \quad f_0 T = 2$ (integer number of cycles) (4.25)

Therefore, if the carrier wave completes k number of cycles, then we have,

$$f_0 T = k \tag{4.26}$$

Where k is an integer. Hence, for all integer values of k, $\sin(4\pi k) = 0$ and therefore

$$\left\{\frac{x_{01}(T)-x_{02}(T)}{\sigma}\right\}^2_{max} = \frac{2P_sT}{N_0}$$

$$\left\{\frac{x_{01}(T)-x_{02}(T)}{\sigma}\right\}^2_{max} = \sqrt{\frac{2P_sT}{N_0}} \tag{4.27}$$

Substituting this value in the expression for P_e (equation 4.17) we get, the probability of error for an ASK system with matched filter detection, as

$$P_e = \frac{1}{2}erfc\left\{\frac{1}{2\sqrt{2}}\cdot\sqrt{\frac{2P_ST}{N_0}}\right\} = \frac{1}{2}erfc\left\{\sqrt{\frac{P_ST}{4N_0}}\right\} \tag{4.28}$$

We know that $P_sT = E$, the energy of one bit and hence P_e can be written as

$$P_e = \frac{1}{2}erfc\left\{\sqrt{\frac{E}{4N_0}}\right\} \tag{4.29}$$

However, the probability of error for a non-coherent detection of ASK also depends on the ratio $\frac{E_b}{N_0}$ and is given as

$$P_e = \frac{1}{2} e^{\frac{E_b}{2N_0}} \tag{4.30}$$

It may be noted that for non-coherent detection, $\frac{E_b}{N_0}$ >> for obtaining reasonable performance.

4.3 BINARY PHASE SHIFT KEYING (BPSK)

In a BPSK scheme, a binary '1' is represented by a carrier of amplitude 'A', frequency 'f_c' with phase of 'ϕ_1' while a binary '0' by a sinusoidal carrier of amplitude of 'A', frequency 'f_c' with phase of ϕ_2. Generally, $\phi_1 = 0$ and $\phi_2 = \pi$, which means that the difference in phase of the two carriers used for representing logic '0' and logic '1' is 180°.

Mathematically,

$$s(t) = \begin{cases} A_c \cdot \cos(2\pi f_c t) \; \textit{for binary symbol} \, 1 \\ A_c \cdot \cos(2\pi f_c t + \pi) \; \textit{for binary symbol} \, 0 \end{cases} \tag{4.31}$$

4.3.1 Generation of BPSK Waves

A product modulator can be used to generate BPSK. The inputs to the product modulator are the sinusoidal carrier and the binary bit stream in polar form (Binary PAM signal, (BPAM).

$$s_{\text{BPSK}}(t) = s_{\text{BPAM}}(t) \,.\, A_c \,.\, \cos(2\pi f_c t) \tag{4.32}$$

This is shown in figure 4.11(a). Figure 4.11 (b) gives a product modulator that can generate a BPSK wave.

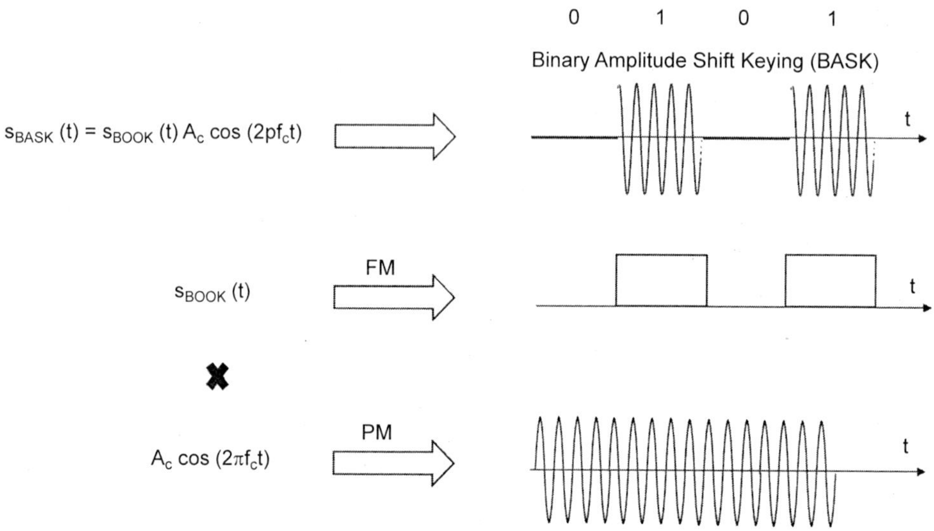

(b)

Fig. 4.11 (a) Generation of BPSK wave (b) Product Modulator

Let us consider a binary sequence 101101. The BPSK wave corresponding to this binary bit stream is as shown in figure 4.12. The binary sequence is converted into an NRZ signal b(t) and then a BPSK signal is generated.

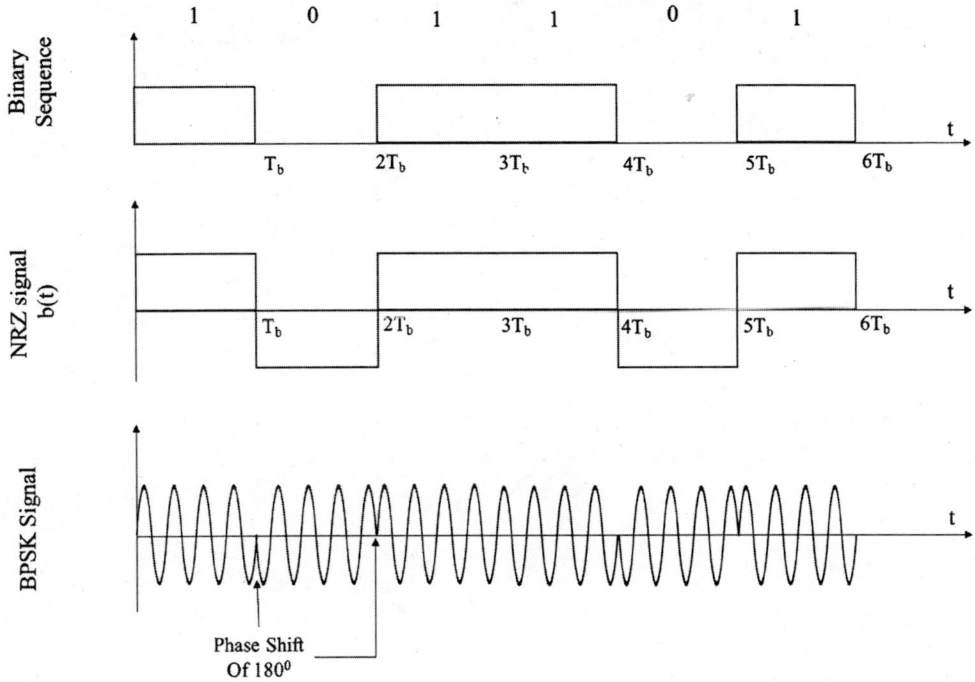

Fig. 4.12 BPSK waveform generation

Suppose

$$s(t) = A\cos(2\pi f_o t) \tag{4.33}$$

$$P = \frac{1}{2}A^2 \tag{4.34}$$

$$A = \sqrt{2P} \tag{4.35}$$

When there is a change in symbol the phase of the carrier signal is changed by 180 degrees (π radians).

For instance, let us consider the expression for symbol '1',

$$s_1(t) = \sqrt{2P}\cos(2\pi f_o t) \tag{4.36}$$

And for symbol '0',

$$s_2(t) = \sqrt{2P}\cos(2\pi f_o t + \pi) = -\sqrt{2P}\cos(2\pi f_o t) \tag{4.37}$$

The BPSK signal hence can be written as

$$s(t) = b(t)\sqrt{2P}\cos(2\pi f_o t) \tag{4.38}$$

Where $b(t)$ is the NRZ signal generated from the binary sequence. $b(t) = \pm 1$ whenever the incoming data bit is '1' and it is – 1 whenever the incoming data bit is '0'. This is depicted in figure 4.13 wherein a Bipolar NRZ level encoder and balanced modulator produce a BPSK signal.

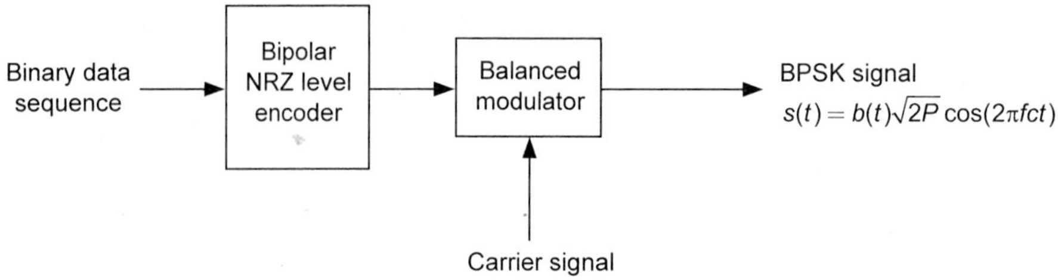

Fig. 4.13 Generation of BPSK signal using bipolar NRZ level encoder and balanced modulator

The geometrical representation (signal space diagram or constellation diagram) for a BPSK system is shown in figure 4.14. The BPSK waveform can be represented as,

$$s(t) = b(t)\sqrt{2P}\cos(2\pi f_o t) \tag{4.39}$$

$$s(t) = b(t)\sqrt{PT_b}\sqrt{\frac{2}{T_b}}\cos(2\pi f_o t) \tag{4.40}$$

Let

$$\phi_1(t) = \sqrt{\frac{2}{T_b}}\cos(2\pi f_o t) \tag{4.41}$$

$$s(t) = b(t)\sqrt{PT_b}\,\phi_1(t) \tag{4.42}$$

Here $b(t)$ is simply ± 1.

$$E_b = PT_b$$

$$s(t) = \pm\sqrt{E_b}\,\phi_1(t) \tag{4.43}$$

The signal space diagram for BPSK will have two points on $\phi_1(t)$. One will be at $\pm\sqrt{E_b}$ and other will be at $-\sqrt{E_b}$ as shown in figure 4.14.

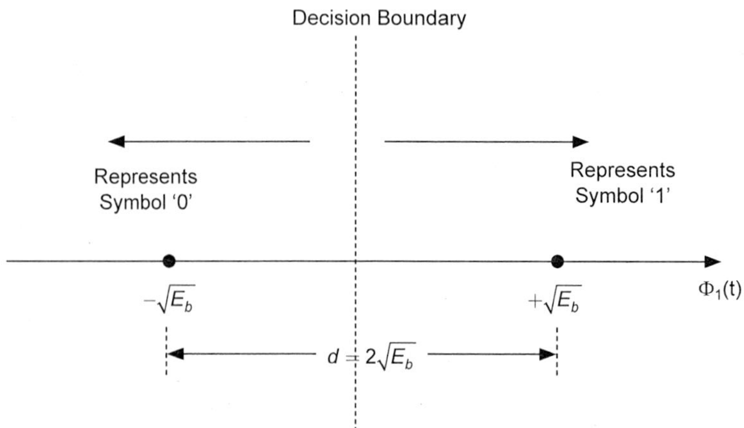

Fig. 4.14 Signal space representation of BPSK

Two signal points are separated by,

$$d = \pm\sqrt{E_b} - (-\sqrt{E_b})$$

$$d = 2\sqrt{E_b} \tag{4.44}$$

4.3.2 Detection of BPSK Waves

The demodulation scheme for detection of BPSK wave is shown in figure 4.15, that employs a multiplier which is used to multiply the incoming BPS wave with a locally generated carrier, an integrator, and a decision device (that can be a comparator or a threshold device) whose output is logic '1' if a prefixed threshold is exceeded and logic '0' if the integrated output is less than the prefixed threshold. The fixing of threshold level is very important in coherent detection of BPSK.

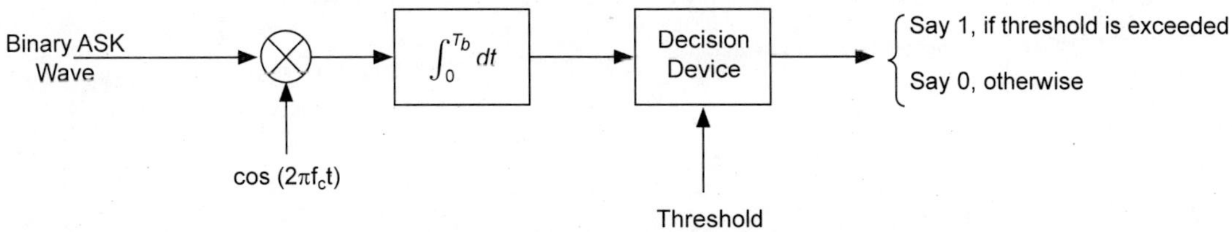

Fig. 4.15 Detection of BPSK wave

A comprehensive scheme to recover the baseband signal from a BPSK wave is shown in figure 4.16.

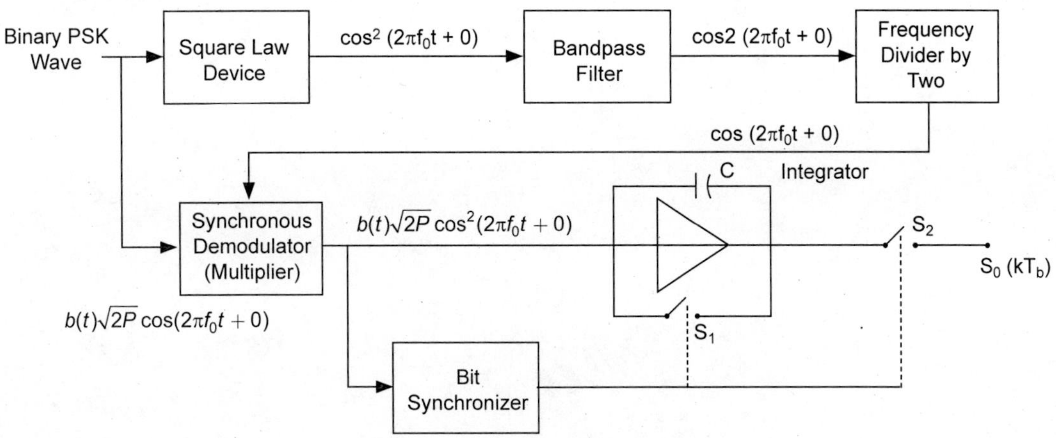

Fig. 4.16 BPSK demodulation scheme

$$b(t)\sqrt{2P}\cos(2\pi f_o t + \theta) \times \cos(2\pi f_o t + \theta) = b(t)\sqrt{2P}\cos^2(2\pi f_o t + \theta)$$

$$= b(t)\sqrt{2P} \times \frac{1}{2}[1 + \cos 2(2\pi f_o t + \theta)] = b(t)\sqrt{2P} \times \frac{1}{2}[1 + \cos 2(2\pi f_o t + \theta)]$$

$$= b(t)\sqrt{\frac{P}{2}} \times [1 + \cos 2(2\pi f_o t + \theta)] \tag{4.45}$$

In the kth bit interval

$$s_0(kT_b) = b(kT_b)\sqrt{\frac{P}{2}}\int_{(k-1)T_b}^{kT_b}[1+\cos 2(2\pi f_o t+\theta)]\,dt$$

$$= b(kT_b)\sqrt{\frac{P}{2}}\int_{(k-1)T_b}^{kT_b}[1+\cos 2(2\pi f_o t+\theta)]\,dt$$

$$= b(kT_b)\sqrt{\frac{P}{2}}\left[\int_{(k-1)T_b}^{kT_b}1\,dt+\int_{(k-1)T_b}^{kT_b}\cos 2(2\pi f_o t+\theta)\,dt\right]$$

$$s_0(kT_b) = b(kT_b)\sqrt{\frac{P}{2}}\int_{(k-1)T_b}^{kT_b}1\,dt$$

$$s_0(kT_b) = b(kT_b)\sqrt{\frac{P}{2}}[kT_b-(k-1)\,T_b]$$

$$s_0(kT_b) = b(kT_b)\sqrt{\frac{P}{2}}\,T_b \tag{4.46}$$

$$s_0(kT_b) \propto b(kT_b)$$

4.3.3 Power Spectral Density (PSD) and Bandwidth (BW) of BPSK

Referring to figure 4.13, we first determine the PSD of a NRZ baseband pulse, which is shown in figure 4.17.

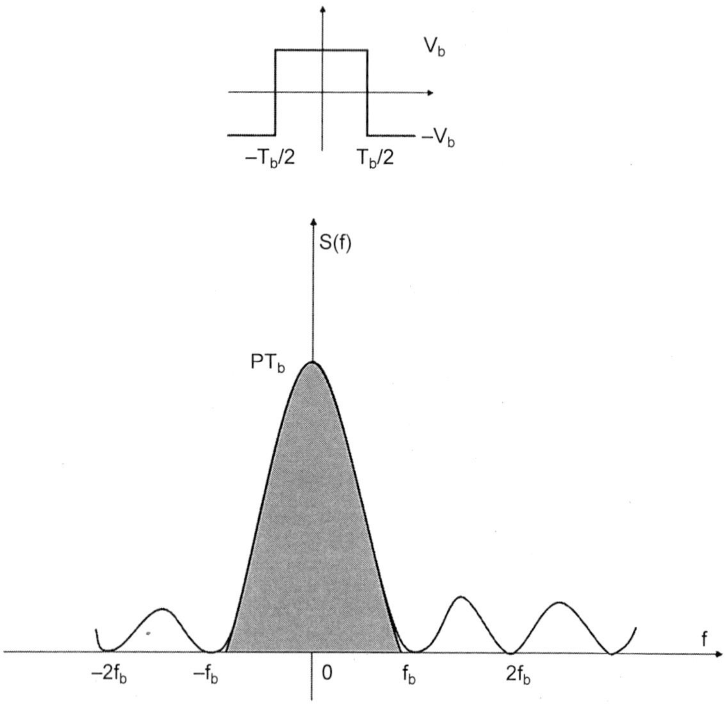

Fig. 4.17 PSD of a NRZ pulse

The FT of a single NRZ pulse is given by

$$X(f) = V_b T_b \frac{\sin(\pi f T_b)}{\pi f T_b} \tag{4.47}$$

For many such positive and negative pulses, the PSD is given by

$$S(f) = \frac{\overline{|X(f)|^2}}{T_s} = \frac{V_b^2 T_b^2}{T_s}\left[\frac{\sin(\pi f T_b)}{\pi f T_b}\right]^2 \tag{4.48}$$

The PSD of the baseband signal $b(t)$ is,

$$S(f) = V_b^2 T_b \left[\frac{\sin(\pi f T_b)}{\pi f T_b}\right]^2 \tag{4.49}$$

The PSD of a BPSK signal is then given by,

$$S_{BPSK}(f) = V_b^2 T_b \left\{\frac{1}{2}\left[\frac{\sin(\pi(f_0 - f)T_b)}{\pi(f_0 - f)T_b}\right]^2 + \frac{1}{2}\left[\frac{\sin(\pi(f_0 + f)T_b)}{\pi(f_0 + f)T_b}\right]\right\}$$

$$S_{BPSK}(f) = \frac{PT_b}{2}\left\{\left[\frac{\sin(\pi(f_0 - f)T_b)}{\pi(f_0 - f)T_b}\right]^2 + \left[\frac{\sin(\pi(f_0 + f)T_b)}{\pi(f_0 + f)T_b}\right]^2\right\} \tag{4.50}$$

The same has been shown in figure 4.18.

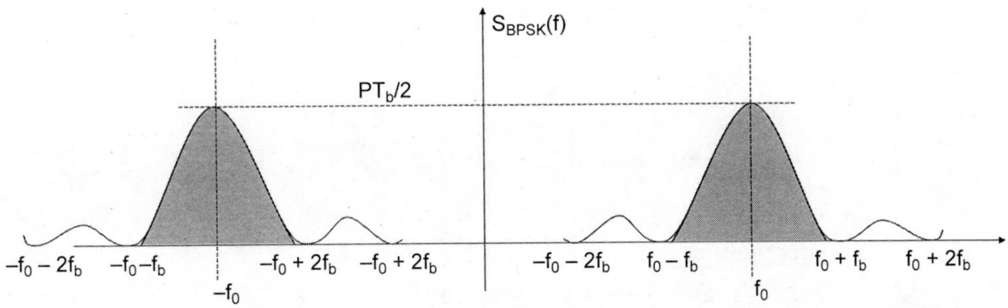

Fig. 4.18 PSD of a BPSK signal

The bandwidth of BPSK signal hence can be obtained by looking at the PSD of the BPSK signal, which is nothing but the difference between the highest frequency and the lowest frequency of the main lobe.

$$BW = (f_0 + f_b) - (f_0 - f_b) = 2f_b \tag{4.51}$$

We also define bandwidth efficiency for a BPSK signal by looking at the required channel bandwidth for 90% in-band power which is given by (refer to figure 4.19),

$$b_{h-90\%} = 2R_b \tag{4.52}$$

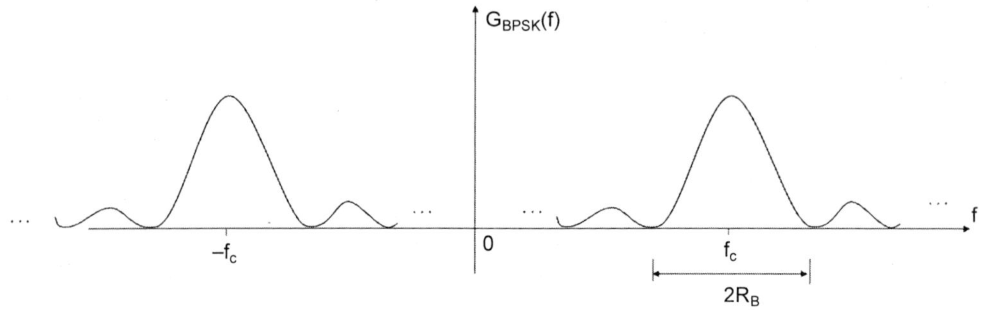

Fig. 4.19 Bandwidth from PSD of BPSK

The BW efficiency or spectral efficiency can be defined as the transmission rate that can be transmitted over a given bandwidth in a particular communication system given by ratio of bit rate (f_b) to bandwidth (BW)

i.e., $$\text{Spectral efficiency} = f_b / BW = f_b / 2f_b = 0.5 \tag{4.53}$$

4.3.4 Probability of Error (P_e) of BPSK

We have seen in section 4.3.1, that a coherent BPSK system the coordinates of the message points in the constellation diagram are $+\sqrt{E_b}$ and $-\sqrt{E_b}$ and the decision boundary can be shown at the origin as shown in figure 4.20.

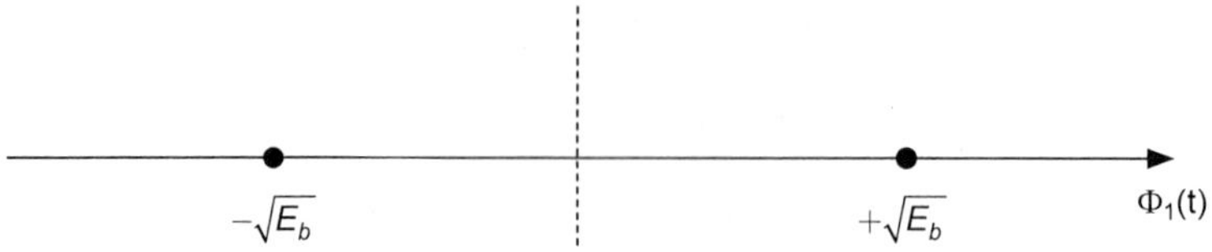

Fig. 4.20 Constellation diagram of BPSK with decision boundary

This is for a correlator receiver output of a BPSK system under noiseless condition. Assuming the received signal is added with additive white gaussian noise (AWGN) signal $w(t)$ as shown in the correlation receiver as shown in figure 4.21. We have two possibilities of making an erroneous decision:

1. When signal $s_2(t)$ is transmitted, the noise affects the receiver decision in such a way that receiver decodes the signal as $s_1(t)$ if the received signal point lies in the region with $x_1 > 0$.
2. When signal $s_1(t)$ is transmitted, the noise affects the receiver decision in such a way that receiver decodes the signal as $s_2(t)$ if the received signal point lies in the region with $x_1 < 0$.

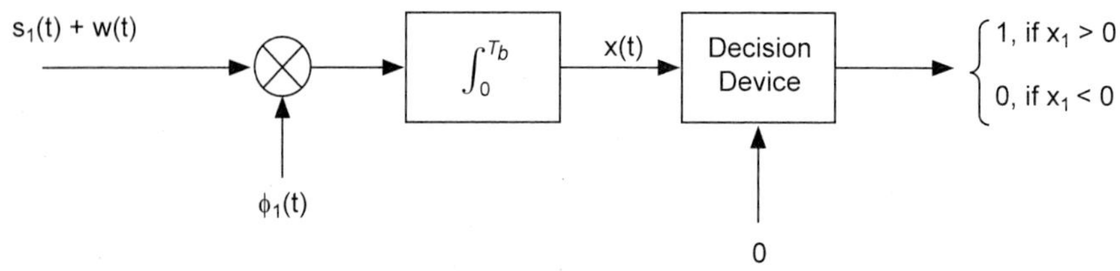

Fig. 4.21 Coherent BPSK receiver

In the first case the observable signal level x_1 is obtained by integrating the received signal with noise multiplied by $\phi_1(t)$ and integrated over the bit duration T_b. ie.

$$x_1 = \int_0^{T_b} x(t)\phi_1(t)dt$$

$$x_1 = \int_0^{T_b} [s_1(t)+w(t)]\phi_1(t)dt = -\sqrt{E_b} + \int_0^{T_b} w(t)\phi_1(t)dt \quad (4.54)$$

x_1 is a Gaussian process with mean and variance given by

$$\overline{x_1} = E[x_1] \quad (4.55)$$

$$\overline{x_1} = E\left[-\sqrt{E_b} + \int_0^{T_b} w(t)\phi_1(t)\,dt\right] = -\sqrt{E_b} \quad (4.56)$$

$$\sigma^2 = E[(x_1 - \overline{x_1})^2]$$

$$\sigma^2 = E\left[\left(\int_0^{T_b} w(t)\phi_1(t)dt\right)^2\right] = E\left[\int_0^{T_b}\int_0^{T_b} w(t)w(u)\phi_1(t)\phi_1(u)dtdu\right]$$

$$= \int_0^{T_b}\int_0^{T_b} E[w(t)w(u)]\phi_1(t)\phi_1(u)dtdu$$

$$= \int_0^{T_b}\int_0^{T_b} \frac{N_0}{2}\delta(t-u)\phi_1(t)\phi_1(u)\,dtdu$$

$$= \frac{N_0}{2}\int_0^{T_b} \phi_1^2(t)\,dt = \frac{N_0}{2} \quad (4.57)$$

Hence, the conditional PDF of given that symbol '0' was transmitted is given by,

$$f(x_1|0) = \frac{1}{\sqrt{2\pi\sigma}}\exp\left[-\frac{(x_1-\overline{x_1})^2}{2\sigma^2}\right] = \frac{1}{\sqrt{\pi N_0}}\exp\left[-\frac{(x_1+\sqrt{E_b})^2}{N_0}\right]$$

Now, the probability of error when symbol was sent and was received is given by,

$$P_{10} = \int_0^{\infty} f(x_1|0)\,dx_1$$

$$P_{10} = \frac{1}{\sqrt{\pi N_0}}\int_0^{\infty} \exp\left[-\frac{(x_1+\sqrt{E_b})^2}{N_0}\right]dx_1$$

Putting $z = \frac{1}{\sqrt{N_0}}(x_1+\sqrt{E_b})$, we have

$$P_{10} = \frac{1}{\sqrt{\pi}}\int_{\sqrt{\frac{E_b}{N_0}}}^{\infty} \exp[-(z)^2]dz = \frac{1}{2}\,erfc\left(\sqrt{\frac{E_b}{N_0}}\right) \quad (4.58)$$

Where

$$erfc(u) = \frac{1}{\sqrt{\pi}}\int_u^{\infty} \exp[-(z)^2]\,dz$$

Considering equiprobable symbols, we can write the probability of error when symbol '1' was transmitted and symbol '0' was received as,

$$P_{01} = P_{10} = \frac{1}{2} erfc\left(\sqrt{\frac{E_b}{N_0}}\right) \tag{4.59}$$

The average probability of symbol error can be thus obtained by considering the average of $P_{01} = P_{10}$ which is equal to

$$P_e = \frac{1}{2} erfc\left(\sqrt{\frac{E_b}{N_0}}\right) \tag{4.60}$$

4.4 BINARY FREQUENCY SHIFT KEYING (BFSK)

In BFSK, the frequency of the carrier is changed with respect to the incoming data as already explained in section 4.1.2. Two signals, $s_1(t)$ and $s_2(t)$ are used in coherent BFSK systems. $s_1(t)$ is used to represent a '1' and $s_2(t)$ represents a symbol '0'.

Mathematically,

$$s_1(t) = \sqrt{\frac{2E_b}{T_b}} \cos(2\pi f_1 t)$$

$$s_2(t) = \sqrt{\frac{2E_b}{T_b}} \cos(2\pi f_2 t) \tag{4.61}$$

Two basis functions of unit energy $\phi_1(t)$ and $\phi_2(t)$ are needed.

They are given by,

$$\phi_1(t) = \sqrt{\frac{2}{T_b}} \cos(2\pi f_1 t)$$

$$\phi_2(t) = \sqrt{\frac{2}{T_b}} \cos(2\pi f_2 t) \tag{4.62}$$

4.4.1 BFSK Modulator

The BFSK modulator basically requires two basis functions. It is as shown in figure 4.22.

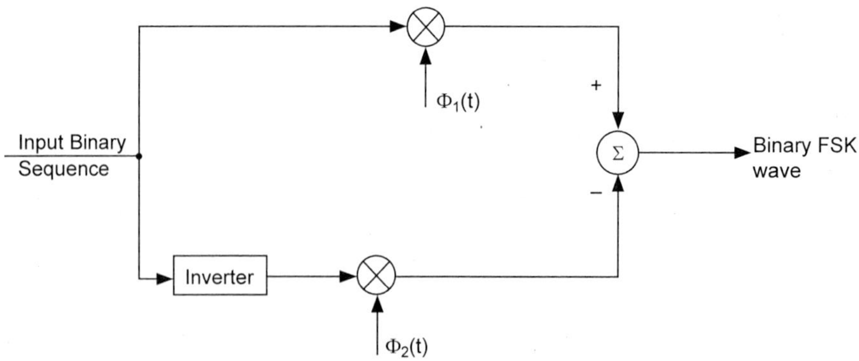

Fig. 4.22 BFSK modulator

Consider a digital input sequence 1011001. The waveforms are as shown in figure 4.23.

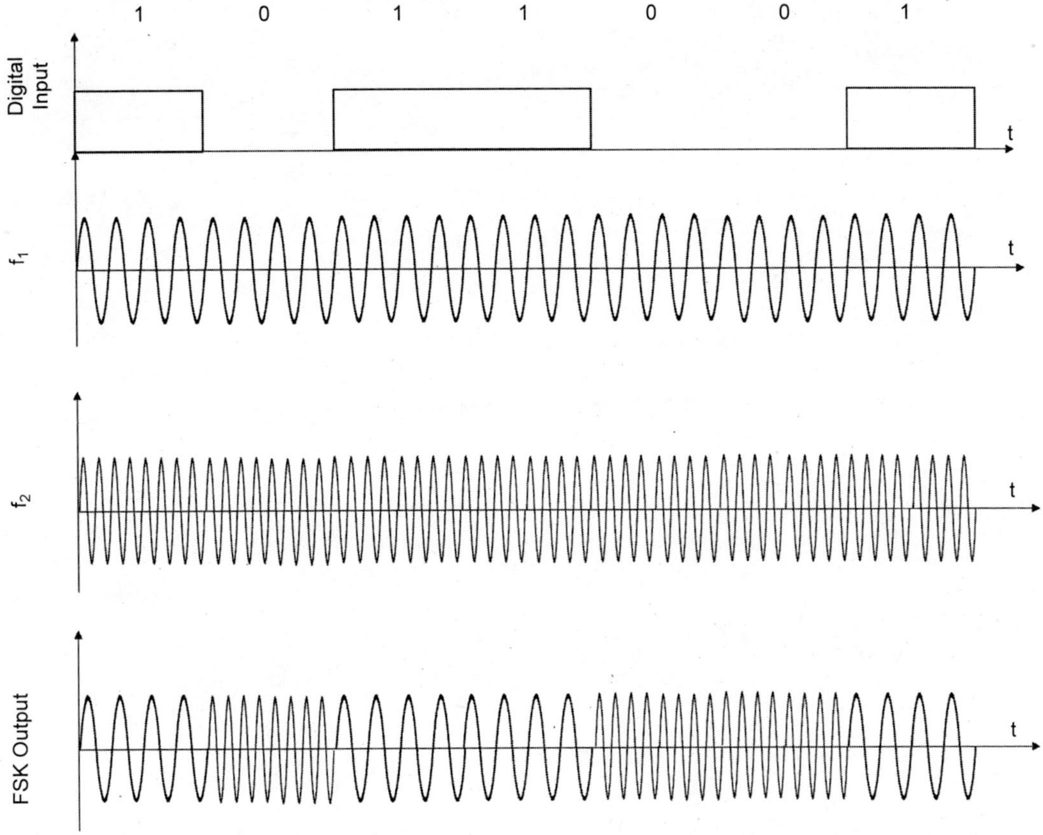

Fig. 4.23 Waveforms for the data 1011001

Coherent and non-coherent BFSK receivers are as shown in figure 4.24 and figure 4.25 respectively.

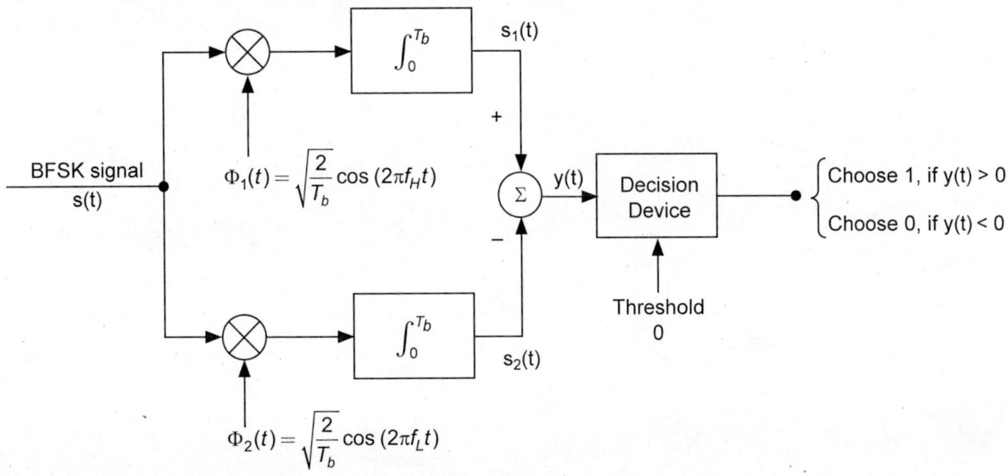

Fig. 4.24 Coherent BFSK receiver

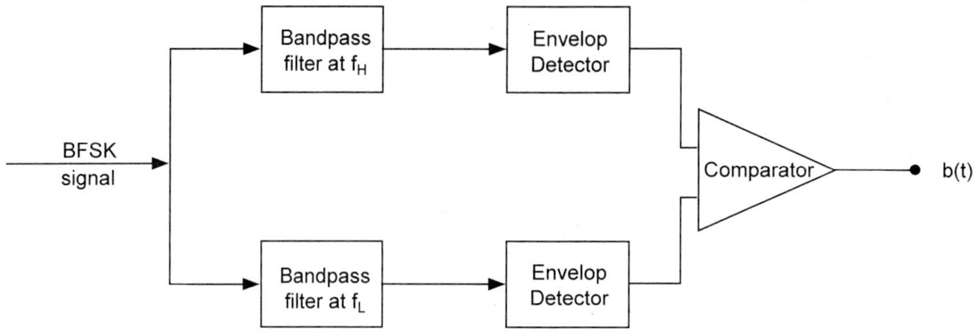

Fig. 4.25 Non-coherent BFSK receiver

Geometrical representation of BFSK(Constellation Diagram) is as shown in figure 4.26.

$$f_H = mf_b$$

And

$$f_L = nf_b \tag{4.63}$$

Here $f_b = \dfrac{1}{T_b}$, then the carriers will be

$$\phi_1(t) = \sqrt{\frac{2}{T_b}}\cos(2\pi mf_b t)$$

$$\phi_2(t) = \sqrt{\frac{2}{T_b}}\cos(2\pi mf_b t)$$

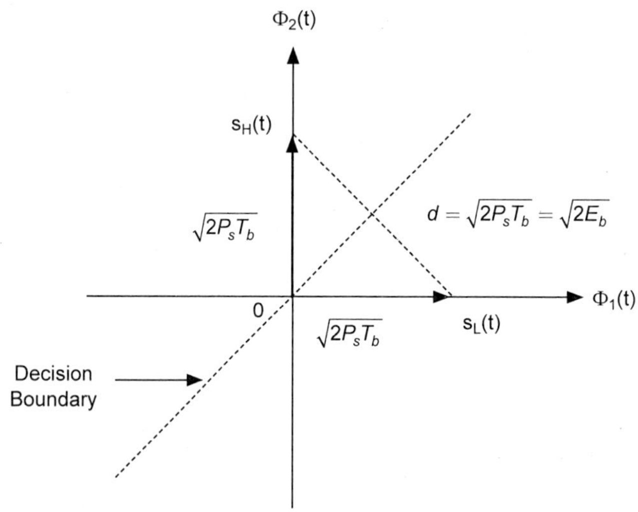

Fig. 4.26 Constellation diagram of BFSK

4.4.2 PSD and Bandwidth of FSK

In BFSK, the frequency of the carrier signal is varied in accordance with the binary data. However, the phase is not altered. As the binary system has two possible symbols, we have two frequency components. If the change in the frequency is denoted by Ω, we can mathematically represent the signals as follows:

If $$b(t) = 1, s_H(t) = \sqrt{2P_s}\cos(2\pi f_0 + \Omega)t$$

If $$b(t) = 1, s_L(t) = \sqrt{2P_s}\cos(2\pi f_0 - \Omega)t \tag{4.64}$$

$$s(t) = \sqrt{2P_s}\cos[(2\pi f_0 + d(t)\,\Omega)\,t] \tag{4.65}$$

In other words, carrier frequency is $f_0 + \left(\frac{\Omega}{2\pi}\right)$ corresponding to the symbol being '1'. And it is $f_0 - \left(\frac{\Omega}{2\pi}\right)$ for the symbol being '0'.

That is

$$f_H = f_0 + \left(\frac{\Omega}{2\pi}\right) \text{ for symbol '1'}$$

$$f_H = f_0 - \left(\frac{\Omega}{2\pi}\right) \text{ for symbol '0'} \tag{4.66}$$

$$s(f) = \sqrt{\frac{P_s}{2}}\left\{\delta(f - f_H) + \delta(f + f_L) + \frac{P_s T_b}{2}\left\{\frac{\sin(\pi f_H T_b)}{\pi f_H T_b}\right\}^2 + \frac{P_s T_b}{2}\left\{\frac{\sin(\pi f_L T_b)}{\pi f_L T_b}\right\}^2\right\} \tag{4.67}$$

f_H and f_L are selected such that

$$f_H - f_L = 2f_b$$

$$BW \text{ of } BFSK = 2f_b + 2f_b = 4f_b \tag{4.68}$$

$$BW(BFSK) = 2 \times BW(BPSK)$$

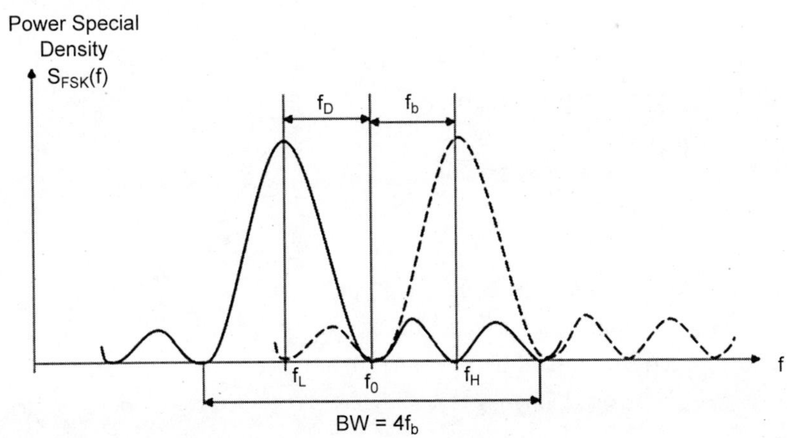

Fig. 4.27 Bandwidth of BFSK

4.5 QUADRIPHASE SHIFT KEYING (QPSK)

QPSK has twice the bandwidth efficiency of BPSK since 2 bits are transmitted in a single modulation symbol. The data input $d_k(t)$ is divided into an inphase stream $d_I(t)$ and a quadrature stream $d_Q(t)$.

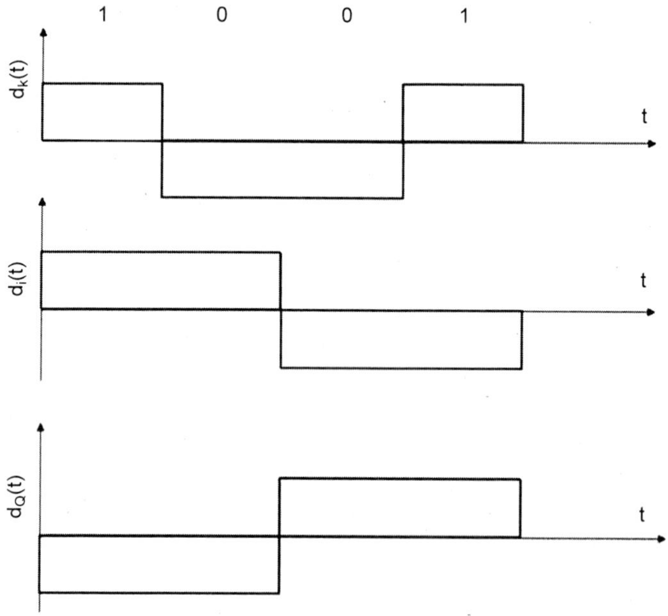

Fig. 4.28 QPSK inphase and qudrature streams

The phase of the carrier signal can take any of the following values:

$\frac{\pi}{4}, \frac{3\pi}{4}, \frac{5\pi}{4}$ and $\frac{7\pi}{4}$

$$s_i(t) = \begin{cases} \sqrt{\frac{2E}{T}} \cos\left[2\pi f_c t + (2i-1)\frac{\pi}{4}\right], & 0 \le t \le T \\ 0, & Elsewhere \end{cases}$$

Where $i = 1, 2, 3, 4$ (4.69)

E is the transmitted signal energy per symbol

T is the symbol duration

$$f_c = \frac{n}{T} \tag{4.70}$$

(Note : $T = 2T_b$)

Each possible value of the phase corresponds to a unique dibit.

For example, 10 for $i = 1$, 00 for $i = 2$, 01 for $i = 3$, 11 for $i = 4$

Only a single bit is changed from one dibit to the next.

The transmitted signal can be written as

$$s_i(t) = \sqrt{\frac{2E}{T}} \cos\left[2\pi f_c t + (2i-1)\frac{\pi}{4}\right]$$

$$s_i(t) = \sqrt{\frac{2E}{T}} \cos[2\pi f_c t] \cos\left[(2i-1)\frac{\pi}{4}\right] - \sqrt{\frac{2E}{T}} \sin[2\pi f_c t] \sin\left[(2i-1)\frac{\pi}{4}\right]$$

$$s_i(t) = s_{i1}\,\phi_1(t) + s_{i2}\,\phi_2(t) \tag{4.71}$$

Where

$$\phi_1(t) = \sqrt{\frac{2}{T}} \cos[2\pi f_c t]$$

$$\phi_2(t) = \sqrt{\frac{2}{T}} \cos[2\pi f_c t]$$

Input Dibit	Phase of QPSK	s_{i1}	s_{i2}
10	$\frac{\neq}{4}$	$\sqrt{\frac{E}{2}}$	$-\sqrt{\frac{E}{2}}$
00	$\frac{3\neq}{4}$	$-\sqrt{\frac{E}{2}}$	$-\sqrt{\frac{E}{2}}$
01	$\frac{5\neq}{4}$	$-\sqrt{\frac{E}{2}}$	$\sqrt{\frac{E}{2}}$
11	$\frac{7\neq}{4}$	$\sqrt{\frac{E}{2}}$	$\sqrt{\frac{E}{2}}$

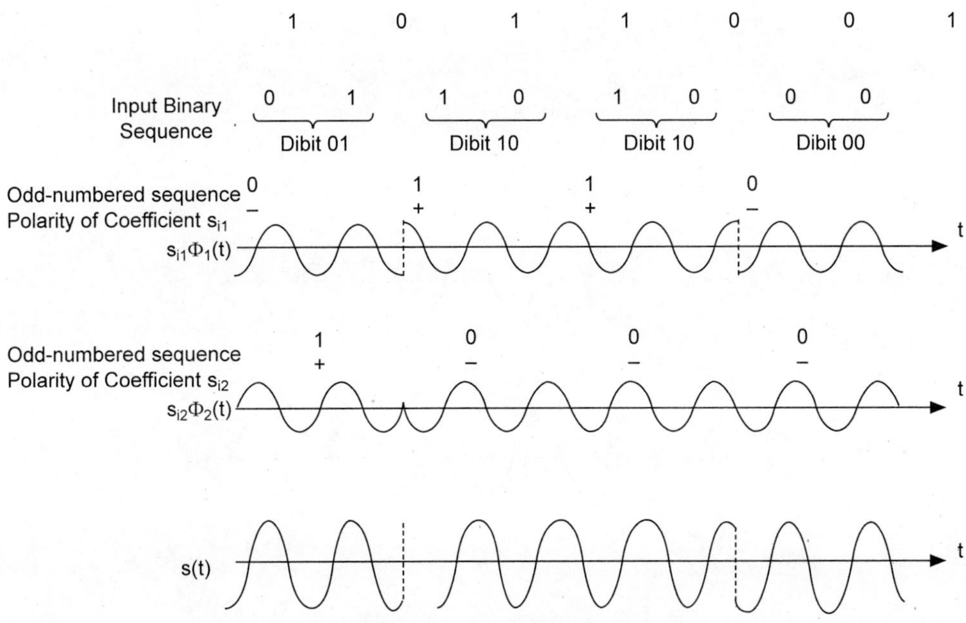

Fig. 4.29 QPSK waveforms for the data 01101000

Example 4.1: If the input binary sequence is $b(k) = \{1, -1, 1, -1, -1, -1, 1, 1\}$, determine the transmitted phase sequence (show odd and even sequences) and also sketch the transmitted waveform for QPSK.

Solution:

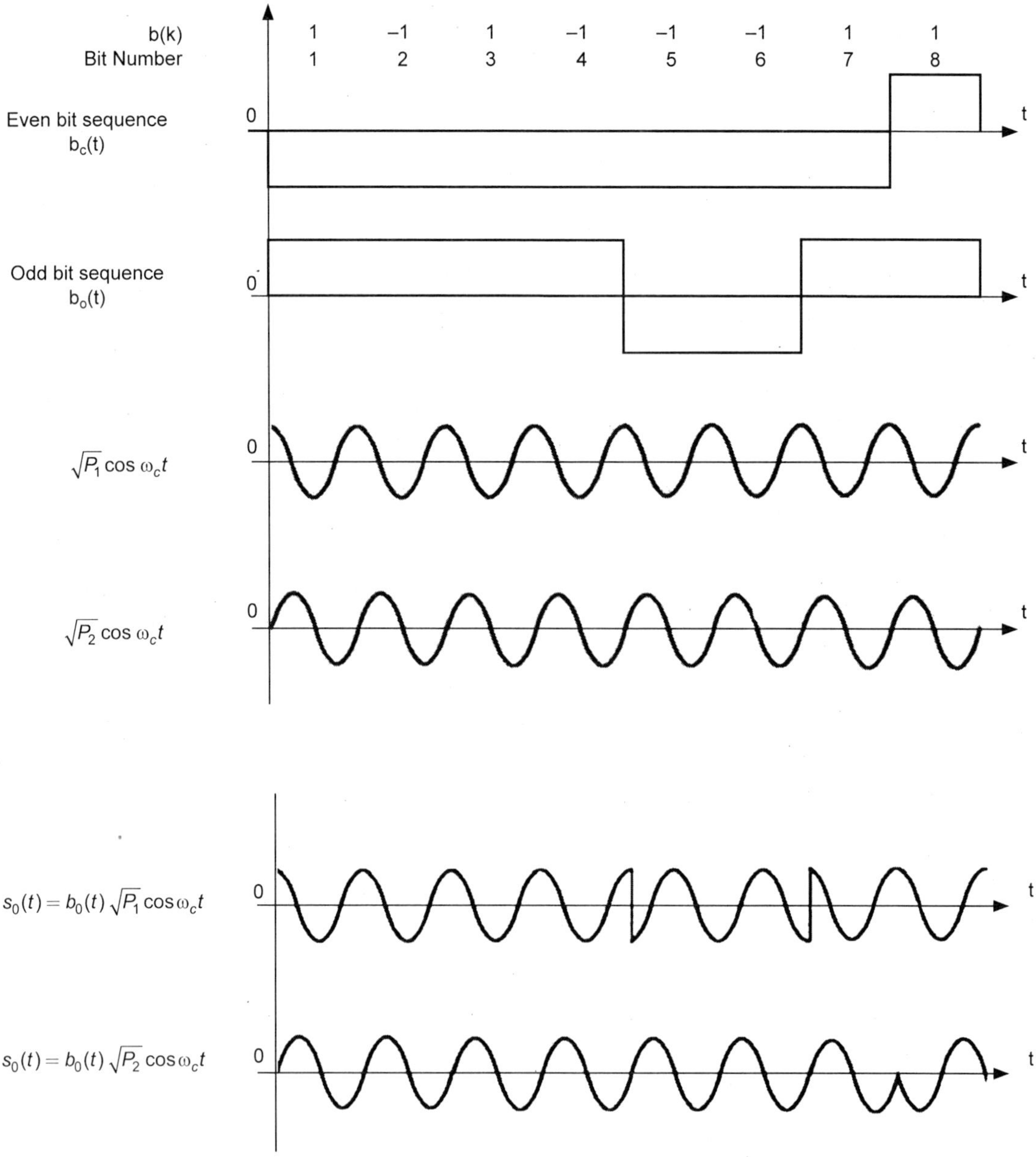

Fig. 4.30 QPSK waveforms for example 4.1

4.5.1 Generation of Coherent QPSK

The QPSK generator is as shown in figure 4.31. The first block in the generator is the NRZ level encoder which converts the binary information into polar form. The demultiplexer splits this signal into two sequences. Using the orthogonality principle of the basis functions $\phi_1(t)$ and $\phi_2(t)$, BPSK signals can be generated at the output.

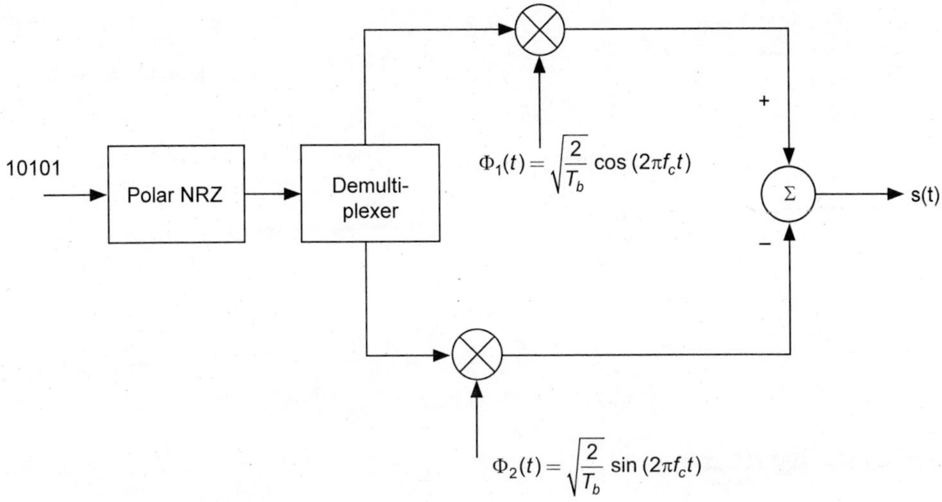

Fig. 4.31 QPSK generator

Constellation of QPSK is as shown in figure 4.32.

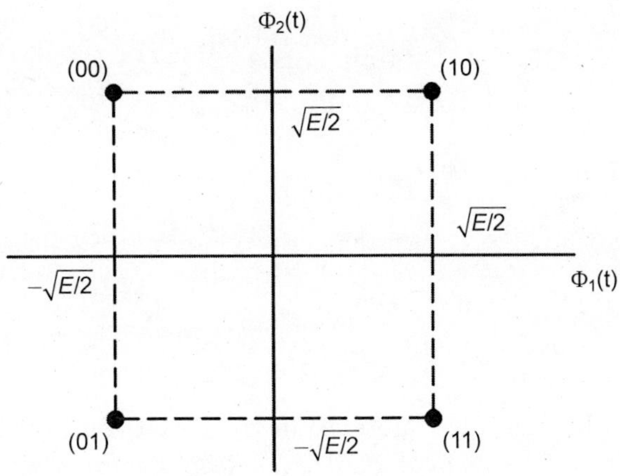

Fig. 4.32 QPSK constellation diagram

QPSK has twice the bandwidth efficiency of BPSK since 2 bits are transmitted in a single modulation symbol.

4.5.2 Detection of Coherent QPSK Signals

Non-coherent detection of QPSK signals is shown in figure 4.33.

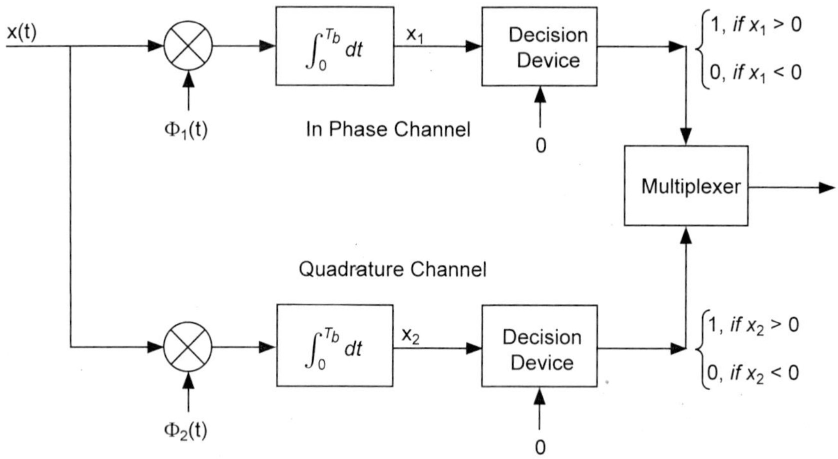

Fig. 4.33 Non-coherent detection of QPSK

4.5.3 Probability of Error

Let the received signal be

$$x(t) = s_1(t) + w(t) \tag{4.72}$$

Observation elements are

$$x_1 = \int_0^{Tb} x(t)\,\phi_1(t)\,dt$$

$$x_1 = \pm\sqrt{E_b} + \int_0^{Tb} w(t)\phi_1(t)dt \tag{4.73}$$

$$x_2 = \int_0^{Tb} x(t)\,\phi_1(t)\,dt$$

$$x_2 = \pm\sqrt{E_b} + \int_0^{Tb} w(t)\phi_1(t)dt \tag{4.74}$$

We can consider a coherent QPSK as two coherent BPSK systems connected in parallel and having carriers in phase quadrature.

$$p = \frac{1}{2}erfc\left(\sqrt{\frac{E/2}{N_0}}\right) = \frac{1}{2}erfc\left(\sqrt{\frac{e}{2N_0}}\right) \tag{4.75}$$

As the bit error in the in phase and quadrature channels of the coherent QPSK systems are statistically independent, the average probability of a correct decision resulting from the combined actions of the two channels is

$$p_c = (1 - p)^2$$

$$p_c = \left(1 - \frac{1}{2}erfc\left(\sqrt{\frac{E}{2N_0}}\right)\right)^2 = 1 - erfc\left(\sqrt{\frac{E}{2N_0}}\right) + \frac{1}{4}erfc^2\left(\sqrt{\frac{E}{2N_0}}\right) \tag{4.76}$$

Therefore, the average error probability in a coherent QPSK is

$$p_e = 1 - p_c = erfc\left(\sqrt{\frac{E}{2N_0}}\right) - \frac{1}{4}erfc^2\left(\sqrt{\frac{E}{2N_0}}\right) \approx erfc\left(\sqrt{\frac{E}{2N_0}}\right) \quad (4.77)$$

If $\frac{E}{2N_0} >> 1$

As two bits represent a symbol in QPSK, energy of the transmitted signal is two times E_b.

$$E = 2E_b$$

Also, $p_e \approx erfc\left(\sqrt{\frac{E}{2N_0}}\right)$

BER of QPSK is given by

$$BER = \frac{1}{2}erfc\left(\sqrt{\frac{E}{2N_0}}\right) \quad (4.78)$$

Comparing equation (4.78) with (4.60), it can be seen that the probability of error for a coherent QPSK is same as that of a coherent BPSK provided bit rate and $\frac{E}{N_0}$ being the same. However, QPSK uses only half the channel bandwidth as that of BPSK.

4.6 DIFFERENTIAL PSK (DPSK)

Carrier synchronizers generally cannot differentiate whether or not they are locked to the carrier phase. This may lead to the large values of bit errors. In a differential scheme, the data are encoded into the change from interval to interval.

A differential BPSK scheme usually abbreviated as DPSK, works as follows: If the present and previous binary data symbols are the same, phase 0° is transmitted. If the present data symbols is opposite to the previous one, phase is transmitted. Special differential detector circuits have been designed that detect DPSK without a separate carrier synchronizer circuit.

DPSK is especially useful in systems that require rapid acquisition of carrier synchronization. An example of this is a network that sends random short bursts of data. The spectrum of DPSK is identical to that of BPSK, and its error probability converges to BPSK's as the channel SNR grows. Figure 4.34 and figure 4.35 give the idea about generation and detection of DPSK signal.

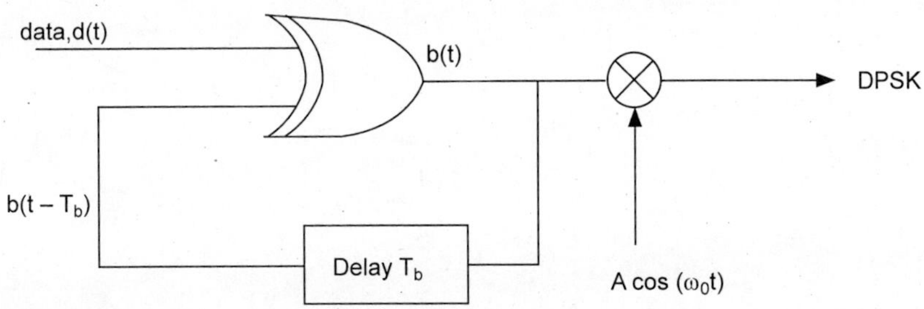

Fig. 4.34 DPSK modulator

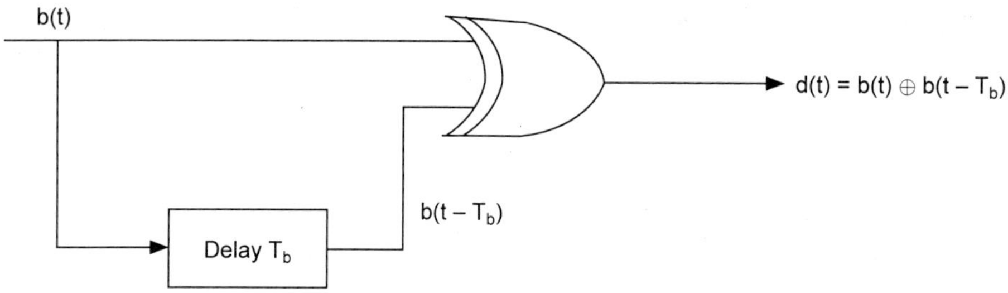

Fig. 4.35 Detector circuit for DPSK

Example 4.2: Consider a binary data stream 01001011101 is to be communicated to the receiver using DBPSK. Assume $f_c = 2 \times R_b$ (where R_b is bit rate) and the baseband signal is unipolar NRZ.

(a) Sketch the waveforms of differential encoder and modulator output.

(b) Show that the DBPSK detector circuit reconstructs the actual information in the absence of noise.

Solution:

(a) Waveforms are as shown in figrue 4.36.

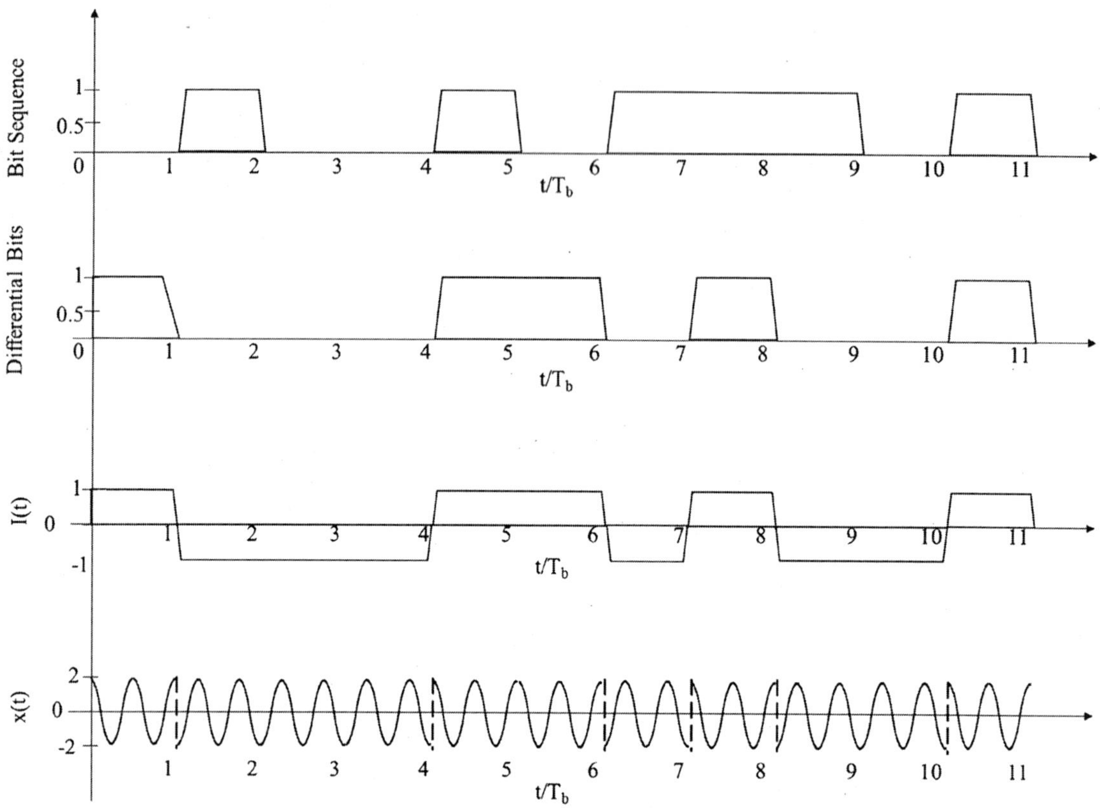

Fig. 4.36 DPSK waveforms for example 4.2

(b)

Differentially encoded bits	1	1	0	0	0	1	1	0	1	0	0	1
Threshold comparison sign		+	-	+	+	-	+	-	-	-	+	-
Decoded differential bit $\hat{d}$	1	1	0	0	0	1	1	0	1	0	0	1
Regenerated data bits $\hat{d}$		0	1	0	0	1	0	1	1	1	0	1

4.7 OFFSET QPSK (OQPSK)

In an offset QPSK modulation baseband quadrature signal $Q(t)$ is delayed by T_b relative to inphase signal $I(t)$. The modulator circuit for OQPSK is as shown in figure 4.37.

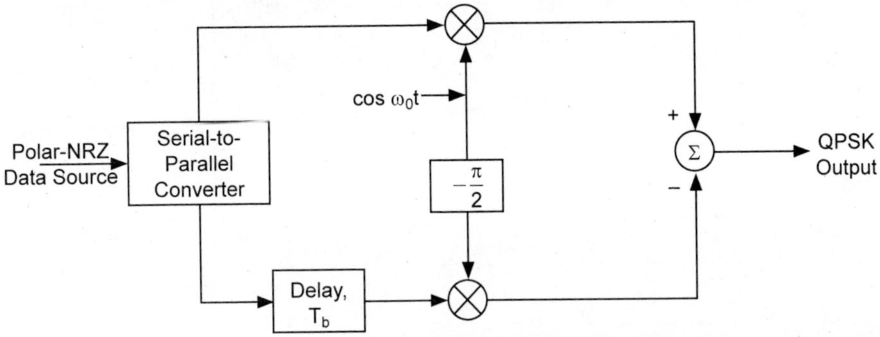

Scan here to know more

Fig. 4.37 OQPSK modulator

One bit delay introduced at the quadrature rail makes the largest phase change in the modulated signal as $\pm\pi/2$ per bit interval. This was $\pm\pi$ per symbol interval (2 bits) in case of QPSK. Therefore, OQPSK offers smaller and more frequent phase changes and hence resulting in low fluctuations in amplitude following bandlimiting.

The OQPSK receiver is as shown in figure 4.38. It can be seen from the figure that the demodulator is a modified version of the demodulator for QPSK.

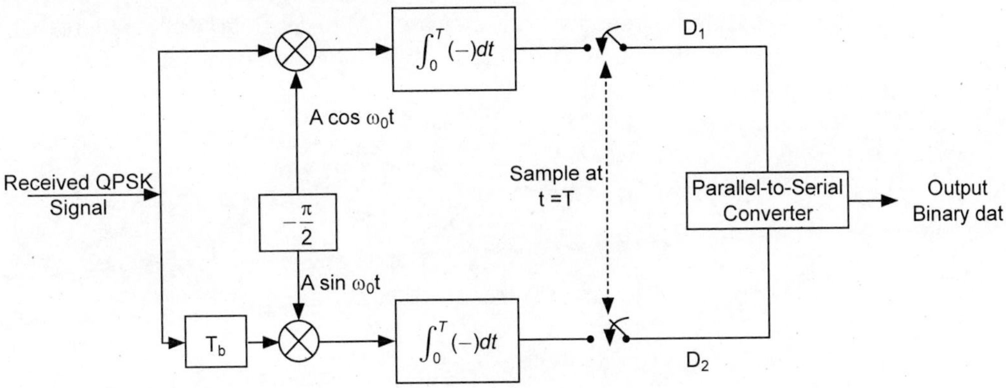

Fig. 4.38 OQPSK demodulator

Integration on lower integrator is over each symbol interval, However, its intervals are denoted by T_b relative to the upper processor channel. Decision values D_1 occurs at times $T_b + T$, $T_b + 2T$, $T_b + 3T$ and so on, where D_2 occurs at times $2T$, $3T$, $4T$ and so on.

Addition of a delay T_b synchronizes values of D_1 with that of D_2 for use in the converter. As the quadrature modulation properties of OQPSK is same as that of QPSK, it has same average probability of bit error as QPSK.

Example 4.3: Consider a binary data 01001011101 is to be generated using OQPSK modulation. Assume $f_c = R_b$ and the pulse shape is unipolar rectangular. Sketch the inphase, quadrature phase baseband signal and final OQPSK waveform.

Solution:

The waveforms are as shown in figure 4.39.

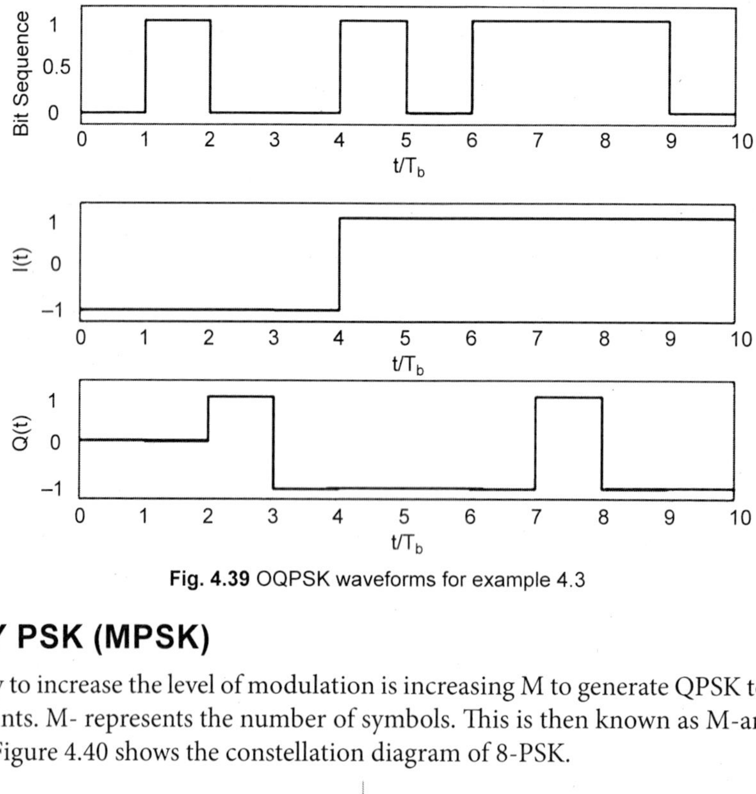

Fig. 4.39 OQPSK waveforms for example 4.3

4.8 M-ARY PSK (MPSK)

The simplest way to increase the level of modulation is increasing M to generate QPSK to more than four constellation points. M- represents the number of symbols. This is then known as M-ary PSK, where M is a power of 2. Figure 4.40 shows the constellation diagram of 8-PSK.

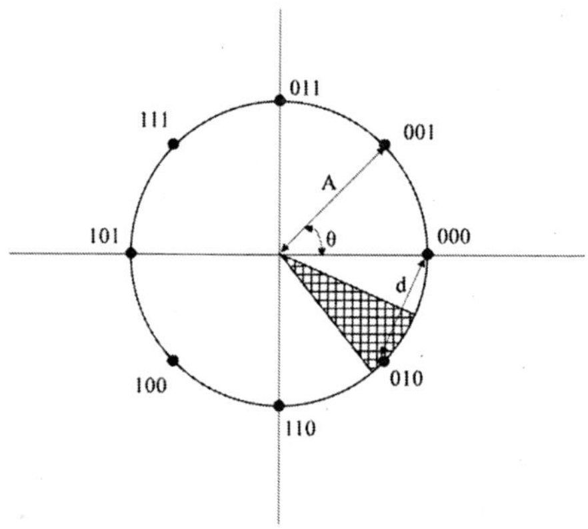

Fig. 4.40 Constellation diagram of 8-PSK

The constellation points may be defined mathematically by expressing the data as

$$d = Ae^{\frac{2\pi ij}{M}} = A\left[\cos\left(\frac{2\pi i}{M}\right) + j\sin\left(\frac{2\pi i}{M}\right)\right] \tag{4.79}$$

$$i = 0, 1, 2, \ldots M - 1 \tag{4.79}$$

Most popular one is to add the angle $\frac{\pi}{M}$ to the arguments, so that the points are placed symmetrically around the axe, rather than on them.

Example 4.4: Sketch the 8-ary PSK modulated waveform for the binary sequence 100101111010. Assume data sequence is unipolar NRZ.

Solution:

The waveforms are as shown in figure 4.41.

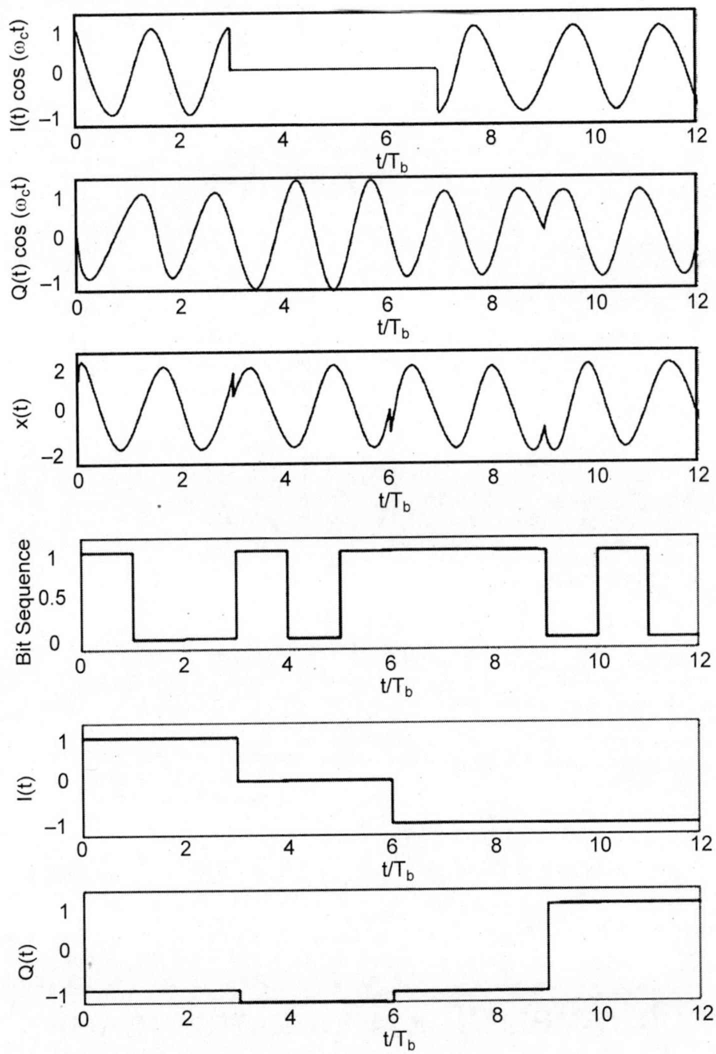

Fig. 4.41 8-PSK waveforms for example 4.4

A symbol error occurs if the received symbol is displayed by noise so that it lies closer to an erroneous constellation point than to the correct one. For the symbol 010 in the previous constellation diagram, this will occur if it is displaced outside the region shown shaded, known as the decision region of the point. The boundaries of the decision region are the perpendicular bisectors of the lines joining the point to its immediate neighbours.

Again, we can calculate the probability of displacement over each of these boundaries using the same formula for BPSK and again the symbol error probability will be approximately twice this because there are two boundaries.

$$P_e = 2Q\left(\frac{d}{2\sigma}\right) = 2Q\left(\frac{2A\sin\left(\frac{\theta}{2}\right)}{2\sigma}\right) = 2Q\left(\frac{A\sin\left(\frac{\theta}{2}\right)}{\sigma}\right)$$

$$P_e = 2Q\left(\sin\left(\frac{\pi}{M}\right)\sqrt{\frac{E}{N_0}}\right) = 2Q\left(\sin\left(\frac{\pi}{M}\right)\sqrt{\frac{2kE_b}{N_0}}\right) \tag{4.80}$$

The labelling of the constellation has been chosen so that any pair of adjacent points differ only in one bit (this is known as Gray code labelling) and therefore a symbol error is liekly to result in only one out of k bit errors. Hence the BER is

$$p_b = \frac{2}{k}Q\left(\sin\left(\frac{\pi}{M}\right)\sqrt{\frac{2kE_b}{N_0}}\right) \tag{4.81}$$

For 8 = PSK this evaluates as

$$p_b = \frac{2}{3}Q\left(0.937\sqrt{\frac{E_b}{N_0}}\right)$$

And for 16-PSK

$$p_b = \frac{1}{2}Q\left(0.552\sqrt{\frac{E_b}{N_0}}\right)$$

As M increases, we can observe that spectrum efficiency increases. But power efficiency reduces.

4.9 QUADRATURE AMPLITUDE MODULATION (QAM)

Figure 4.42 shows the constellation diagram for 16-ary PSK.

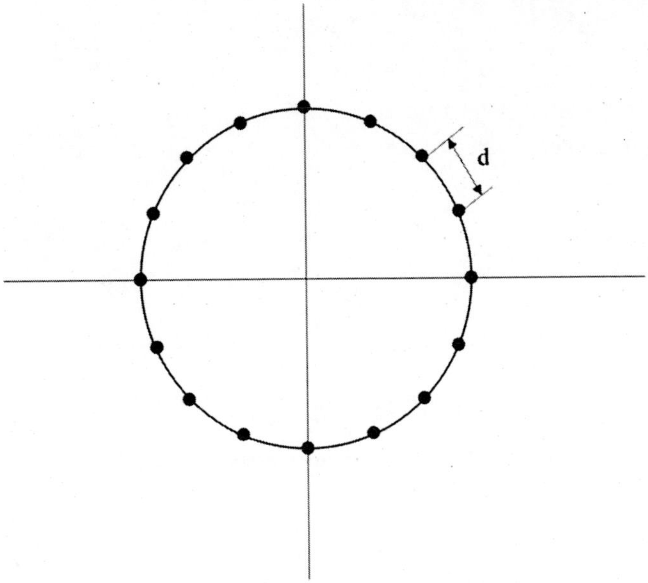

Fig. 4.42 Constellation diagram for 16-ary PSK

Here all 16 constellation points are distributed around the circumference of a circle and are therefore rather closely spaced. The bit error probability equation $P_b = Q\left(\frac{d}{2\sigma}\right)$ shows that the error depends on the distance between constellation points and hence this is undesirable.

A more effective distribution would be obtained by spreading the points across the centre of the diagram. Figure 4.43 shows a distribution of the 16 points on a rectangular grid, which achieves this.

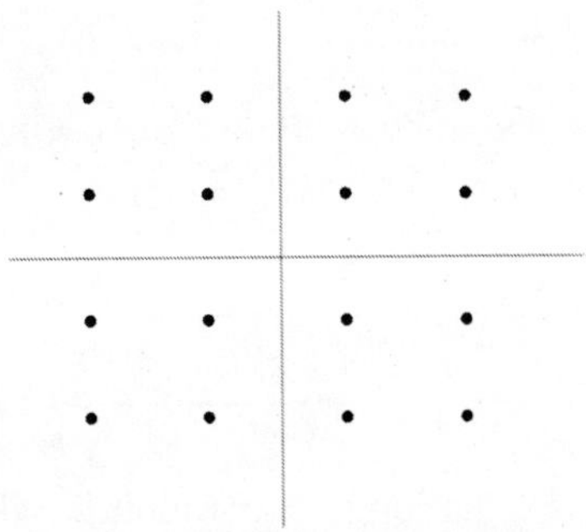

Fig. 4.43 16-QAM constellation diagram

Note that the mean square distance of points from the origin and hence the average signal power is the same in both cases. The minimum spacing between points, however is increased by a factor of approximately 1.6 in the latter constellation. This latter constellation is known as Quadrature Amplitude Modulation (QAM), because it may be formed by a form of four level amplitude modulation of the in-phase and quadrature-phase components of the signal separately. This may be mathematically expressed as,

$$d = a(2i - k + 1) + ja(2l - k + 1) \quad i, l = 0, 1, \ldots k - 1$$
$$k = \sqrt{M},\ M = 4, 16, 64, 256, \ldots \tag{4.82}$$

Where the spacing between constellation points is 2a.

Figure 4.44 shows the decision region of the constellation points labelled 1000 in the 16-QAM signal space diagram.

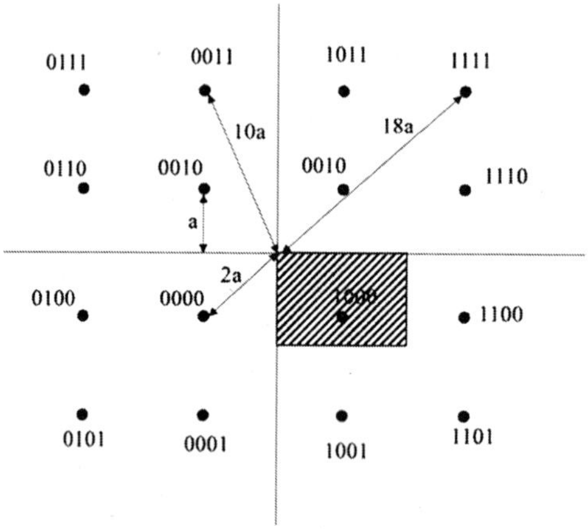

Fig. 4.44 Decision region for 16-QAM

This has four faces, since the point has four immediate neighbours at distance $d = 2a$. Hence the symbol error probability for this point is given by $4Q\left(\frac{d}{2a}\right)$. However, the points on the periphery of the constellation, there are fewer neighbours and hence the average symbol error probability is

$$P_e = (nn)_{avg}\, Q\left(\frac{d}{2\sigma}\right) P_e = (nn)_{avg}\, Q\left(\frac{a}{\sigma}\right) \tag{4.83}$$

Where the average number of immediate neighbours for 16-QAM

$$(nn)_{avg} = \frac{(4\times 4) + (8\times 3) + (4\times 2)}{16} = 3$$

In general

$$(nn)_{avg} = \frac{4\times(k-2)^2 + 8\times(k-2) + 8}{M}$$

For QAM constellation the power is no longer a constant for all points. The average power for 16 QAM is given by:

$$(avg)^2 = \frac{4\times 2a^2 + 8\times 10a^2 + 4\times 18a^2}{16} = 10a^2 \tag{4.84}$$

Thus for 16- QAM the symbol error probability is

$$P_e = 3Q\left(\frac{a}{\sigma}\right) = 3Q\left(\sqrt{\frac{(Avg)^2}{10\sigma^2}}\right) = 3Q\left(\sqrt{\frac{2E}{10N_0}}\right) \tag{4.85}$$

From the previous constellation diagram, we can notice that neighbouring labels differ only by one bit (Gray code) and therefore a symbol error will usually lead to one bit error out of four bits. Hence the BER:

$$P_b = \frac{3}{4}Q\left(\sqrt{\frac{2E}{10N_0}}\right) = \frac{3}{4}Q\left(\sqrt{\frac{4E_b}{4N_0}}\right) \tag{4.86}$$

The BER performance plot as shown in figure 4.45 tells that 16-QAM has an advantage of about 4dB compared with 16-PSK, which is due to the more even distribution of points and the resulting increased minimum distance between the constellation points.

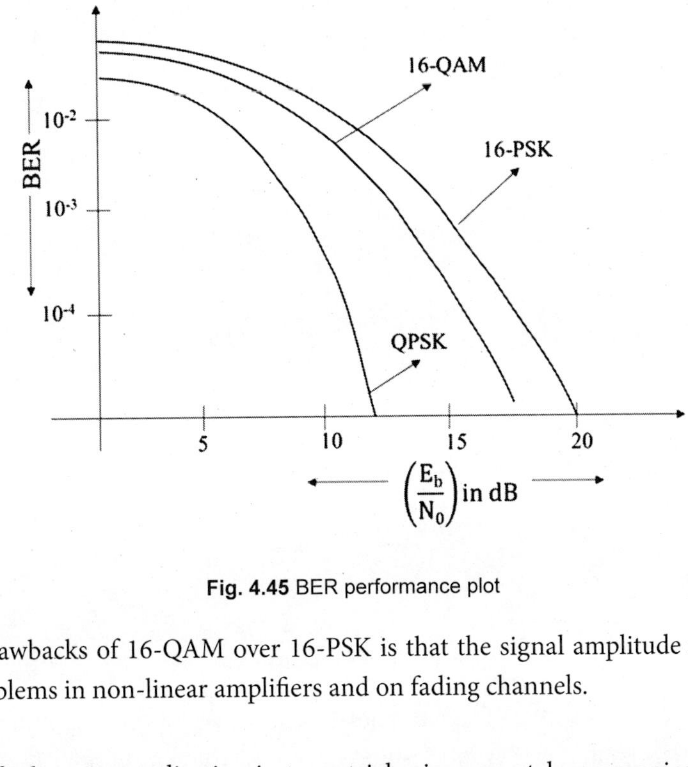

Fig. 4.45 BER performance plot

One of the drawbacks of 16-QAM over 16-PSK is that the signal amplitude now is varying. This could result in problems in non-linear amplifiers and on fading channels.

Applications:

M-ary QAM finds major application in terrestrial microwave telecommunications. These systems are required to transmit very high data rates in limited bandwidth and the power budget is not restrictive. Tall microwave towers are commonly used to prinvide a direct line of sight path, together with high gain dish antennas. Hence, they are bandwidth limited and bandwidth efficient modulation is highly desirable. For this reason, QAM modulation up to 256-QAM is widelt used and even higher levels have been proposed. The main difficulties experienced with higher order QAM is due to multipath effects, which give rise to occasional deep fades.

The new digital broadcast systems, both land and satellite are in general bandwidth limited because of high data rates required to supply hjgh quality broadcasr signals. Hence, the effieinct digitial modulation schemes like 64-QAM are used for this purpose.

4.10 MINIMUM SHIFT KEYING (MSK)

MSK is a non-linear binary modulation. Modulation can be achieved with binary FSK with modulation index h = 0.5. This results the power spectral density (PSD) with suppressed sidelobes and the most the modualted power is being concnetrated in main lobe only. This will result in spectrum efficient modulation scheme.

The value of h results in an interesting property of the effective constellation diagram, as we may see by considering the pahse change which occurs in the course of one bit period T_b:

$$\Delta\theta = \pm w_a T_b = h\pi = \frac{\pi}{2} \tag{4.87}$$

w_d is called frequency shift or frequency difference. Hence the constellation diagram observed at the end of each symbol period is as shown in figure 4.46 with $\pi/2$ shift between each constelaltion point.

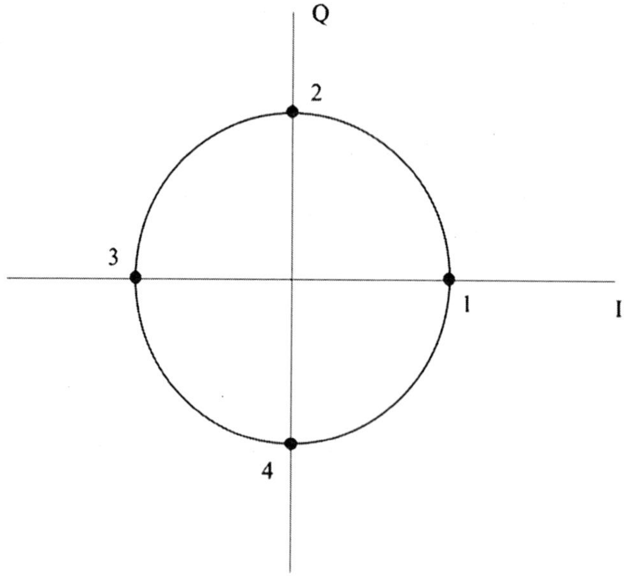

Fig. 4.46 Constellation diagram

Note that between symbols, phase changes linearly with time and the amplitude remains constant, so between symbols the signal moves evenly around the circle from one constellation point to another. We can also note that the signal never remains on the same constellation point: it moves to one of its neighbours. For example, from point 1 it will move to point 2 (for data '1') or 4 (for '0') then from point 2 to 3 or 1 etc.

The constellation closely resembles that of QPSK. This results in another interesting property. If we consider the I component amplitude as the signal moves from point 2 to 1 and then either back to 2 or to 4, we observe that it follows a half-sine function. Similarly, for the Q-component in moving from 1 to 2 to 3 (or back to 1). This suggests that the signal can be decomposed into the sum of time-shifted half sine pulses on I and Q with amplitudes ±1 depending on the data. In other words, it is effectively a linear modulation scheme with signalling filter has impulse response equal to half-sine pulse with two-bit duration.

In the receiver side, at the end of each bit interval, the demodulator must decide between the two opposite points of the constellation diagram, i.e it should effectively be regarded as tow interleaved constellations. Hence the BER performance is the same as that of BPSK (or QPSK) i.e,

$$P_e = Q\left(\sqrt{\frac{2E_b}{N_0}}\right) \tag{4.88}$$

One popular receiver diagram for MSK is mentioned in the figure 4.47.

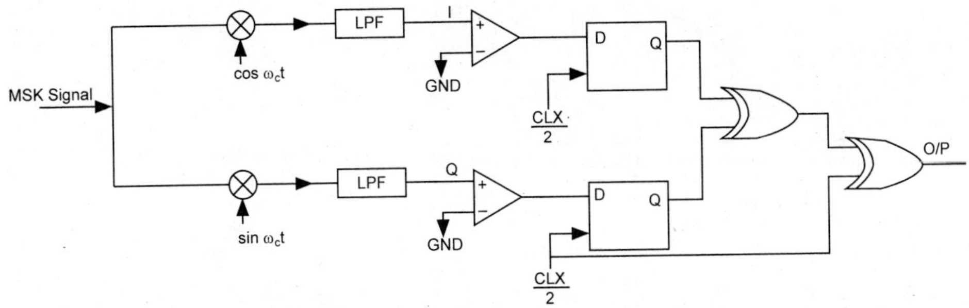

Fig. 4.47 MSK decoder circuit

Example 4.5: Consider a binary message stream 01001011101 is to be transmitted using MSK modualtion. Assume that carrier frequency is equal to data rate. Baseband pulse is assumed to Unipolar NRZ. Sketch inphase and quadratute waveforms. Finally show the wavefrom for MSK signal.

Solution:

Waveforms are as shown in figure 4.48.

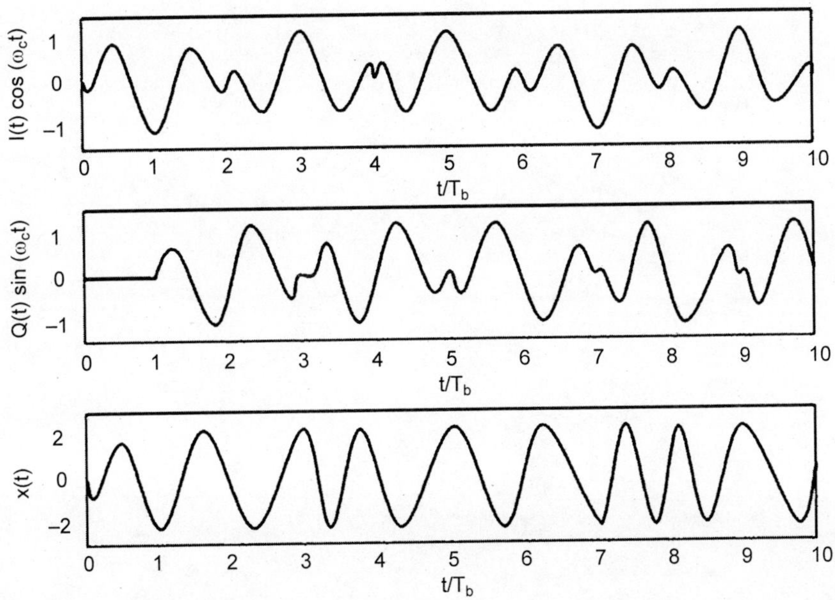

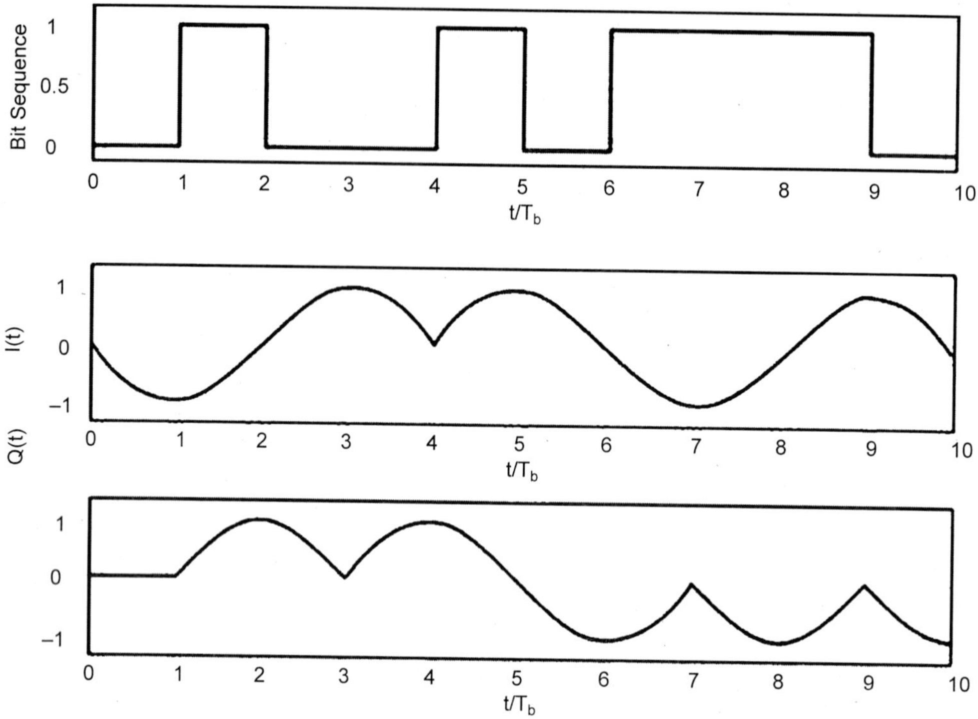

Fig. 4.48 MSK waveforms for example 4.5

UNIT SUMMARY

- A binary ASK signal is generated by sending a carrier signal $A_c\cos(2\pi f_c t)$, whenever the information bit is '1' and by sending a '0' if the information bit is '0'.
- ASK modulated signal is

$$s(t) = \sqrt{\frac{2}{T_b}} \cdot b(t) \cdot \cos(2\pi f_c t)$$

- The probability of error for an ASK system

$$P_e = \frac{1}{2} erfc\left\{\frac{1}{2\sqrt{2}} \cdot \sqrt{\frac{2P_s T}{N_0}}\right\} = \frac{1}{2} erfc\left\{\sqrt{\frac{P_s T}{4N_0}}\right\}$$

- In a BPSK scheme, a binary '1' is represented by a sinusoidal carrier of amplitude 'A', frequency 'f_c' with phase of 'ϕ_1' while a binary '0' by a sinusoidal carrier of amplitude of 'A', frequency 'f_c' with phase of ϕ_2.
- BPSK signal can be expressed as

$$s(t) = \begin{cases} A_c \cdot \cos(2\pi f_c t) \; for\ binary\ symbol\ 1 \\ A_c \cdot \cos(2\pi f_c t + \pi) \; for\ binary\ symbol\ 0 \end{cases}$$

- The PSD of a BPSK signal is then given by,

$$S_{BPSK}(f) = \frac{PT_b}{2}\left\{\left[\frac{\sin(\pi(f_0 - f)T_b}{\pi(f_0 - f)T_b}\right] + \left[\frac{\sin(\pi(f_0 + f)T_b}{\pi(f_0 + f)T_b}\right]^2\right\}$$

- The probability of error for an BPSK

$$P_e = \frac{1}{2} erfc\left(\sqrt{\frac{E_b}{N_0}}\right)$$

- In BFSK, the frequency of the carrier is changed with respect to the incoming data. Two signals, $s_1(t)$ and $s_2(t)$ are used in coherent BFSK systems. $s_1(t)$ is used to represent a '1' and $s_2(t)$ represents a symbol '0'.

$$s_1(t) = \sqrt{\frac{2E_b}{T_b}} \cos(2\pi f_1 t)$$

$$s_2(t) = \sqrt{\frac{2E_b}{T_b}} \cos(2\pi f_2 t)$$

- BW of BFSK = $2f_b + 2f_b = 4f_b$
- QPSK has twice the bandwidth efficiency of BPSK since 2 bits are transmitted in a single modulation symbol.
- The transmitted signal for a QPSK system can be written as

$$s_i(t) = \sqrt{\frac{2E}{T}} \cos\left[2\pi f_c t + (2i - 1)\frac{\pi}{4}\right]$$

- Bit error rate of QPSK is

$$BER = \frac{1}{2} erfc\left(\sqrt{\frac{E}{2N_0}}\right)$$

- DPSK, works as follows: If the present and previous binary data symbols are the same, phase 0⊠ is transmitted. If the present data symbols is opposite to the previous one, phase π is transmitted.
- In an offset QPSK modulation baseband quadra signal $Q(t)$ is delayed by T_b relative to inphase signal $I(t)$.
- The simplest way to increase the level of modulation is increasing M to generate QPSK to more than four constellation points. M- represents the number of symbols. This is then known as M-ary PSK, where M is a power of 2.
- BER for MPSK is

$$P_b = \frac{2}{k} Q\left(\sin\left(\frac{\pi}{M}\right)\sqrt{\frac{2kE_b}{N_0}}\right)$$

- BER for a QAM

$$P_b = \frac{3}{4} Q\left(\sqrt{\frac{2E}{10N_0}}\right) = \frac{3}{4} Q\left(\sqrt{\frac{4E_b}{4N_0}}\right)$$

- MSK or Minimum Shift Keying is a non-linear binary modulation. Modulation can be achieved with binary FSK with modulation index $h = 0.5$.
- BER for MSK

$$P_e = Q\left(\sqrt{\frac{2E_b}{N_0}}\right)$$

EXERCISE

Numerical Problems

1. If the input binary sequence is b(k)={-1,1,1,1,-1,-1,1,-1}, determine the transmitted phase sequence (show odd and even sequences) and also sketch the transmitted waveform for QPSK.
2. Consider a binary data stream 10011110011 is to be transmitted using DBPSK. Let $f_c = 2 \times R_b$ (where R_b is bit rate) and the baseband signal is unipolar NRZ. Sketch the waveforms at the output of differential encoder and modulator. Also show that the DBPSK detector can reconstructs the original information in the absence of noise.
3. Consider a binary data 1001010011011 is to be generated using OQPSK modulation. Assume that $f_c = R_b$ and the pulse shape is unipolar rectangular. Sketch the inphase, quadrature phase baseband signal and final OQPSK waveform.

4. Consider a message sequence 1011011010101. Sketch the 8-ary PSK modulated waveform assuming data sequence is unipolar NRZ.
5. Consider MSK modulation scheme is used to tranmsit a binary message 11010001011. Assume that carrier frequency is equal to data rate. Baseband pulse is assumed to be in Unipolar NRZ. Sketch inphase and quadratute waveforms. Also show MSK wavefrom.

Descriptive Type Questions

1. Derive the expression for probability of error in a BASK system.
2. With the help of a neat block diagram explain the generator and detector blocks of an BPSK modulation scheme.
3. Explain coherent and non-coherent detection of BFSK.
4. Explain the generation process of QPSK modulation scheme.
5. Explain MPSK in detail.
6. With the help of constellation diagram, explain the concept of decision region in 16-QAM.
7. Explain the decoding process of MSK.

Objective Type Questions

1. Bandwidth of a BPSK system is
   a. $2f_b$
   b. f_b
   c. $4f_b$
2. State True or false
   BFSK requires two basis functions.
3. The relationship between the bandwidths of BPSK and BFSK is
   a. BW (BFSK) = 2 × BW (BPSK)
   b. BW (BPSK) = 2 × BW (BFSK)
   c. BW (BFSK) = 2 × BW (BPSK)
   d. BW (BFSK) = BW (BPSK)
4. State True or false
   A coherent QPSK system achieves the same average probability of bit error as a coherent binary PSK system for the same bit rate and the same E/N_0 but uses only half the channel bandwidth.
5. State True or false
   Average error probability in a OQPSK system is as that of QPSK.

KNOW MORE

Jagadeesh Chandra Bose

Image Courtesy:

https://commons.wikimedia.org/wiki/File:J.C.Bose.JPG

Jagadeesh Chandra Bose was born on 30th November 1858 in Bengal presidency. He is known for his discoveries on plants, He invented a device called crescograph used to measure the growth of plants. He also has made remarkable contribution in the area of microwave radio research. He established Bose Institute in Kolkata in 1917. It is considered to be one of the oldest research institutions in India. He has in numerous awards and recognitions to his credit. He dies in the year 1937.

FURTHER READING

[1] Haykin, Simon. "Digital Communications", John Wiley, New York, 2001.

[2] Sklar, Bernad. "Digital Communication: Functions and Applications", Prenice Hall., 1988.

[3] K. Sam Shanmugam , « Digital and Analog Communication Systems», John Wiley, New York, 2006.

[4] M. Kulkarni and Farooq Husain, "Analog and Digital Communication Systems", Umesh Publications, New Delhi, 2005.

[5] K. N. Hari Bhat and D. Ganesh Rao, "Digital Communications", Third Edition, Pearson, 2012.

5 Information Theory

UNIT SPECIFICS

Through this unit we have discussed the following aspects:

- Definition of information content and measure of information.
- Average information content of a source (Entropy)
- Channels for communication
- Mutual Information of a channel
- Channel capacity theorem

RATIONALE

Till the recent past, information was considered to be an abstract quantity that cannot be measured. However, Shannon in his remarkable paper has given a mathematical structure to measure information. This chapter consists of two main parts. In the first half, we discuss the measure of information and average amount of information content by an information source. At the later part, we discuss on communication channels and the maximum rate at which information can be sent through a channel. This chapter lays a foundation for the study of information theory and coding.

PRE-REQUISITES

- Theory of Probabilities
- Basic Communication Systems

UNIT OUTCOMES

At the end of this unit the student will be able to

U5-O1: Determine the self-information content of message

U5-O2: Compute the entropy of a zero-memory source for the given source statistics

U5-O3: Define continuous and discrete communication channels

U5-O4: Explain the concepts of channel entropies and mutual information

U5-O5: Define channel capacity theorem

MAPPING OF UNIT OUTCOMES WITH COURSE OUTCOMES

Unit-5 Outcomes	EXPECTED MAPPING WITH COURSE OUTCOMES (1- Weak Correlation; 2- Medium correlation; 3- Strong Correlation)					
	CO 1	CO 2	CO 3	CO4	CO 5	CO 6
U5-O1	1	-	-	-	3	-
U5-O2	1	-	-	-	3	-
U5-O3	-	-	-	-	3	-
U5-O4	-	-	-	-	3	-
U5-O5	-	-	-	-	3	-

5. 1 INTRODUCTION

Today's world is world of information. Information is defined as any message or event. Until 1948, when Claude E. Shannon published his remarkable paper "Mathematical Theory on Communication" in Bell System Technical journal, information was considered to be an abstract entity which cannot be measured. Nevertheless, in his work, Shannon has given a strong mathematical base to measure and analyse information.

5.2 INFORMATION MEASURES

Let us consider the following two events:

- A few places in Japan experienced earthquake last night
- A few places of Karnataka experienced earthquake last night

Both statements given above represent an event of earthquake. However, it is evident that the amount of information conveyed by both statements is different. The event of earthquake is common in Japan and hence it conveys lesser amount of information as compared to the event of earthquake in Karnataka. Thus, we can conclude that the amount of information conveyed by a message or an event is dependent on the probability of occurrence of that event. The events that are more likely to occur convey less information and that are less likely occur convey more information.

Let I_k be the amount of information conveyed by a message or an event, say m_k. This information is termed as Self-information content of the message or event. Let p_k be the probability of occurrence of m_k. We can now list the facts related to self-information content of the message m_k.

- Self-information I_k is inversely proportional to p_k.

$$I_k \propto \frac{1}{p_k} \tag{5.1}$$

- Self-information cannot be negative. Nevertheless, it can be zero.
  That is
  $I_k \geq 0$ (5.2)
- Definite events convey no information. In other words,
  If $p_k = 1, I_k = 0$ (5.3)
- The amount of information conveyed collectively by two or more independent events is the sum of the self-information of the individual events.
  $I(m_i, m_j) = I_i + I_j$ (5.4)

The only mathematical operator satisfying all conditions from (5.1) to (5.4) is a Logarithmic operator.

Therefore, the self-information content of a message m_k, can be defined as

$$I_k = \log_r \left(\frac{1}{p_k} \right) units \quad (5.5)$$

The unit of self-information is dependent on the value of 'r', base of the logarithm used.

If 'r' = 2, unit is bits

If 'r' = e, unit is nats

And for 'r' = 10, unit is decits or Hatleys

For our entire discussion in this book, we restrict the value of 'r' to 2. Hence the unit for self-information considered in this book is bits.

Therefore (5.5) becomes

$$I_k = \log_2 \left(\frac{1}{p_k} \right) bits \quad (5.6)$$

Example 5.1: Consider an event of tossing a fair coin. What is the amount of information conveyed if the outcome is Head?

Solution:

As the coin is a fair coin, probability of getting a Head is equal to the probability of getting a tail = 0.5.

Therefore, self-information content is given by,

$$I_k = \log_2 \left(\frac{1}{p_k} \right) bits$$

$$I = \log_2 \left(\frac{1}{0.5} \right) = 1\, bits$$

Example 5.2: Consider a memoryless source emitting three symbols say, s_1,s_2 & s_3. Let the probabilities of occurrence of each of these symbols are 0.4, 0.5 and 0.1 respectively. Find the self-information contents of s_1,s_2 & s_3.

Solution:

Self-information content is given by,

Self-information content of

Self-information content of

Self-information content of

NOTE: It can be seen from this example that the event that is less likely occur conveys more information.

5.3 SHANNON ENTROPY

Shannon entropy or simply entropy gives a measure of average amount of information conveyed by a zero-memory source. It is also termed as average amount of uncertainty or average amount of surprise.

Consider a memoryless or a zero-memory source S. Let this source is capable of emitting 'q' possible symbols. Hence the source alphabet can be defined as

$$S = \{ s_1 , s_2, ...s_q \} \tag{5.7}$$

Scan here to know more

Let the probability of occurrences of these symbols be

$$P = \{ p_1, p_2 , ... p_q \} \tag{5.8}$$

Then, the entropy of this source can be mathematically defined as follows:

$$H(S) = \sum_{k=1}^{q} p_k \log_2\left(\frac{1}{p_k}\right) \text{ bits / message symbols} \tag{5.9}$$

5.3.1 Differential Entropy

The expression for the entropy given by (5.9) corresponds to discrete signals. Considering a continuous random variable 'X' with a probability density function . Then, we can define a differential entropy as follows:

$$h(X) = \int_{-\infty}^{\infty} P_X(x)\log_2\left(\frac{1}{P_X(x)}\right)dx \tag{5.10}$$

Example 5.3: For the source given in the example 5.2, find the entropy.

Solution:

Entropy of a zero-memory source is given by

$$H(S) = \sum_{k=1}^{q} p_k \log_2\left(\frac{1}{p_k}\right) \text{ bits / message symbols}$$

Given:

$$S = \{ s_1, s_2, s_3 \}$$

$$P = \{ 0.4,0.5,0.1 \}$$

Using these in the equation of entropy, we will get

$$H(S) = 0.4\log_2\left(\frac{1}{0.4}\right)+0.5\log_2\left(\frac{1}{0.5}\right)+0.1\log_2\left(\frac{1}{0.1}\right)=1.361\, bits/sym$$

Example 5.4: Repeat the previous example considering the source statistics as P = {0.4,0.3,0.3}

Solution:

Entropy of a zero-memory source is given by

$$H(S) = \sum_{k=1}^{q} p_k \log_2\left(\frac{1}{p_k}\right) \text{ bits / message symbols}$$

Given:

$$S = \{ s_1, s_2, s_3 \}$$

$$P = \{ 0.4,0.3,0.3 \}$$

Using these in the equation of entropy, we will get

$$H(S) = 0.4\log_2\left(\frac{1}{0.4}\right)+0.3\log_2\left(\frac{1}{0.3}\right)+0.3\log_2\left(\frac{1}{0.3}\right)=1.571\, bits/sym$$

Example 5.5: Repeat the previous example considering the source statistics as P = $\left\{\frac{1}{3}, \frac{1}{3}, \frac{1}{3}\right\}$

Solution:

Entropy of a zero-memory source is given by

$$H(S) = \sum_{k=1}^{q} p_k \log_2\left(\frac{1}{p_k}\right) \text{ bits / message symbols}$$

Given:

$$S = \{ s_1, s_2, s_3 \}$$

$$P = \left\{\frac{1}{3}, \frac{1}{3}, \frac{1}{3}\right\}$$

Using these in the equation of entropy, we will get

$$H(S) = \frac{1}{3}\log_2\left(\frac{1}{1/3}\right) + \frac{1}{3}\log_2\left(\frac{1}{1/3}\right) + \frac{1}{3}\log_2\left(\frac{1}{1/3}\right) = 1.585\, bits / sym$$

5.3.2 Properties of Entropy

From the examples 5.3, 5.4 and 5.5, it can be seen that closer the probabilities of individual symbols larger the value of the entropy. The value of the entropy will be maximum if all symbols are equally likely to occur. This is called as extremal property of entropy. The properties of entropy can be summarized as follows:

1. Entropy is a continuous function of probabilities.
2. Entropy is a symmetric function with respect to its arguments.
3. **Maximum Entropy:** Entropy attains its maxima when all probabilities are same and equal to

   $pk = \frac{1}{q}$ and is given by

   $H_{max} = \log_2 q$ bits / sym (5.11)

4. **Entropy of an extended source**: If the original source 'S' is extended to nth extension, then the entropy of the extended source is related to the entropy of the original source by the following relation:

   $H(S^n) = n \times H(S)$ (5.12)

5.4 COMMUNICATION CHANNELS

A channel is a medium through which the information is transmitted from source to the destination. A typical communication channel is shown in figure 5.1.

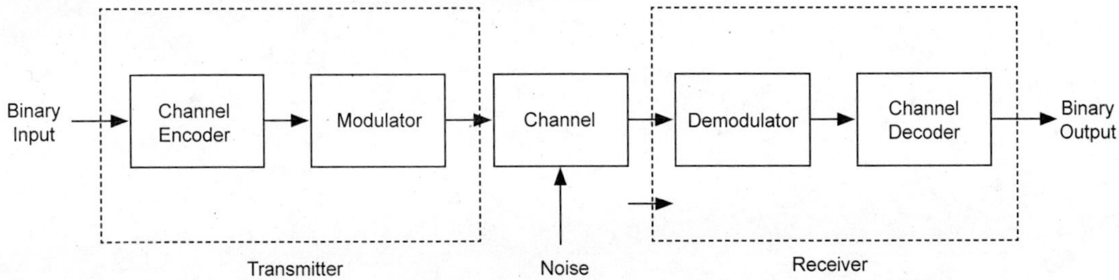

Fig. 5.1 Communication channel

5.4.1 Discrete Communication Channel

A channel is said to be a discrete communication channel it its input is coming from one of the 'r' possible symbols of the input alphabet and output is one of the 's' discrete symbols from the output alphabet.

For instance, consider a discrete communication channel whose input alphabet consists of 3 symbols given by:

$$X = \{x_1, x_2, x_3\}$$

Output of the channel is one of the 3 possible symbols from the following alphabet:

$$Y = \{y_1, y_2, y_3\}$$

Let the probability of receiving the symbol provided is transmitted into the channel be p $\left(y_1/x_1\right)$

Similarly, the probability of receiving the symbol provided is transmitted into the channel be p $\left(y_1/x_1\right)$ and so on.

Then the corresponding matrix that represents the channel is called as channel matrix and it is denoted by P $\left(Y/X\right)$ and it is given by,

$$\text{P}\left(Y/X\right) = \begin{bmatrix} p(y_1/x_1) & p(y_2/x_1) & p(y_3/x_1) \\ p(y_2/x_1) & p(y_2/x_2) & p(y_3/x_2) \\ p(y_3/x_1) & p(y_3/x_2) & p(y_3/x_3) \end{bmatrix} \tag{5.13}$$

The dimensions of the channel matrix is $r \times s$. Where 'r' indicates the number of possible input symbols (number of symbols in the input alphabet) and 's' indicates the number of symbols in the output alphabet of the channel. It is evident that the sum of all elements of a row in the channel matrix is always unity.

The channel can also be represented by its channel diagram. Pictorial representation of a channel matrix gives the channel diagram. The channel diagram representation of the discrete channel given in (5.13) is as shown in Figure 5.2.

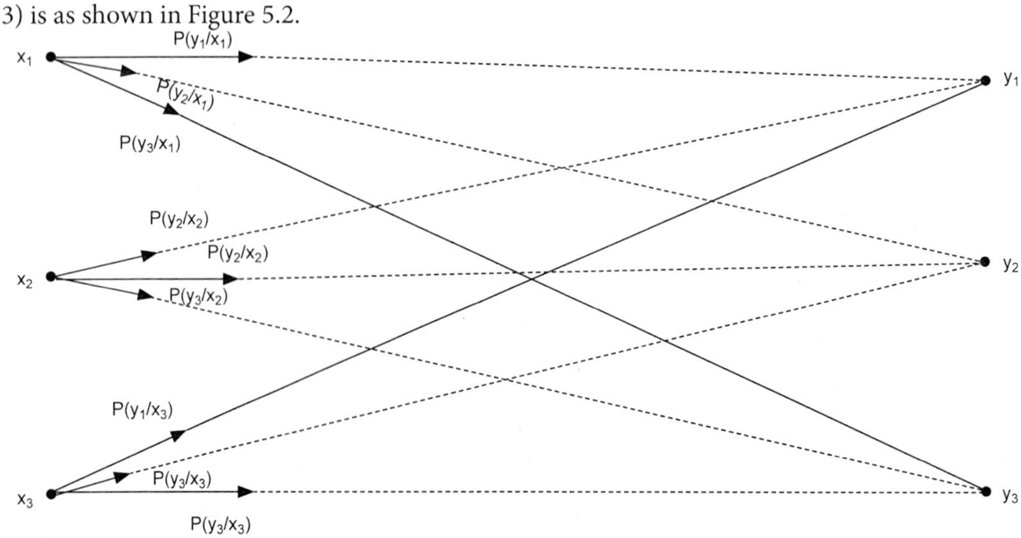

Fig. 5.2 Channel diagram representation of the channel

Consider the channel matrix as given in (5.13). Let the probabilities of the input to the channel be

$$P(X) = \{p(x_1), p(x_2)\, p(x_3)\} \tag{5.14}$$

We can now define another probability matrix for the channel called Joint Probability Matrix (JPM). This matrix represents the probability of being transmitted and being received. We can now write the JPM for the channel represented in (5.13) as follows:

$$P(X,Y) = P\left(Y/X\right) \times P(X) \tag{5.15}$$

It is to be noted that the multiplication here does not indicate the matrix multiplication, instead it is the multiplication of the input probabilities row wise to the channel matrix.

$$P(X,Y) = \begin{bmatrix} p(y_1/x_1)\times p(x_1) & p(y_2/x_1)\times p(x_1) & p(y_3/x_1)\times p(x_1) \\ p(y_2/x_1)\times p(x_2) & p(y_2/x_2)\times p(x_2) & p(y_3/x_2)\times p(x_2) \\ p(y_3/x_1)\times p(x_3) & p(y_3/x_2)\times p(x_3) & p(y_3/x_3)\times p(x_3) \end{bmatrix}$$

$$P(X,Y) = \begin{bmatrix} p(x_1, y_1) & p(x_1, y_2) & p(x_1, y_3) \\ p(x_2, y_1) & p(x_2, y_2) & p(x_2, y_3) \\ p(x_3, y_1) & p(x_3, y_2) & p(x_3, y_3) \end{bmatrix} \tag{5.16}$$

It is evident that if we add all elements a row of a JPM, we will get the respective input probability and if we add all elements of a particular column of a JPM, we will get the corresponding output probability.

$$\sum_{j=1}^{s} p(x_i, y_j) = p(x_i) \tag{5.17}$$

$$\sum_{i=1}^{r} p(x_i, y_j) = p(y_j) \tag{5.18}$$

Clearly

$$\sum_{i=1}^{r}\sum_{j=1}^{s} p(x_i, y_j) = 1 \tag{5.19}$$

Example 5.6: Consider a discrete communication channel with 3 inputs and 4 outputs. The incomplete channel matrix of that channel is as given below. Complete the channel matrix and also draw its channel diagram.

$$P(Y/X) = \begin{bmatrix} 0.5 & 0.2 & * & 0.1 \\ 0.4 & 0.1 & 0.5 & * \\ 0.3 & * & 0.2 & 0.4 \end{bmatrix}$$

Solution:

We know that the sum of all elements of a row of a channel matrix is unity.

Therefore, the third element of first row, $p(y_3/x_1)$ is given by

$p(y_3/x_1) = 1 - (0.5 + 0.2 + 0.1) = 0.2$

Similarly

$p(y_4/x_2) = 1 - (0.3 + 0.2 + 0.4) = 0.1$

And

$p(^{y_2}/x_3) = 1 - (0.3 + 0.2 + 0.4) = 0.1$

Therefore, the complete channel matrix is given by,

$$P(^{Y}/_{X}) = \begin{bmatrix} 0.5 & 0.2 & 0.2 & 0.1 \\ 0.4 & 0.1 & 0.5 & 0 \\ 0.3 & 0.1 & 0.2 & 0.4 \end{bmatrix}$$

The channel diagram is shown in figure 5.3

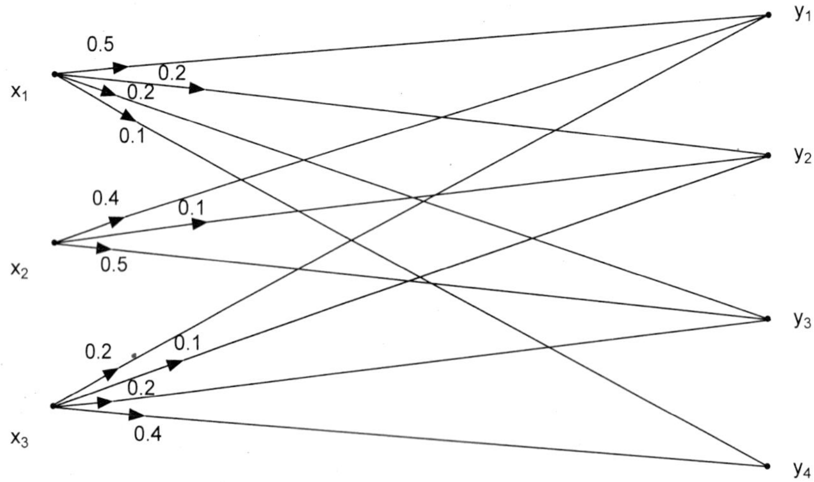

Fig. 5.3 Channel diagram for the channel given in example 5.6

5.4.2 Binary Communication Channel

A channel that has exactly two input and two output lines is called as a binary channel. The channel matrix for a binary channel is as given below:

$$P(^{Y}/_{X}) = \begin{bmatrix} p & 1-p \\ 1-q & q \end{bmatrix} \tag{5.20}$$

Where 'p' is the probability of a symbol '0' is transmitted and is received and 'q' is the probability of a symbol '1' is transmitted and '1' is received.

Fig. 5.4 represents a typical binary communication channel.

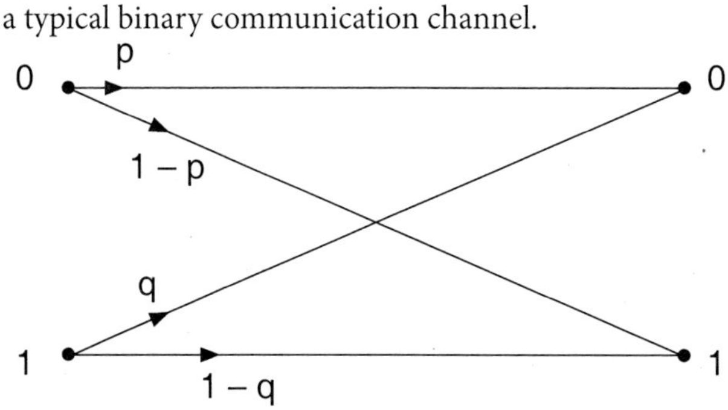

Fig. 5.4 Binary communication channel

A binary channel is said to be a binary symmetric channel if the probabilities and are equal.

$$P\left(Y/X\right) = \begin{bmatrix} p & 1-p \\ 1-p & p \end{bmatrix} \tag{5.21}$$

5.5 CHANNEL ENTROPIES

The following entropies can be defined for a discrete communication channel.

Entropy at the input, H (X)

The entropy $H(X)$ denotes the average amount of uncertainty as observed at the input side of the channel. The entropy at the input side of the channel can be obtained if the probabilities of input symbols are known. It is defined as

$$H(X) = \sum_{i=1}^{r} p(x_i)\log_2\left(\frac{1}{p(x_i)}\right) bits/sym \tag{5.22}$$

Entropy at the output, H (Y)

The entropy $H(X,Y)$ denotes the average amount of uncertainty as observed at the output side of the channel. The entropy at the output side of the channel can be obtained if the probabilities of output symbols are known. It is defined as

$$H(Y) = \sum_{j=1}^{s} p(y_j)\log_2\left(\frac{1}{p(y_j)}\right) bits/sym \tag{5.22}$$

Joint Entropy H (X ,Y)

The entropy denotes the average amount of uncertainty as observed jointly at the input and output sides of the channel. To find the joint entropy of the channel, we need the joint probability matrix, . It is defined as

$$H(X,Y) = \sum_{i=1}^{r}\sum_{j=1}^{s} p(x_i, y_j)\log_2\left(\frac{1}{p(x_i, y_j)}\right) bits/sym \tag{5.23}$$

Conditional Entropy H (X/Y)

The conditional entropy $H(X/Y)$ denotes the average amount of uncertainty at the input provided the output is known. It is defined as

$$H(X/Y) = \sum_{i=1}^{r}\sum_{j=1}^{s} p(x_i, y_j)\log_2\left(\frac{1}{p(x_i, y_j)}\right) bits/sym \tag{5.24}$$

Conditional Entropy H (Y/X)

The conditional entropy $H(Y/X)$ denotes the average amount of uncertainty at the output provided the input is known. It is defined as

$$H(Y/X) = \sum_{i=1}^{r}\sum_{j=1}^{s} p(x_i, y_j)\log_2\frac{1}{p(y_j/x_i)} bits/sym \tag{5.25}$$

It can be noted that

$$H(X,Y) = H(X/Y) + H(Y) = H(Y/X) + H(X) \tag{5.26}$$

The proof for (5.26) is out of the scope of this book.

Example 5.7: Consider a binary symmetric channel with a transition probability of = 0.8. The inputs are equally likely to occur. Draw the channel diagram. Also find:

i. H (X)

ii. H (Y)

iii. H (X , Y)

iv. H (X / Y)

v. H (Y / X)

Solution:

The channel diagram is as shown in figure 5.5

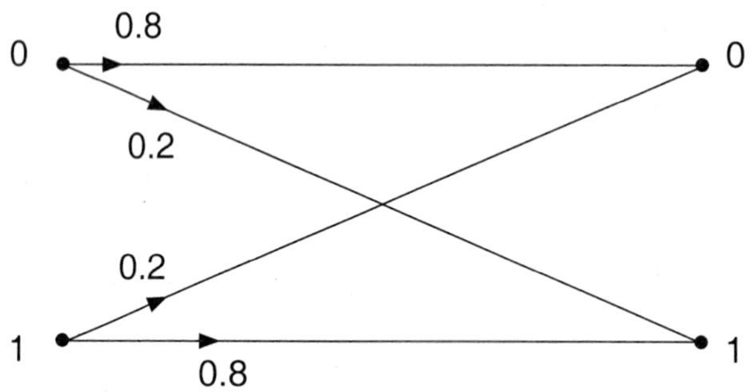

Fig. 5.5 Channel diagram

As input symbols are equally likely to occur.

$$P(X) = \{0.5, 0.5\}$$

$$H(X) = \sum_{i=1}^{r} p(x_1)\log_2\left(\frac{1}{p(x_i)}\right) bits/sym$$

$$= 0.5\log_2\frac{1}{0.5} + 0.5\log_2\frac{1}{0.5} = 1\, bits/sym$$

To find $H(Y)$ we need $P(Y)$. The probabilities $P(Y)$ by adding the elements column-wise in a JPM. To find JPM, consider the relation

$$P(X, Y) = P(^{Y}/_{X}) \times P(X)$$

$$P(^{Y}/_{X}) = \begin{bmatrix} 0.8 & 0.2 \\ 0.2 & 0.8 \end{bmatrix}$$

Therefore $P(X, Y)$ becomes

$$P(X, Y) = \begin{bmatrix} 0.4 & 0.1 \\ 0.1 & 0.4 \end{bmatrix}$$

Output probabilities can be obtained by adding the elements column-wise.

$$P(Y) = \{0.5, 0.5\}$$

$$H(Y) = \sum_{j=1}^{s} p(y_j)\log_2\left(\frac{1}{p(y_j)}\right) \textit{ bits/sym}$$

$$= 0.5\log_2\frac{1}{0.5} + 0.5\log_2\frac{1}{0.5} = 1 \textit{ bits/sym}$$

The joint entropy can be obtained as follows

$$H(X, Y) = \sum_{i=1}^{r}\sum_{j=1}^{s} p(x_i, y_j)\log_2\frac{1}{p(x_i, y_j)} \textit{ bits/sym}$$

$$= 0.4\log_2\frac{1}{0.4} + 0.1\log_2\frac{1}{0.1} + 0.1\log_2\frac{1}{0.1} + 0.4\log_2\frac{1}{0.4} = 1.7219 \textit{ bits/sym}$$

The conditional entropy $H(Y/X)$ can be calculated as follows

$$H(X, Y) = \sum_{i=1}^{r}\sum_{j=1}^{s} p(x_i, y_j)\log_2\frac{1}{p(y_j/x_i)} \textit{ bits/sym}$$

$$= 0.4\log_2\frac{1}{0.8} + 0.1\log_2\frac{1}{0.2} + 0.2\log_2\frac{1}{0.2} + 0.4\log_2\frac{1}{0.8} = 0.7219 \textit{ bits/sym}$$

It can also obtained using the relation

$(X, Y) = H(Y/X) + H(X)$

$H(Y/X) = H(X, Y) - H(X) = 0.7219$ *bits/sym*

Similarly,

$H(X/Y) = H(X,Y) - H(Y) = 0.7219$ *bits/sym*

5.6 MUTUAL INFORMATION

We know that $H(X)$ denotes the average amount of uncertainty at the input side of the channel and $H(X/Y)$ is the average amount of uncertainty at the input side of the channel provided we have observed the output of the channel. Clearly, $H(X/Y) \le H(X)$. The difference $H(X) - H(X/Y)$ is called as the mutual information of the channel.

Therefore, mutual information of a communication channel $I(X, Y)$ is defined as:

$$I(X,Y) = H(X) - H(X/Y) \tag{5.27}$$

From (5.26)

$$H(X,Y) = H(X,Y) - H(Y)$$

Using this in (5.27) we get,

$$I(X,Y) = H(X) + H(Y) - H(X,Y) \tag{5.28}$$

The relations of mutual information and channel entropies can be collectively represented by a graphical representation as shown in Figure 5.6.

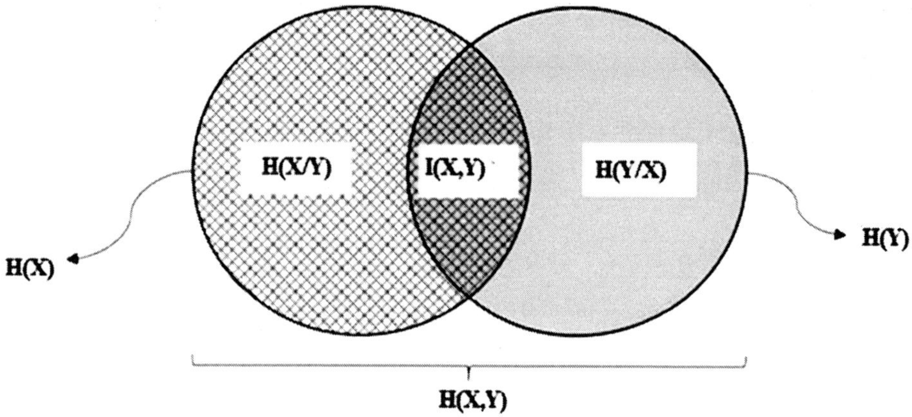

Fig. 5.6 Mutual information and channel entropies

5.6.1 Properties of Mutual Information

1. Mutual Information $I(X, Y)$ is symmetric with respect to its arguments
$$I(X, Y) = I(Y, X) \tag{5.29}$$
2. Mutual Information $I(X, Y)$ is always non negative
$$I(X,Y) > 0 \tag{5.30}$$
3. As a continuation of property (1), mutual information can also be represented as
$$I(X,Y) = H(Y) - H(Y/X) \tag{5.31}$$

5.6.2 Average Rate of Information Transmission

The average rate of information at the information source is given by,

$$R_t = H(X) \times r_s \tag{5.32}$$

Where r_s is the symbol rate at the source.

However, when the information is sent over a channel, we lose some information due to noise in the channel and hence the actual information received at the receiver will be less than $H(X)$ and it is denoted by the mutual information of the channel $I(X, Y)$.

Thus, the average rate of information transmitted over a discrete communication channel can be now defined as,

$$R_{tr} = I(X,Y) \times r_s = [H(X) - H(X/Y)] \times r_s$$

$$= [H(Y) - H(Y/X)] \times r_s \tag{5.33}$$

Example 5.8: Determine the mutual information and average rate of information transmission for the discrete communication channel shown in Figure 5.7. Consider the probabilities of the input symbols as $P(X) = \left\{\frac{1}{3}, \frac{2}{3}\right\}$. Consider the symbol rate $r_s = 1000$ symbols / sec.

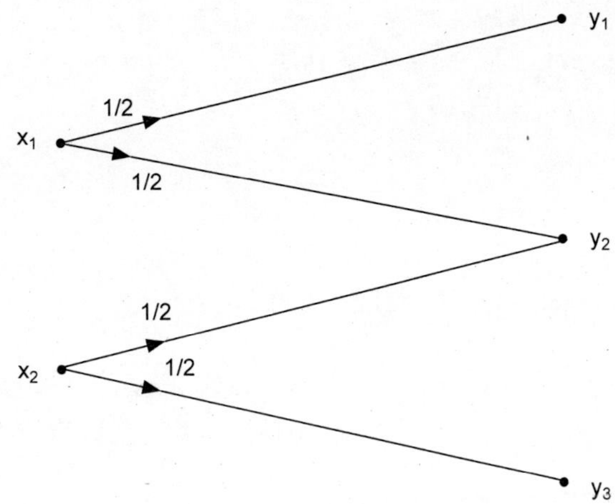

Fig. 5.7 Communication channel

Solution:

The channel matrix for the channel given in Figure 5.7 is as given below:

$$P\left(Y/X\right) = \begin{bmatrix} \frac{1}{2} & \frac{1}{2} & 0 \\ 0 & \frac{1}{2} & \frac{1}{2} \end{bmatrix}$$

Given

$$P(X) = \left\{\frac{1}{3}, \frac{2}{3}\right\}$$

$$P(X, Y) = P(Y/X) \times P(X)$$

$$P(X, Y) = \begin{bmatrix} \frac{1}{6} & \frac{1}{6} & 0 \\ 0 & \frac{1}{3} & \frac{1}{3} \end{bmatrix}$$

We can now find the probabilities of the output symbols by adding the elements of the JPM column-wise.

$$P(Y) = \left\{\frac{1}{6}, \frac{1}{2}, \frac{1}{3}\right\}$$

$$H(Y) = \sum_{j=1}^{s} p(y_j)\log_2\left(\frac{1}{p(y_j)}\right) \textit{bits/sym}$$

$$= \frac{1}{6}\log_2\frac{1}{1/6} + \frac{1}{2}\log_2\frac{1}{1/2} + \frac{1}{3}\log_2\frac{1}{1/3} = 1.46\ \textit{bits/sym}$$

$$H(Y/X) = \sum_{i=1}^{r}\sum_{j=1}^{s} p(x_i, y_j)\log_2 \frac{1}{p(y_j/x_i)} \; bits/sym$$

$$= \frac{1}{2}\log_2 \frac{1}{1/6} + \frac{1}{2}\log_2 \frac{1}{1/6} + \frac{1}{2}\log_2 \frac{1}{1/3} + \frac{1}{2}\log_2 \frac{1}{1/3} = 4.16 \; bits/sym$$

$$I(X, Y) = H(Y) - H\left(\frac{Y}{X}\right) = 2.7 \; bits/sym$$

Average rate of information transmitted over a discrete communication channel is given by,

$$R_{tr} = I(X, Y) \times r_s = 2700 \text{ bps}$$

5.7 CHANNEL CAPACITY

The capacity of a discrete communication channel is defined as the maximum rate at which the information is transmitted over the channel. Shannon in his channel capacity theorem states that as long as the rate at which the information is transmitted over a channel is less than or equal to the capacity of the channel, we can achieve smaller bit errors by using suitable channel coding techniques. On the other hand, if the rate at which the information transmitted over the channel is greater than the capacity of the channel, then the error free transmission is not possible irrespective of the channel coding techniques being used.

The capacity of the channel is therefore defined as

$$C = Max\,\{R_{tr}\} = \text{Max}\,\{\text{I}(X,Y) \times r_s = \text{Max}\,\{\text{I}(X,Y)\} \times r_s \tag{5.34}$$

5.7.1 Channel Capacity using Muroga's Method

This is applicable to find the channel capacity of channels with equal number of input and output symbols. Consider a channel with three input and three output symbols. Let the corresponding channel matrix be

$$P\,(Y/X) = \begin{bmatrix} p_{11} & p_{12} & p_{13} \\ p_{21} & p_{22} & p_{23} \\ p_{31} & p_{32} & p_{33} \end{bmatrix} \tag{5.35}$$

The following equations can be defined

$$\begin{bmatrix} p_{11} & p_{12} & p_{13} \\ p_{21} & p_{22} & p_{23} \\ p_{31} & p_{32} & p_{33} \end{bmatrix} \begin{bmatrix} Q_1 \\ Q_2 \\ Q_3 \end{bmatrix} = \begin{bmatrix} p_{11}\log_2 p_{11} + p_{12}\log_2 p_{12} + p_{13}\log_2 p_{13} \\ p_{21}\log_2 p_{21} + p_{22}\log_2 p_{22} + p_{23}\log_2 p_{23} \\ p_{31}\log_2 p_{31} + p_{32}\log_2 p_{32} + p_{33}\log_2 p_{33} \end{bmatrix} \tag{5.36}$$

The unknowns Q_1, Q_2 and Q3 can be obtained by solving the simultaneous equations obtained by expanding (5.36).

Finally, the capacity of the channel can be obtained as follows:

$$C = \log_2 [\, 2^{Q_1} + 2^{Q_2} + 2^{Q_3}] \tag{5.37}$$

Example 5.9: Find the capacity of the channel using Muroga's method whose channel matrix is given by

$$P(Y/X) = \begin{bmatrix} 0.5 & 0 & 0.5 \\ 0.1 & 0.7 & 0.2 \\ 0 & 0.4 & 0.6 \end{bmatrix}$$

Solution:

Using Muroga's method, the simultaneous equations can be constructed as follows:

$$\begin{bmatrix} 0.5 & 0 & 0.5 \\ 0.1 & 0.7 & 0.2 \\ 0 & 0.4 & 0.6 \end{bmatrix}\begin{bmatrix} Q_1 \\ Q_2 \\ Q_3 \end{bmatrix} = \begin{bmatrix} 0.5\log_2 0.5 + 0.5\log_2 0.5 \\ 0.1\log_2 0.1 + 0.7\log_2 0.7 + 0.2\log_2 0.2 \\ 0.4\log_2 0.4 + 0.6\log_2 0.6 \end{bmatrix}$$

$$0.5\, Q_1 + 0.5\, Q_3 = -1$$

$$0.1\, Q_1 + 0.7\, Q_2 + 0.2\, Q_3 = -1.157$$

$$0.4\, Q_2 + 0.6\, Q_3 = -0.971$$

Solving the equations, we will get

$$Q_1 = -1.219$$

$$Q_2 = -1.255$$

$$Q_3 = -0.781$$

The capacity of the channel is given by

$$C = \log_2 [2^{Q1} + 2^{Q2} + 2^{Q3}]$$

$$C = \log_2 [2^{-1.219} + 2^{-1.255} + 2^{-0.781}] = 0.516 \text{ bits / sym}$$

5.8 CONTINUOUS CHANNELS

In general, any information that is to be conveyed is analog in nature. A part of the communication system where the input and output of the channel belong to continuous sample space is called continuous channel. It can be noted that the various entropies defined for discrete communication channel can be defined for continuous channels as well in the similar manner. The summations are replaced with the integrations in the continuous time channel entropies and mutual information.

5.9 SHANNON HARTLEY LAW

Consider a bandlimited Gaussian channel in the presence of AWGN. Shannon Hartley theorem for the channel capacity states that the capacity of a bandlimited Gaussian channel with AWGN is given by

$$C = B \log 2 \left[1 + \frac{S}{N}\right] \; bits / sec \tag{5.38}$$

Scan here to know more

Where

B is the bandwidth of the channel in Hz

S is the signal power in Watts

N is the noise power in Watts

Example 5.10: Find the capacity of the Gaussian channel with a bandwidth of 10 MHz and the SNR is 10 dB.

Solution:

From Shannon-Hartley theorem

$$C = B \log_2 \left[1+\frac{S}{N}\right] \; bits / sec$$

$$\left[\frac{S}{N}\right]_{dB} = 10 \; dB$$

$$10 \log_{10} \frac{S}{N} = 10 \; dB$$

$$\frac{S}{N} = 10$$

$$C = B \log_2 \left[1+\frac{S}{N}\right] bits/\sec$$

$$C = 10 \times 10^6 \times \log_2 [\, 1 + 10 \,] = 34.56 \times 10^6 \text{ bits/sec}$$

UNIT SUMMARY

- The self-information content of a message m_k, can be defined as

  $I_k = \log_r \left(\frac{1}{p_k}\right)$ bits

- The entropy of a source is defined as follows:

  $H(S) = \sum_{k=1}^{q} p_k \log_2 \left(\frac{1}{p_k}\right)$ bits/message symbols

- Differential entropy can be defined as follows:

  $h(X) = \int_{-\infty}^{\infty} p_X(x) \log_2 \left(\frac{1}{p_X(x)}\right) dx$

- Properties of Entropy
  - Entropy is a continuous function of probabilities.
  - Entropy is a symmetric function with respect to its arguments.
  - Maximum Entropy: Entropy attains its maxima when all probabilities are same and equal to $p_k = \frac{1}{q}$ and is given by

    $H_{max} = \log_2 q$ bits/sym

- Entropy of an extended source: If the original source 'S' is extended to n^{th} extension, then the entropy of the extended source is related to the entropy of the original source by the following relation:

  $H(S^n) = n \times H(S)$

- Channel matrix for a discrete communication channel is given by,

$$P\left(\frac{Y}{X}\right)=\begin{bmatrix} p\left(\frac{y_1}{x_1}\right) & p\left(\frac{y_2}{x_1}\right) & p\left(\frac{y_3}{x_1}\right) \\ p\left(\frac{y_2}{x_1}\right) & p\left(\frac{y_2}{x_2}\right) & p\left(\frac{y_3}{x_2}\right) \\ p\left(\frac{y_3}{x_1}\right) & p\left(\frac{y_3}{x_2}\right) & p\left(\frac{y_3}{x_3}\right) \end{bmatrix}$$

- Joint Probability Matrix is given by
  $P(X, Y) = P(Y/X) \times P(X)$
- A channel that has exactly two input and two output lines is called as a binary channel.
- Entropy at the input, H(X): The entropy H(X) denotes the average amount of uncertainty as observed at the input side of the channel.

$$H(X) = \sum_{i=1}^{r} p(x_i)\log_2\left(\frac{1}{p(x_i)}\right) \text{bits/sym}$$

- Entropy at the output, H(Y): The entropy H(Y) denotes the average amount of uncertainty as observed at the output side of the channel.

$$H(Y) = \sum_{j=1}^{s} p(y_j)\log_2\left(\frac{1}{p(y_j)}\right) \text{bits/sym}$$

- Joint Entropy H(X, Y): The entropy H(X, Y) denotes the average amount of uncertainty as observed jointly at the input and output sides of the channel.

$$H(X, Y) = \sum_{i=1}^{r}\sum_{j=1}^{s} p(x_i, y_j)\log_2 \frac{1}{p(x_i, y_j)} \text{ bits/sym}$$

- Conditional Entropy H(X/Y): The conditional entropy H(X/Y) denotes the average amount of uncertainty at the input provided the output is known.

$$H(X, Y) = \sum_{i=1}^{r}\sum_{j=1}^{s} p(x_i, y_j)\log_2 \frac{1}{p(x_i, y_j)} \text{ bits/sym}$$

- Conditional Entropy H(Y/X): The conditional entropy H(Y/X) denotes the average amount of uncertainty at the output provided the input is known.

$$H(X, Y) = \sum_{i=1}^{r}\sum_{j=1}^{s} p(x_i, y_j)\log_2 \frac{1}{p(y_i, x_j)} \text{ bits/sym}$$

- Mutual information of a communication channel I(X, Y) is defined as:
  $I(X, Y) = H(X) - H(X/Y)$
- Mutual Information I(X, Y) is symmetric with respect to its arguments
  $I(X, Y) = I(Y, X)$
- Mutual Information I(X, Y) is always non negative
  $I(X, Y) \geq 0$
- Mutual information can also be represented as
  $I(X, Y) = H(Y) - H(Y/X)$

- Average rate of information transmitted over a discrete communication channel can be now defined as,

  $R_{tr} = I(X, Y) \times r_s = [H(X) - H(X/Y)] \times r_s = [H(Y) - H(Y/X)] \times r_s$

- The capacity of a discrete communication channel is defined as the maximum rate at which the information is transmitted over the channel.

  $C = \text{Max}\{R_{tr}\} = \text{Max}\{I(X, Y) \times r_s\} = \text{Max}\{I(X,Y)\} \times r_s$

- Shannon Hartley theorem for the channel capacity states that the capacity of a bandlimited Gaussian channel with AWGN is given by

  $$C = B\log_2\left[1+\frac{S}{N}\right] \text{bits/sec}$$

EXERCISE

Numerical Problems

1. Let 'X' and 'Y' are two independent variables that can take a value of either '1' or '-1'. If P(X='1') = P(X= '-1') = P(Y='1') = P(Y='-1') =0.5. Find the average amount of information conveyed by the function (X+Y).
2. Consider that a bin has 6 Red balls, 4 Blue balls and 5 Green balls. In each event a ball is picked from the bin and its color is observed and the ball is kept back to the bin. The balls are only distinguishable with their colors.
   i. What is the information conveyed if the ball picked is Blue?
   ii. What is the entropy of the event?
   iii. If one of the balls can be recolored, which ball is to be recolored to which color so as to achieve maximum entropy?
3. Consider that a professor has called students for an extra class. There were four free class rooms R1, R2, R3 and R4 where the class can be engaged. The probability of the professor taking class in any of these class rooms is the same. Calculate the amount of information conveyed by the event, if the class is taken at R3?
4. Consider a memoryless source emitting three symbols say, s_1, s_2, s_3. Let the probabilities of occurrence of each of these symbols are 0.3, 0.4 and 0.3 respectively. Find the self- information contents of s_1, s_2 & s_3. Also find the entropy of the source.
5. Consider a discrete communication channel with 3 inputs and 4 outputs. The incomplete channel matrix of that channel is as given below. Complete the channel matrix and also draw its channel diagram.

$$P(Y/X) = \begin{bmatrix} * & 0 & 0.8 & 0.1 \\ 0.5 & * & 0.3 & 0.2 \\ 0.1 & 0.6 & 0.2 & * \end{bmatrix}$$

6. Consider a channel with the following joint probability matrix.

$$P\,(Y\,/X) = \begin{bmatrix} 0.2 & 0.1 & 0.1 \\ 0.1 & 0.1 & 0.1 \\ 0.1 & 0 & 0.2 \end{bmatrix}$$

Find

i. $H(X)$

ii. $H(Y)$

iii. $H(X,Y)$

iv. $H(X/Y)$

v. $H(Y/X)$

vi. $I(X,Y)$

7. Find the capacity of a binary symmetric channel with an error probability of 0.1.
8. Find the capacity of the Gaussian channel with a bandwidth of 50 MHz and the SNR is 20 dB.

Descriptive Type Questions

1. Justify the use of logarithm function to find the self-information of a message.
2. Define entropy of a zero-memory source. List the properties of entropy.
3. With help of an example explain how a channel can be represented with its channel matrix and channel diagram.
4. What is mutual information? List the properties of mutual information.
5. Explain how the capacity of the channel can be obtained using Muroga's method?
6. State Shannon-Hartley theorem to find the channel capacity.

Objective Type Questions

1. The information I in bits contained in a message with probability of occurrence given P is.

a. $\log 2\ \frac{1}{P}$

b. $\log_2 P$

c. $\log_2 \frac{1}{2P}$

d. $P\,\mathrm{lof}_2 \frac{1}{P}$

2. State True or False: Entropy is also called as average amount of surprise.

a. True

b. False

3. State True or False: Self information can take negative values.
   a. True
   b. False
4. The self-information of definite event is
   a. 0
   b. 1
   c. Infinite
   d. Cannot be determined
5. The entropy for the event of a fair coin tossing is
   a. 0.811 bit/sym
   b. 1.5 bit/sym
   c. 0.5 bit/sym
   d. 1 bit/sym
6. For which value(s) of p is the binary entropy function H(p) maximized?
   a. 0
   b. 0.5
   c. 1
   d. 0.25 and 0.75
7. Which one of the following statements is not true?
   a. Efficiency of a source would be maximum if all its symbols are equiprobable.
   b. The average rate of information conveyed by a source is directly proportional to its entropy.
   c. Self-information content of a message can be negative.
   d. Entropy of a source is upper bounded by $\log_2 M$ bits/sym, where M is the total number of symbols emitted by the source.
8. Sum of all elements of a channel matrix is 1.
   a. True
   b. False
9. The maximum rate of error free data transmission is upper bounded by the channel capacity.
   a. True
   b. False
10. Measure of the average uncertainty about the channel input after the channel output has been observed is given by
    a. H(Y/X)
    b. H(X/Y)
    c. H(X, Y)
    d. I(X, Y)
11. The sum of all elements of a row of the matrix P(Y/X) is always unity
    a. True
    b. False
12. What is the channel matrix for a Binary Symmetric Channel with the error probability of 0.4.
    a. $\begin{bmatrix} 0.6 & 0.4 \\ 0.6 & 0.4 \end{bmatrix}$
    b. $\begin{bmatrix} 0.6 & 0.4 \\ 0.4 & 0.6 \end{bmatrix}$
    c. $\begin{bmatrix} 0.4 & 0.6 \\ 0.6 & 0.4 \end{bmatrix}$
    d. $\begin{bmatrix} 0.4 & 0.6 \\ 0.4 & 0.6 \end{bmatrix}$

KNOW MORE

Claude Shannon

Image Courtesy:
https://commons.wikimedia.org/wiki/File:ClaudeShannon_MFO3807.jpg

Claude Elwood Shannon (April 30, 1916 – February 24, 2001), "The Father of Information Theory" was an American engineer. At the age of 21 doing his masters at MIT, he wrote a thesis giving an insight into the usage of Boolean concepts in solving electromechanical problems. He also has contributed a lot in the field of cryptanalysis during World War II. He had two Bachelor degrees, one in electrical engineering and the other in mathematics. His paper "A Mathematical Theory of Communication" which was published in two parts of the Bell System Technical Journal is considered to be one of the most promising works in the field of information theory.

A MATHEMATICAL THEORY OF COMMUNICATION

By C. E. SHANNON

INTRODUCTION

The recent development of various methods of modulation such as PCM and PPM which exchange bandwidth for signal-to-noise ratio has intensified the interest in a general theory of communication. A basis for such a theory is contained in the important papers of Nyquist and Hartley on this subject. In the present paper we will extend the theory to include a number of new factors, in particular the effect of noise in the channel, and the savings possible due to the statistical structure of the original message and due to the nature of the final destination of the information.

The fundamental problem of communication is that of reproducing at one point either exactly or ap-proximately a message selected at another point. Frequently the messages have meaning, that is they refer to or are correlated according to some system with certain physical or conceptual entities. These semantic aspects of communication are irrelevant to the engineering problem. The significant aspect is that the actual message is one selected from a set of possible messages. The system must be designed to operate for each possible selection, not just the one which will actually be chosen since this is unknown at the time of design.

If the number of messages in the set is finite then this number or any monotonic function of this number can be regarded as a measure of the information produced when one message is chosen from the set, all choices being equally likely. As was pointed out by Hartley the most natural choice is the logarithmic function. Although this definition must be generalized considerably when we consider the influence of the statistics of the message and when we have a continuous range of messages, we will in all cases use an essentially logarithmic measure.

The logarithmic measure is more convenient for various reasons:

1. It is practically more useful. Parameters of engineering importance such as time, bandwidth, number of relays, etc., tend to vary linearly with the logarithm of the number of possibilities. For example, adding one relay to a group doubles the number of possible states of the relays. It adds I to the base 2 logarithm of this number. Doubling the time roughly squares the number of possible messages, or doubles the logarithm, etc.
2. It is nearer to our intuitive feeling as to the proper measure. This is closely related to (1) since we in-tuitively measures entities by linear comparison with common standards. One feels, for example, that two punched cards should have twice the capacity of one for information storage, and two identical channels twice the capacity of one for transmitting information.
3. It is mathematically more suitable. Many of the limiting operations are simple in terms of the loga-rithm but would require clumsy restatement in terms of the number of possibilities.

The choice of a logarithmic base corresponds to the choice of a unit for measuring information. If the base 2 is used the resulting units may be called binary digits, or more briefly bits, a word suggested by J. W. Tukey. A device with two stable positions, such as a relay or a flip-flop circuit, can store one bit of information. N such devices can store N bits, since the total number of possible states is 2^N and $\log_2 2^N = N$. If the base 10 is used the units may be called decimal digits. Since

$$\log_2 M = \log_{10} M / \log_{10} 2$$
$$= 3.32 \log_{10} M.$$

Nyquist, H., "Certain Factors Affecting Telegraph Speed." Bell System Technical Journal. April 1924, p. 324, "Certain Topics in Telegraph Transmision Theory." ALEE Truns 47. April 1928, p. 617.

Hartley, R. V. L. "Transmision of Information, Bell System Technical Journal, July 1928, p. 535.

FURTHER READING

[1] M. Kulkarni and K. S. Shivaprakasha, "Information Theory and Coding", Wiley (India), 2015.

[2] Ranjan Bose, "Information Theory Coding and Cryptography", Tata McGraw Hill, 2007.

[3] Haykin, Simon. "Digital Communications", John Wiley, New York, 2001.

[4] Sklar, Bernad. "Digital Communication: Functions and Applications", Prenice Hall., 1988.

[5] K. Sam Shanmugam , " Digital and Analog Communication Systems", John Wiley, New York, 2006.

[6] M. Kulkarni and Farooq Husain, "Analog and Digital Communication Systems", Umesh Publications, New Delhi, 2005.

6 Coding Techniques

UNIT SPECIFICS

Through this unit we have discussed the following aspects:

- Define linear block codes
- Encoding and decoding process for a given data using linear block code
- Define and distinguish soft and hard decision decoding
- Explain Hamming codes, RS codes and Concatenated codes
- Appreciate the concept of convolution codes. Explain different encoding and decoding techniques of convolution codes
- Detail the concept of LDPC and Turbo codes

RATIONALE

One of the major advantages of digital communication is that the digital communication systems are more immune to noise. In other words, the reconstruction of information can be better performed in digital communication systems over analog communication. In order to perform error detection and correction, a few parity bits are to be introduced in the message sequence. This process of calculated addition of redundancy facilitating the receiver to perform error detection and corrections is called as error control coding. This unit gives an insight into a few channel coding techniques used in digital communication systems.

PRE-REQUISITES

- Linear Algebra
- Basic Communication Systems

UNIT OUTCOMES

At the end of this unit the student will be able to

U6-O1. Determine the codewords for a given linear block code

U6-O2. Compute error detecting and correcting capabilities of a given linear block code

U-O3. Explain Hamming, RS and concatenated codes

U-O4. Determine the codewords for a given data using convolution codes

U-O5. Decode the given convolution code sequence using Viterbi algorithm

U-O6. Explain LDPC and Turbo codes

MAPPING OF UNIT OUTCOMES WITH COURSE OUTCOMES

Unit-6 Outcomes	EXPECTED MAPPING WITH COURSE OUTCOMES (1- Weak Correlation; 2- Medium correlation; 3- Strong Correlation)					
	CO 1	CO 2	CO 3	CO4	CO 5	CO 6
U6-O1		1	-	-	3	-
U6-O2		-	-	-	3	-
U6-O3		-	-	-	3	-
U6-O4		-	-	-	3	-
U7-O5		-	-	-	3	-

6.1 INTRODUCTION

Advancements in the performances of information and storage systems are becoming important in the modern era of communication. In his phenomenal work, Shannon has suggested that by employing proper encoding technique, one can achieve a better performance in storage and information communication systems, without compromising the rate of information transmission. In this unit we will discuss various classes of encoding and decoding techniques used to perform error detection and error correction operations. The computational blocks performing these tasks are called channel encoders and channel decoders and process is known as error control coding.

6.2 RATIOANLE FOR ERROR CONTROL CODING

Data being transmitted over a channel is likely to get corrupted due to the presence of noise during communication. Thus, there has to be a proper mechanism being devised to detect the error in the received sequence.

In order to understand the principle of channel coding, consider a scenario where the information source is capable of generating four symbols say A,B,C and D. Let the source encoder uses a fixed length encoding scheme and the code words be

$A - 0\,0$

$B - 0\,1$

$C - 1\,0$

$D - 1\,1$

Please note that the same table is to be used at the receiver for decoding operation. Consider that the following message is to be transmitted to the receiver.

ABADDAC

The corresponding bit sequence being transmitted is

00 01 00 11 11 00 10

Let us assume that the noise present in the channel has corrupted 3rd, 7th and 10th bits of the code sequence. Therefore, the received sequence is

00 11 00 01 10 00 10

The receiver now performs the decoding operation considering two bits at a time. As the first two bits are '00', the receiver refers to the code table and decodes this sequence as '*A*'. Next two bits are

'11' (though the transmitted bits were '01'). In this case despite the presence of error, receiver could not realize this and it incorrectly decodes the sequence as . Similarly, the other symbols are decoded.

The decoded information will be,

ADABCAC

The three-bit errors resulted in incorrect decoding of 3 symbols. The reason behind receiver not detecting the errors in the received sequence is that there was no redundancy. All combinations of two-bit sequences were valid code vectors. In other words, each error has changed one valid code vector into another valid code vector. Thus, receiver could not distinguish a genuine vector with the erroneous one.

We can overcome this shortcoming by introducing a parity in the code vector for each of the symbols. Let us assume for even parity and the third bit in every code is chosen appropriately such that the number of ones in the code vector is even. The modified code vectors for the example considered are as follows:

$A - 0\,0\,0$

$B - 0\,1\,1$

$C - 1\,0\,1$

$D - 1\,1\,0$

Now consider the same message

ABADDAC

The corresponding bit sequence being transmitted is

000 011 000 110 110 000 101

Considering 3rd, 7th and 10th being erroneous as in the previous case, the received vector becomes,

001 011 100 010 110 000 101

The decoding at the receiver follows the same procedure, except that it takes 3 bits at a time. The first three bits are and it does not correspond to any of the valid code vector in the table. Thus, the receiver can make out that atleast one bit in this code vector is corrupted. Likewise it can properly detect the error for other two cases as well.

It can be noted that out of eight possible 3-bit combinations, only four combinations are valid code vectors. Hence if the receiver receives any of the four unused combinations, it can detect the presence of error. It is also worth noting at this point that if an error pattern converts a valid code vector into another valid code vector, then the error can not be detected. It is obvious that more the number of parity bits added, better will be the error detecting capability of the code.

Thus, an error control coding can be defined as a procedure of adding redundant bits, also called as parity bits or check bits through mathematical calculations so as to facilitate the receiver to detect the presence of error(s) in the received sequence. A more sophisticated code can also enable the receiver to correct the error(s) to some extent.

6.3 TYPES OF CHANNEL CODES

Error control codes or channel codes are classified into two broad categories. Namely,

- Block Codes
- Convolution Codes

Block Codes: In this case, the channel encoder takes 'k' bit information at once and generates a code vector of length 'n' bits by introducing '$n - k$' parity bits. They are represented by a two-tuple notation . (n,k).

Convolution Codes: Convolution codes take the input in a continuous manner and generate the output. One of the major differences between block codes and convolution codes is that the output of the block codes depends only on the present data block. Whereas, convolution codes depend on previous input bits as well. In other words, convolution coders possess memory.

6.4 LINEAR BLOCK CODE

Linear block codes are a class of block codes where the linear combination of two or more valid code vectors would also result in a valid code vector. Like any other block code, an (n,k) linear block code takes 'k' bits of information at once and generates an 'n' bit code vector by introducing an $(n - k)$ bits of parity.

The block diagram representation of a general (n,k) linear block code is as shown in figure 6.1

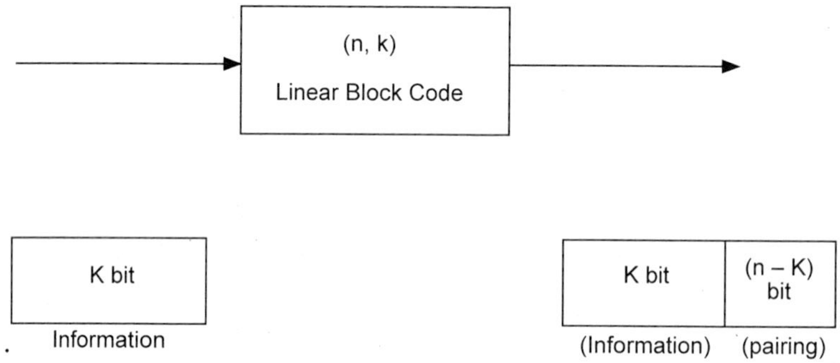

Scan here to know more

Fig. 6.1 A general block diagram of an linear block code

The codes of type as depicted in figure 6.1 are called systematic codes as we can separate data and parity bits in the code vector. Please note that we are restricting our discussions to systematic codes only.

6.4.1 Generator Matrix

The code vector for an (n, k) linear block code can be obtained from the following relation

$$C = D \times G \quad 6.1)$$

Where

C is the code vector of length 'n' bits.

D is the message vector of length 'k' bits.

G is the generator matrix of dimension $k \times n$.

The general structure of the generator matrix is as follows:

$$G = [I_k : P] \quad (6.2)$$

Where

I_k is the Identity matrix of dimension $k \times k$.

P is the Parity matrix of dimension $k \times (n - k)$.

Example 6.1: Consider a (6, 3) Linear Block Code with the following generator matrix.

$$G = \begin{bmatrix} 100101 \\ 010011 \\ 001111 \end{bmatrix}$$

Find all possible code vectors.

Solution: As the value of $k = 3$. The number of possible valid data combinations is $2^3 = 8$.

Code vector can be determined considering equation (6.1)

$$C = D \times G$$

For the data $D = 0\ 0\ 0$, $C = [0\ 0\ 0]\begin{bmatrix}100101\\010011\\001111\end{bmatrix} = [0\ 0\ 0\ 0\ 0\ 0]$

For the data $D = 0\ 0\ 1$, $C = [\ 0\ 0\ 1]\begin{bmatrix}100101\\010011\\001111\end{bmatrix} = [0\ 0\ 1\ 1\ 1\ 1]$

For the data $D = 0\ 1\ 0$, $C = [\ 0\ 1\ 0]\begin{bmatrix}100101\\010011\\001111\end{bmatrix} = [0\ 1\ 0\ 0\ 1\ 1]$

Similarly, the code vectors for other five combinations can be obtained.

Thus, all possible valid code vectors are:

Data	Code Vector
0 0 0	[0 0 0 0 0 0]
0 0 1	[0 0 1 1 1 1]
0 1 0	[0 1 0 0 1 1]
0 1 1	[0 1 1 1 0 0]
1 0 0	[1 0 0 1 0 1]
1 0 1	[1 0 1 0 1 0]
1 1 0	[1 1 0 1 1 0]
1 1 1	[1 1 1 0 0 1]

6.4.2 Parity Check Matrix (H)

For a given generator matrix G, we can define another matrix of dimension $(n-k) \times n$ called as parity check matrix denoted by H.

The parity check matrix H can be defined as

$$H = [P^T : I_{n-k}] \tag{6.3}$$

where

P^T is the transpose of the parity matrix of dimension $(n - k) \times k$

I_{n-k} is the identity matrix of dimension $(n - k) \times (n - k)$

It is to be noted that the product of generator matrix with the transpose of the parity check matrix is always zero.

That is

$$GH^T = 0 \tag{6.4}$$

Example 6.2: Find the parity check matrix for the generator matrix given in example 6.1. Also verify that $GH^T = 0$.

Solution: The parity check matrix is given by

$$H = [P^T : I_{n-k}]$$

The given generator matrix is

$$G = \begin{bmatrix} 100101 \\ 010011 \\ 001111 \end{bmatrix}$$

The parity matrix P can be extracted from the generator matrix as follows:

$$P = \begin{bmatrix} 101 \\ 011 \\ 111 \end{bmatrix}$$

Therefore, the parity check matrix is given by,

$$H = \begin{bmatrix} 101100 \\ 011010 \\ 111001 \end{bmatrix}$$

$$GH^T = \begin{bmatrix} 100101 \\ 010011 \\ 001111 \end{bmatrix} \times \begin{bmatrix} 100 \\ 010 \\ 001 \\ 101 \\ 011 \\ 111 \end{bmatrix} = \begin{bmatrix} 000 \\ 000 \\ 000 \end{bmatrix}$$

6.4.3 Syndrome Calculation

Like how a generator matrix is used at the encoder side to find the code vectors for the data sequences, at the decoder side, parity check matrix is used for detection and correction of errors. In order to perform this task, a parameter called syndrome is computed at the receiver.

Let us consider an (n,k) linear block code with 'C' being the transmitted vector and 'R' is the received vector. Assume that an error pattern 'E' had affected the transmitted signal during communication.

Therefore,

$$R = C + E \tag{6.5}$$

It is to be noted that as the addition represented in equation (6.5) is over binary, it is basically an EXOR operation being performed.

The syndrome S can be now computed as follows:

$$S = RH^T \tag{6.6}$$

Using equation (6.5) in equation (6.6),

$$S = (C + E)\ H^T$$

$$S = CH^T + EH^T \qquad 6.7)$$

We know that

$$C = DG$$

Therefore equation (6.7) becomes

$$S = DGH^T + EH^T \tag{6.8}$$

But from equation (6.4)

$$GH^T = 0$$

Therefore, the first term of the RHS of equation (6.8) is zero. Thus, the simplified expression for the syndrome becomes,

$$S = EH^T \tag{6.9}$$

From equation (6.9) it is clear that the syndrome is dependent only on the error pattern and thus if there are no errors introduced during transmission, i.e. $E = 0$, the syndrome will be zero.

To summarize, the procedure to detect the presence of error can be given as follows:

- Consider the received vector R.
- Compute the syndrome using the relation
  $S = RH^T$
- If the value of the syndrome is non zero then the received vector is erroneous. If the syndrome obtained is zero then either the received vector is error free or the error pattern has converted one valid code vector into another valid code vector.

Syndrome calculation for an (n,k) linear block code also facilitates the correction of single bit errors. The procedure to detect the location of the error in the received vector is as follows:

- If the syndrome is non zero, the received vector is erroneous.
- To locate the position of the error, compare the syndrome with the rows of matrix. To whichever the row it is matching, the corresponding bit from the left in the received vector is erroneous. It is because of the fact that and the syndrome will be the corresponding row in the matrix based on the error bit from the left as indicated by the error vector
- Once the error is located, the correction can be made by just inverting the error bit in the received vector.

Please note that the procedure detailed above can be used to correct only single bit errors.

Example 6.3: For the given (6, 3) linear block code in example 3.1, find the syndromes for the following received vectors:

i. $R_1 = 001000$

ii. $R_2 = 011111$

iii. $R_3 = 111101$

iv. $R_4 = 110110$

Also, correct the single bit errors if any.

Solution:

The generator matrix for the given problem is

$$G = \begin{bmatrix} 100101 \\ 010011 \\ 001111 \end{bmatrix}$$

And the parity check matrix is given by,

$$H = \begin{bmatrix} 101100 \\ 011010 \\ 111001 \end{bmatrix}$$

Syndrome can be computed using the relation,

$$S = RH^T$$

i.

$$R_1 = 001000$$

$$S_1 = R_1H^T$$

$$S_1 = [001000] \times \begin{bmatrix} 100 \\ 010 \\ 001 \\ 101 \\ 011 \\ 111 \end{bmatrix} = [001]$$

As the syndrome is non zero, the received vector is erroneous. And the syndrome obtained is matching to the third row of the H^T matrix. Therefore, third bit from the left in the received vector is erroneous.

Therefore, the corrected vector is

$$R'_1 = 000000$$

It can be verified from example 3.1 that the vector $[000000]$ is a valid code vector and $[001000]$ is not.

ii.

$$R_2 = 01111$$

$$S_2 = R_2H^T$$

$$S_1 = [011111] \times \begin{bmatrix} 100 \\ 010 \\ 001 \\ 101 \\ 011 \\ 111 \end{bmatrix} = [010]$$

As the syndrome is non zero, the received vector is erroneous and the syndrome obtained is matching to the second row of the H^T matrix. Therefore, second bit from the left in the received vector is erroneous.

Therefore, the corrected vector is

$$R'_2 = 001111$$

iii.

$$R_3 = 111101$$

$$S_3 = R_3H^T$$

$$S_3 = [111101] \times \begin{bmatrix} 100 \\ 010 \\ 001 \\ 101 \\ 011 \\ 111 \end{bmatrix} = [010]$$

As the syndrome is non zero, the received vector is erroneous. And the syndrome obtained is matching to the fourth row of the H^T matrix. Therefore, fourth bit from the left in the received vector is erroneous.

Therefore, the corrected vector is

$$R'_3 = 111001$$

iv. $$R_4 = 110110$$

$$S_4 = R_4 H^T$$

$$S_4 = [110110] \times \begin{bmatrix} 100 \\ 010 \\ 001 \\ 101 \\ 011 \\ 111 \end{bmatrix} = [000]$$

As the syndrome is zero, the received vector is error free.

Please note that a zero syndrome can also indicate the presence of an undetectable error.

6.4.4 Error Detecting and Correcting Capabilities of a Linear Block Code

As discussed in the previous sections, receiver can detect the presence of error in the received sequence as long as the error pattern has not converted a valid code vector into another valid code vector. We can now formally define the error detecting and correcting capabilities of a Linear Block Code.

In order to do so, we need to define the a few distance parameters of a linear block codes as given below:

i. *Hamming Distance:*

Hamming distance is defined between the two code vectors. It is defined as the number of bit positions in which two code vectors differ.

Example: Consider $C_1 = 001101$ and $C_2 = 101011$. The code vectors C_1 and C_2 are different in 1st, 4th and 5th bit positions.

Therefore, $d(C_1, C_2) = 3$

ii. *Hamming Weight, HW :*

Hamming weight of a code vector is defined as the number of non-zero elements in it. For a binary code vector, it is defined as the number of $1's$ present in the code vector.

Example: Consider $C_3 = 101101$. It has four 1's.

Therefore, $H_W(C_3) = 4$

iii. *Minimum Hamming Distance, d_{min}*:

The minimum Hamming distance of an (n,k) linear block code is defined as the smallest Hamming distance between any two code vectors of the code. It can be noted that the minimum Hamming distance is also equal to the smallest Hamming weight of a non-zero code vector. However, the proof is out of the scope of this book.

We can now define the error detecting and error correcting capabilities of a linear block code as follows:

$$\text{Error Detecting Capability} = d_{min} - 1 \tag{6.10}$$

$$\text{Error Correcting Capability} = \left\lfloor \frac{d_{\min} - 1}{2} \right\rfloor \tag{6.11}$$

Where [⋯] denotes the previous integer value if the value is a fraction.

Example 6.4: For the given (6, 3) linear block code in example 3.1, find the error detecting and correcting capabilities of the code.

Solution:

We already have calculated all possible valid code vectors in Example 6.1. To find the error detecting and correcting capabilities of the code, we need to find the value of Hamming weights of all non-zero code vectors.

The following table gives the Hamming weights of all non-zero code vectors.

Data	Code Vector	Hamming Weight
0 0 0	[0 0 0 0 0 0]	-
0 0 1	[0 0 1 1 1 1]	4
0 1 0	[0 1 0 0 1 1]	3
0 1 1	[0 1 1 1 0 0]	3
1 0 0	[1 0 0 1 0 1]	3
1 0 1	[1 0 1 0 1 0]	3
1 1 0	[1 1 0 1 1 0]	4
1 1 1	[1 1 1 0 0 1]	4

The minimum amongst all Hamming weights is '3'. Therefore $d_{min} = 3$.

Error Detecting Capability = $d_{min} - 1 = 3 - 1 = 2$

$$\text{Error Correcting Capability} = \left\lfloor \frac{d_{\min} - 1}{2} \right\rfloor = \left\lfloor \frac{3-1}{2} \right\rfloor = 1$$

Therefore, the given equation (6, 3) linear block code is capable of correcting all errors upto 2 bits and can correct all single bit errors.

Example 6.5 : Consider a (7, 4) Linear Block Code with the Generator matrix given by,

$$G = \begin{bmatrix} 1000111 \\ 0100011 \\ 0010101 \\ 0001110 \end{bmatrix}$$

(a) Find all possible code vectors.
(b) Find the parity check matrix of this code.
(c) Find the error detecting and correcting capabilities of the code.

Solution:

(a) We can find all possible code vectors using the relation
$C = D \times G$

For the data $D = 0\,0\,0\,0$, $C = [0\,0\,0\,0] \begin{bmatrix} 1000111 \\ 0100011 \\ 0010101 \\ 0001110 \end{bmatrix} = [0\,0\,0\,0\,0\,0\,0]$

For the data $D = 0\,0\,0\,1$, $C = [0\,0\,0\,1] \begin{bmatrix} 1000111 \\ 0100011 \\ 0010101 \\ 0001110 \end{bmatrix} = [0\,0\,0\,1\,1\,1\,0]$

For the data $D = 0\,0\,1\,0$, $C = [0\,0\,1\,0] \begin{bmatrix} 1000111 \\ 0100011 \\ 0010101 \\ 0001110 \end{bmatrix} = [0\,0\,1\,0\,1\,0\,1]$

For the data $D = 0\,0\,1\,1$, $C = [0\,0\,1\,1] \begin{bmatrix} 1000111 \\ 0100011 \\ 0010101 \\ 0001110 \end{bmatrix} = [0\,0\,1\,1\,0\,1\,1]$

Similarly, the code vectors for other combinations can be obtained.

Thus, all possible valid code vectors are:

Data	Code Vector	Hamming Weight
0	0 0 0 0 0 0 0	-
0 0 0 1	0 0 0 1 1 1 0	3
0 0 1 0	0 0 1 0 1 0 1	3

0 0 1 1	0 0 1 1 0 1 1	4
0 1 0 0	0 1 0 0 0 1 1	3
0 1 0 1	0 1 0 1 1 0 1	4
0 1 1 0	0 1 1 0 1 1 0	4
0 1 1 1	0 1 1 1 0 0 0	3
1 0 0 0	1 0 0 0 1 1 1	4
1 0 0 1	1 0 0 1 0 0 1	3
1 0 1 0	1 0 1 0 0 1 0	3
1 0 1 1	1 0 1 1 1 0 0	4
1 1 0 0	1 1 0 0 1 0 0	3
1 1 0 1	1 1 0 1 0 1 0	4
1 1 1 0	1 1 1 0 0 0 1	4
1 1 1 1	1 1 1 1 1 1 1	7

(b) The minimum amongst all Hamming weights is '3'. Therefore $d_{\min} = 3$.

Error Detecting Capability = $d_{\min} - 1 = 3 - 1 = 2$

Error Correcting Capability = $\left\lfloor \frac{d_{\min} - 1}{2} \right\rfloor \left\lfloor \frac{3-1}{2} \right\rfloor = 1$

6.5 BOUNDS ON (N,K) LINEAR BLOCK CODES

6.5.1 Singleton Bound

In an (n, k) linear binary block code, let A (n, d_{min}) denotes the maximum number of binary block codes of length 'n' and minimum Hamming distance 'd_{min}'. Then the Singleton bound can be defined as

$$|A\,(n, d_{\min})| \le 2^{n - d_{min} + 1} \tag{6.12}$$

Where [⋯] denotes the cardinality of the set $A(n, d_{min})$.

We know that the number of possible valid code vectors for an (n, k) linear binary block codes is 2^k. Therefore,

$$|A\,(n, d_{min})| = 2^k$$

Using this in (6.12),

$$2^k \le 2^{(n - dmin + 1)}$$

$$\Rightarrow \quad k \le n - d_{min} + 1$$

Or

$$d_{min} \le n - k + 1 \tag{6.13}$$

6.5.2 Hamming Bound

The number of distinct possible syndromes for an (n, k) linear block code should be at least equal to number of possible correctable error patterns. Therefore, if an (n, k) linear block code is capable of correcting 't' bit errors, then

$$2^{n-k} \geq \sum_{i=0}^{t} C_i^n \tag{6.14}$$

The above inequality is called as Hamming bound. All (n, k) linear block codes satisfy relation as shown in equation (6.14). Codes for which the inequality given in (6.14) turns out to be an equality are called perfect codes.

6.5.3 Gilbert–Varshamov (GV) Bound

In an (n, k) linear binary block code, let $A(n, d_{\min})$ denotes the maximum number of binary block codes of length 'n' and minimum Hamming distance '$d_{\min}$'. Then the GV bound can be defined as

$$|A\,(n, d_{min})| \geq \frac{2^n}{\sum_{i=0}^{d_{\min}} C_i^n} \tag{6.15}$$

6.5.4 McEliece-Rodemich-Rumsey-Welch (MRRW) Bound

For an (n, k) linear binary block code, we can define an $(n, (n - k)$ dual code. The parity check matrix of the original (n, k) linear binary block code is used as a generator matrix to generate all code vectors of an $(n, (n - k)$ dual code. Therefore, the number of valid code vectors of a dual code is .

MRRW bound states that the dual codes have essentially small covering radius compared to the original code. Covering radius is defined as the minimum radius when placed around each vector covers all vectors. In other words, it can also be defined as the number of error bits it can correct if hard decision decoding is used.

Example 6.6 : Determine which of the following linear binary block codes are perfect codes?

a. (7,4) code with a $d_{\min} = 3$

b. (6,3) code with a $d_{\min} = 3$

Solution:

From the definition of Hamming Bound, an (n, k) linear binary block code is said to be a perfect code if the inequality present in the equation (6.14) turns out to be an equality.

That is,

$$2^{n-k} = \sum_{i=0}^{t} C_i^n$$

a. Given $n = 7$, $k = 4$ and $d_{min} = 3$.

$$t = \left\lfloor \frac{d_{\min} - 1}{2} \right\rfloor = \left\lfloor \frac{3-1}{2} \right\rfloor = 1$$

$$2^{n-k} = 2^{7-4} = 2^3 = 8$$

and,

$$\sum_{i=0}^{t} C_i^n = \sum_{i=0}^{1} C_i^7 = C_0^7 + C_1^7 = 8$$

$$\Rightarrow \qquad 2^{n-k} = \sum_{i=0}^{t} C_i^n$$

Therefore, (7, 4) linear block code is a perfect code.

b. Given $n = 6$, $k = 3$ and $d_{\min} = 3$.

$$t = \left\lfloor \frac{d_{\min} - 1}{2} \right\rfloor = \left\lfloor \frac{3-1}{2} \right\rfloor = 1$$

$$2^{n-k} = 2^{6-3} = 2^3 = 8$$

and,

$$\sum_{i=0}^{t} C_i^n = \sum_{i=0}^{1} C_i^6 = C_0^6 + C_1^6 = 7$$

$$\Rightarrow \qquad 2^{n-k} \neq \sum_{i=0}^{t} C_i^n$$

Nevertheless, Hamming bound is satisfied.

$$2^{n-k} \geq \sum_{i=0}^{t} C_i^n$$

Therefore, (6, 3) linear block code is not a perfect code.

6.6 SOFT AND HARD DECISION DECODING

Decoding is one of the most crucial tasks in any communication system. As the channel is likely to be noisy and would introduce errors during communication, making a proper decision at the decoder plays an important role in the performance of the system. As long as the received vector matches with a valid code vector, decoding can be performed easily. However, decoding becomes more challenging if the received vector is not matching with any of the valid code vector.

There are two broad categories of decoding namely, hard decision and soft decision decoding.

6.6.1 Hard Decision Decoding

In case of hard decision decoding, the receiver takes individual bits and makes a decision in favor of either bit '1' or bit '0'. This decision is made based on the threshold chosen. If the received bit pulse is greater than the chosen threshold, the decision is made in favor of bit '1'. Else it is made in favor of bit '0'. It is to be noted that the decision is hard and is not concerned with how close the received pulse is to the threshold value. Generally Hamming distance is used as the distance measure for hard decision decoding.

To make the concepts clearer, consider an example of the following linear block codes:

A – 0 0 0

B – 0 1 1

C – 1 0 1

D – 1 1 0

Let us consider that the voltages used to represent bits '0' and '1' are 0.2 V and 4.2 V respectively.

Consider that the message B (bit sequence '0 1 1) is sent to the receiver. The corresponding voltage levels sent are [0.2V, 4.2V, 4.2V]. Due to the noise characteristics of the channel let the received pulses be [0.5V, 2.1V, 4.0V]. Considering the threshold value of the voltage as 2.1V, the decoding can be done as follows:

First value is 0.5V which is less than the threshold, so decode it as bit `0`

Second value is 2.1V which is less than the threshold, so decode it as bit `0`

Third value is 4.0V which is greater than the threshold, so decode it as bit `1`

Therefore, the decoded sequence is 0 0 1. But receiver knows that 0 0 1 is not a valid code sequence. Hence it considers the Hamming distance of the received sequence with all valid code vectors and the decision is made in favor of the valid code vector with which the decoded sequence exhibits the minimum Hamming distance.

Thus, the Hamming distance with all valid code vectors can be computed as follows:

Valid Code Vector	Decoded Vector	Hamming Distance
0 0 0	0 0 1	1
0 1 1	0 0 1	1
1 0 1	0 0 1	1
1 1 0	0 0 1	3

It is seen from the above table that the minimum value of the Hamming distance is 1 and it is appearing at three places (that is 0 0 0, 0 1 1 and 1 0 1). In other words, decoded sequence exhibits equal closeness with three of the valid code vectors. Now the decoder makes an arbitrary decision in favor of one of the three valid code vectors with equal probability. Thus, it can be seen that in hard decision decoding there is a scope for ambiguity.

6.6.2 Soft Decision Decoding

Unlike hard decision, soft decision decoding considers some degree of reliability. It considers Euclidian distance as the distance measure unlike Hamming distance in Hard decision decoding.

Considering the same scenario as considered for hard decision decoding. After receiving the pulse , [0.5V, 2.1V, 4.0V], receiver considers the Euclidian distance of the received sequence with all valid code vectors and decision is made in favor of the valid code vector with which the decoded sequence exhibits the minimum Euclidian distance.

The Euclidian distances can be calculated as follows:

Valid Code Vector	Received Pulse	Euclidian Distance
0 0 0 0.2, 0.2, 0.2	0.5, 2.1, 4.0	$(0.2 - 0.5)^2 + (0.2 - 2.1)^2 + (0.2 - 4.0)^2 = 18.14$
0 1 1 0.2, 4.2, 4.2	0.5, 2.1, 4.0	$(0.2 - 0.5)^2 + (4.2 - 2.1)^2 + (4.2 - 4.0)^2 = 4.54$
1 0 1 4.2, 0.2, 4.2	0.5, 2.1, 4.0	$(4.2 - 0.5)^2 + (0.2 - 2.1)^2 + (4.2 - 4.0)^2 = 17.34$
1 1 0 4.2, 4.2, 0.2	0.5, 2.1, 4.0	$(4.2 - 0.5)^2 + (4.2 - 2.1)^2 + (0.2 - 4.0)^2 = 32.54$

As the Euclidian distance of the received pulse is minimum with the code vector '0 1 1', the received pulse is decoded '0 1 1' as without any ambiguity.

Thus, it can be seen from the example that although hard decision decoding is a faster approach, its performance is inferior compared to soft decision decoding. In other words, soft decision decoding assures better reliability on decoding.

6.7 HAMMING CODES

Hamming codes are one of the popular linear block codes. They are a sub class of linear block codes with a minimum Hamming distance $d_{min} = 3$. Thus they are single error correcting codes.

If we define a variable 'm' as $m = (n - k)$, the Hamming codes can be formally defined with the following parameters:

Length of the code vector : $n = 2^m - 1$

Data bits : $k = 2^m - m - 1$

Number of parity bits : $(n - k) = 3$

Minimum Hamming distance : $d_{\min} = 3$

Error correcting capability : $t = 1$

It can be noted that Hamming codes form a class of perfect codes. As an example, if $m = (n - k) = 3$, the Hamming code will have the following parameters:

$n = 2^m - 1 = 7$ and $k = 2^m - m - 1 = 4$ Hence it is a (7,4) linear block code. The code considered in Example 6.5 is therefore a Hamming code.

6.8 REED SOLOMON (RS) CODES

Reed Solomon (RS) Codes are one of the popular coding schemes. They are a special class of block codes mainly used in storage applications.

For a q-ary RS codes, the parameters can be defined as follows:

Length of the code vector : $n = q - 1$

Data bits : k

Number of parity bits : $(n - k) = 2t$

Error correcting capability : t

Scan here to know more

6.9 CONCATENATED CODES

As per the Shannon theorem on channel capacity one can achieve reliable data transmission over a noisy channel as long as the rate at which the data is transmitted is less than the capacity of the channel. More sophisticated the channel coding used, better will be the reliability achieved. This necessitates code vectors with longer length. Concatenated codes are one such code designed for this purpose. They were designed to obtain long codes with a reasonably less complex decoding procedure.

A concatenated code consists of two encoders, namely outer encoder and inner encoder. Similarly at the decoder side, we have inner decoder and outer decoder.

The figure 6.2 presents the general block diagram of a concatenated code.

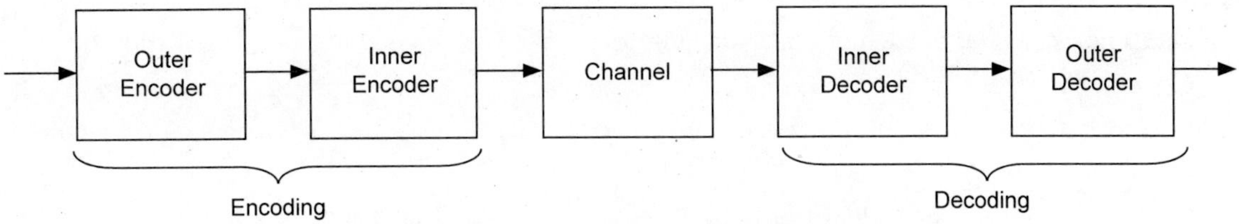

Fig. 6.2 A general block diagram of a concatenated code

The outer encoder takes the input from the bit stream and generates the code vector. The output of the outer encoder is taken as the input to the inner encoder where the code bits are considered as the data bits. Inverse operation is performed at the decoding stage.

Generally, RS codes are used for outer encoder and convolution codes are used for inner encoder. The concept of convolution codes is detailed in Section 6.10.

6.10 CONVOLUTION CODES

We have discussed block codes in the previous sections. Block codes take input bits in blocks, compute parity bits and generates a block of output bits. In case of block codes, the code vector of the present instance depends only on the present value of the input bits. Unlike block codes, in case of convolution codes, the present output bits are dependent not only on the present values of the input but also on the past input values. This necessitates the presence of memory elements. Thus, the major difference between block and convolution codes is that convolution codes possess memory.

Convolution codes are characterized by a triplet (n, k, m)

Where,

'k' indicates the number of input lines to the encoder

'n' indicates the number of output lines from the encoder

and 'm' indicates the number of memory elements in the encoder

A typical (2,1,2) convolution encoder is as shown in figure 6.3.

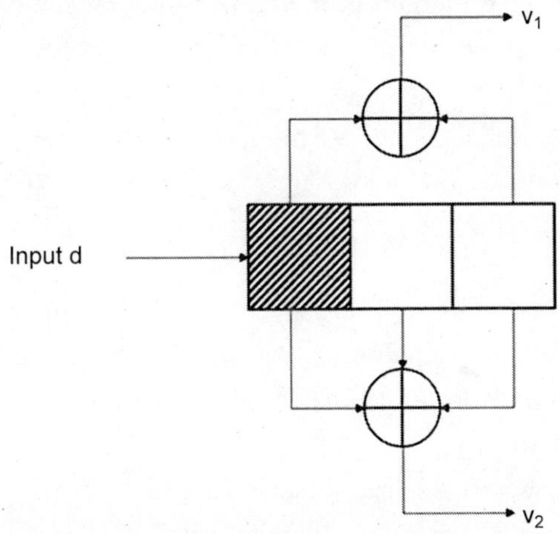

Fig. 6.3 convolution encoder

It is clear from the figure 6.3, that the encoder has one input line and two output lines with two memory elements.

Let us now consider the definitions of few important parameters used in convolution coding.

Code Rate:

It is defined as the ratio of number of input lines to that of output lines for a given convolution encoder.

$$R = {}^{k}/_{n} \tag{6.16}$$

For the convolution code given in figure 6.3, the rate is $R = 1/2$.

Constraint Length:

As the convolution codes possess memory, the present input bit will have its implications not only to the present output bits but also to the output bits of the future instances. The constraint length gives a measure of how many output bits are affected by a single input bit. It is denoted by 'L'.

Considering the encoder given in figure 6.3, the input applied at a present time instance will be there in the encoder for next two clock cycles as well (as there are two memory elements). Thus, one bit of input applied at the present time instance will affect output bits for three-time instances. Therefore, the constraint length for (2, 1, 2) convolution encoder shown in figure 6.3 is $L = 3 \times 2 = 6$ In other words, one bit of input will impact six output bits. This more sophisticated structure of convolution codes enables them to assure better coding performance over block codes.

In general, for an (n, k, m) convolution code the constraint length is given by,

$$L = n \times (m + 1) \tag{6.17}$$

6.10.1 Encoding using Time Domain Approach

Convolution codes can be viewed as a linear time invariant systems and hence the code vectors of convolution encoder can be obtained by performing convolution of the input sequence with the impulse responses or generator sequences of the encoder. The generator sequences for the convolution encoder can be obtained by considering the connection patterns to the summers present. For instance, consider the (2, 1, 2) convolution code as presented in figure 3.3. The first summer has a connection from the input and from the second memory element. Thus, the generator sequence for the first output is

$g_1 = (1\ 0\ 1)$

Similarly, to find the generator sequence for the second output consider the connection pattern for the second summer. It has connections from the input and from both memory elements. Therefore, the second generator sequence is given by,

$g_2 = (1\ 1\ 1)$

It can be seen from the above discussions that the length of the generator sequence is equal to $(m + 1)$ and the number of generator sequences is equal to number of output lines, n.

To find the code vector for an input sequence, we need to perform convolution of the generator sequences with the input sequence.

Let us now find the code vectors for the message $d = (1\ 1\ 0\ 1)$.

The output sequences v_1 and v_2 can be obtained as follows:

$v_1 = d * g_1$

Mathematically it can be defined as

$$v_i^l = \sum_{j=0}^{m} d_{l-j} g_i^j$$

$$\Rightarrow \quad v_1^l = \sum_{j=0}^{2} d_{l-j} g_1^j \tag{6.18}$$

We have

$$g_1 = (1\ 0\ 1)$$

Therefore

$$g_1^0 = 1,\ g_1^1 = 0 \text{ and } g_1^2 = 1$$

Similarly

$$g_2^0 = 1,\ g_2^1 = 1 \, and \, g_2^2 = 1$$

Using these in equation (6.18)

$$v_1^l = d_l g_1^0 + d_{l-1} g_1^1 + d_{l-2} g_1^2$$

$$v_1^l = d_l + d_{l-2}$$

$$d = (1\ 1\ 0\ 1)$$

$$v_1^0 = d_0 + d_{-2}$$

$d_0 = 1$ and $d_{-2} = 0$ (Assuming the input sequence to exist only for positive values of time)

$$\therefore \quad v_1^0 = 1$$

Similarly,

$$v_1^1 = d_1 + d_{-1}$$

$$d_1 = 1 \text{ and } d_{-1} = 0$$

$$v_1^1 = 1$$

And so on.

Calculating in the similar manner, all bits of the output can be obtained as follows:

$$v_1 = (1\ 1\ 1\ 0\ 0\ 1)$$

Similarly,

$$v_2 = \mathrm{d} \times \mathrm{g}_2$$

$$\Rightarrow \quad v_2^1 = \sum_{j=0}^{2} d_{l-j} g_2^j$$

$$v_2^l = d_l g_2^0 + d_{l-1} g_2^1 + d_{l-2} g_2^2$$

$$v_2^l = d_l + d_{l-1} + d_{i-2}$$

Following the same steps as that for the calculation of v_2, we will get

$$v_2 = (1\ 0\ 0\ 0\ 1\ 1)$$

To find the overall output consider the outputs instance by instance.

For example, at the first instance when $l = 0$, $v_1^0 = 1$ and $v_2^0 = 1$. Therefore, the output at the instance $l =$ 0 is $v^0 = 11$. Similarly, the output for the instance $l = 1$ is $v^1 = 10$ and so on.

The overall output sequence can be hence written as,

$v = (11, 10, 10, 00, 01, 11)$

It can be seen from the above example that for an input of length 4, the length of the output sequences are 6 bits each. This can be explained as follows: due to the presence of two memory elements, the input that was fed into the encoder at the present instance lasts for next two clock cycles as well. Thus, after the last input bit is fed into the encoder, the output bits are to be observed for two more clock cycles. During these two clock cycles, input bits are to be assumed as 0s. In general, for any (n, k, m) convolution code, for a message of length 'l', the output is to be observed for '$l + m$' clock cycles.

Example 6.7: Consider the convolution encoder shown in figure 6.4.

Determine

a. The values of n, k and m.

b. Code rate

c. Constraint length.

d. Generator sequences.

e. Output using time domain approach for the message $d = (1\ 1\ 1\ 0\ 1)$.

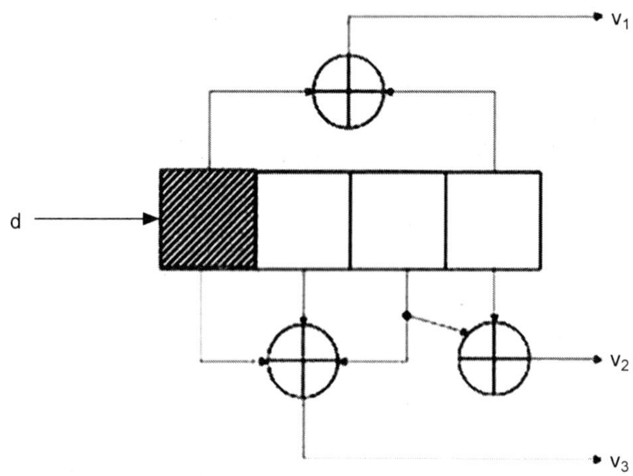

Fig. 6.4 Convolution encoder

Solution:

a. The values of n, k and m are

$n = 3$

$k = 1$

$m = 3$

Hence it is a $(3, 1, 3)$ convolution code.

b. Code rate, $R = k/n = 1/3$

c. Constraint Length, $L = n \times (m + 1) = 3 \times (3 + 1) = 12$.

d. There are three generator sequences as there are three output lines.

$g_1 = (1\ 0\ 0\ 1)$

$g_2 = (0\ 0\ 1\ 1)$

$g_3 = (1\ 1\ 1\ 0)$

f. To find the output sequence, consider the message $d = (1\ 1\ 1\ 0\ 1)$.

$v_1 = d * g_1 = (1\ 1\ 1\ 0\ 1) * (1\ 0\ 0\ 1) = (1\ 1\ 1\ 1\ 0\ 1\ 0\ 1)$

$v_2 = d * g_2 = (1\ 1\ 1\ 0\ 1) * (0\ 0\ 1\ 1) = (0\ 0\ 1\ 0\ 0\ 1\ 1\ 1)$

$v_3 = d * g_3 = (1\ 1\ 1\ 0\ 1) * (1\ 1\ 1\ 0) = (1\ 0\ 1\ 0\ 0\ 1\ 1\ 0)$

Therefore, the overall output is given by,

$v = (101, 100, 111, 100, 000, 111, 011, 110)$

6.10.2 Encoding using Transform Domain Approach

We know that, convolution in time domain is equivalent to multiplication in transform domain. Using this property, we can find the code vectors for a given message by representing the message and generator sequences in polynomial domain and then taking inverse transformation.

Therefore, in general the procedure to find the code vector for a convolution code using transform domain approach is as follows:

$$v_1(x) = d(x) \times g_1(x)$$
$$v_2(x) = d(x) \times g_2(x)$$
$$v_3(x) = d(x) \times g_3(x)$$

And so on.

The overall code vector polynomial can be obtained as follows:

$$v(x) = v_1(x^n) + xv_2(x^n) + x^2v_3(x^n) + \ldots\ldots \quad (6.19)$$

Considering the example of the convolution encoder as shown in figure 6.3,

We have $g_1 = (1\ 0\ 1)$

$g_2 = (1\ 1\ 1)$

Considering the same message, $d = (1\ 1\ 0\ 1)$

The polynomial representations of generator sequences and message sequence are:

$$g_1(x) = (1 + x^2)$$
$$g_2(x) = (1 + x + x^2)$$
$$d(x) = (1 + x + x^3)$$

The code vectors in polynomial domain can be written as follows:

$$v_1(x) = d(x) \times g_1(x) = (1 + x + x^3) \times (1 + x^2) = (1 + x + x^2 + x^5)$$

It is to be noted that the addition is in binary and hence $(x^3 + x^3) = 0$.

The polynomial $v_1(x)$ obtained is matching with the bit sequence (1 1 1 0 1) obtained in time domain approach.

Similarly, the second code sequence can be obtained as follows:

$$v_2(x) = d(x) \times g_2(x) = (1 + x + x^3) \times (1 + x + x^2) = (1 + x^4 + x^5)$$

To find the overall code polynomial consider the expression (6.18)

$$v(x) = v_1(x^2) + xv_2(x^2)$$
$$v(x) = (1 + x^2 + x^4 + x^{10}) + x(1 + x^8 + x^{10}) = 1 + x^2 + x^4 + x^{10} + x + x^9 + x^{11}$$
$$v(x) = 1 + x + x^2 + x^4 + x^9 + x^{10} + x^{11}$$

The binary representation of the code polynomial gives the required code vector.

$$v = (11, 10, 10, 00, 01, 11)$$

This is exactly the same vector that we have obtained using time domain approach.

Example 6.8: Consider the convolution encoder shown in example 6.7, find the code vector for the message $d = (1\ 1\ 1\ 0\ 1)$ using transform domain approach.

Solution:

We have

$$g_1 = (1\ 0\ 0\ 1) = 1 + x^3$$
$$g_2 = (0\ 0\ 1\ 1) = x^2 + x^3$$
$$g_3 = (1\ 1\ 1\ 0) = 1 + x + x^2$$

Considering the same message, $d = (1\ 1\ 1\ 0\ 1) = 1 + x + x^2 + x^4$

The code vectors in polynomial domain can be written as follows:

$$v_1(x) = d(x) \times g_1(x) = (1 + x + x^2 + x^4) \times (1 + x^3) = (1 + x + x^2 + x^3 + x^5 + x^7)$$
$$v_2(x) = d(x) \times g_2(x) = (1 + x + x + x^4) \times (x^2 + x^3) = (x^2 + x^5 + x^6 + x^7)$$
$$v_3(x) = d(x) \times g_3(x) = (1 + x + x^2 + x^4) \times (1 + x + x^2) = (1 + x^2 + x^5 + x^6)$$

The overall output is Sgiven by,

$v(x) = v_1(x^3) + xv_2(x^3) + x^2 v_3(x^3)$

$v(x) = (1 + x^3 + x^6 + x^9 + x^{15} + x^{21}) + x(x^6 + x^{15} + x^{18} + x^{21}) + x^2(1 + x^6 + x^{15} + x^{18})$

$v(x) = (1 + x^3 + x^6 + x^9 + x^{15} + x^{21}) + (x^7 + x^{16} + x^{19} + x^{22}) + (x^2 + x^8 + x^{17} + x^{20})$

$v(x) = 1 + x^2 + x^3 + x^6 + x^7 + x^8 + x^9 + x^{15} + x^{16} + x^{17} + x^{19} + x^{20} + x^{21} + x^{22}$

The corresponding binary sequence is given by,

$v = (101, 100, 111, 100, 000, 111, 011, 110)$

6.10.3 Representation of Convolution Codes

As convolution codes possess memory, like any other sequential circuits, convolution codes can also be represented using state diagram representation.

In order to write the state diagram for a convolution encoder, we need to first write the state table. Consider the encoder shown in figure 6.3. The generator sequences for the given encoder are as follows:

$$g_1 = (1\ 0\ 1)$$
$$g_2 = (1\ 1\ 1)$$

As we have two memory elements in the encoder, there are four possible states it can take on. Let us define the states for the given (2, 1, 2) encoder as follows:

$S_0 : 0\ 0$

$S_1 : 0\ 1$

$S_2 : 1\ 0$

$S_3 : 1\ 1$

Input can be either a bit '0' or a bit '1' for each of the possible states. The output bits and next states of the memory elements for each of the possible states can be represented in the form of a state table as follows:

State Table

Present State	Input	Next State	Output
$S_0 : 0\,0$	0	$S_0 : 00$	00
	1	$S_2 : 1\,0$	11
$S_1 : 0\,1$	0	$S_0 : 0\,0$	11
	1	$S_2 : 1\,0$	00
$S_2 : 1\,0$	0	$S_1 : 0\,1$	01
	1	$S_3 :1\,1$	10
$S_3 : 1\,1$	0	$S_1 :0\,1$	10
	1	$S_3 : 1\,1$	01

It is to be noted that the present state to next state transition is dependent only on the shift operation and not on the connection pattern in the encoder. Nevertheless, the output bits are dependent on the connection pattern in the encoder diagram.

State Diagram

State diagrams give the pictorial representation of the state table. Let the circles indicate the states. Let transition from a state when the input is '0' be represented using a solid line and that for an input being '1' be represented using dotted line.

The state diagram representation of the (2, 1, 2) convolution encoder is given in figure 6.5.

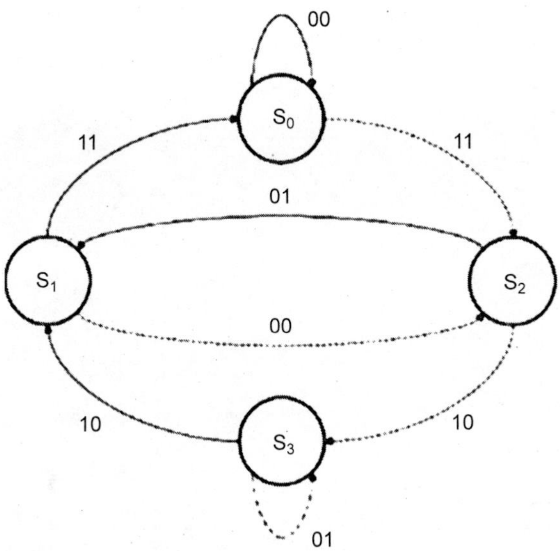

Fig. 6.5. State diagram representation of a encoder given in example 6.3

Despite its ease of representation, state diagrams do not give timing information. In other words, from the state diagram representation, we cannot make out the timing instance of the encoder. Thus, a more sophisticated method to represent convolution code is needed. Tree diagram is one such method.

Tree Diagram:

Tree diagram gives a more structured information about the encoder. In this representation, each transition is considered as a branch of the tree and transitions represent the next state and the corresponding output bits. Each transition is also associated with the time instance.

As tree diagram representation considers the timing information, we have to decide on the number of stages for which the tree diagram is to be written. As discussed in Section 6.10.1, for any (n, k, m) convolution code, for a message of length '*l*', the output is to be observed for '*l* + *m*' clock cycles. For the first '*l*' clock cycles transitions correspond to the actual input and last '*m*' stages correspond to the output due to effect of past input bits in the memory.

Therefore, for a message of length '*l*', the tree diagram shall have '*l* + *m*' stages in which for the first '*l*' stages the transitions are to be presented for both cases: input being a bit '0' or a bit '1' . The last '*m*' stages have the transitions corresponding to '0' input only.

Consider the (2, 1, 2) convolution encoder as shown in figure 6.3. The corresponding state table and state diagram representations were already discussed. Now let us consider the tree diagram representation of the same. Suppose that the length of the input is four bits. Therefore, the corresponding tree diagram has six stages out of which for the first four stages the transitions corresponding to bit and bit are considered and for the last two stages only the transitions corresponding to bit '0' are considered. Figure 6.6 gives the corresponding tree diagram representation. Let the transitions moving upwards correspond to input being and that of downwards correspond to input being .

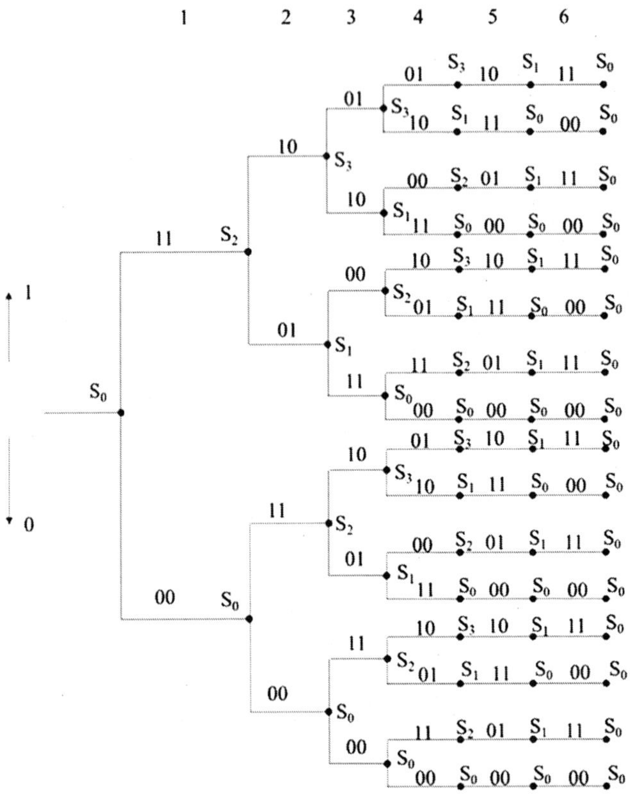

Fig. 6.6. Tree diagram representation of a encoder given in example 6.3

Let us find the code vector for the input sequence $d = (1\ 1\ 0\ 1)$.

The output sequences can be obtained by traversing through the respective branches of the tree diagram.

To start with, the tree diagram is initialized to be in state S_0. The first bit in the message is '1'. Hence traverse upwards, the state reached is S_2 and the corresponding output bits are '1 1'.

Now from that state, as the second bit of the message is '1', traverse upwards. The next state reached is S_3 and the corresponding output bits are '1 0'.

Similarly for the next two input bits traversing appropriately, we will get the output bits '1 0' and '0 0'.

Now we have reached to last two stages of the tree diagram where the output bits are to be determined considering input as '0' s. Thus, the output bits for the next two stages are '0 1' and '1 1'.

Therefore, the overall output can be obtained as:

$$v = (11, 10, 10, 00, 01, 11)$$

Which is same as the one we obtained using time domain and transform domain approaches.

This shows that the tree diagram is a more efficient way of representing convolution codes as compared to state diagrams. However, the main drawback of this representation is the increased complexity for longer input sequence. Nevertheless, the presence of redundant transitions in each stage of the tree diagram can be explored to have a better representation of the convolution coder. This has resulted in Trellis diagram representation.

Trellis Diagram:

Like tree diagram representation, Trellis representation of convolution codes also considers the timing information. However, the Trellis gives a more compact and efficient representation of a convolution code.

The Trellis diagram representation of the (2, 1, 2) convolution encoder as shown in figure 6.3 is presented in figure 6.7. In Trellis representation, it can be seen that the four levels on the vertical axis indicate the states of the encoder. The timing instances are considered on the top as similar to tree diagram representation. As the encoder is assumed to be in all zero state initially, only the state is present at the beginning of the instance 1. As there are two possible states can transit to, we have transitions to states and corresponding to the inputs '0' and '1' respectively at the beginning of the instance 2. The process continuous for first stages and transitions correspond to input '0' are only considered for the last stages.

It can be seen from the diagram that unlike tree diagram representation, in Trellis representation, the number of transitions in each stage does not increase exponentially. The output bits for each transition are not written in the representation for the sake of better legibility. Here also the length of the input is considered to be four and hence the Trellis diagram is written for six stages. Solid lines indicate transitions corresponding to input being a bit and dotted lines represent that for an input of bit.

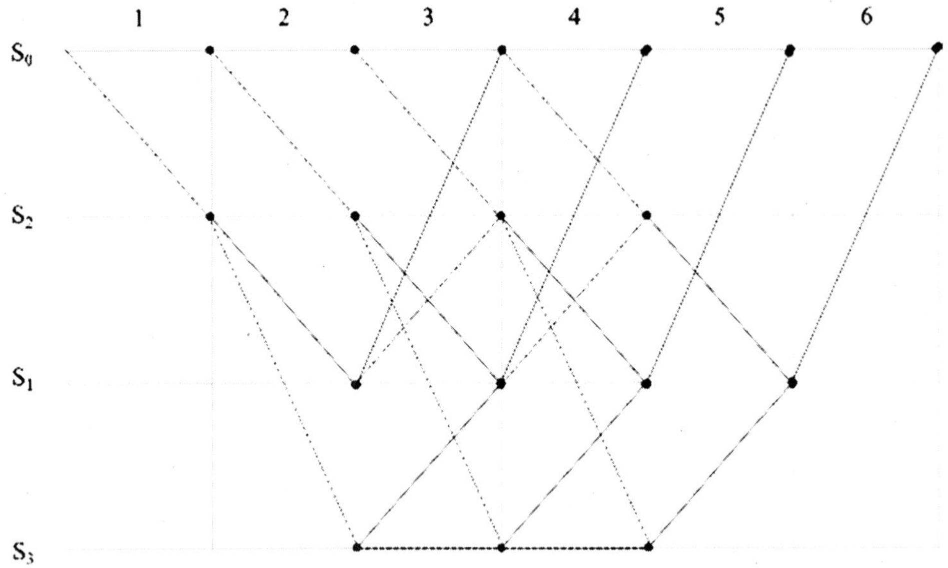

Fig. 6.7. Trellis diagram representation of a encoder given in example 6.3

6.10.4 Viterbi Decoding

Viterbi algorithm is one of the most popular decoding algorithms for convolution codes. The procedure is similar to find a shortest path between two nodes in a weighted network. Viterbi algorithm can be either a soft decision or a hard decision decoding. As discussed in Section 6.6, hard decision decoding uses Hamming distance for metric computation whereas, soft decision decoding uses Euclidian distance. In this chapter we restrict our discussions to hard decision Viterbi decoding algorithm.

In order to understand the decoding process, let us define a few terminologies used in decoding process:

Branch Metric Mn (s_i, s_j) : This is the metric of the transition branch from state s_i to state s_j at the instance 'n'. As mentioned earlier, this is the Hamming distance between the expected output for that transition with the received sequence at the instance 'n'.

State Metric $S_M(s_j)$: This is a measure of the cumulative metric of the state 'si' at the instance '$n - 1$' and the branch metric $M_n(s_i, s_j)$.

$$S_M(s_j) = M_n(s_i, s_j) + S_M(s_i) \tag{6.20}$$

Survivor Path: If a state can be reached by more than one incoming transition, each transition gives a different state metric. In such cases, the transition offering the least state metric is to be considered and other transitions are to be discarded.

For instance, if the node s_j can be reached from two nodes say s_i and s_k, the state metric can be computed as follows:

$$S_M(s_j) = \text{Min}\,\{[M_n(s_i, s_j) + S_M(s_i)], [M_n(s_k, s_j) + S_M(s_k)]\} \tag{6.21}$$

The path that offers a minimum metric is called as the survivor path.

Example 6.9: Consider a convolution code with the following generator sequences:

$g_1 = (1\ 0\ 1)$

$g_2 = (1\ 1\ 1)$

a. Find the code vector for the message $d = (1\ 0\ 0\ 1\ 1)$ using time domain approach.
b. Verify your answer using transform domain approach.
c. Consider that second and tenth bit in the transmitted vector received erroneously due to the presence of noise. Using, hard decision Viterbi decoding algorithm, obtain the message sequence.

Solution:

a. The values of n, k and m are

$n = 2$

$k = 1$

$m = 2$

The given generator sequences are

$g_1 = (1\ 0\ 1)$

$g_2 = (1\ 1\ 1)$

To find the output sequence, consider the message $d = (1\ 0\ 0\ 1\ 1)$.

$v_1 = d \times g_1 = (1\ 0\ 0\ 1\ 1) \times (1\ 0\ 1) = (1\ 0\ 1\ 1\ 1\ 1\ 1)$

$v_2 = d \times g_2 = (1\ 0\ 0\ 1\ 1) \times (1\ 1\ 1) = (1\ 1\ 1\ 1\ 0\ 0\ 1)$

Therefore, the overall output is given by,

$v = (11{,}01{,}11{,}11{,}10{,}10{,}11)$

b. We have

$g_1 = (1\ 0\ 1) = 1 + x^2$

$g_2 = (\ 1\ 1\ 1) = 1 + x + x^2$

Considering the same message, $d = (1\ 0\ 0\ 1\ 1) = 1 + x^3 + x^4$

The code vectors in polynomial domain can be written as follows:

$v_1(x) = d(x) \times g_1(x) = (1+x^3 + x^4) \times (1 + x^2) = (1 + x^2 + x^3 + x^4 + x^5 + x^6)$

$v_2(x) = d(x) \times g_2(x) = (1 + x^3 + x^4) \times (1 + x + x^2) = (1 + x + x^2 + x^3 + x^6)$

The overall output is given by,

$v(x) = v_1(x^2) + xv_2(x^2)$

$v(x) = (1 + x^4 + x^6 + x^8 + x^{10} + x^{12}) + x(1 + x^2 + x^4 + x^6 + x^{12})$

$v(x) = 1 + x^4 + x^6 + x^8 + x^{10} + x^{12} + x + x^3 + x^5 + x^7 + x^{13}$

$v(x) = 1 + x + x^3 + x^4 + x^5 + x^6 + x^7 + x^8 + x^{10} + x^{12} + x^{13}$

The corresponding binary sequence is given by,

$v = (11, 01, 11, 11, 10, 10, 11)$

Which is same as that of the time domain approach.

c. Considering second and tenth bit in the transmitted vector recevied erroneously, the recevied vector become.

$r = (10, 01, 11, 11, 11, 10, 11)$

As the message is of lenth 5, we need to consider the Trellis diagram for seven stage of which for the first stage transitions corresponding tp input '0' and '1' are to be considered and for the last two stages transitions corresponding to input '0' are to be considered.

The Trellis diagram for the given convolution code for seven stage is as shown in figure 6.8.

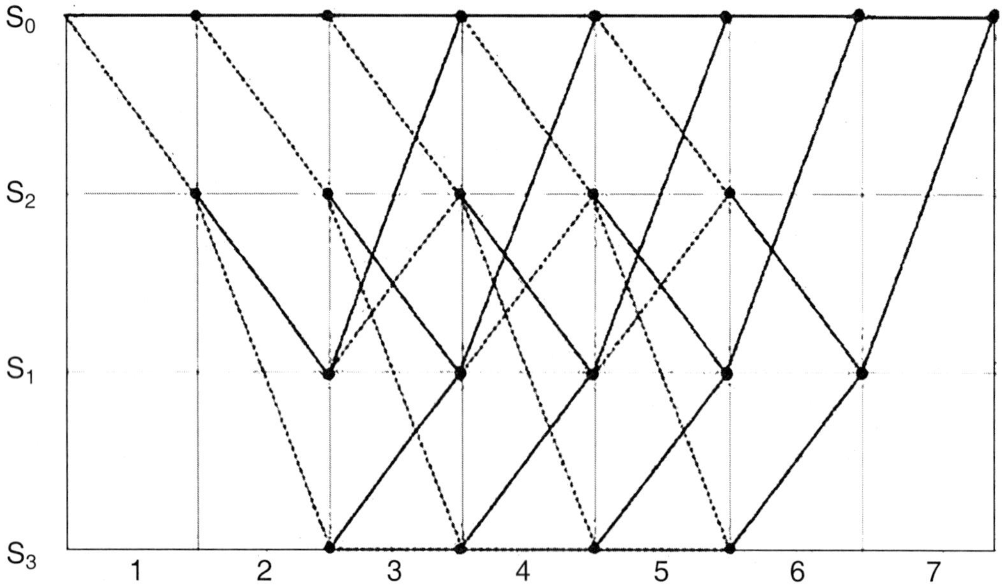

Fig. 6.8. Trellis diagram representation

To find the decoded sequence, consider the received sequence written stage - wise in the Trellis diagram. At any stage for the branch metric computation. e need to consider the Hamming distance of this sequence with the expected output for the corresponding transition branch as the state table.

The initial state S_0 is assumed to have a metric of '0'. In the next level, there are two possible transitions, one is to S_0 and the another is to S_2. From S_0 to S_0 the expected output sequence is '00' and the first two bits of the received sequence is '10', Hamming distance between the two sequences is 1 which is the corresponding branch metric. Therefore, the metric for the state S_0 at the beginning of the second instance is given by the sum of the branch metric and the metric of the predecessor S_0 i.e. $1 + 0 = 1$. Similarly the branch metric for the transition S_0 to S_2 is also 1 and hence the metric for the state S_1 at the beginning of the second instance is also $1 + 0 = 1$. The same procedure is continued to find the metrics for all nodes in the Trellis diagram. Whenever there are two branches destined at the same node, calculate the metrics from both branches and retain the minimum one as discussed in equation (6.21).

In the process of computing the state metrics, determine the survivor path and cancel out the other paths. Once the state metric computation is done for all states, traverse back from the last state towards the source node by traversing through uncrossed transitions only. If the traversing is through a dotted line, note the corresponding input as '1', else note it as '0'.

The detailed decoding procedure for the given convolution code is presented in figure 6.9.

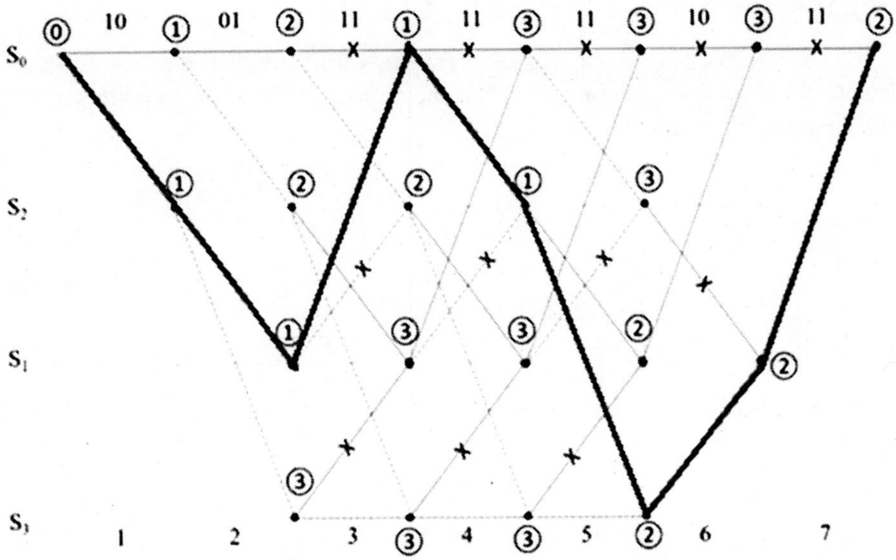

Scan here to know more

Fig. 6.9 Decoding using Viterbi algorithm

The decoded sequence from the figure 6.9, is '1 0 0 1 1 0 0'.

Please note that the last two '0's indicate the additional '0's that were loaded to the encoder after the complete input sequence is fed in order to get the complete response.

Therefore, the decoded message sequence is

$$d = \text{'1 0 0 1 1'}$$

Which is same as the original message. The metric of '2' for the final node indicates the presence of two errors in the received sequence.

6.10.5 BCJR Decoding

BCJR algorithm is named after Bahl Cocke Jelinek and Raviv who have proposed this technique for decoding convolution codes. Like Viterbi algorithm, BCJR decoding also works on Trellis diagram. However, BCJR tries to minimize the bit error rate by considering the maximization of a- posteriori probability, $P\ ((d_i = d_i\ |r)$ that is the probability of correct detection of a bit d_i for a given received sequence.

Viterbi algorithm is a maximum likelihood decoding whereas BCJR is a bitwise maximum a-posteriori probability (MAP) decoder. Despite both work on Trellis representation of the convolution code, Viterbi makes one pass on the Trellis from initial to final stage and decides upon the most likely output. Whereas, BCJR makes two passes on the Trellis because of which we will not only get the decoded sequence but also get a-posteriori likelihood ratio for each message bit. Such output is called as soft output. This bit-wise MAP information is useful in some applications like Turbo decoders etc.

It can be noted that the MAP decoders are of importance if the convolution decoders are used as a part of a larger systems. In which case the probabilistic information about the message bits will have a significant impact on the performance of the systems connected further.

6.11 TURBO CODES

As discussed in section 6.9, concatenated codes achieve better transmission rates. Turbo codes are a class of powerful error control codes consisting of concatenated connection of convolution codes in parallel. They are capable of achieving data rates closer to Shannon limit.

The general block diagram of a rate 1⁄3 Turbo encoder is as shown in figure 6.10.

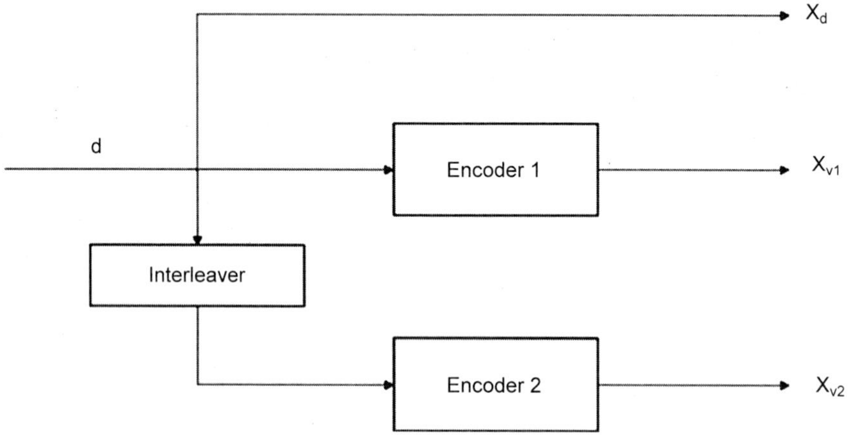

Fig. 6.10 A rate 1⁄3 turbo encoder

As seen from figure 6.10, it consists of two convolution encoders. Although, same input is considered for both encoders, it is fed directly to the first encoder and fed through an interleaver to the second encoder. Interleaver does reordering of the bits. Design of interleavers plays an important role in the performance of Turbo codes. One of the output lines is directly from the input, generating a systematic code.

Let X_d, X_{v1} and X_{v2} are the data and parity bits transmitted by the Turbo encoder. The corresponding received sequences at the receiver be Y_d, Y_{v1} and Y_{v2}. A typical Turbo decoder is shown in figure 6.11.

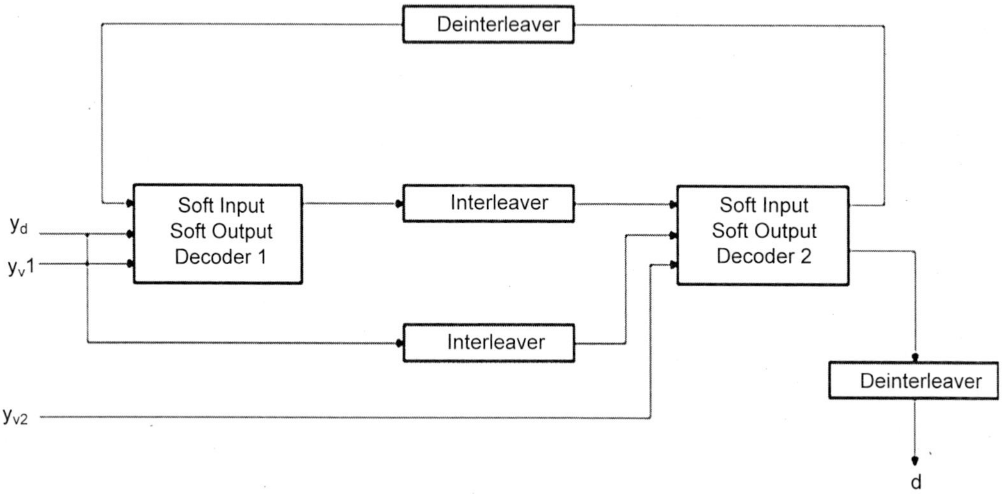

Fig. 6.11 A rate 1⁄3 turbo decoder

Similar to two encoders being used at the transmitter side, two decoders are used at the receiver. Decoder 1 is a counter part for encoder 1 at the transmitter side and decoder 2 is that for encoder 2. As already discussed in the previous section, the term Soft Input Soft Output Decoders implies that the output of the decoder not only presents the decoded data but also gives some probabilistic information about the data being decoded.

It is seen from figure 6.11 that the received sequence on the first line, Y_d is given to both decoders, directly to decoder 1 and through interleaver to decoder 2. The other two sequences Y_v1 and Y_v2 are appropriately given to the decoders 1 and 2. Also, there is a third input applied to both decoders. This is the probabilistic information about the message as obtained from the soft decoders. Decoder 1 feeds this probabilistic information to decoder 2 and vice versa. Interleaver and deinterleavers are used appropriately so as to assure the order of the message for which the probabilistic information is fed is same as the order in which the data is fed into the decoders. This process is carried in iterations till an equilibrium is reached. After this stage, the decoded sequence can be obtained from decoder 2 through a deinterleaver.

6.12 LOW DENSITY PARITY CHECK CODES

Low Density Parity Check (LDPC) Codes were first introduced in early 1960s but they have become popular only after early 1990s. LDPC codes are a class of linear block code with a few additional properties. As the name indicates, LDPC codes have low density parity check matrix. In other words, the number of 1's in the parity check matrix of the code is very less compared to the number of 0's. Such parity check matrices are called as sparse matrix. An LDPC code is said to be a regular LDPC code if the number of 1's in every row and every column of the parity check matrix is same.

A regular LDPC code can be characterized by the triplet (n, w_c, w_r)

Where,

'n' is the length of the code vector

'w_c' is the number of 1' s in every column of the parity check matrix

'w_r' is the number of 1' s in every row of the parity check matrix

Scan here to know more

LDPC codes offer better performance for the length of the code vector being long. In some cases, they perform better than concatenated codes discussed in the previous sections. The major difference between Turbo codes and LDPC codes is that the Turbo codes have low encoding complexity and high decoding complexity. But LDPC codes offer a higher complexity in encoding and relatively lower complexity in decoding.

UNIT SUMMARY

- An error control coding can be defined as a procedure of adding redundant bits, also called as parity bits or check bits through mathematical calculations so to facilitate the receiver to detect the presence of error (*s*) and in the received sequence.
- Error control codes or channel codes are classified into two broad categories. Namely, block Codes and convolution Codes
- Block Codes: Channel encoder takes 'k' bit information at once and generates a code vector of length 'n' bits by introducing '$n - k$' parity bits. They are represented by a two-tuple information (n,k).

- Convolution Codes: Convolution codes, takes the input in a continuous manner and generates the output. One of the major differences between block codes and convolution codes is that the output of the block codes depends only on the present data block whereas, convolution codes depend on previous input bits as well.
- Linear Block Codes are a class of block codes where the linear combination of two or more valid code vector would also result in a valid code vector.
- The code vector for an (n, k) linear block code can be obtained from the following relation

  $C = D \times G$

  Where

  C is the code vector of length 'n' bits.

  D is the message vector of length 'k' bits.

  G is the generator matrix of dimension $k \times n$.
- The generator structure of the Generator Matrix is as follows:

  $G = [I_k : P]$

  Where

  I_k is the Identity matrix of dimension $k \times k$.

  P is the Parity matrix of dimension $k \times (n - k)$.
- The parity check matrix H can be defined as

  $H = [P^T : (n - k)\,]$

  where

  P^T is the transpose of the parity matrix of dimension $(n - k) \times k$

  $I\,(n - k)$ is the identity matrix of dimension $(n{-}k) \times (n - k)$
- Product of generator matrix with the transpose of the parity check matrix is always zero.
- Hamming distance is defined between the two code vectors. It is defined as the number of bit positions in which two code words differ.
- Hamming weight of a code vector is defined as the number of non zero elements in it. For a binary code vector it is defined as the number of 1's present in the code vector.
- The minimum Hamming distance of an (n, k) linear block code is defined as the smallest Hamming distance between any two code vectors of the code.
- Error Detecting Capability of an (n, k) linear block code = $d_{\min} - 1$
- Error Correcting Capability of an (n, k) linear block code = $\left\lfloor \dfrac{d_{\min} - 1}{2} \right\rfloor$
- There two broad categories of decoding namely, hard decision and soft decision decoding.
- Hamming codes are one of the popular linear block codes. They are a sub class of linear block codes with a minimum Hamming distance $d_{\min} = 3$.
- Concatenated codes were designed to obtain long codes with a reasonably less complex decoding procedure.
- Convolution codes are characterized by a triplet (n, k, m)

Where,

'k' indicates the number of input lines to the encoder

'n' indicates the number of output lines to the encoder

'm' indicates the number of memory elements in the encoder

- Code rate is defined as the ratio of number of input lines to that of output lines.

  $R = {}^{k}\!/_{n}$
- The constraint length gives a measure of how many output bits are affected by a single input bit.
- Convolution codes can be encoded in time domain approach by performing the convolution of the message with the generator sequences.
- Convolution codes can be represented using state diagrams, tree diagrams and trellis diagrams.
- Turbo codes are a class of powerful error control codes consists of concatenated connection of convolution codes in parallel.
- LDPC codes have low density parity check matrix. In other words, the number of 1's in the parity check matrix of the code is very less compared to the number of 0's.

EXERCISE

Numerical Problems

1. Consider a (6,3) linear block code with generator matrix

$$G = \begin{bmatrix} 100111 \\ 010110 \\ 001101 \end{bmatrix}$$

Find:

i. All possible code vectors

ii. Minimum Hamming distance

iii. Parity check matrix

iv. Obtain the syndrome for the received vector (1 1 1 0 0 0)

2. For a systematic (6,3) linear block code, the parity matrix is

$$P = \begin{bmatrix} 1 & 0 & 1 \\ 0 & 1 & 1 \\ 1 & 1 & 0 \end{bmatrix}$$

Determine

i. All possible code vectors

ii. Minimum Hamming distance

iii. Parity check matrix

iv. Calculate syndrome for the received vector (1 1 1 0 0 1)

3. Consider a (5,1) repetition code whose generator matrix is given as

$$G = [1:1\ 1\ 1\ 1]$$

   i. All possible code vectors
   ii. Parity check matrix

4. Draw the state diagram, tree diagram and trellis diagram representation of a (3,1,2) convolution code whose generator polynomials are given by:

   $g_1(x) = (1 + x + x^2)$, $g_2(x) = (1 + x)$ and $g_3(x) = (1 + x^2)$

   Consider a (3,1,3) with convolution code whose impulse response sequences are given as

   $g_1 = (1\ 0\ 1\ 1)$

   $g_2 = (1\ 1\ 1\ 1)$

   $g_3 = (1\ 1\ 0\ 1)$.

   i. Draw the corresponding encoder diagram.
   ii. Considering the message sequence as d=(1 1 0 0 1), find the code vector using time-domain approach.
   iii. Recompute the code vector for the data sequence given in the previous sub question using transform-domain approach.

6. Consider a (3,1,2) convolution encoder with the generator sequences $g_1 = (1\ 1\ 0)$, $g_2 = (1\ 1\ 1)$ and $g_3 = (1\ 0\ 1)$.
   i. Draw its encoder diagram.
   ii. Find the code rate and constraint length.
   iii. Considering the message sequence as d=(1 0 1 0 1 1), find the code vector using time-domain approach.
   iv. Verify answer obtained in (iii) using transform domain approach.

7. Consider a (2,1,2) convolution code having the generator sequences $g_1 = (1\ 1\ 1)$ and $g_2 = (1\ 0\ 1)$. Draw its Trellis Diagram. Hence decode the sequence (11, 11, 10, 01, 00, 10, 11) using Hard Decision Viterbi decoding algorithm.

Descriptive Type Questions

1. Define the following with reference to linear block codes:
   i. Hamming distance
   ii. Hamming weight
   iii. Minimum Hamming distance
2. Explain how single errors can be corrected using syndrome computation in linear block codes?
3. What are RS codes? Explain in detail.
4. Distinguish Hard and Soft Decision decoding algorithms.
5. Distinguish block codes and convolution codes.
6. Explain the procedure of Viterbi decoding of convolution codes.
7. Explain in detail, the encoding and decoding process of Turbo Codes.
8. What are LDPC codes? Explain.

Objective Type Questions

1. What is the dimension of a parity matrix in an (n, k) linear block code?
   (a) $n \times (n - k)$ (b) $k \times (n - k)$
   (c) $(n - k) \times n$ (d) $(n - k) \times k$
2. State True or False
   The product of the generator matrix with the transpose of the parity check matrix in an (n,k) linear block code is always zero.
   (a) True (b) False
3. The length of the output for a (3,1,3) convolution code for the message $d = (1\ 0\ 1\ 1)$ is
   (a) 14 (b) 21
   (c) 28 (d) 35
4. The length of the generator sequencc for a (3,1,2) convolution code is
   (a) 3 (b) 2
   (c) 4 (d) 5
5. The maximum number of encoder output bits that can be affected by a single input bit in a convolution encoder is known as
   (a) Constraint length (b) Code Length
   (c) Code Rate (d) None of the Above
6. For a (2,1,2) convolution code $g_1 = (0\ 1\ 1)$ and $g_2 = (1\ 0\ 1)$. The output when $d = (0\ 1)$ is
   (a) (00, 01, 00, 11) (b) (00, 01, 10, 11)
   (c) (00, 01, 01, 11) (d) (00, 01, 11, 11)
7. What is the code rate of a (4,1,3) convolution code?
   (a) 1⁄4 (b) 1⁄3
   (c) 3⁄4 (d) None of the above

KNOW MORE

Image Courtesy: https://commons.wikimedia.org/wiki/File:Evariste_galois.jpg

Galois Filed (GF) is considered to be one of the biggest milestones in the area of communication. It plays a vital role in the field of error control coding and cryptography. It is named after Galois, whose efforts are highly remarkable and phenomenal.

Galois was imprisoned for some political reasons and was killed at the age of just 21. Nevertheless, the work of Galois is one of the most appreciated contributions towards the shift from traditional to modern algebra.

Image Courtesy: https://commons.wikimedia.org/wiki/File:10-08ViterbiBIG.jpg

Andrew James Viterbi was born in 1935 in Bergamo, Italy. He along with his parents has later shifted to United States as refugees. In 1967, he proposed a novel algorithm to decode convolution codes. The algorithm has become very popular and is used in most of the modern applications including cell phones. It is to be worth noted that Viterbi did not file a patent on his algorithm.

PREFACE

The Noisy Channel Coding Theorem discovered by C. E. Shannon in 1948 of fered communication engineers the possibility of reducing error rates on noisy channels to negligible levels without sacrificing data rates. The primary obstacle to the practical use of this theorem has been the equipment complexity and the computation time required to decode the noisy received data.

This monograph presents a technique for achieving high data rates and neg-ligible error probabilities on noisy channels with a reasonable amount of equip ment. The advantages and disadvantages of this technique over other techniques for the same purpose are neither simple nor clear-cut, and depend primarily upon the channel and the type of service required. More important than the particular technique, however, is the hope that the concepts here will lead to new and better coding procedures.

The chapters of the monograph are arranged in such a way that with the exception of Chapter 5 each chapter can be read independently of the others. Chapter 1 sets the background of the study, summarizes the results, and briefly compares low-density coding with other coding schemes. Chapter 2 analyzes the distances between code words in low-density codes and Chapter 3 applies these results to the problem of bounding the probability of decoding error that can be achieved for these codes on a bread class of binary-input channels. The results of Chapter 3 can be immediately applied to any code or class of codes for which the distance properties can be bounded. Chapter 4 presents a simple decoding algorithm for these codes and Analyzes the resulting error probabil ity. Chapter 5 brielly extends all the previous results to multi-input channels, and Chapter 6 presents the results of-eomputer simulation of the low-density decoding algorithm.

The work reported here is an expanded and revised version of my doctoral dissertation, completed in 1960 in the Department of Electrical Engineering. MIT. I am grateful to my thesis supervisor, Professor Peter Elias, and to my thesis readers, Professors Robert M. Fano and John M. Wozencraft, for assistance and encouragement both during the course of the thesis and later.

This research was made possible in part by support extended by the Research Laboratory of Electronics of the Massachusetts Institute of Technology, which is supported in part by the U.S. Army, the Air Force Office of Scientific Research, and the Office of Naval Research; additional support was received through the National Science Foundation (Grant G-16526) and the National Institute of Health (Grant MH-04737-03)

Much of Chapter 1 is reprinted with permission of the editors from an article by the author in the Transactions of the L.R.E, IT 9, раде 21 то 28. The experimental results in Chapter 6 were obtained in part through the support of the Rome Air Development Center and in part through the support of the M.LT. Computation Center.

Cambridge, Mass

July, 1963 Robert G. Gallager

FURTHER READING

[1] M. Kulkarni and K. S. Shivaprakasha, "Information Theory and Coding", Wiley (India), 2015.

[2] Ranjan Bose, "Information Theory Coding and Cryptography", Tata McGraw Hill, 2007.

[3] Richerd E Blahut, "Algebraic Codes for Data Transmission", Cambridge University Press; UK, 2003.

[4] W E Ryan and S Lin, "Channel Codes: Classical and Modern", Cambridge University Press; UK, 2009.

[5] T K Moon, "Error Control Coding: Mathematical Methods and Algorithms", John Wiley and Sons, New Jersey, 2005.

[6] Haykin, Simon. "Digital Communications", John Wiley, New York, 2001.

[7] Sklar, Bernad. "Digital Communication: Functions and Applications", Prenice Hall., 1988.

[8] K. Sam Shanmugam , " Digital and Analog Communication Systems", John Wiley, New York, 2006.

[9] M. Kulkarni and Farooq Husain, "Analog and Digital Communication Systems", Umesh Publications, New Delhi, 2005.

Appendix

APPENDIX-I
MATLAB SIMULATION EXPERIMENTS

1. Matlab Code for Generation of signals and sequences

To generate various signals and sequences (Periodic and aperiodic), such as Unit Impulse, Unit Step, Square, Saw tooth, Triangular, Sinusoidal, Ramp, Sinc.

PROGRAM:

```
% Generation of signals and sequences
clc;
clear all;
close all;
%~~~~~~~~~~~~~~~~~~~~~~~~~~~~~~~~~~~~~~
%generation of unit impulse signal
t1=-1:0.01:1
y1=(t1==0);
subplot(2,2,1);
plot(t1,y1);
xlabel('time');
ylabel('amplitude');
title('unit impulse signal');
%generation of impulse sequence
subplot(2,2,2);
stem(t1,y1);
xlabel('n');
ylabel('amplitude');
title('unit impulse sequence');
%~~~~~~~~~~~~~~~~~~~~~~~~~~~~~~~~~~~~~~~
%generation of unit step signal
t2=-10:1:10;
```

```
y2=(t2>=0);
subplot(2,2,3);
plot(t2,y2);
xlabel('time');
ylabel('amplitude');
title('unit step signal');
%generation of unit step sequence
subplot(2,2,4);
stem(t2,y2);
xlabel('n');
ylabel('amplitude');
title('unit step sequence');
%~~~~~~~~~~~~~~~~~~~~~~~~~~~~~~~~~~~~~~~~
%generation of square wave signal
t=0:0.002:0.1;
y3=square(2*pi*50*t);
figure;
subplot(2,2,1);
plot(t,y3);
axis([0 0.1 -2 2]);
xlabel('time');
ylabel('amplitude');
title('square wave signal');
%generation of square wave sequence
subplot(2,2,2);
stem(t,y3);
axis([0 0.1 -2 2]);
xlabel('n');
ylabel('amplitude');
title('square wave sequence');
%~~~~~~~~~~~~~~~~~~~~~~~~~~~~~~~~~~~~~~~~
%generation of sawtooth signal
y4=sawtooth(2*pi*50*t);
subplot(2,2,3);
plot(t,y4);
axis([0 0.1 -2 2]);
xlabel('time');
```

```
ylabel('amplitude');
title('sawtooth wave signal');
%generation of sawtooth sequence
subplot(2,2,4);
stem(t,y4);
axis([0 0.1 -2 2]);
xlabel('n');
ylabel('amplitude');
title('sawtooth wave sequence');
%~~~~~~~~~~~~~~~~~~~~~~~~~~~~~~~~~~~~~~~~
%generation of triangular wave signal
y5=sawtooth(2*pi*50*t,.5);
figure;
subplot(2,2,1);
plot(t,y5);
axis([0 0.1 -2 2]);
xlabel('time');
ylabel('amplitude');
title(' triangular wave signal');
%generation of triangular wave sequence
subplot(2,2,2);
stem(t,y5);
axis([0 0.1 -2 2]);
xlabel('n');
ylabel('amplitude');
title('triangular wave sequence');
%~~~~~~~~~~~~~~~~~~~~~~~~~~~~~~~~~~~~~~~~~~~
%generation of sinusoidal wave signal
y6=sin(2*pi*40*t);
subplot(2,2,3);
plot(t,y6);
axis([0 0.1 -2 2]);
xlabel('time');
ylabel('amplitude');
title(' sinusoidal wave signal');
%generation of sinu s o i d a l wave sequence
subplot(2,2,4);
```

```
stem(t,y6);
axis([0 0.1 -2 2]);
xlabel('n');
ylabel('amplitude');
title('sinusoidal wave
sequence');
%~~~~~~~~~~~~~~~~~~~~~~~~~~~~~~~~~~~~~~~~
%generation of ramp signal
y7=t;
figure;
subplot(2,2,1);
plot(t,y7);
xlabel('time');
ylabel('amplitude');
title('ramp signal');
%generation of ramp sequence
subplot(2,2,2);
stem(t,y7);
xlabel('n');
ylabel('amplitude');
title('ramp sequence');
%~~~~~~~~~~~~~~~~~~~~~~~~~~~~~~~~~~~~~~~~
%generation of sinc signal
t3=linspace(-5,5);
y8=sinc(t3);
subplot(2,2,3);
plot(t3,y8);
xlabel('time');
ylabel('amplitude');
title(' sinc signal');
%generation of sinc sequence
subplot(2,2,4);
stem(y8);
xlabel('n');
ylabel('amplitude');
title('sinc sequence');
```

Result: Various signals & sequences generated using Matlab software.

Outputs

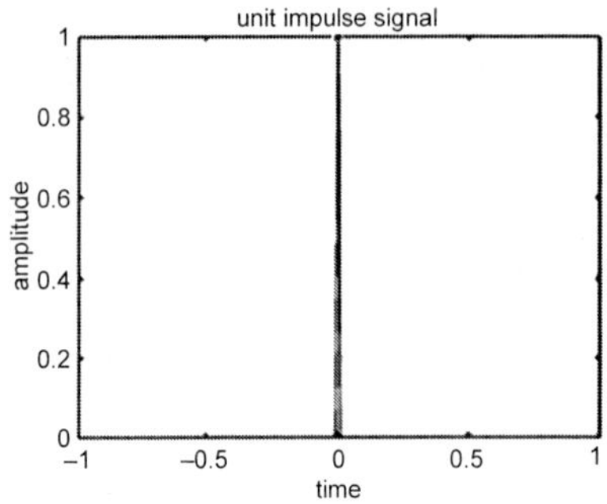

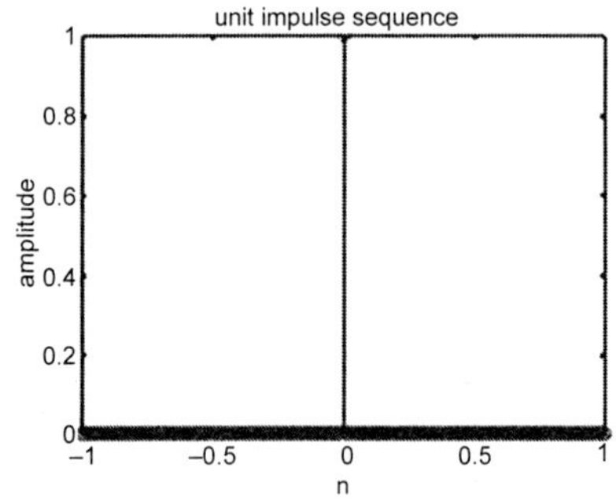

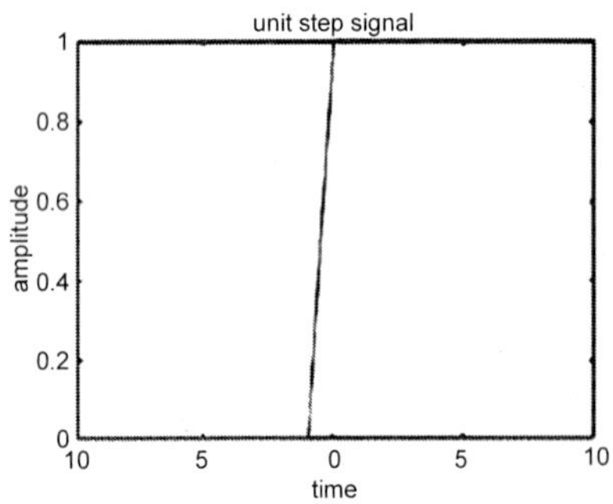

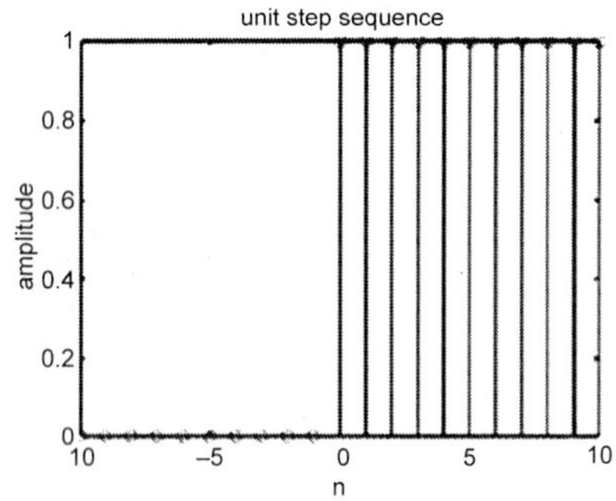

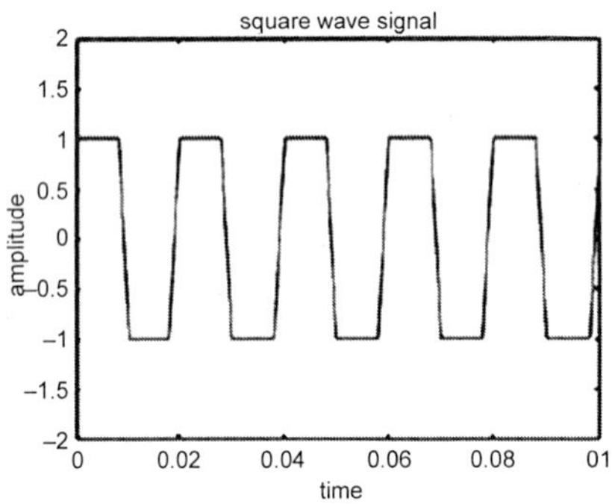

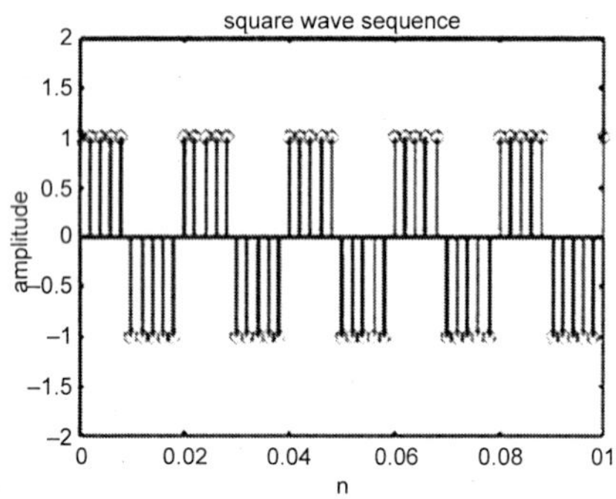

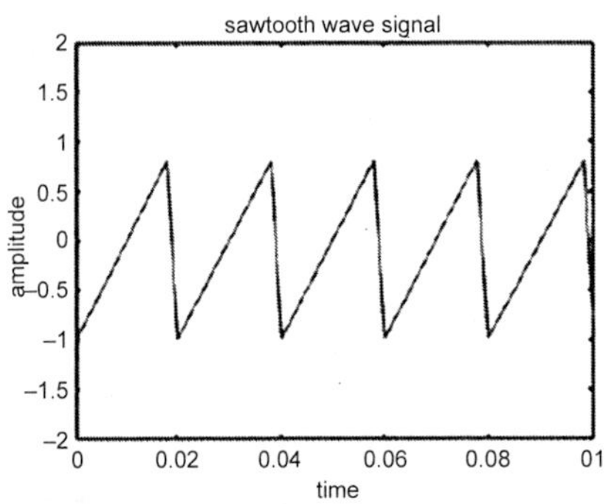

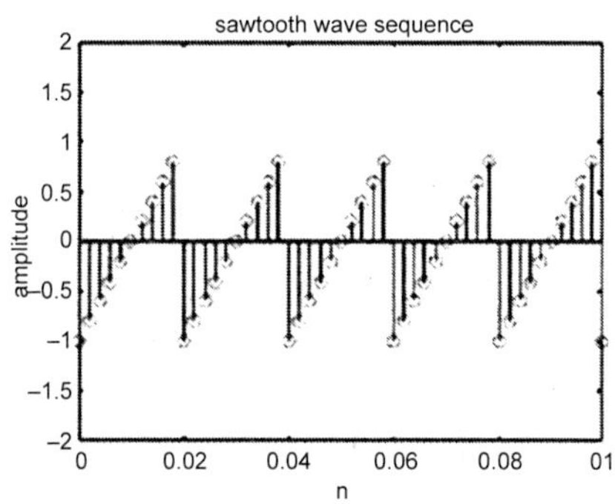

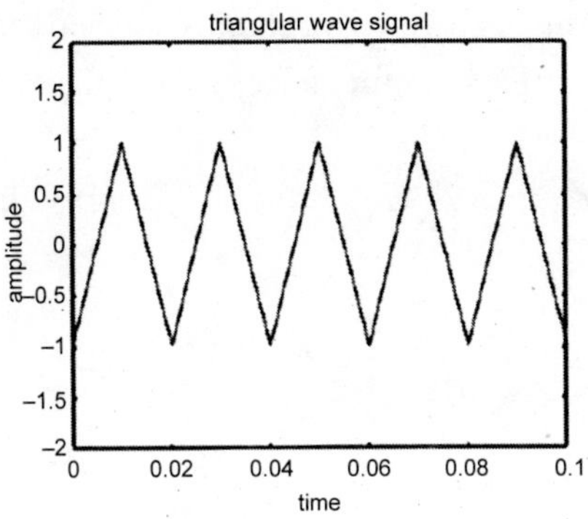
triangular wave signal
amplitude
time

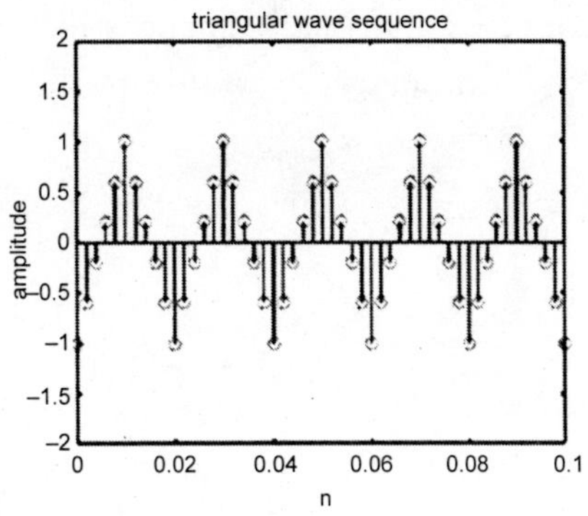
triangular wave sequence
amplitude
n

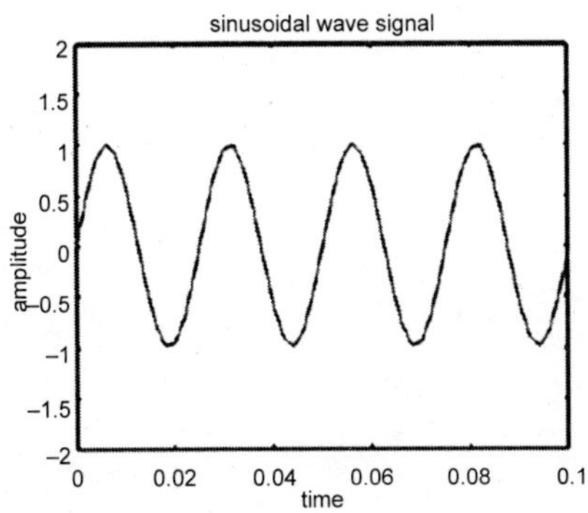
sinusoidal wave signal
amplitude
time

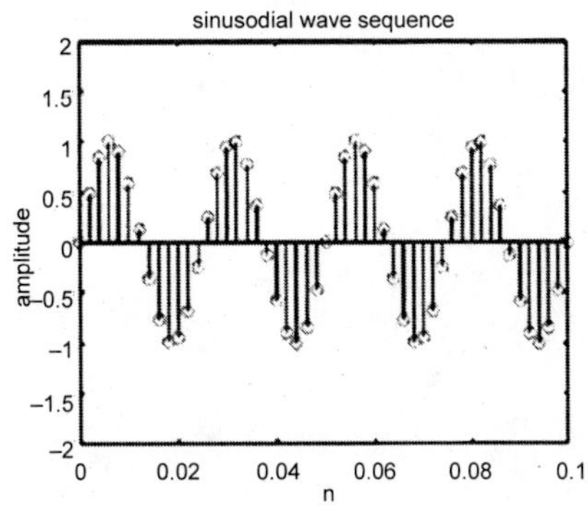
sinusodial wave sequence
amplitude
n

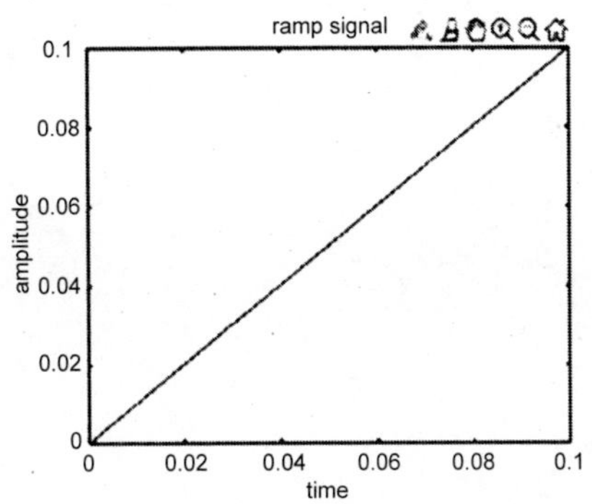
ramp signal
amplitude
time

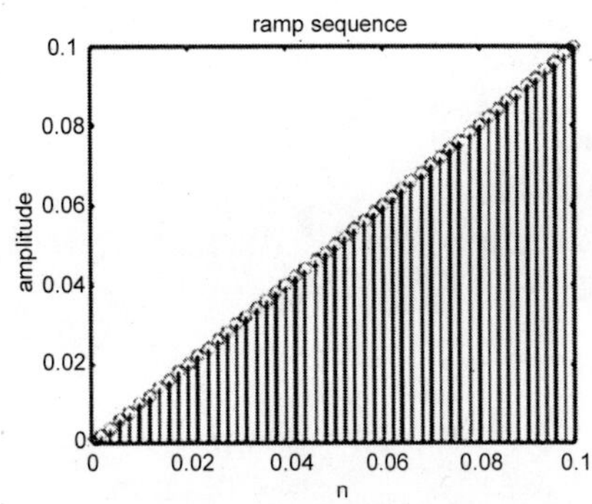
ramp sequence
amplitude
n

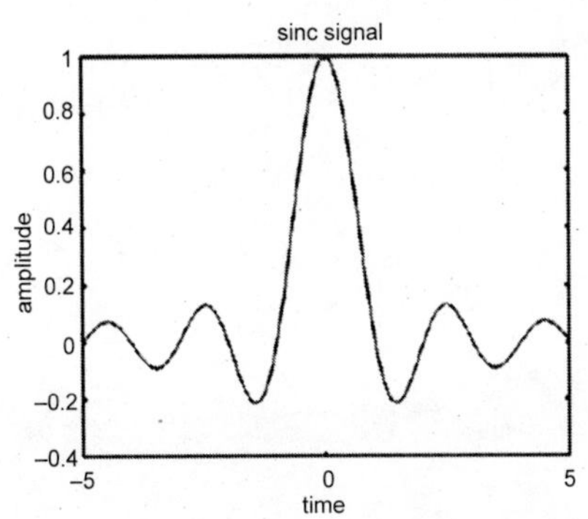
sinc signal
amplitude
time

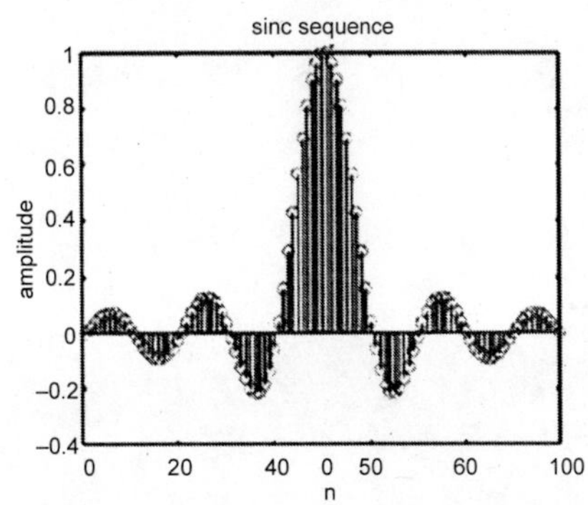
sinc sequence
amplitude
n

2. Basic Operations on Signals and sequences: Perform the operations on signals and sequences such as addition, multiplication, scaling, shifting, folding and also compute energy and power.

Program:

```
clc;
clear all;
close all;
%~~~~~~~~~~~~~~~~~~~~~~~~~~~~~~~~~~~~~~~~~~~~~~~~~~~
% generating two input signals
t=0:.01:1;
x1=sin(2*pi*4*t);
x2=sin(2*pi*8*t);
subplot(2,2,1);
plot(t,x1);
xlabel('time');
ylabel('amplitude');
title('input signal 1');
subplot(2,2,2);
plot(t,x2);
xlabel('time');
ylabel('amplitude');
title('input signal 2');
% addition of signals
y1=x1+x2;
subplot(2,2,3);
plot(t,y1);
xlabel('time');
ylabel('amplitude');
title('addition of two signals');
% multiplication of signals
y2=x1.*x2;
subplot(2,2,4);
plot(t,y2);
xlabel('time');
ylabel('amplitude');
```

```
title('multiplication of two signals');
% scaling of a signal1
A=2;
y3=A*x1;
figure;
subplot(2,2,1);
plot(t,x1);
xlabel('time');
ylabel('amplitude');
title('input signal')
subplot(2,2,2);
plot(t,y3);
xlabel('time');
ylabel('amplitude');
title('amplified input signal');
% folding of a signal1
h=length(x1);
nx=0:h-1;
subplot(2,2,3);
plot(nx,x1);
xlabel('nx');
ylabel('amplitude');
title('input signal')
y4=fliplr(x1);
nf=-fliplr(nx);
subplot(2,2,4);
plot(nf,y4);
xlabel('nf');
ylabel('amplitude');
title('folded signal');
%shifting of a signal 1
figure;
subplot(3,1,1);
plot(t,x1);
```

```
xlabel('time t');
ylabel('amplitude');
title('input signal');
subplot(3,1,2);
plot(t+2,x1);
xlabel('t+2');
ylabel('amplitude');
title('right shifted signal');
subplot(3,1,3);
plot(t-2,x1);
xlabel('t-2');
ylabel('amplitude');
title('left shifted signal');
%~~~~~~~~~~~~~~~~~~~~~~~~~~~~~~~~~~~~~~~~~~~~~~~~~~~
%operations on sequences
n1=1:1:9;
s1=[1 2 3 0 5 8 0 2 4];
figure;
subplot(2,2,1);
stem(n1,s1);
xlabel('n1');
ylabel('amplitude');
title('input sequence1');
s2=[1 1 2 4 6 0 5 3 6];
subplot(2,2,2);
stem(n1,s2);
xlabel('n2');
ylabel('amplitude');
title('input sequence2');
% addition of sequences
s3=s1+s2;
subplot(2,2,3);
stem(n1,s3);
xlabel('n1');
```

```
ylabel('amplitude');
title('sum of two sequences');
% multiplication of sequences
s4=s1.*s2;
subplot(2,2,4);
stem(n1,s4);
xlabel('n1');
ylabel('amplitude');
title('product of two sequences');
%~~~~~~~~~~~~~~~~~~~~~~~~~~~~~~~~~~~~~~~~~~~~~~~
% program for energy of a sequence
z1=input('enter the input sequence');
e1=sum(abs(z1).^2);
disp('energy of given sequence is');e1
% program for energy of a signal
t=0:pi:10*pi;
z2=cos(2*pi*50*t);
e2=sum(abs(z2).^2);
disp('energy of given signal is');e2
% program for power of a sequence
p1=(sum(abs(z1).^2))/length(z1);
disp('power of given sequence is');p1
% program for power of a signal
p2=(sum(abs(z2).^2))/length(z2);
disp('power of given signal is');p2
OUTPUT:
enter the input sequence[1 3 2 4 1]
energy of given sequence is
e1 = 31
energy of given signal is
e2 = 5.2898
power of given sequence is
p1 = 6.2000
power of given signal is
p2 = 0.4809
```

Result: Various operations on signals and sequences are performed.

Outputs:

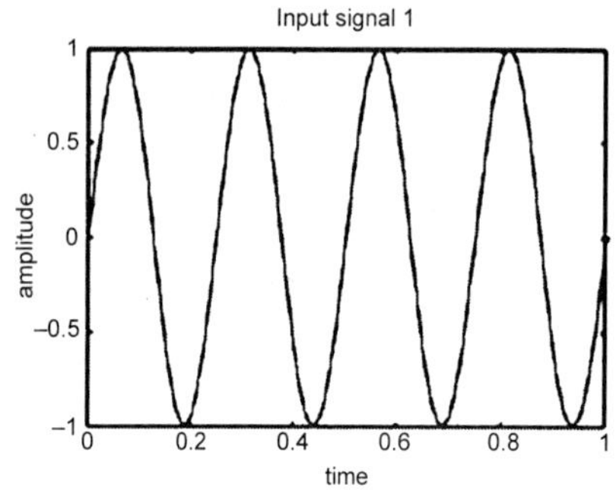

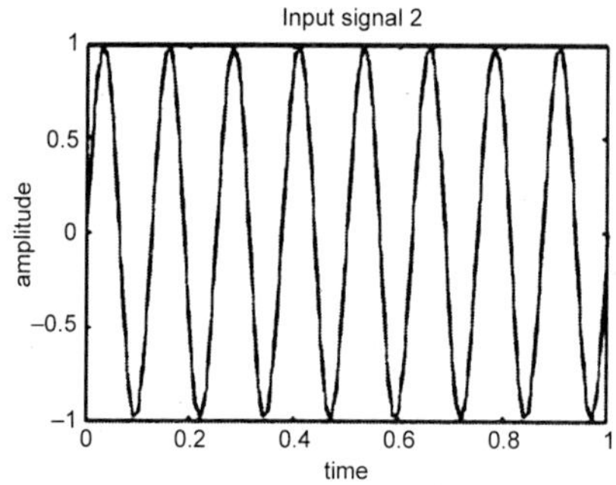

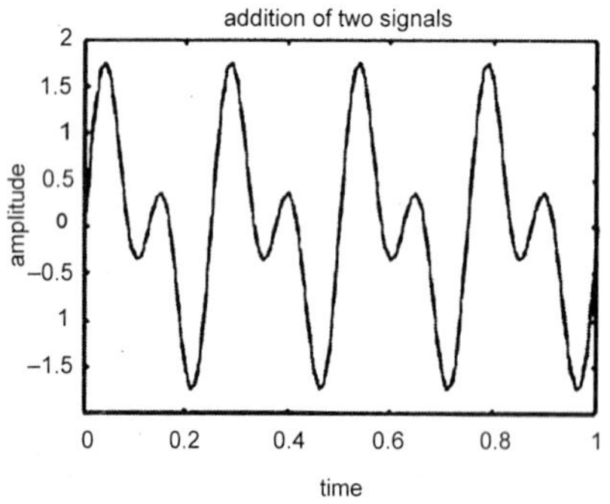

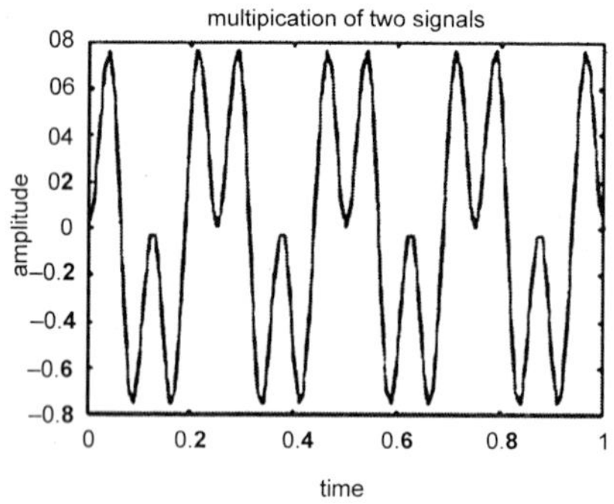

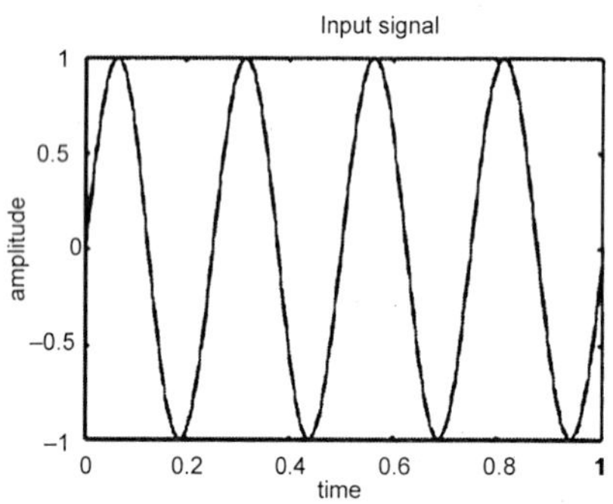

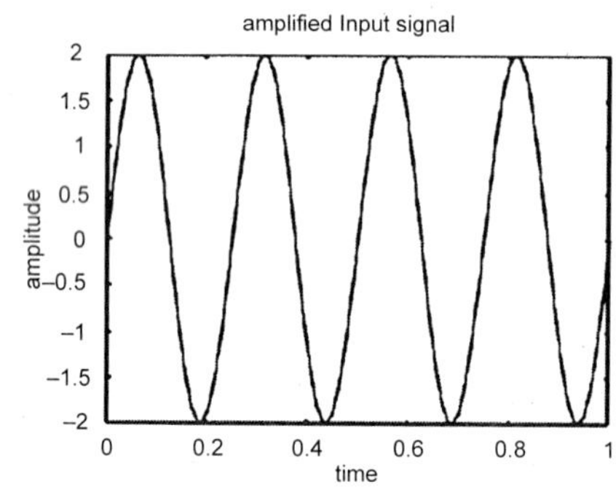

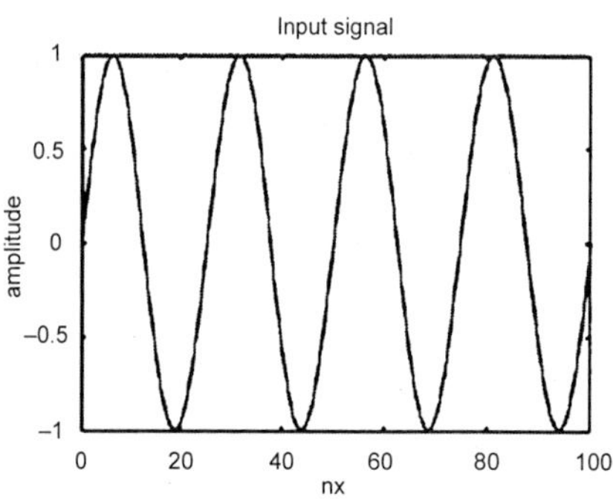

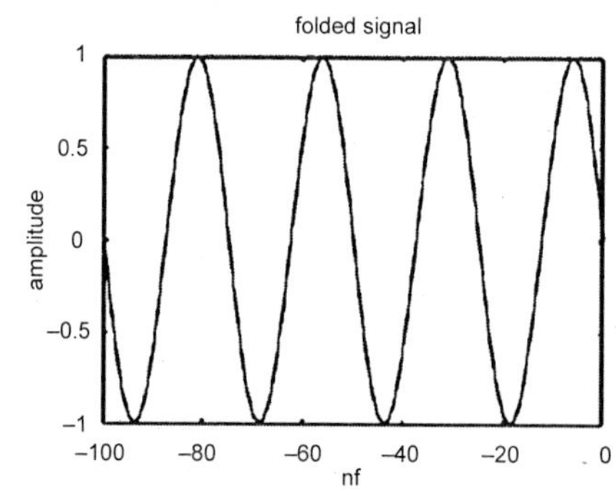

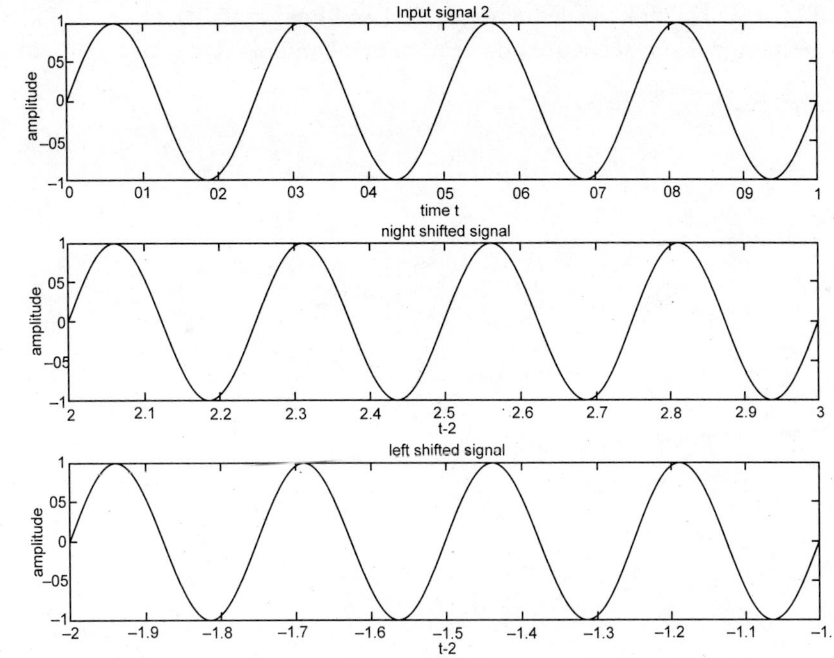
Input signal 2
amplitude
time t
night shifted signal
amplitude
t-2
left shifted signal
amplitude
t-2

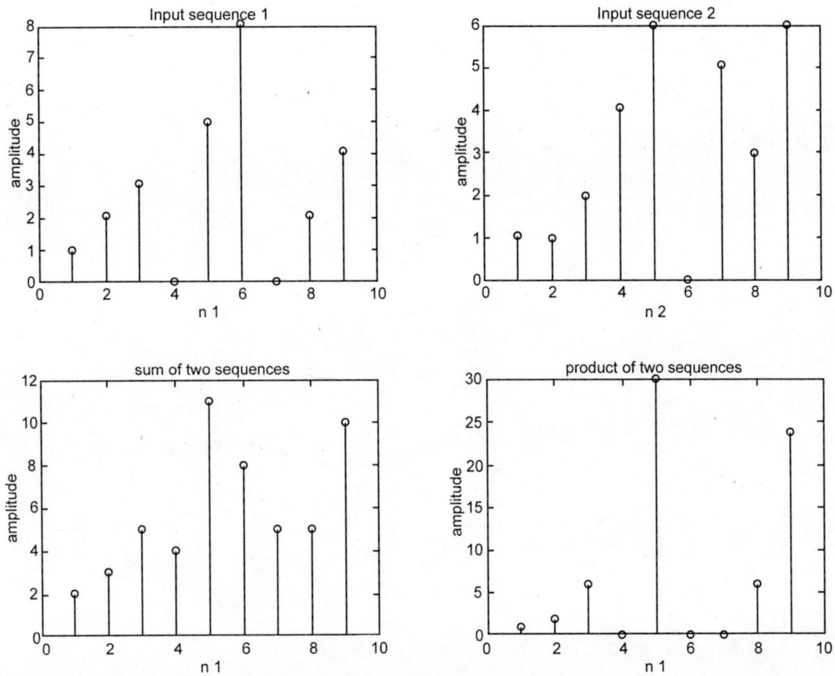
Input sequence 1
amplitude
n 1
Input sequence 2
amplitude
n 2
sum of two sequences
amplitude
n 1
product of two sequences
amplitude
n 1

3. Even and odd parts of signal and sequence & Real and imaginary parts of Signal: Finding even and odd part of the signal and sequence and also find real and maginary parts of signal.

Program:

```
clc
close all;
clear all;
%Even and odd parts of a signal
t=0:.001:4*pi;
x=sin(t)+cos(t); % x(t)=sint(t)+cos(t)
subplot(2,2,1)
plot(t,x)
xlabel('t');
ylabel('amplitude')
title('input signal')
y=sin(-t)+cos(-t); % y(t)=x(-t)
subplot(2,2,2)
plot(t,y)
xlabel('t');
ylabel('amplitude')
title('input signal with t= -t')
even=(x+y)/2;
subplot(2,2,3)
plot(t,even)
xlabel('t');
ylabel('amplitude')
title('even part of the signal')
odd=(x-y)/2;
subplot(2,2,4)
plot(t,odd)
xlabel('t');
ylabel('amplitude');
title('odd part of the signal');
% Even and odd parts of a sequence
x1=[0,2,-3,5,-2,-1,6];
n=-3:3;
y1= fliplr(x1);%y1(n)=x1(-n)
figure;
subplot(2,2,1);
stem(n,x1);
xlabel('n');
ylabel('amplitude');
```

```
title('input sequence');
subplot(2,2,2);
stem(n,y1);
xlabel('n');
ylabel('amplitude');
title('input sequence with n= -n');
even1=.5*(x1+y1);
odd1=.5*(x1-y1);
% plotting even and odd parts of the sequence
subplot(2,2,3);
stem(n,even1);
xlabel('n');
ylabel('amplitude');
title('even part of sequence');
subplot(2,2,4);
stem(n,odd1);
xlabel('n');
ylabel('amplitude');
title('odd part of sequence');
title('odd part of sequence');
% plotting real and imaginary parts of the signal
x2=sin(t)+j*cos(t);
figure;
subplot(3,1,1);
plot(t,x2); xlabel('t');
ylabel('amplitude');
title('input signal');
subplot(3,1,2)
plot(t,real(x2));
xlabel('time');
ylabel('amplitude');
title('real part of signal');
subplot(3,1,3)
plot(t,imag(x2));
xlabel('time');
ylabel('amplitude');
title('imaginary part of signal');
```

RESULT: Even and odd part of the signal and sequence, real and imaginary parts of signal are computed.

Outputs:

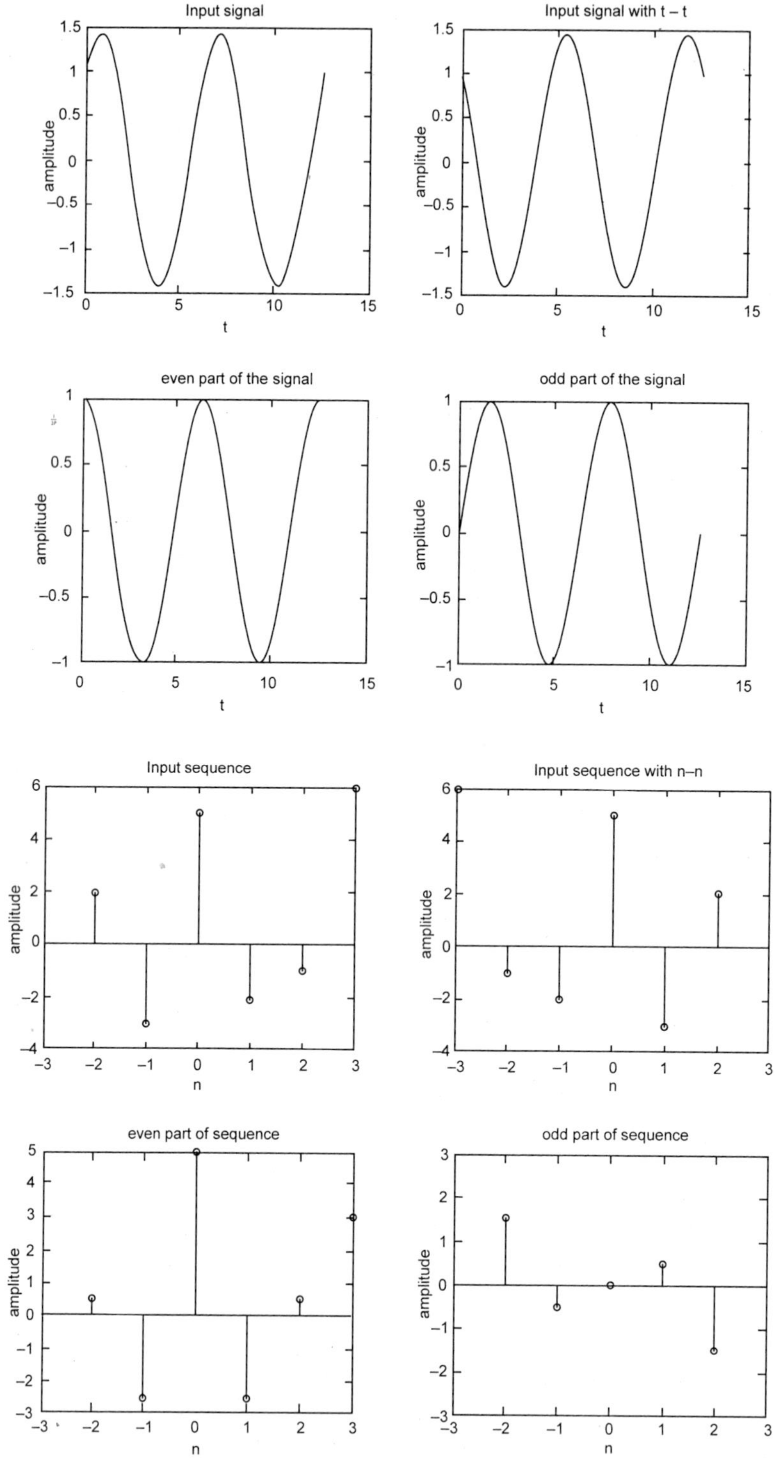

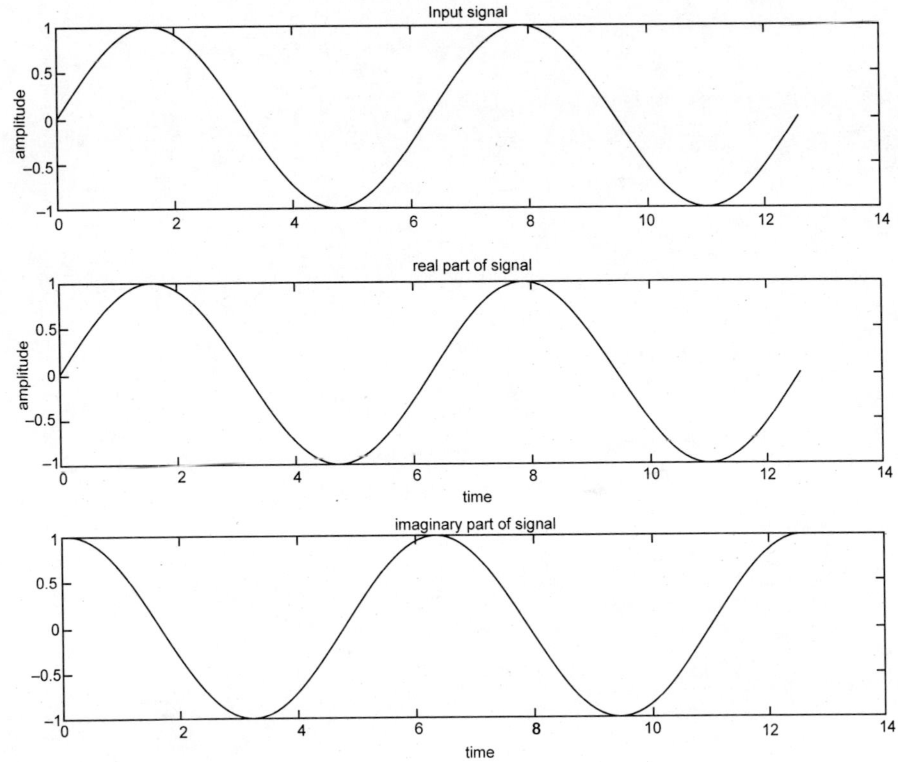

4. Convolution between signals & sequences

Write the program for convolution between two signals and also between two sequences.

Program:

```
clc;
close all;
clear all;
%program for convolution of two sequences
x=input(‘enter input sequence: ‘);
h=input(‘enter impulse response: ‘);
y=convo(x,h);
subplot(3,1,1);
stem(x);
xlabel(‘n’);
ylabel(‘x(n)’);
title(‘input sequence’)
subplot(3,1,2);
stem(h);
```

```
xlabel('n');
ylabel('h(n)');
title('impulse response sequence')
subplot(3,1,3);
stem(y);
xlabel('n');
ylabel('y(n)');
title('linear convolution')
disp('linear convolution y=');
disp(y)
%program for signal convolution
t=0:0.1:10;
x1=sin(2*pi*t);
h1=cos(2*pi*t);
y1=convo(x1,h1)
;
figure;
subplot(3,1,1);
plot(x1);
xlabel('t');
ylabel('x(t)');
title('input signal')
subplot(3,1,2);
plot(h1);
xlabel('t');
ylabel('h(t)');
title('impulse response')
subplot(3,1,3);
plot(y1);
xlabel('n');
ylabel('y(n)');
title('linear convolution');
%Custom Code for Convolution
function [y] = convo(x, h)
l1 = length(x);
```

```
l2 = length(h);
N = l1 + l2 - 1;
for n = 1 : 1 : N
y(n) = 0;
for k = 1 : 1 : l1
if(n - k + 1 >= 1 & n - k + 1 <= l2)
    y(n) = y(n) + x(k) * h(n - k + 1);
                          end
                    end
             end
     end
```

RESULT: convolution between signals and sequences is computed.

Output:

```
enter input sequence: [1 3 4 5]
enter impulse response: [2 1 4]
linear convolution y = 2 7 15 26 21 20
```

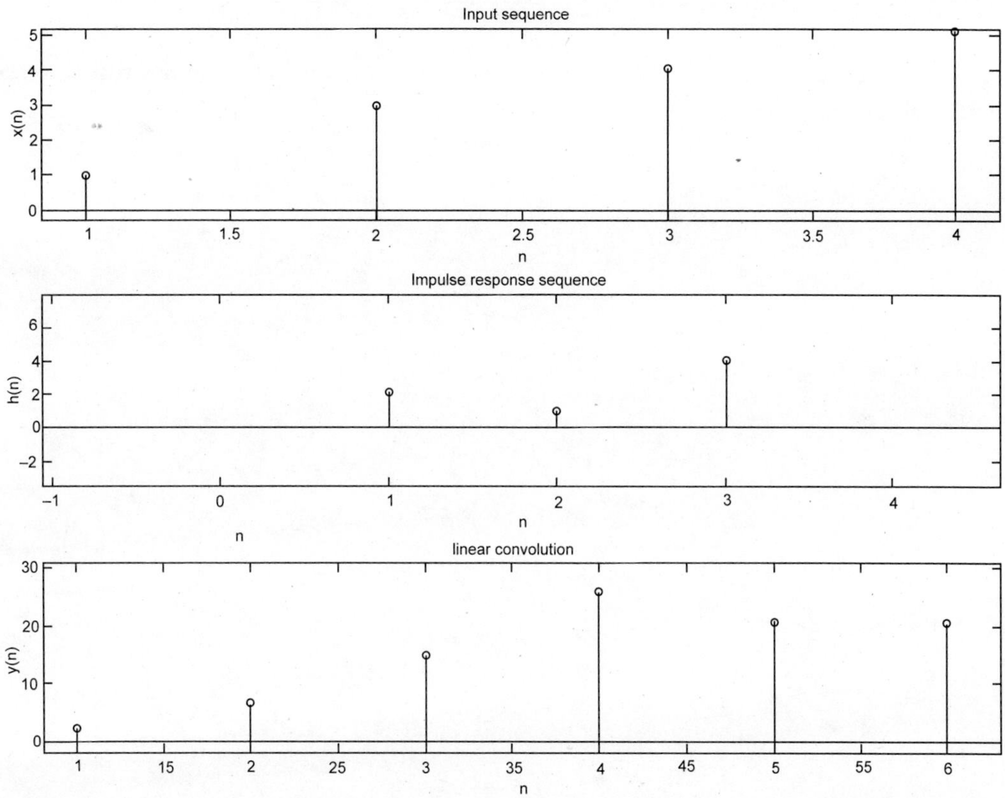

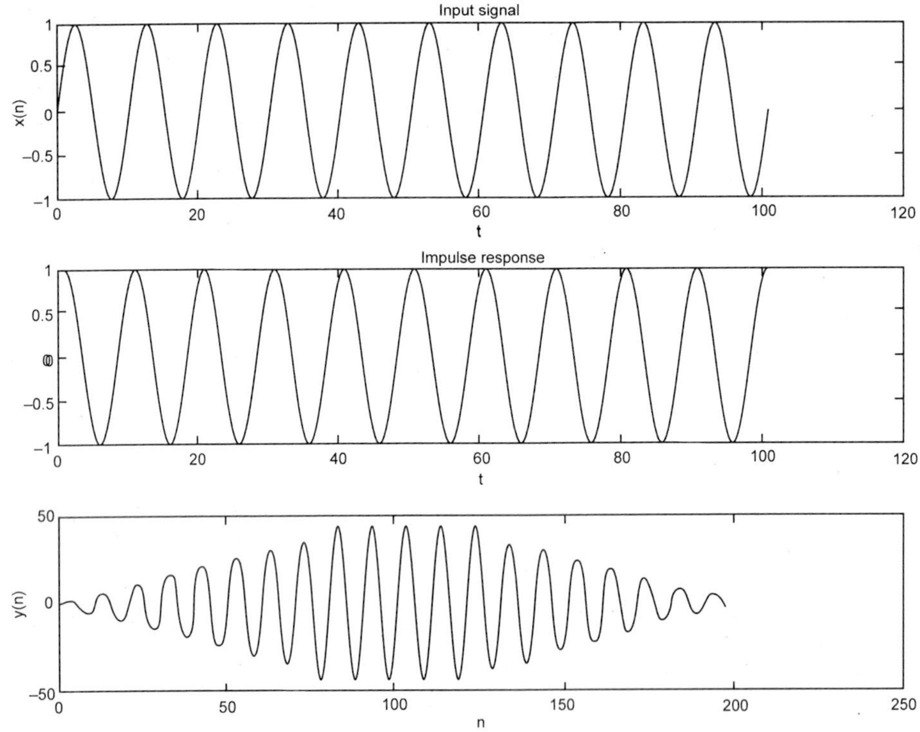

5. Auto correlation and Cross correlation: To compute Auto correlation and Cross correlation between signals and sequences.

Program: n

```
clc;

close all;

clear all;

x(n)x(n 1)

% two input sequences

x=input('enterinput sequence');

h=input('enter the impulse suquence');

subplot(2,2,1); stem(x); xlabel('n');

ylabel('x(n)');

title('input sequence');

subplot(2,2,2);

stem(h);
```

```
xlabel('n'); ylabel('h(n)');
title('impulse sequence');
% cross correlation between two sequences
y=corr(x,h);
subplot(2,2,3);
stem(y);
xlabel('n');
ylabel('y(n)');
title(' cross correlation between two sequences ');
% auto correlation of input sequence
z=corr(x,x);
subplot(2,2,4);
stem(z);
xlabel('n');
ylabel('z(n)');
title('auto correlation of input sequence');
% cross correlation between two signals
% generating two input signals
t=0:0.2:10;
x1=3*exp(-2*t);
h1=exp(t);
figure;
subplot(2,2,1);
plot(t,x1);
xlabel('t');
ylabel('x1(t)');
title('input signal');
subplot(2,2,2);
plot(t,h1);
xlabel('t');
```

```
ylabel('h1(t)');
title('impulse signal');
% cross correlation
subplot(2,2,3);
z1=corr(x1,h1); plot(z1);
xlabel('t');
ylabel('z1(t)'); title('cross
correlation ');
% auto correlation
subplot(2,2,4);
z2=corr(x1,x1);
plot(z2);
xlabel('t');
ylabel('z2(t)');
title('auto correlation ');
function [y] = corr(x, h)
n=length(x);
m=length(h);
k=n+m-1;
x=[x zeros(1,k-n)]';
h=wrev(h);
h=[h zeros(1,k-m)]';
for i=1:k
c(:,i)=circshift(x,i-1);
end
y=c*h;
end
```

Result: Auto correlation and Cross correlation between signals and sequences is computed.

Output: enter input sequence [1 2 5 7]

enter the impulse sequence [2 6 0 5 3]

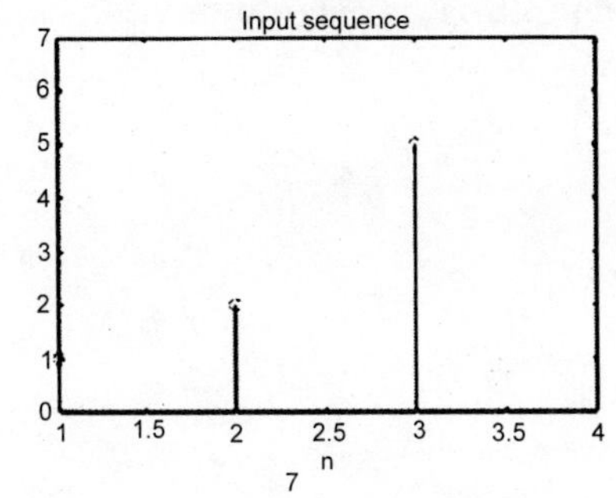
Input sequence
n

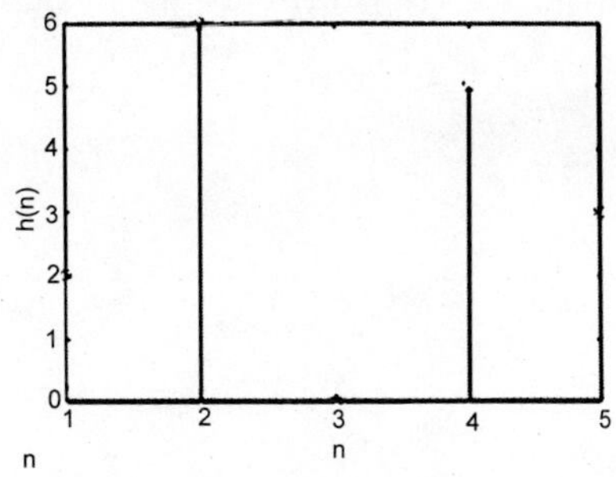
h(n)
n

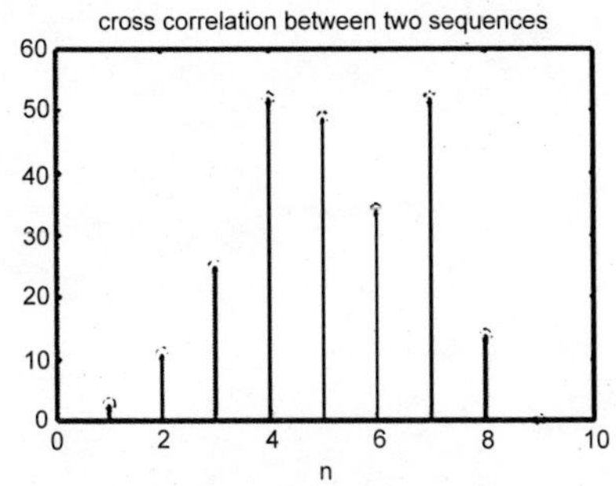
cross correlation between two sequences
n

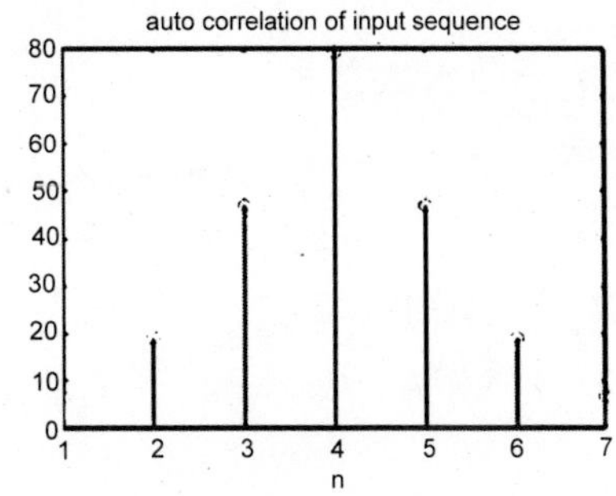
auto correlation of input sequence
n

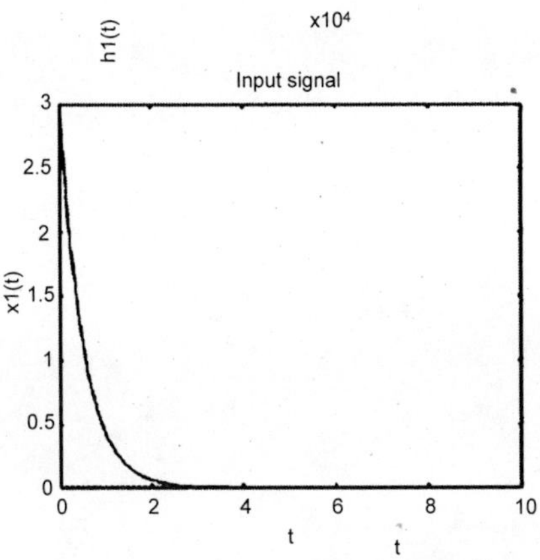
Input signal
x1(t)
t

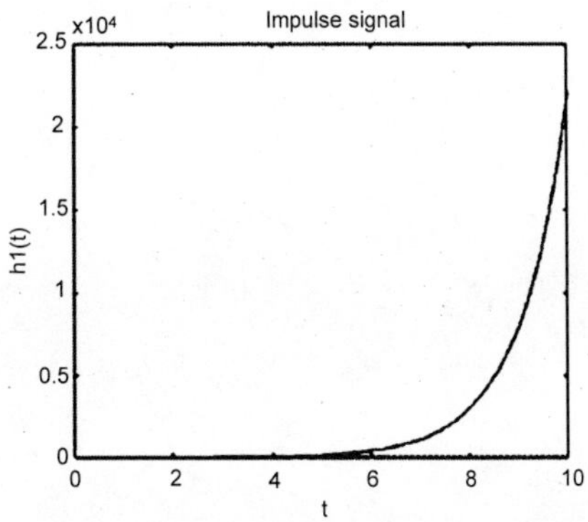
x10⁴
Impulse signal
h1(t)
t

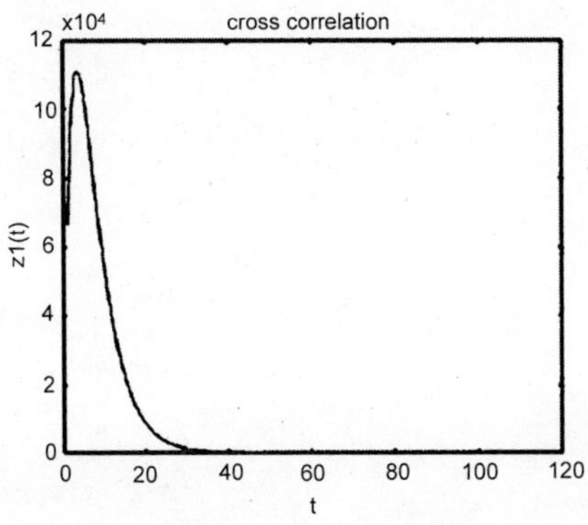
x10⁴
cross correlation
z1(t)
t

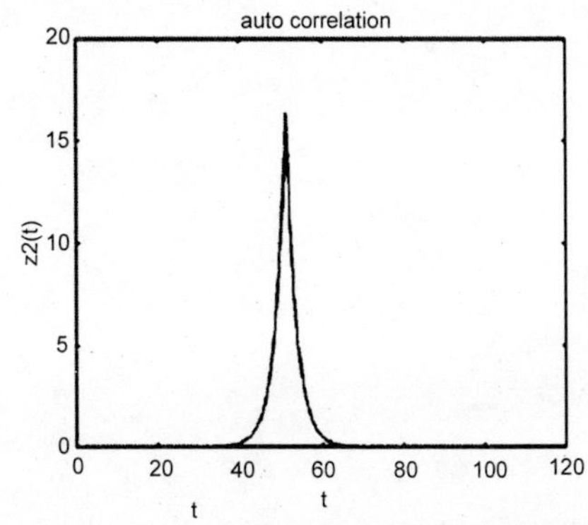
auto correlation
z2(t)
t

6. Finding the Fourier Transform of a given signal and plotting its magnitude and phase spectrum

Program:

```
clc;
clear all;
close all;
fs=1000;
N=1024; % length of fft sequence
t=[0:N-1]*(1/fs);
% input signal
x=0.8*cos(2*pi*100*t);
subplot(3,1,1);
plot(t,x);
axis([0 0.05 -1 1]);
grid; xlabel('t');
ylabel('amplitude');
title('input signal');
% Fourier transform of given signal
x1=fft(x);
% magnitude spectrum
k=0:N-1;
Xmag=abs(x1);
subplot(3,1,2);
plot(k,Xmag);
grid;
xlabel('t');
ylabel('amplitude');
title('magnitude of fft signal')
%phase spectrum
Xphase=angle(x1);
subplot(3,1,3);
plot(k,Xphase);
grid;
xlabel('t');
ylabel('angle');
title('phase of fft signal');
```

Result: Magnitude and phase spectrum of FFT of a given signal is plotted.

Output:

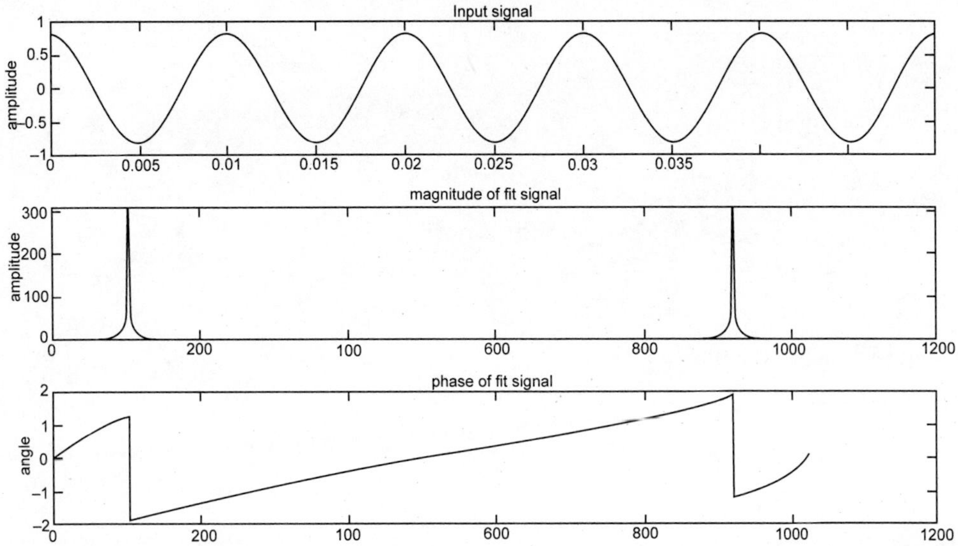

7. Verification of Wiener-Khinchin Theorem

Program:

```
clc;
clear all;
close all;
t=0:0.1:2*pi;
%input signal
x=sin(2*t);
subplot(3,1,1);
plot(x);
xlabel('time');
ylabel('amplitude');
title('input signal');
%autocorrelation of input signal
xu=xcorr(x,x);
%fft of autocorrelation signal
y=fft(xu);
subplot(3,1,2);
plot(abs(y));
xlabel('f');
ylabel('amplitude');
title('fft of autocorrelation of input signal');
%fourier transform of input signal
```

```
y1=fft(x);
%finding the power spectral density
y2=(abs(y1)).^2;
subplot(3,1,3);
plot(y2);
xlabel('f');
ylabel('magnitude');
title('PSD of input signal');
```

Result: Wiener-Khinchin relation is verified.

Output:

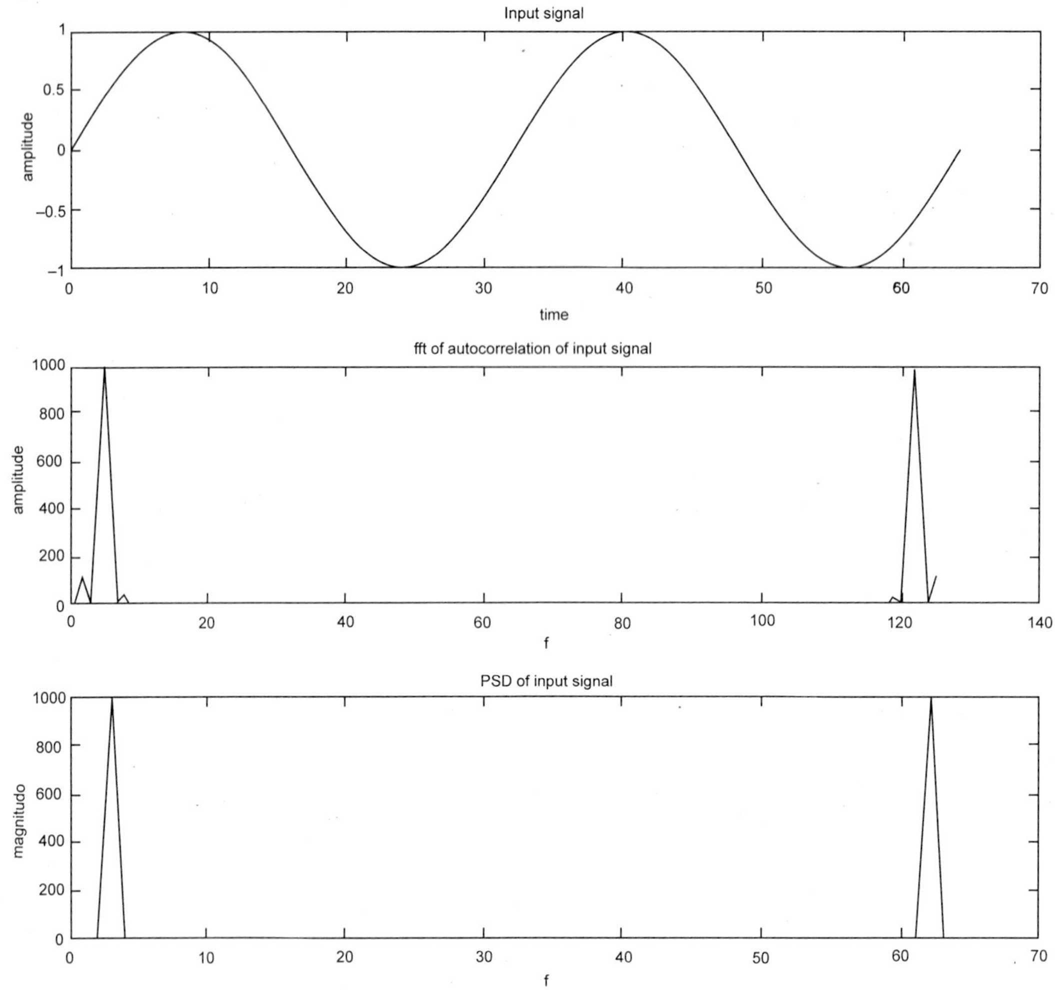

8. Sampling Theorem Verification

Program 1:

```
% Verification of Sampling Theorem (Single Tone)
clc; clear; close
all;fs = 1000;
Ts = 1/fs;
t = 0:Ts:1-Ts; % Time Axis (Determines the smoothness of the Signal)
f = -fs/2 : 1 : fs/2 - 1; % Frequency axis (Determines the smoothness of
theSignal)
T = 0.1; % Time Period of the input signal
fm = 1/T;% Highest frequency component in the input signalfs1 = 1.5*fm;
% Less than Nyquist
Sampling frequency
fs2 = 2*fm; % Nyquist Sampling frequency
fs3 = 10*fm; % Greater than Nyquist Sampling frequencyTs1 = 1/fs1; % Less
than Nyquist
Sampling interval
Ts2 = 1/fs2; % Nyquist Sampling interval
Ts3 = 1/fs3; % Greater than Nyquist Sampling interval
Fs1 = -fs1/2 : 1 : fs1/2 - 1; % Frequency axis to plot spectrum of the
signalsampled with Less than Nyquist Sampling frequency
Fs2 = -fs2/2 : 1 : fs2/2 - 1; % Frequency axis to plot spectrum of the
signalsampled with Nyquist Sampling frequency
Fs3 = -fs3/2 : 1 : fs3/2 - 1; % Frequency axis to plot spectrum of the
signalsampled with Greater than Nyquist Sampling frequency
length(Fs1);l2=length(Fs2);l3=length(Fs3);%lengthsoffrequencyaxisused to
compute FFT
%% Input Signal to sampler
x = cos(2*pi*fm*t); % Input Signal to be sampled
X = fftshift(abs(fft(x)/fs)); % Magnitude spectrum of input Signal
%% Input signal Sampled with fs1 (< Nyquist rate)n = 0:1:40;
x1 = cos(2*pi*fm*n*Ts1);% Sampled signal with < Nyquist rate
X1 = fftshift(abs(fft(x1,l1)/fs1)); % Magnitude Spectrum of Sampled
signalwith < Nyquist rate
%% Input signal Sampled with fs2 (= Nyquist rate)
x2 = cos(2*pi*fm*n*Ts2); % Sampled signal with = Nyquist rate
X2 = fftshift(abs(fft(x2,l2)/fs2)); % Magnitude Spectrum of Sampled
signalwith = Nyquist rate
%% Input signal Sampled with fs3 (> Nyquist rate) x3=cos(2*pi*fm*n*Ts3);
% Sampled signal
with > Nyquist rate
```

```
X3 = fftshift(abs(fft(x3,l3)/fs3)); % Magnitude Spectrum of Sampled signal
with > Nyquist rate
%% Plots in time domain figure
subplot(2,2,1) % Plot of Input signal
plot(t,x);ylim([-1.2,1.2]);                              xlabel('time');
ylabel('x(t)');title('Continous time
Input signal');grid;
subplot(2,2,2) % Plot of Sampled signal with < Nyquist rate
s t e m ( n * T s 1 , x 1 ) ; x l i m ( [ 0 , 1 ] ) ; y l i m ( [ - 1 . 2 , 1 . 2 ] ) ;
xlabel('time');ylabel('x(n)');
title('Discrete time signal with fs<2fm'); hold on;
subplot(2,2,2); plot(n*Ts1,x1); grid;
subplot(2,2,3) % Plot of Sampled signal with = Nyquist rate stem(n*Ts2,x2);
xlim([0,1]);ylim([-1.2,1.2]);xlabel('time');ylabel('x(n)');
title('Discrete time signal with fs=2fm'); hold
on;subplot(2,2,3); plot(n*Ts2,x2); grid;
subplot(2,2,4) % Plot of Sampled signal with > Nyquist rate
s t e m ( n * T s 3 , x 3 ) ; x l a b e l ( ' t i m e ' ) ; y l i m ( [ - 1 . 2 , 1 . 2 ] ) ;
ylabel('x(n)');title('Discrete time
signal with fs>2fm')
hold on;subplot(2,2,4); plot(n*Ts3,x3); grid;
%% Plots in
Frequency domain
figure
subplot(2,2,1) % Plot of Spectrum of Input signal
plot(f,X);xlim([-100,100]);  ylim([0,0.6]);xlabel('Frequency');ylabel('X
(f)');
title('Spectrum of Input Signal');
subplot(2,2,2) % Plot of spectrum of the signal sampled with Less than
NyquistSampling frequency
plot(Fs1,X1);                        xlim([-100,100]);xlabel('Frequency');
ylabel('X1(f)');title('Spectrum for
fs<2fm');
subplot(2,2,3)  %  Plot  of  spectrum  of  the  signal  sampled  with  the
NyquistSampling frequency
plot(Fs2,X2); xlim([-100,100]);ylim([0,2]);xlabel('Frequency');ylabel('X
2(f)');
title('Spectrum for fs=2fm');
subplot(2,2,4)  % Plot  of  spectrum  of  the  signal  sampled  with  Greater
thanNyquist Sampling
frequency
plot(Fs3,X3);xlim([-100,100]);ylim([0,0.3]); xlabel('Frequency');ylabel(
```

```
'X3(f)');
title('Spectrum for fs>2fm');
```

Result: Sampling theorem is verified.

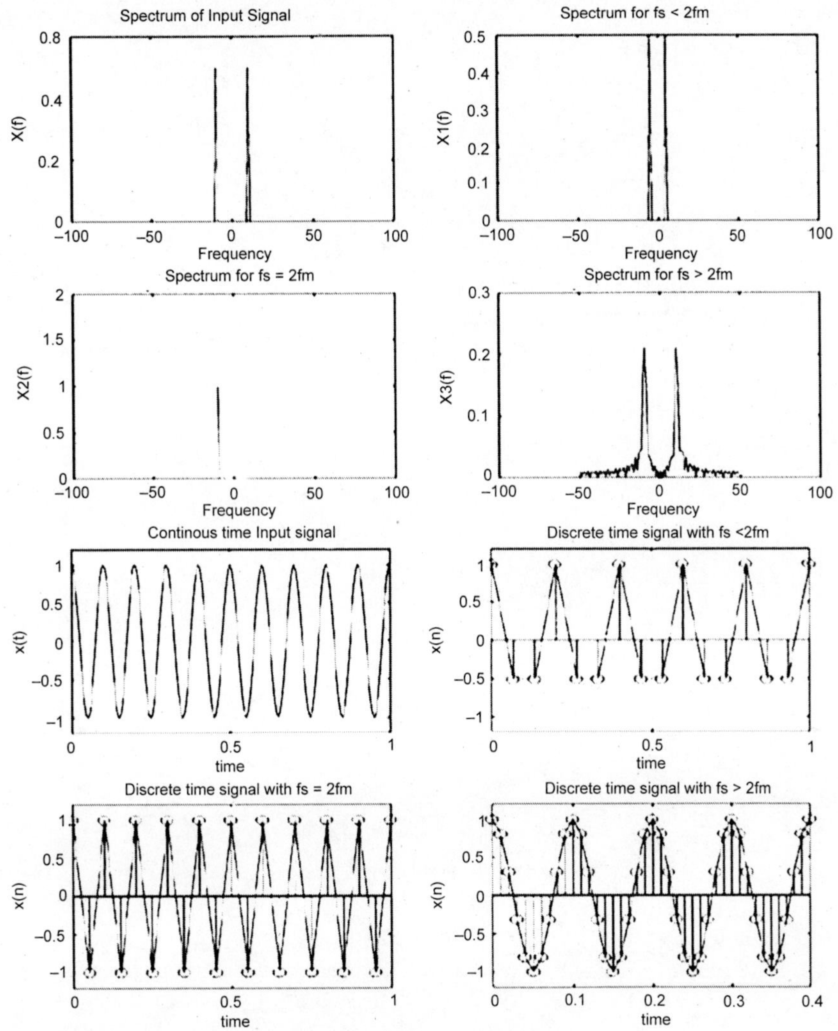

Program 2:

```
% Verification of Sampling Theorem (Multi Tone)
clc; clear; close all; fs = 1000;
Ts = 1/fs;
t = 0:Ts:1-Ts; % Time Axis (Determines the smoothness of the Signal)
f = -fs/2 : 1 : fs/2 - 1; % Frequency axis (Determines the smoothness of the
Signal)
T = 0.1; % Time Period of the input signal
fm = 1/T;% Highest frequency component in the input signal
%% Input Signal to sampler
```

```
x =
cos(2*pi*fm*t)+0.9*cos(2*pi*2*fm*t)+0.8*cos(2*pi*3*fm*t)+0.7*cos(2*pi*4*fm*t)+0
.6*cos(2*pi*5*fm*t)+0.5*co
s(2*pi*6*fm*t)+0.4*cos(2*pi*7*fm*t)+0.3*cos (2*pi*8*fm*t)+0.2*cos(2*pi*9*fm*t)+0
.1*cos(2*pi*10*fm*t); %
Input Signal to be sampled
X = fftshift(abs(fft(x)/fs)); % Magnitude spectrum of input Signal
fmax = 10*fm;
fs1 = 1.5*fmax; % Less than Nyquist Sampling frequency
fs2 = 2*fmax; % Nyquist Sampling frequency
fs3 = 10*fmax; % Greater than Nyquist Sampling frequency
Ts1 = 1/fs1; % Less than Nyquist Sampling interval
Ts2 = 1/fs2; % Nyquist Sampling interval
Ts3 = 1/fs3; % Greater than Nyquist Sampling interval
Fs1 = -fs1/2 : 1 : fs1/2 - 1; % Frequency axis to plot spectrum of the signal
sampled with Less than Nyquist
Sampling frequency
Fs2 = -fs2/2 : 1 : fs2/2 - 1; % Frequency axis to plot spectrum of the signal
sampled with Nyquist Sampling
frequency
Fs3 = -fs3/2 : 1 : fs3/2 - 1; % Frequency axis to plot spectrum of the signal
sampled with Greater than
Nyquist Sampling frequency
l1 = length(Fs1);l2 = length(Fs2);l3 = length(Fs3); % lengths of frequency axis
used to compute FFT
%% Input signal Sampled with fs1 (< Nyquist rate)
n = 0:1:400;% Controls the width of sampling interval
x1
=cos(2*pi*fm*n*Ts1)+0.9*cos(2*pi*2*fm*n*Ts1)+0.8*cos(2*pi*3*fm*n*Ts1)+0.7*cos(2
*pi*4*fm*n*Ts1)+0.6*c
os(2*pi*5*fm*n*Ts1)+0.5*cos(2*pi*6*fm*n*Ts1)+0.4*cos(2*pi*7*fm*n*Ts1)+0.3*cos(2
*pi*8*fm*n*Ts1)+0.2*c
os(2*pi*9*fm*n*Ts1)+0.1*cos(2*pi*10*fm*n*Ts1);
X1 = fftshift(abs(fft(x1,l1)/fs1)); % Magnitude Spectrum of Sampled signal with <
Nyquist rate
%% Input signal Sampled with fs2 (= Nyquist rate)
x2 =
cos(2*pi*fm*n*Ts2)+0.9*cos(2*pi*2*fm*n*Ts2)+0.8*cos(2*pi*3*fm*n*Ts2)+0.7*cos(2*
pi*4*fm*n*Ts2)+0.6*co
s(2*pi*5*fm*n*Ts2)+0.5*cos(2*pi*6*fm*n*Ts2)+0.4*cos(2*pi*7*fm*n*Ts2)+0.3*cos(2*
pi*8*fm*n*Ts2)+0.2*cos
(2*pi*9*fm*n*Ts2)+0.1*cos(2*pi*10*fm*n*Ts2); % Sampled signal with = Nyquist rate
X2 = fftshift(abs(fft(x2,l2)/fs2)); % Magnitude Spectrum of Sampled signal with =
Nyquist rate
%% Input signal Sampled with fs3 (> Nyquist rate)
x3
```

```
=cos(2*pi*fm*n*Ts3)+0.9*cos(2*pi*2*fm*n*Ts3)+0.8*cos(2*pi*3*fm*n*Ts3)+0.7*cos(2
*pi*4*fm*n*Ts3)+0.6*c
os(2*pi*5*fm*n*Ts3)+0.5*cos(2*pi*6*fm*n*Ts3)+0.4*cos(2*pi*7*fm*n*Ts3)+0.3*cos(2
*pi*8*fm*n*Ts3)+0.2*c
os(2*pi*9*fm*n*Ts3)+0.1*cos(2*pi*10*fm*n*Ts3); % Sampled signal with > Nyquist
rate
X3 = fftshift(abs(fft(x3,13)/fs3)); % Magnitude Spectrum of Sampled signal with >
Nyquist rate
%% Plots in time domain
figure
subplot(2,2,1) % Plot of Input signal
plot(t,x);ylim([-1.2,1.2]);  xlabel('time');  ylabel('x(t)');  title('Continous
time Input signal');grid;
subplot(2,2,2) % Plot of Sampled signal with < Nyquist rate stem(n*Ts1,x1);
xlim([0,1]);
ylim([-1.2,1.2]); xlabel('time'); ylabel('x(n)'); title('Discrete time signal
with fs<2fm');
hold on; subplot(2,2,2); plot(n*Ts1,x1); grid;
subplot(2,2,3) % Plot of Sampled signal with = Nyquist rate stem(n*Ts2,x2);
xlim([0,1]);
ylim([-1.2,1.2]);xlabel('time'); ylabel('x(n)'); title('Discrete time signal with
fs=2fm');
hold on;subplot(2,2,3); plot(n*Ts2,x2); grid;
subplot(2,2,4)  %  Plot  of  Sampled  signal  with  >  Nyquist  rate
stem(n*Ts3,x3);xlabel('time');
ylim([-1.2,1.2]);
ylabel('x(n)');
title('Discrete time signal with fs>2fm')
hold on;subplot(2,2,4); plot(n*Ts3,x3); grid;
%% Plots in Frequency domain
figure
subplot(2,2,1) % Plot of Spectrum of Input signal
plot(f,X);
xlim([-100,100]);
ylim([0,0.6]);
xlabel('Frequency'); ylabel('X(f)'); title('Spectrum of Input Signal');
subplot(2,2,2) % Plot of spectrum of the signal sampled with Less than Nyquist
Sampling frequency
plot(Fs1,X1);      xlim([-100,100]);xlabel('Frequency');      ylabel('X1(f)');
title('Spectrum for fs<2fm');
subplot(2,2,3) % Plot of spectrum of the signal sampled with the Nyquist Sampling
frequency
plot(Fs2,X2);
xlim([-100,100]);
ylim([0,2]);
xlabel('Frequency'); ylabel('X2(f)'); title('Spectrum for fs=2fm');
```

```
subplot(2,2,4) % Plot of spectrum of the signal sampled with Greater than Nyquist
Sampling frequency
stem(Fs3,X3); xlim([-150,150]);
ylim([0,0.3]);
xlabel('Frequency'); ylabel('X3(f)'); title('Spectrum for fs>2fm');
```

9. Pulse code Modulation

Result:

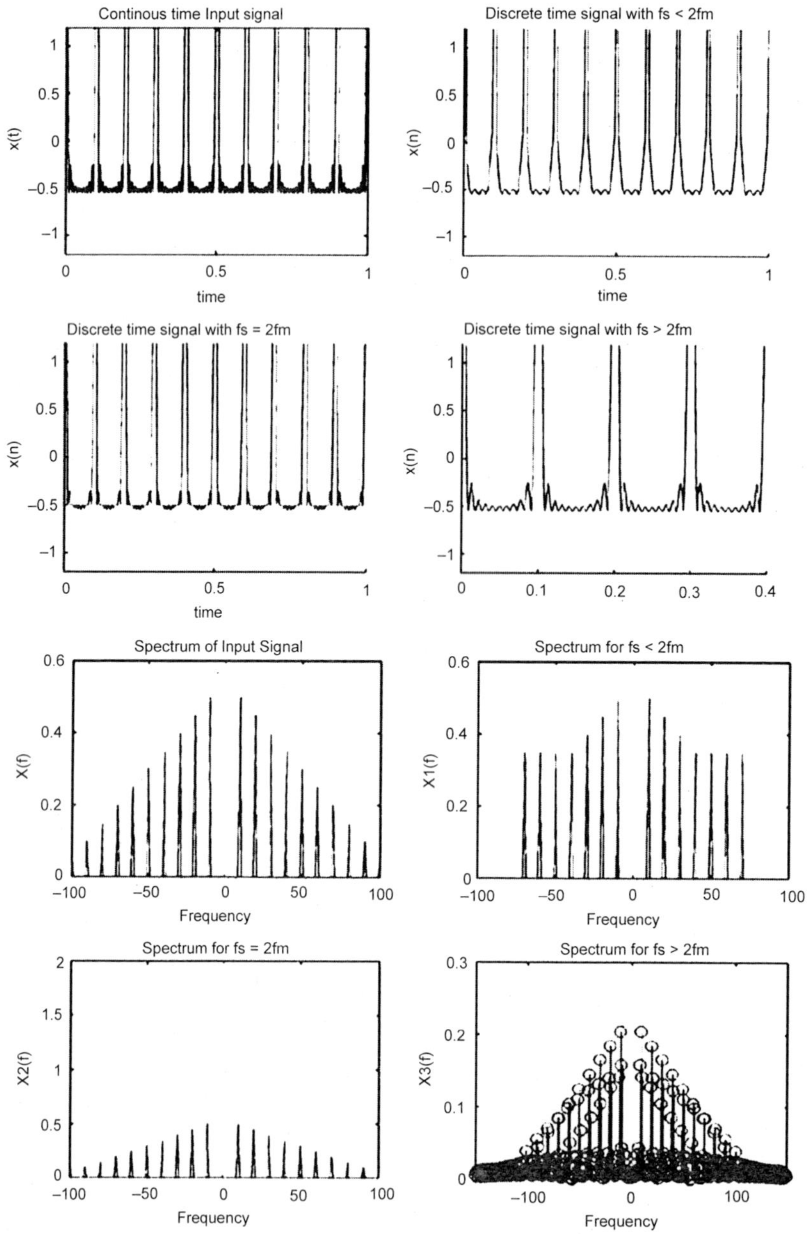

```
% Pulse code modulation and Demodulation
clc;
clear ;
close all;
n = 12; % n-bit PCM system
L = 2^n;% # voltage levels
fss = 10000;% Determines the smoothness of the Signal
Tss = 1/fss; % Determines the smoothness of the Signal
t = 0:Tss:1-Tss; % Time Axis
T = 0.1; % Time Period of the input signal
fm = 1/T;% Highest frequency component in the input signal
fs = 20*fm; % Greater than Nyquist Sampling frequency
Ts = 1/fs;
%% Input Signal to sampler (Signal generation where Amplitude of signal
is 10v)
vmax = 10 ;% Amplitude of input signal
x = vmax* cos(2*pi*fm*t); % Input Signal to be sampled
%% Input signal Sampled greaterthan Nyquist rate)
m = 0:1:4000; % # samples required to construct sampled signal
y = 10*cos(2*pi*fm*m*Ts); % Sampled signal with > Nyquist rate
%% Quantization Process
vmin = -vmax;
del = (vmax-vmin)/L; % step size
partition = vmin : del : vmax; % Voltage levels between vmin and vmax
with difference of del
binary_code = vmin-(del/2) : del : vmax+(del/2); % codebook having
quantized values
[indx , quantv] = quantiz(y,partition,binary_code);% Quantization
process indx contain index number and quantv contain quantized values
l_ind = length(indx);
l_quantv = length(quantv);
for i = 1:l_ind % For loop to avoid -ve index number
   if(indx(i)~=0) % To make index as binary decimal so
                    started from 0 to N = 2^n.
```

```
  indx(i) = indx(i)-1;
end
end
%% Encoding Process
binary_code_TX = de2bi(indx,'left-msb'); % Convert decimal to Binary
(o/p
is a matrix )
code_Tx = [];
for i = 1 : length(m)
code_Tx = [code_Tx, binary_code_TX(i,:)]; % convert code matrix to a
coded row vector ( Serial binary data)
end
code_Tx;
%% Demodulation of PCM Signal
% Decoding (De-Quantization)
binary_code_RX = reshape(code_Tx,n,length(code_Tx)/n);%reshape(X,M,N)
or
reshape(X,[M,N]) returns the M-by-N matrix...
...whose elements
are taken columnwise from X.
code_Rx = bi2de(binary_code_RX','left-msb'); % Getback the index in
decimal form
x_quant = del*code_Rx+vmin+(del/2); % getback Quantized values
% Low Pass Filtering
N = 5;% Order of Butterworth Filter
Wn = 4*fs/fss; %Normalized cut-of frequency
[B,A] = butter(N,Wn,'low');% Selecting Butterworth LPF of order N
x_tilde = filter(B,A,x_quant);% Implementing Filter
%% Plots in time Domain
figure
subplot(3,1,1) % Plot of Input signal
plot(t,x);xlim([0,0.2]);ylim([-11,11]);           xlabel('time');
```

```
ylabel('x(t)');
title('Continous time Input signal');grid;
subplot(3,1,2) % Plot of Sampled signal with > Nyquist rate
stem(m*Ts,y);xlabel('time');xlim([0,0.2]);ylim([-11,11]);
ylabel('x(n)');
title('Discrete time signal with fs>2fm');grid;
subplot(3,1,3) % Plot of quantized signal
stem(m*Ts,x_quant);grid on;xlim([0,0.2]); % Display the quantized
values
title ('Quantized Signal');
xlabel(' Time');
ylabel('Amplitude');
figure
subplot(3,1,1);
stairs(code_Tx);% Display the encoded signal
grid on; axis([0 100 -2 3]); title('Encoded Signal');
xlabel(' Time');
ylabel('Amplitude');
subplot(3,1,2);
plot(m*Ts,x_quant); % plot De-quantized signal
grid on;xlim([0,0.2]);ylim([-11,11]);
title('De-Quantized signal');
xlabel(' Time');
ylabel('Amplitude');
subplot(3,1,3);
plot(m*Ts,x_tilde); % plot demodulated signal
grid on;xlim([0,0.5]);ylim([-11,11]);
title('demodulated signal');
xlabel(' Time');
ylabel('Amplitude');
Results : n = 3 Bit PCM
```

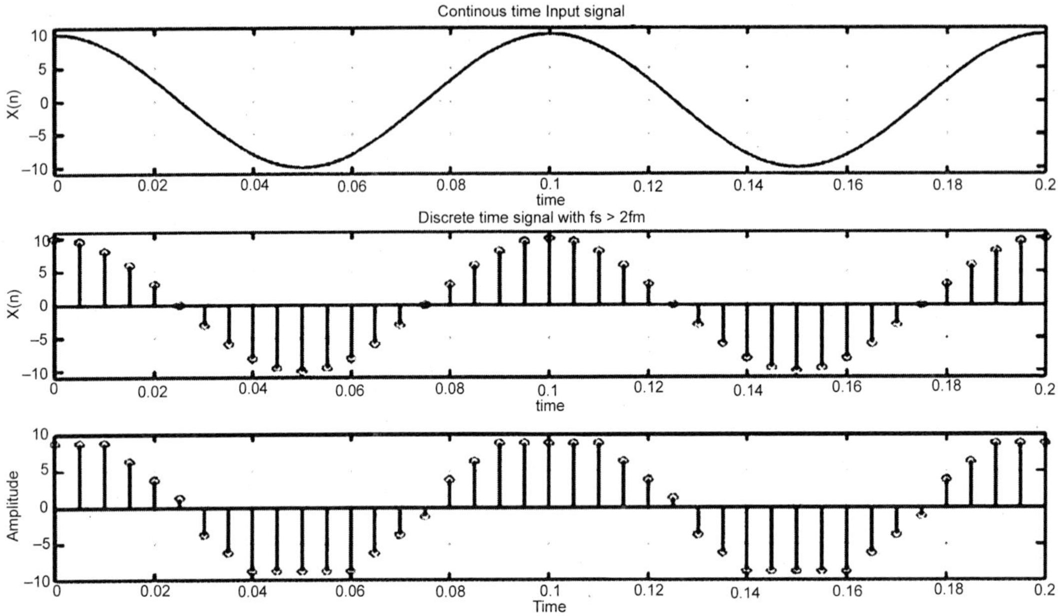

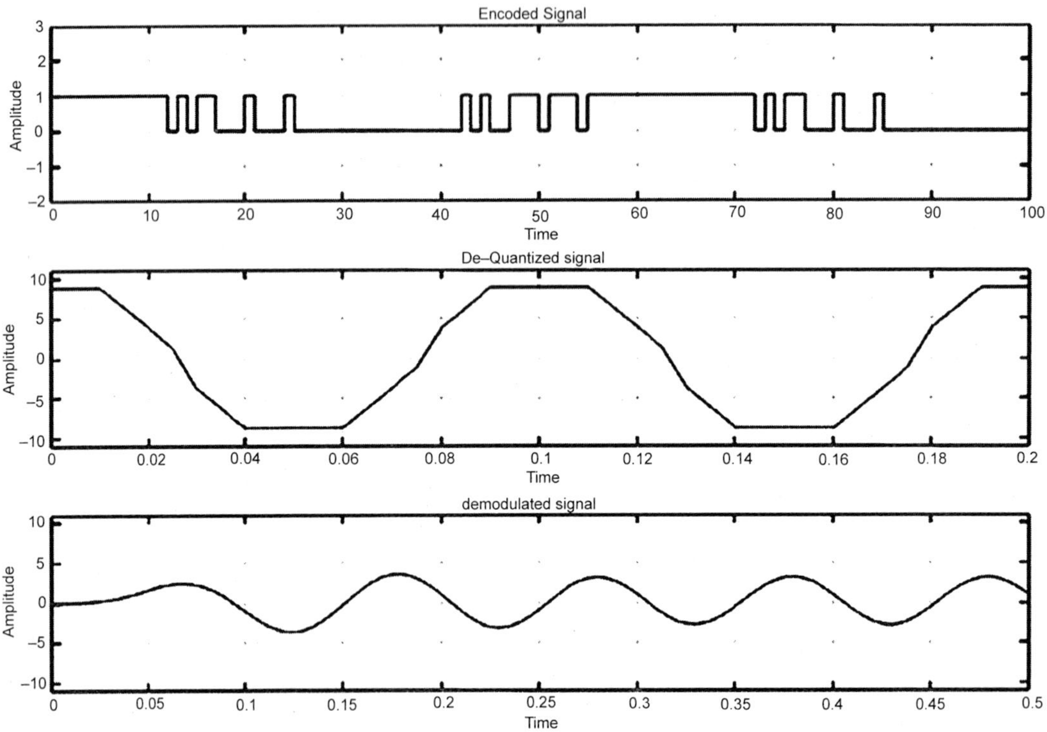

Results : n = 12 Bit PCM

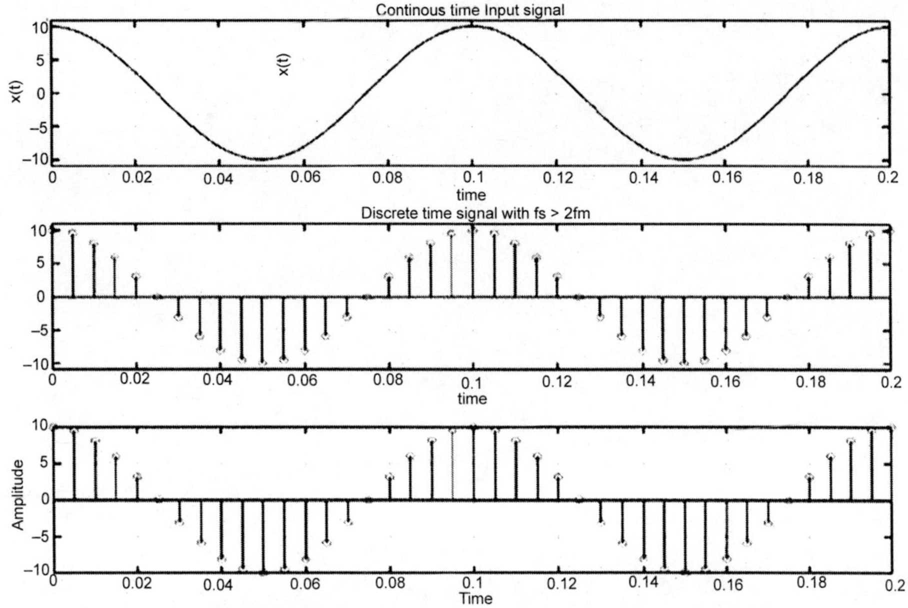
Continous time Input signal
x(t)
time
Discrete time signal with fs > 2fm
time
Amplitude
Time

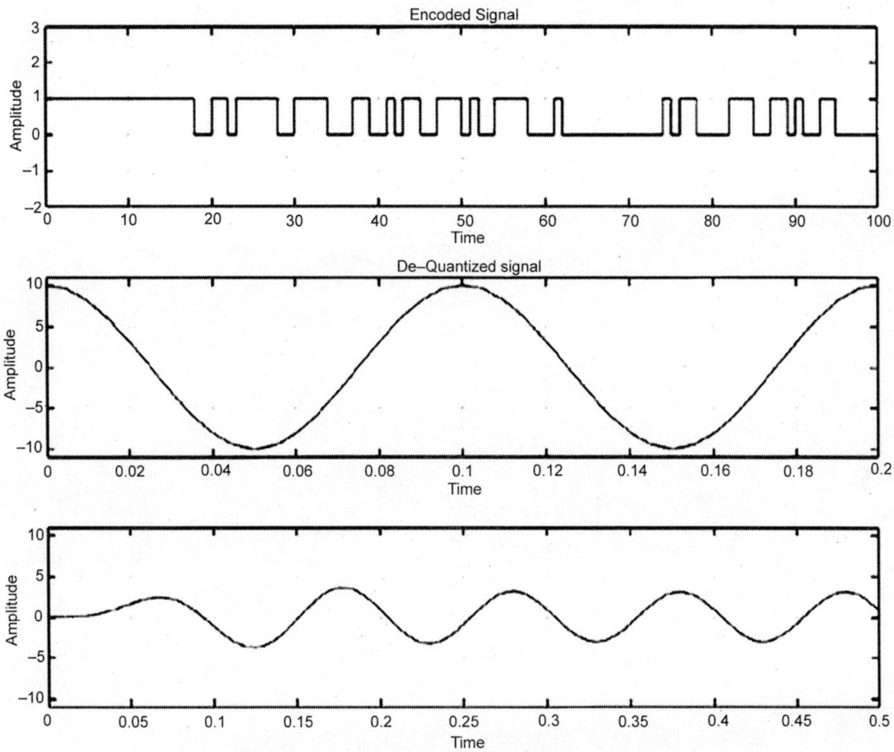
Encoded Signal
Amplitude
Time
De–Quantized signal
Amplitude
Time
Amplitude
Time

10. Delta Modulation

```
% Delta modulation
clc;
clear;
close all;
fm = 4;
fs = 20*fm;
Ts = 1/fs;
vm = 2;% Amplitude of the modulating signal
t = 0 : Ts : 1;
x = vm*cos(2*pi*fm*t);% Modulating signal
del = (2*pi*vm*fm)/fs;% Step size selection to avoid slope overload
distortion
%% Quantization
for n = 1 : length(x)
    if n==1
        e(n) = x(n); %error for n = 1
        eq(n) = del*sign(e(n));
% Quantization for n = 1(sign(X) returns 1 if the element is greater
than zero, 0 if it equals zero and -1 if it is less than zero.)
        xq(n) = eq(n);
    else
        e(n) = x(n)-xq(n-1);
        eq(n) = del*sign( e(n));
        xq(n) = eq(n)+xq(n-1);
    end
end
%% Demodulation
for n = 1 : length(x)
    if n==1
        xqr(n) = eq(n);
    else
        xqr(n) = eq(n)+xq(n-1);
    end
end
%% Reconstruction ( Filtering)
N = 2;
fc = 2*(2*fm/fs); % Take slightly higher cutoff frequency
[num,den] = butter(N,fc); % Butterworth filter
x_tilde = filter(num,den,xqr);% Lowpass filtering
figure
```

```
plot(t,x);  ylim([-2.5,2.5]);hold  on;  stem(t,x);legend('Modulating
Signal','Sampled Signal');
grid on;xlabel('time');ylabel('amplitude');title('Sampled signal');
figure
stairs(t,xq);ylim([-3,3]);holdon;stem(t,x);holdon;plot(t,x,'green');
grid  on;xlabel('time');ylabel('amplitude');title('Delta  Modulated
signal');
legend('Delta  Modulated  Signal','Sampled  Signal','I/P  Modulating
Signal');
figure
plot(t,xqr); ylim([-3,3]);
grid     on;xlabel('time');ylabel('amplitude');title('Reconstructed
signal (Demodulated Signal)');
figure
plot(t,x_tilde); ylim([-2.5,2.5]);
grid on;xlabel('time');ylabel('amplitude');title('Filtered signal');
```

11. Differential Pulse Code Modulation

```
% Differential Pulse code modulation
clc;
clear;
close all;
fm = 4; % Frequency of modulating signal
fs = 20*fm; % Sampling frequency
Ts = 1/fs; % sampling Interval
vm = 2;% Amplitude of the modulating signal
t = 0 : Ts : 1;
x = vm*cos(2*pi*fm*t);%modulating signal
%% Quantization
for n = 1 : length(x)
    if n==1
        e(n) = x(n);% Error signal
        eq(n) = round (e(n));% Quantization
        xq(n) = eq(n);
    else
        e(n) = x(n)-xq(n-1);
        eq(n) = round( e(n));
        xq(n) = eq(n)+xq(n-1);
        xq(n) = abs(xq(n));
    end
end
%% Demodulation
```

```
for n = 1 : length(x)
    if n==1
        xqr(n) = eq(n);
    else
        xqr(n) = eq(n)+xq(n-1);
    end
end
%% Reconstruction ( Filtering)
N = 2;
fc = 2*(2*fm/fs); % Take slightly higher cutoff frequency
[num,den] = butter(N,fc); % Butterworth filter
x_tilde = filter(num,den,xqr);% Lowpass filtering
figure
plot(t,x); ylim([-2.5,2.5]);hold on; stem(t,x);
grid on;xlabel('time');ylabel('amplitude');title('Sampled signal');
legend('Modulating Signal','Sampled Signal');
figure
plot(t,xqr); ylim([-2.5,2.5]);
grid      on;xlabel('time');ylabel('amplitude');title('Reconstructed
signal (Demodulated Signal)');
figure
plot(t,x_tilde); ylim([-2.5,2.5]);
grid on;xlabel('time');ylabel('amplitude');title('Filtered signal');
```

12. Binary Phase Shift keying (BPSK)

```
% BPSK Modulation
close all;
clear ; clc;
Tb = 0.1;% Bit duration
k = 3; % # cycles
fc = k/Tb;% Carrier frequency
fs = 20*fc; % Sampling Frequency > Nyquist sampling Frequency Ts = 1/
fs; % Sampling Interval
t = 0 : Ts : 1-Ts; % Carrier Signal Time axis
b = 0 : Tb : 1; % Time axis for serial Binary data blockLength =
length(Tb);% Length of Serial Binary data
bits_TX = randi([0,1],[1,blockLength]); % Generation of Serial Binary
Bits
bits_TX = (2*bits_TX-1);
c = cos(2*pi*fc*t); % Carrier Signal
tc = 0:Ts:Tb; % Time axis for carrier within one bit duration Tb
c_Tb = cos(2*pi*fc*tc); % Carrier Signal in one bit duration
```

```
t_BPSK = 0:Ts:(blockLength*length(tc)-1)*Ts;
% For plotting PSK Signal
% Modulation
s_BPSK = [];
for i = 1 : length(bits_TX)
s_BPSK = [s_BPSK, bits_TX(i)*c_Tb]; % BPSK Modulated Signal
end
%% Demodulation by Synchronous Detector (Correlator)
% Multiplier Output
x_Mul = [];
for k = 1 : blockLength
x_Mul = [x_Mul , s_BPSK((k-1)*length(tc)+1 : k*length(tc)).*c_Tb];
%Multiplier output end
% Low pass Filter Output
N = 10; % Filter order
f_cutoff = 2*fc/fs; % Cutoff Frequency
[num,den] = butter(N,f_cutoff); % Butterworth filter y_LPF =
filter(num,den,x_Mul); % Lowpass filtering
%% Sampling at t = Tb and Threshold Detection
for s = 1 : length(y_LPF)
if y_LPF(s) > 0.1 bits_RX(s) = 1;
end
else end
bits_RX(s) = 0;
%% Plots in time domain figure
subplot(3,1,1) stairs(Tb,bits_TX);ylim([-1.5,1.5]);
xlabel('time');
ylabel('Amplitude');
title('Transmitted Bits');
subplot(3,1,2)
plot(t,c);ylim([-1.5,1.5]);
xlabel('time');
ylabel('Amplitude');
title('Carrier Signal');
subplot(3,1,3)
plot(t_BPSK,s_BPSK);ylim([-1.5,1.5]);xlim([0,1]);
xlabel('time');
ylabel('Amplitude');
title('BPSK Signal');
figure subplot(3,1,1)
plot(t_BPSK,x_Mul);ylim([0,1.5]);xlim([0,1]);
```

```
xlabel('time');
ylabel('Amplitude');
title('Multiplier Output');
subplot(3,1,2)
plot(t_BPSK,y_LPF);ylim([0,1.5]);xlim([0,1]);
xlabel('time');
ylabel('Amplitude');
title('LPF Output');
subplot(3,1,3)
plot(t_BPSK,bits_RX);ylim([-1,1.5]);xlim([0,1]);
xlabel('time');
ylabel('Amplitude');
title('Received Bits')
```

RESULTS:

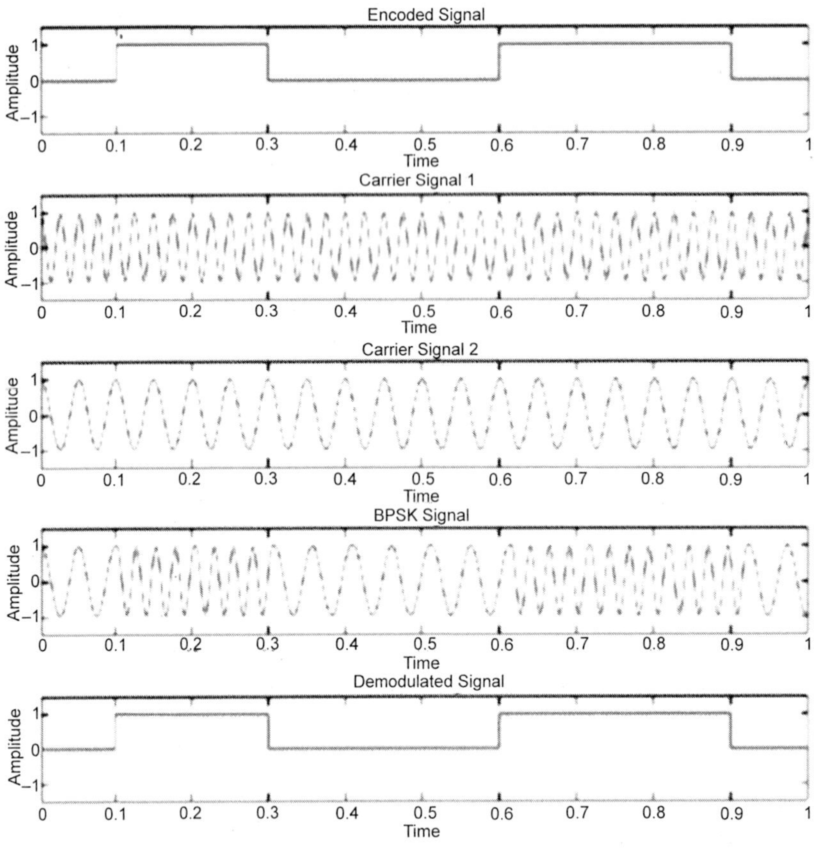

13. Binary Frequency Shift Keying (BFSK)

```
% BFSK Modulation close all;
clear ;
clc;
Tb = 0.1;% Bit duration k1 = 4; % # cycles
k2 = 2; % % # cycles and Make sure K1>k2
fc1 = k1/Tb;% Carrier frequency1 for Bit-1
fc2 = k2/Tb;% Carrier frequency2 for Bit-0
fs = 20*fc2; % Sampling Frequency > Nyquist sampling Frequency
Ts = 1/fs; % Sampling Interval
t = 0 : Ts : 1-Ts; % Carrier Signal Time axis
tb = 0 : Tb : 1; % Time axis for serial Binary data
blockLength = length(tb);% Length of Serial Binary data (# Bits)
bits_TX = randi([0,1],[1,blockLength]); % Generation of Serial Binary
Bits
c11 = cos(2*pi*fc1*t); % Carrier Signal1
c22 = cos(2*pi*fc2*t); % Carrier Signal2
tc = 0:Ts:Tb; % Time axis for carrier with in one bit duration Tb
c1 = cos(2*pi*fc1*tc); % Carrier Signal1 in one bit duration
c2 = cos(2*pi*fc2*tc); % Carrier Signal2 in one bit duration
t_BFSK = 0:Ts:(blockLength*Ts*length(c1)-Ts);% For plotting BFSK
Signal
%% Modulation s_BFSK = [];
for i = 1 : length(bits_TX) if bits_TX(i)==1
y = c1;
else bits_TX(i) == 0 y = c2;
end
s_BFSK = [s_BFSK, y]; % BFSK Modulated Signal
end
%% Demodulation (Correlator)
demod=[];
% Multiplier Output x_Mul1 = [];
x_Mul2 = [];
for k = 1 : blockLength
x_Mul1 = [s_BFSK((k-1)*length(tc)+1 : k*length(tc)).*c1]; % Multiplier
output for Carrier-1
x_Mul2 = [s_BFSK((k-1)*length(tc)+1 : k*length(tc)).*c2]; % Multiplier
output for Carrier-2
% integration
```

```
LPF1 = trapz(x_Mul1); % Integrator output for Carrier-1 LPF2 = trapz(x_
Mul2); % Integrator output for Carrier-2
diff = LPF1-LPF2; % Output of Subtractor
% Threshold Detector if diff>0
demod(k)=1; else
demod(k)=0;
end end
%% Plots in time domain figure
subplot(5,1,1) stairs(tb,bits_TX);ylim([-1.5,1.5]);
xlabel ('time');
ylabel ('Amplitude');
title ('Transmitted Bits');
subplot(5,1,2) plot(t,c11);ylim([-1.5,1.5]);
xlabel ('time');
ylabel ('Amplitude');
title ('Carrier Signal1');
subplot (5,1,3) plot(t,c22);ylim([-1.5,1.5]);
xlabel ('time');
ylabel ('Amplitude');
title ('Carrier Signal2');
subplot (5,1,4)
plot (t_BFSK,s_BFSK);ylim([-1.5,1.5]);xlim([0,1]);
xlabel ('time');
ylabel ('Amplitude');
title ('BFSK Signal');
subplot(5,1,5) stairs(tb,demod);ylim([-1.5,1.5]);
xlabel ('time');
ylabel ('Amplitude');
title ('Demodulated Signal');
```

RESULTS:

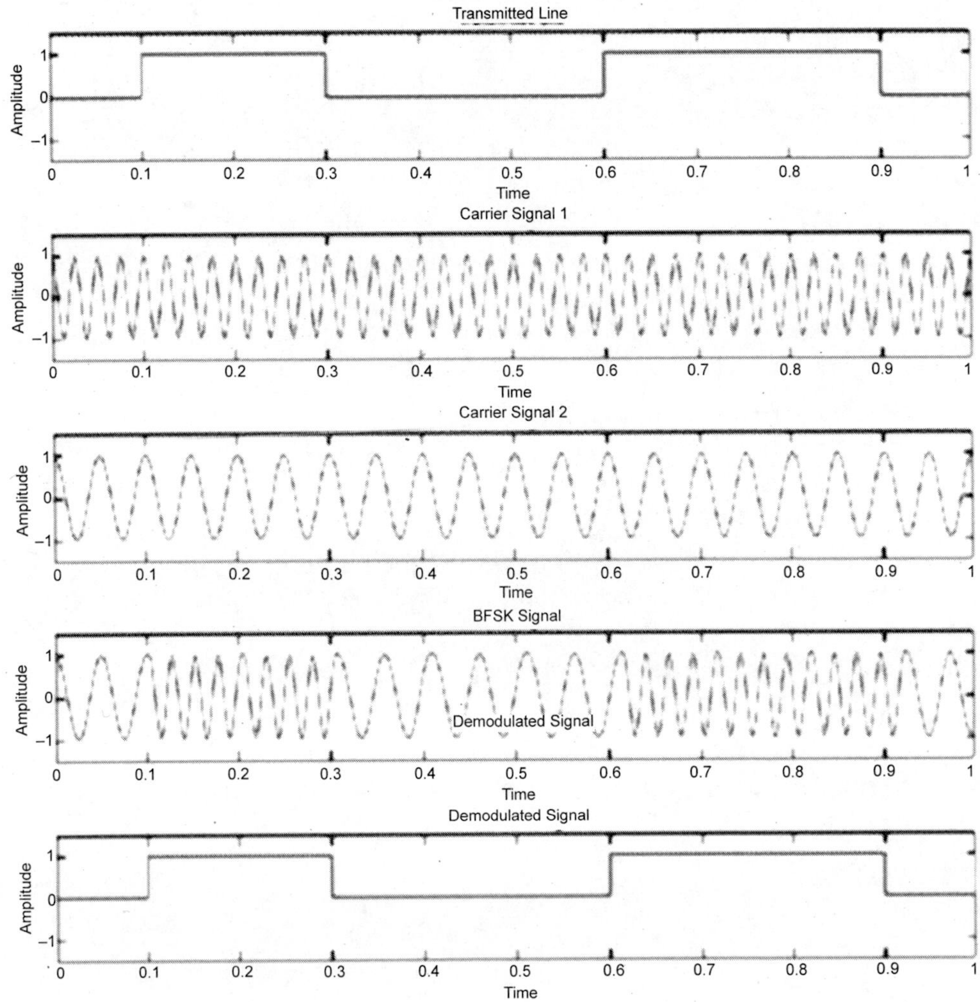

14. BER performance of BPSK system

```
% BER performance of BPSK Modulation under AWGN Channel
%% Initialization close all;
clear ;
clc;
rng('shuffle');
blockLength = 100;% # Symbols in a block of serial data
numBlocks = 10000;% # Iterations to get smooth BER curve
SNRdB = [1:0.5:12];% SNR Vector
Err = zeros(size(SNRdB)); % Error Vector Initialization
SNR = zeros(size(SNRdB)); % SNR Initialization
n = 1;% # Bits Per Symbol (n = 1 For BPSK, n = 2 For QPSK)
```

```
M = 2^n; % # Symbols
%% Transmission, White Gaussian Noise addition, Reception & Decoding
for L = 1:numBlocks % Monte Carlo Simulation
bits = randi([0,M-1],[blockLength,1]); % Generate serial random integers between 0 & M-1 of size 1 X blockLength
ChNoise = (randn(blockLength,1) + 1j*randn(blockLength,1));% Noise Generation of size blockLength X 1(#bits = #Noise samples)
for k = 1 : length(SNRdB) % Since we have to compute BER for different SNR's
SNR(k) = 10^(SNRdB(k)/10); % Absolute SNR computed from SNRdB Txbits = sqrt(SNR(k))*pskmod(bits,M); % Transmitted Bits( Symbols )
Rxbits = Txbits + ChNoise ; % Received Bits( Symbols )from AWGN Channel
DecodedBits = pskdemod(Rxbits,M); % Bits decoded for AWGN Channel
Err(k) = Err(k) + symerr(DecodedBits,bits); % Net ERROR for all iterations(1:NumBlocks)
end end
%% Simulated(Practical) & Theoretical BER Calculations
BER = Err/(blockLength*numBlocks);% AvgBER = Total # Bits received in error / total # Bits transmitted i.e.(=blockLength*iter)
BER_Theoretical = qfunc(sqrt(SNR)); % Theoritical BER For AWGN Channel
%% Plots For Simulated and Theoretical BER
semilogy(SNRdB,BER,SNRdB,BER_Theoretical,'ro','linewidth',2.0);
% Gives Theoritical BER
axis tight;
grid on;
legend('simulated ','Theoretical');
xlabel('SNR(dB)');
ylabel('BER');
title('BER vs SNR(dB)');
```

PROCEDURE:

Type the MATLAB code in editor window.

Run the code and get the BER curves.

Calculate the BER for BPSK Modulation for various SNR values .

Compare theoretical and Simulated BER Curves for BPSK Modulationscheme.

RESULTS:

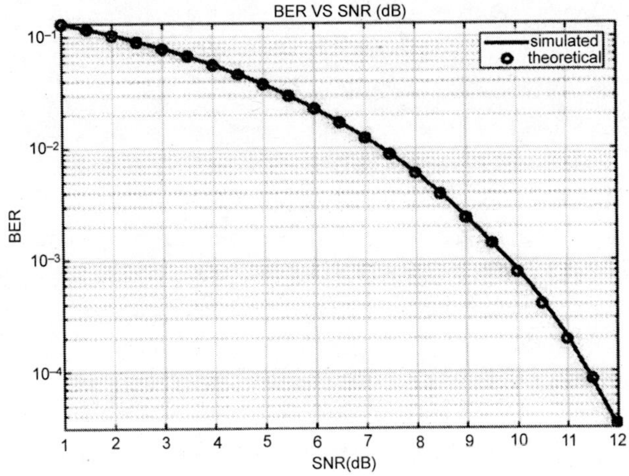

15. BER performance of BFSK system

```
% BER performance of BFSK Modulation under AWGN Channel
%% Initialization close all;
clear ;
clc;
rng('shuffle');
blockLength = 100;% # Symbols in a block of serial data
numBlocks = 1000;% # Iterations to get smooth BER curve
SNRdB = [1:0.5:12];% SNR Vector
Err = zeros(size(SNRdB)); % Error Vector Initialization
SNR = zeros(size(SNRdB)); % SNR Initialization
n = 1;% # Bits Per Symbol (n = 1 For BFSK)
M = 2^n; % # Symbols
Del_f = 8; %Frequency Deviation (or) Seperation in Hz nsamp = 3;% #
samples per symbol
Fs = 4*Del_f; % Sample rate (Hz)
%% Transmission, White Gaussian Noise addition, Reception & Decoding
for L = 1:numBlocks % Monte Carlo Simulation
bits = randi([0,M-1],[blockLength,1]); % Generate serial random
integers between 0 & M-1 of size 1 × blockLength
ChNoise = (randn(blockLength*nsamp,1) + 1j*randn(blockLength*nsamp,1));
% Noise Generation of size blockLength×1(#bits = #Noise samples)
for k = 1 : length(SNRdB) % Since we have to compute BER for different
SNR's
SNR(k) = 10^(SNRdB(k)/10); % Absolute SNR computed from SNRdB
Txbits = sqrt(SNR(k))*fskmod(bits,M,Del_f,nsamp,Fs); % Transmitted
Bits( Symbols )
Rxbits = Txbits +ChNoise ; % Received Bits( Symbols )from AWGN Channel
```

```
DecodedBits = fskdemod(Rxbits,M,Del_f,nsamp,Fs); % Bits decoded for
AWGN Channel
Err(k) = Err(k) + symerr(DecodedBits,bits); % Net ERROR for all
iterations(1:NumBlocks)
end
end
%% Simulated(Practical) & Theoretical BER Calculations
BER = Err/(blockLength*numBlocks);% AvgBER = Total # Bits received in
error / total # Bits transmitted i.e.(=blockLength*iter)
BER_Theoretical = 0.5*erfc(sqrt(SNR/2)); % Theoritical BER For BFSK
under AWGN Channel
%% Plots For Simulated and Theoretical BER
figure semilogy(SNRdB,BER,SNRdB,BER_Theoretical,'ro','linewidth',2.0);
% Gives Theoritical BER
axis tight;
grid on;
legend('simulated ','Theoretical');
xlabel('SNR(dB)');
ylabel('BER');
title('BER vs SNR(dB)For BFSK Modulation ');
```

PROCEDURE:

Type the MATLAB code in editor window.

Run the code and get the BER curves.

Calculate the BER for Various Modulation orders at a given SNR.

Compare theoretical and Simulated BER Curves for BPSK Modulation scheme.

RESULTS:

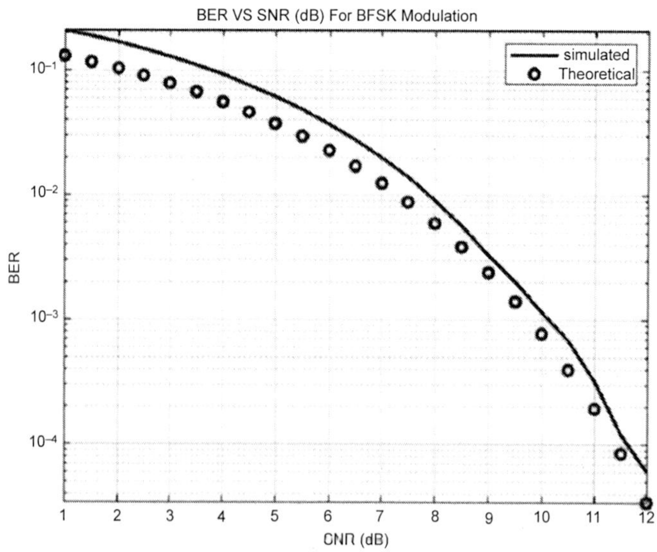

16. BER performance of BQAM system

```
% BER performance of BQAM Modulation under AWGN Channel
%% Initialization close all;
clear ;
clc;
rng('shuffle');
blockLength = 100;% # Symbols in a block of serial data
numBlocks = 10000;% # Iterations to get smooth BER curve
SNRdB = [1:0.5:12];% SNR Vector
Err = zeros(size(SNRdB)); % Error Vector Initialization
SNR = zeros(size(SNRdB)); % SNR Initialization
n = 1;% # Bits Per Symbol (n = 1 For BQAM)
M = 2^n; % # Symbols
%% Transmission, White Gaussian Noise addition, Reception & Decoding
for L = 1:numBlocks % Monte Carlo Simulation
bits = randi([0,M-1],[blockLength,1]); % Generate serial random
integers between 0 & M-1 of size 1 × blockLength
ChNoise = (randn(blockLength,1) + 1j*randn(blockLength,1));
% Noise Generation of size blockLength × 1(#bits = #Noise samples)
for k = 1 : length(SNRdB) % Since we have to compute BER for different
SNR's
SNR(k) = 10^(SNRdB(k)/10); % Absolute SNR computed from SNRdB
Txbits = sqrt(SNR(k))*qammod(bits,M); % Transmitted Bits( Symbols )
Rxbits = Txbits + ChNoise ; % Received Bits( Symbols )from AWGN Channel
DecodedBits = qamdemod(Rxbits,M); % Bits decoded for AWGN Channel
Err(k) = Err(k) + symerr(DecodedBits,bits); % Net ERROR for all
iterations(1:NumBlocks)]
end
end
%% Simulated(Practical) & Theoretical BER Calculations
BER = Err/(blockLength*numBlocks);% AvgBER = Total # Bits received in
error / total # Bits transmitted i.e.(=blockLength*iter)
BER_Theoretical = qfunc(sqrt(SNR)); % Theoritical BER ForQAM under
AWGN Channel
%% Plots For Simulated and Theoretical BER
semilogy(SNRdB,BER,SNRdB,BER_Theoretical,'ro','linewidth',2.0);
%Gives Theoritical BER
axis tight;
grid on;
```

```
legend('simulated ','Theoretical');
xlabel('SNR(dB)');
ylabel('BER');
title('BER vs SNR(dB)');
```

PROCEDURE:

Type the MATLAB code in editor window.
Run the code and get the BER curves.
Calculate the BER for Various Modulation orders at a given SNR.
Compare theoretical and Simulated BER Curves for BPSK Modulation scheme.

RESULTS

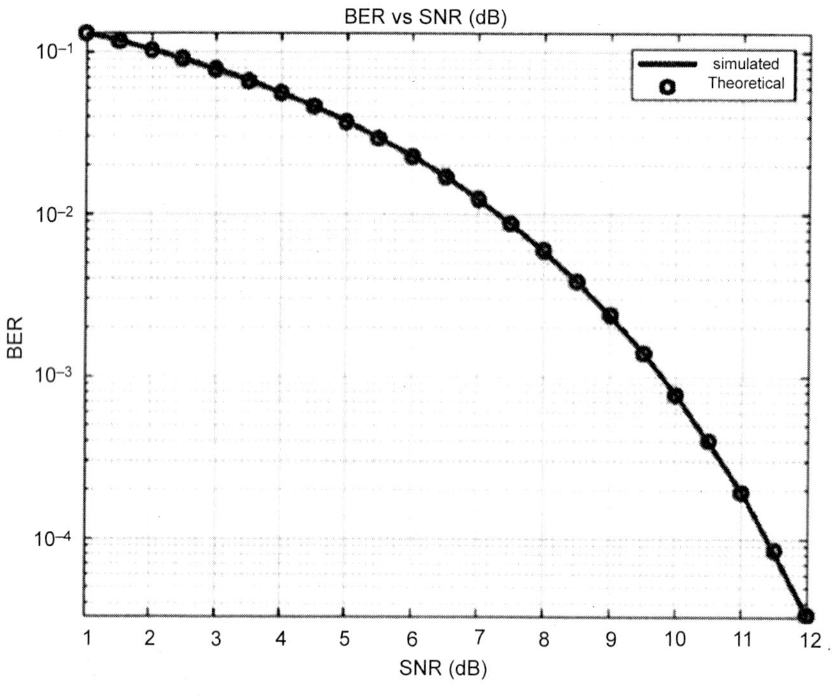

17. BER performance of M-ary PSK system

```
% BER performance of AWGN and Rayleigh Fading System's For M- ary PSK
Modulation
%% Initialization close all;
clear all;
clc;
rng('shuffle');
blockLength = 100;% # Symbols in a block of serial data
numBlocks = 10000;% # Iterations to get smooth BER curve
```

```
SNRdB = [1:0.5:12];
BER = zeros(size(SNRdB));
BER_fad = zeros(size(SNRdB));% Initialization of BER
SNR = zeros(size(SNRdB));
for n = 1:2 % # Bits Per Symbol (n = 1 For BPSK, n = 2 For QPSK)
M = 2^n; % M-ary PSK
%% Transmission, Fading, White Gaussian Noise addition, Reception &
Decoding
for L = 1:numBlocks
bits = randi([0,M-1],[blockLength,1]);
% Generate serial random integers between 0 & M-1 of size 1 X blockLength
h = 1/sqrt(2)*(randn+1j*randn);
% Multi Path Fading channel Coefficient
ChNoise = (randn(blockLength,1) + 1j*randn(blockLength,1));
% Noise Generation os size blockLength X 1(#bits = #Noise samples)
for k = 1 : length(SNRdB)
% Since we have to compute BER for different SNR's
SNR(k) = 10^(SNRdB(k)/10);
% Absolute SNR computed from SNRdB
Txbits = sqrt(SNR(k))*pskmod(bits,M);
% Transmitted Bits( Symbols )
Rxbits = Txbits + ChNoise ;
% Received Bits( Symbols )from AWGN Channel
Rxbits_fad = h*Txbits + ChNoise ;
% Received Bits( Symbols)from Rayleigh Fading Channel
Bitsprocessed_MF_fad = conj(h)*Rxbits_fad;
% Bits Processed using matched filter receiver for Rayleigh Fading
Channel
DecodedBits = pskdemod(Rxbits,M);
% Bits decoded for AWGN Channel
DecodedBits_fad = pskdemod(Bitsprocessed_MF_fad,M);
% Bits decoded for Rayleigh Fading Channel
BER(k) = BER(k) + symerr(DecodedBits,bits);
% Net BER for all iterations(1:NumBlocks)
BER_fad(k) = BER_fad(k) + symerr(DecodedBits_fad,bits);
% Net BER for all iterations(1:NumBlocks)
end
```

```
end
%% Simulated (Practical) BER Calculations & Plots
BER = BER/(blockLength*numBlocks);% AvgBER = Total # Bits received in
error / total # Bits transmitted i.e.(=blockLength*iter)
BER_fad = BER_fad/(blockLength*numBlocks);
semilogy(SNRdB,BER,'linewidth',2.0);
hold on;
semilogy(SNRdB,BER_fad,'linewidth',2.0); % Gives Simulated BER
hold on;
end
%% Theoritical BER Calculations & Plots
BER_Theoritical = qfunc(sqrt(SNR));
% Theoritical BER For AWGN Channel
semilogy(SNRdB,BER_Theoritical,'bo','linewidth',2.0);
% Gives Theoritical BER
hold on;
BER_Theoritical_fad = 0.5*(1-sqrt(SNR./(2+SNR)));
% Theoritical BER For Rayleigh Fading Channel
semilogy(SNRdB,BER_Theoritical_fad,'ro','linewidth',2.0);
%Gives Theoritical BER
Hold on;
axis tight;
grid on;
legend('simulated @ BPSK(AWGN)','simulated @ BPSK(FADING)','simulated
@ QPSK(AWGN)','simulated @ QPSK(FADING)','Theoritical @
BPSK(AWGN)','Theoritical @ BPSK(FADING)');
xlabel('SNR(dB)');
ylabel('BER');
title('BER vs SNR(dB)');
```

PROCEDURE:

Type the MATLAB code in editor window.

Run the code and get the BER curves.

Calculate the BER for Various Modulation orders at a given SNR andtabulate the results.

Compare theoretical and Simulated BER Curves for BPSKModulation scheme.

RESULTS:

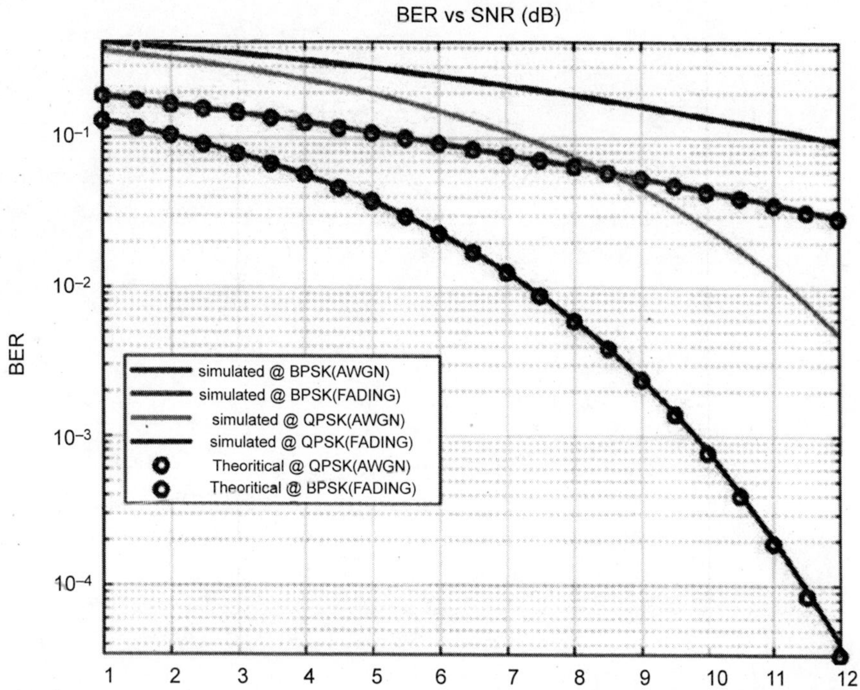

18. BER performance of M-ary QAM system

```
% BER performance of AWGN and Rayleigh Fading System's For M-ary QAM
Modulation
%% Initialization close all;
clear all;
clc;
rng('shuffle');
blockLength = 100;% # Symbols in a block of serial data
numBlocks = 10000;% # Iterations to get smooth BER curve
SNRdB = [1:0.5:12];
BER = zeros(size(SNRdB));
BER_fad    =    zeros(size(SNRdB));%    Initialization    of    BER    SNR    =
zeros(size(SNRdB));
for n = 1:2 % # Bits Per Symbol (n = 1 For B-QAM, n = 2 For 4-QAM)
M = 2^n; % M-ary QAM
%% Transmission, Fading, White Gaussian Noise addition, Reception &
Decoding
for L = 1:numBlocks
bits   =   randi([0,M-1],[blockLength,1]);   %   Generate   serial   random
integers between 0 & M-1 of size 1 × blockLength
```

```
h = 1/sqrt(2)*(randn+1j*randn); % Multi Path Fading channel Coefficient
ChNoise = (randn(blockLength,1) + 1j*randn(blockLength,1));
% Noise Generation os size blockLength × 1(#bits = #Noise samples)
for k = 1 : length(SNRdB) % Since we have to compute BER for different
SNR's
SNR(k) = 10^(SNRdB(k)/10); % Absolute SNR computed from SNRdB
Txbits = sqrt(SNR(k))*qammod(bits,M); % Transmitted Bits( Symbols )
Rxbits = Txbits + ChNoise ; % Received Bits (Symbols)from AWGN Channel
Rxbits_fad = h*Txbits + ChNoise ; % Received Bits (Symbols) from
Rayleigh Fading Channel
Bitsprocessed_MF_fad = conj(h)*Rxbits_fad;
% Bits Processed using matched filter receiver for Rayleigh Fading
Channel
DecodedBits = qamdemod(Rxbits,M); % Bits decoded for AWGN Channel
DecodedBits_fad = qamdemod(Bitsprocessed_MF_fad,M); % Bits decoded
for Rayleigh Fading Channel
BER(k) = BER(k) + symerr(DecodedBits,bits); % Net BER for all
iterations(1:NumBlocks)
BER_fad(k) = BER_fad(k) + symerr(DecodedBits_fad,bits);
% Net BER for all iterations(1:NumBlocks)
end
end
%% Simulated (Practical) BER Calculations & Plots
BER = BER/(blockLength*numBlocks);
% AvgBER = Total # Bits received in error / total # Bits transmitted
i.e.(=blockLength*iter)
BER_fad = BER_fad/(blockLength*numBlocks);
semilogy(SNRdB,BER,'linewidth',2.0);
hold on;
semilogy(SNRdB,BER_fad,'linewidth',2.0); % Gives Simulated BER
hold on;
end
%% Theoritical BER Calculations & Plots
BER_Theoritical = qfunc(sqrt(SNR)); % Theoritical BER For AWGN Channel
semilogy(SNRdB,BER_Theoritical,'bo','linewidth',2.0);        %Gives
Theoritical BER hold on;
BER_Theoritical_fad = 0.5*(1-sqrt(SNR./(2+SNR))); % Theoritical BER
For Rayleigh Fading Channel
semilogy(SNRdB,BER_Theoritical_fad,'ro','linewidth',2.0);
% Gives Theoritical BER
hold on;
axis tight;
grid on;
```

```
legend('simulated
@ B-QAM(AWGN)','simulated    @    B-    QAM(FADING)','simulated    @
4-QAM(AWGN)','simulated     @ 4- QAM(FADING)','Theoritical    @
B-QAM(AWGN)','Theoritical
@ B-QAM(FADING)');
xlabel('SNR(dB)');
ylabel('BER');
title('BER vs SNR(dB) for M-ary QAM');
```

PROCEDURE:

Type the MATLAB code in editor window.

Run the code and get the BER curves.

Calculate the BER for Various Modulation orders at a given SNRand tabulate the results.

Compare theoretical and Simulated BER Curves for BP Modulation scheme.

RESULTS:

19. To design a Linear Block code for the given (n, k).

```
% Input Generator Matrix
g=input('Enter The Generator Matrix: ')
disp ('G = ')
disp ('The Order of Linear block Code for given Generator Matrix is:')

[n,k] = size(transpose(g))
for i = 1:2^k
for j = k:-1:1
if rem(i-1,2^(-j+k+1))>=2^(-j+k)
u(i,j)=1;
else
u(i,j)=0;
end
end
end
u;
disp('The Possible Codewords are :')
c = rem(u*g,2)
disp('The Minimum Hamming Distance dmin for given Block Code is= ')
d_min = min(sum((c(2:2^k,:))'))
% Code Word
r = input('Enter the Received Code Word:')
p = [g(:,k+1:n)];
h = [transpose(p),eye(n-k)];
disp('Hammimg Code')
```

```
ht = transpose(h)
disp('Syndrome of a Given Codeword is :')
s = rem(r*ht,2)
for i = 1:1:size(ht)
if(ht(i,1:n-k)==s)
r(i) = 1-r(i);
break;
end
end
if (s==0)
    disp('No Error')
else
disp('The Error is in bit:')
disp(i)
disp('The Corrected Codeword is :')
disp(r)
end
```

20. To check whether a given code perfect code.

```
G=input('Enter the Generator Matrix');
% G = Generator Matrix of the form [P Ik]
[k n]= size(G); dmin=inf;
for i = 1:(2^k-1)
j = dec2binvec(i,k); j= wrev(j);          % j = message vector
C= j*G;
C = mod(C,2)                             % C is Code matrix
if dmin > nnz(C)
dmin = nnz(C)                            % Hamming Weight of the code vector
C
end
end
dmin                                         %Minimum Hamming Distance
t=floor((dmin-1)/2)                      % No. of correctable errors
s=0;
for i = 0:t
s = s + factorial(n)/(factorial(i)*factorial(n-i)); % Total no. of
possible error combinations
end
if(s == 2^(n-k)) % Hamming Bound Check:
disp('ITS A PEFECT CODE')
else
disp('ITS NOT A PERFECT CODE')
end
```

APPENDIX-II
PRACTICAL EXERCISES: HARDWARE EXPERIMENTS

Expt. No.1 Natural and Flat Top Sampling

OBJECTIVES

To design and implement Flat Top Sampling.
To design and implement Natural Sampling.
Observe and compare the generated waveforms with the simulated waveforms

COMPONENTS USED

Three LF398 IC
Two 47K ohm Resistor
One 0.01 micro farad capacitor
4) +15V and -15V Power Supply

THEORY

Sampling is the reduction of a continuous signal to a discrete signal. A common example is the conversion of a sound wave (a continuous signal) to a sequence of samples (a discrete-time signal). A sample is a value or set of values at a point in time and/or space.

There are three types of sampling:-

1. **Impulse Sampling:** Impulse sampling can be performed by multiplying input signal x(t) with impulse train of period 'T'. Here, the amplitude of impulse changes with respect to amplitude of input signal x(t).

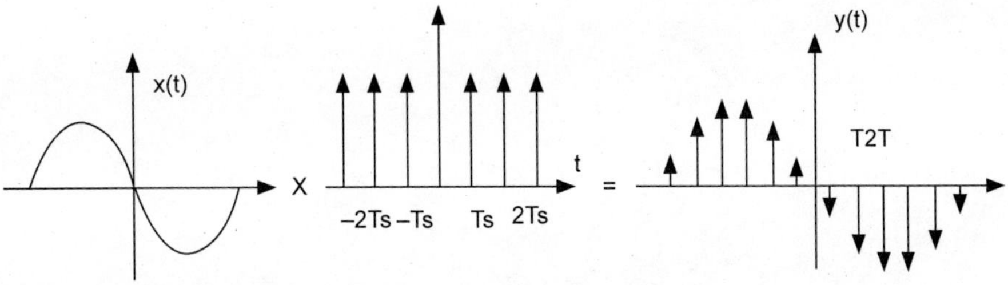

2. **Natural Sampling:** It is similar to impulse sampling except the impulse train is replaced by pulse train.

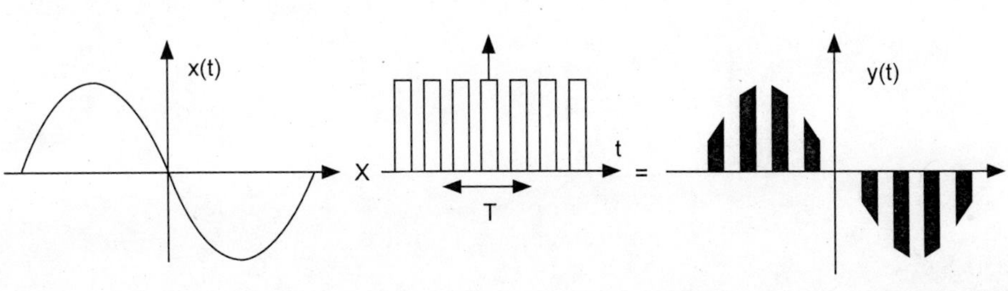

3. **Flat Top Sampling:**

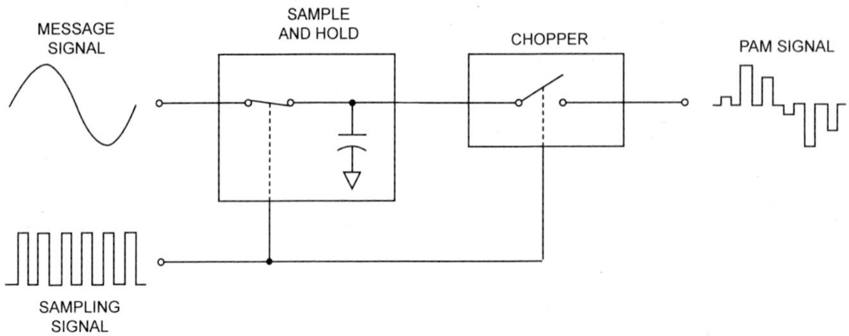

During transmission, noise is introduced at top of the transmission pulse which can be easily removed if the pulse is in the form of flat top. Here, the top of the samples are flat. Flat top sampling uses sample and hold circuit.

CIRCUIT DIAGRAM

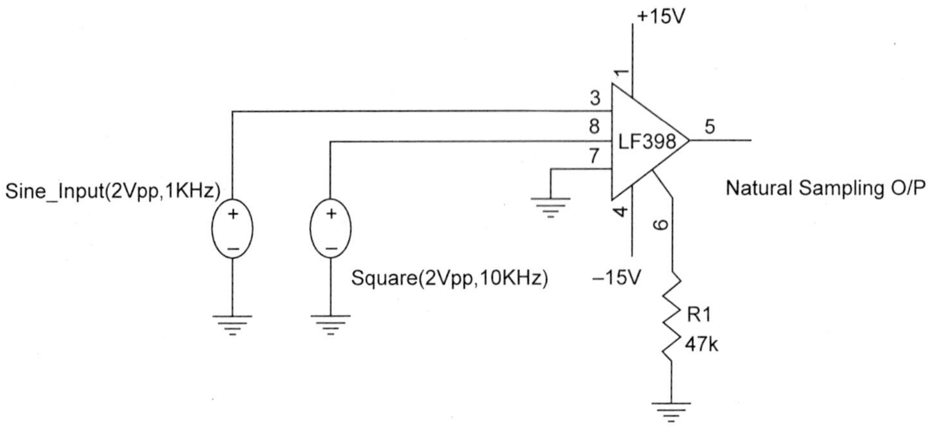

Figure: Natural Sampling

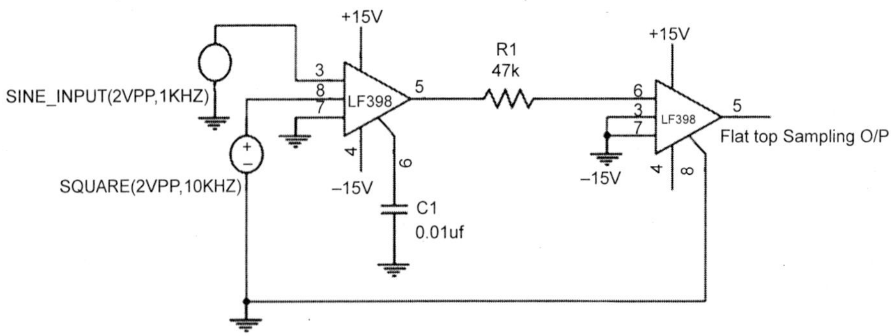

Figure: Flat Top Sampling

PROCEDURE

For flat top sampling, first circuit is connected as per the circuit diagram. Apply sinusoidal signal of 1KHz and amplitude 2Vp-p at pin no. 3of first IC and square wave of frequency 10KHz and amplitude 2Vp-p with 20% duty cycle at pin no. 8 of first IC.

Observe the natural sampled signal and flat top sampled signal at Pin no. 5 of IC LF 398 and pin no. 5 of second IC LF 398 respectively.

WAVEFORMS

Input Signal and outputs: – Below waveforms shows:-

- Input sine waveform (Yellow)
- Output waveforms :-

i. Natural sampled signal (Green)

ii. Flat Top Sampled signal (Blue)

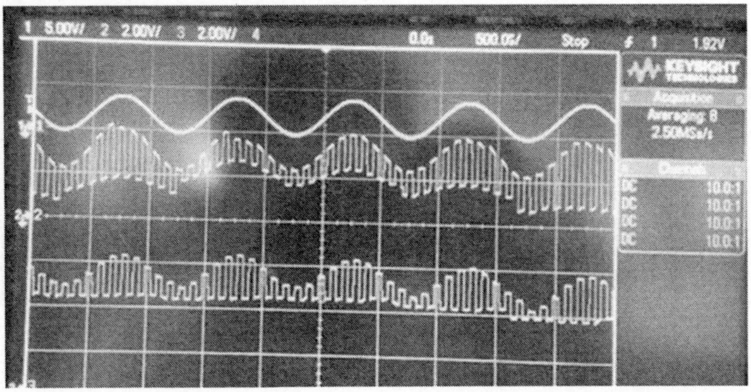

PRECAUTIONS

1. Switch off the experimental kit during making connections.
2. Set the proper amplitude and frequency of the signals to get a correct waveform.
3. All the connections should be right and tight.
4. Supply voltage should not be greater than the required otherwise IC might get damaged.
5. All the ground connections should be properly connected to avoid the distortions.

CONCLUSION

In this section we demonstrated about two types of sampling i.e. Natural Sampling and Flat Top Sampling via HW circuit.

Expt. No. 2. Verification of Sampling Theorem

Aim: To verify the sampling theorem.

Theory:

The analog signal can be converted to a discrete time signal by a process called sampling. The sampling theorem for a band limited signal of finite energy can be stated as,

"A band limited signal of finite energy, which has no frequency component higher than W Hz is completely

described by specifying the values of the signal at instants of time separated by 1/2W seconds."
It can be recovered from knowledge of samples taken at the rate of 2W per second.

Circuit Diagram:

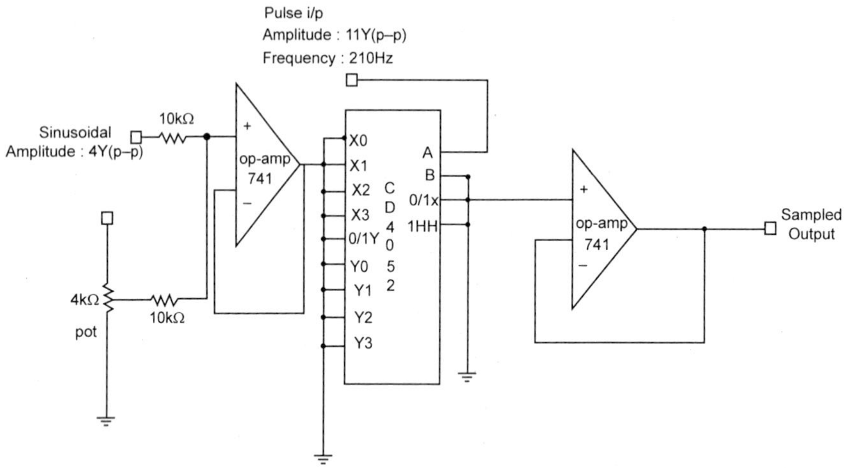

Figure: Sampling Circuit

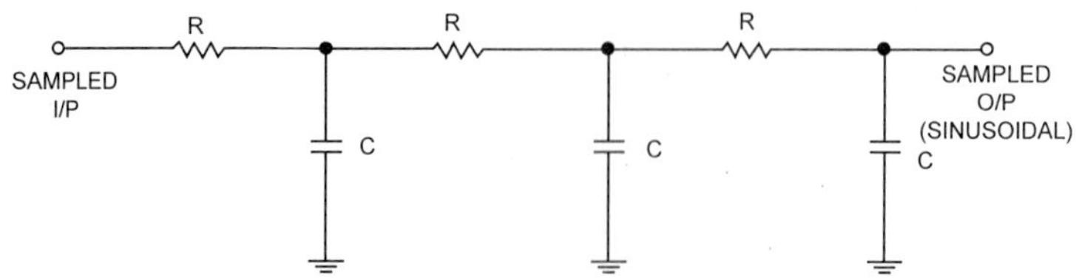

Figure: Reconstructing Circuit

PROCEDURE:

1. The circuit is connected as per the circuit diagram shown in the figure.
2. Switch on the power supply. And set at +11V and -11V.
3. Apply the sinusoidal signal of approximately 4V (p-p) at 105 Hz frequency and pulse signal of 11V (p-p) with frequency between 100Hz and 4 KHz.
4. Connect the sampling circuit output and AF signal to the two inputs of oscilloscope
5. Initially set the potentiometer to minimum level and sampling frequency to 200Hz and observe the output on the CRO. Now by adjusting the potentiometer, vary the amplitude of modulating signal and observe the output of sampling circuit. Note that the amplitude of the sampling pulses will be varying in accordance with the amplitude of the modulating signal.
6. Design the reconstructing circuit. Depending on sampling frequency, R & C values are calculated using the relations Fs = 1/Ts, Ts = RC. Choosing an appropriate value for C, R can be found using the relation R=Ts/C

7. Connect the sampling circuit output to the reconstructing circuit shown in Figure.
8. Observe the output of the reconstructing circuit (AF signal) for different sampling frequencies. The original AF signal would appear only when the sampling frequency is 200Hz or more.

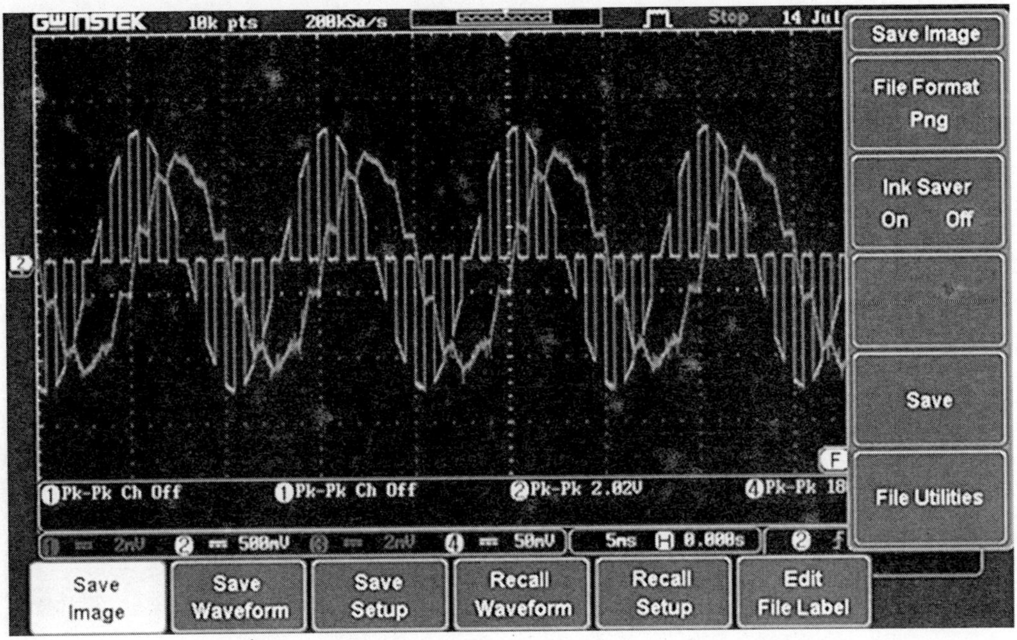

Figure: Sampling and reconstruction output (for fs=2fm)

Note: Verify the sampling conditions, fs<2fm, fs=2fm and fs>2fm.

Result Analysis:

Expt. No. 3. PWM and PPM: Generation

Aim: To generate the pulse width modulated and demodulated signals

Theory:

Pulse Time Modulation is also known as Pulse Width Modulation or Pulse Length Modulation. In PWM, the samples of the message signal are used to vary the duration of the individual pulses. Width may be varied by varying the time of occurrence of leading edge, the trailing edge or both edges of the pulse in accordance with modulating wave. It is also called Pulse Duration Modulation.

In Pulse Position Modulation, both the pulse amplitude and pulse duration are held constant but the position of the pulse is varied in proportional to the sampled values of the message signal. Pulse time modulation is a class of signaling techniques that encodes the sample values of an analog signal on to the time axis of a digital signal and it is analogous to angle modulation techniques. The two main types of PTM are PWM and PPM. In PPM the analog sample value determines the position of a narrow pulserelative to the clocking time. In PPM rise time of pulse decides the channel bandwidth. It has low noiseinterference.

Circuit Diagram:

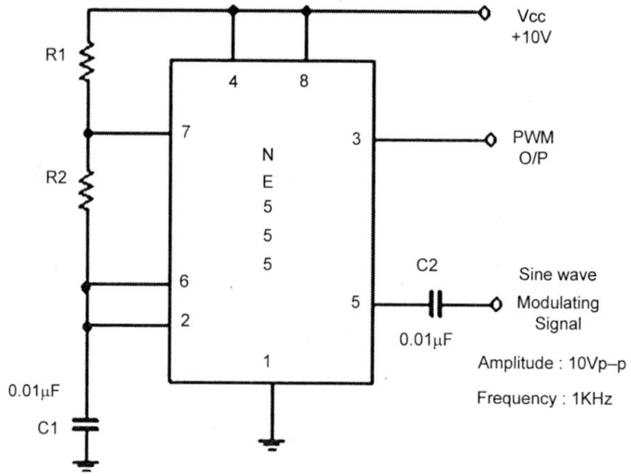

Figure: Circuit diagram for Pulse width modulation (PWM)

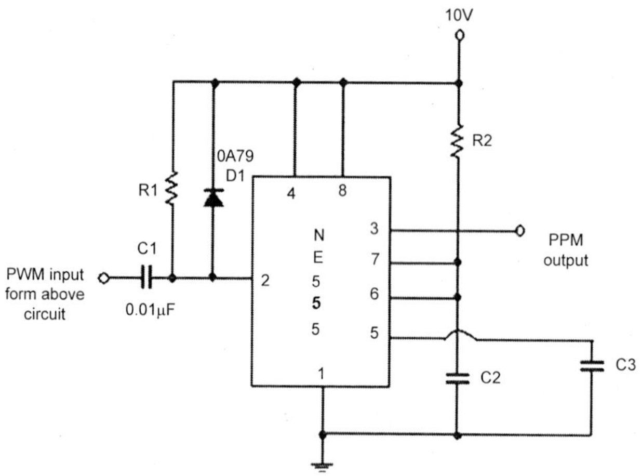

Figure: Circuit diagram for Pulse Position modulation (PPM)

Procedure for PWM:

1. Connect the circuit as per circuit diagram shown in figure.
2. Apply a sinusoidal signal as shown in the circuit diagram.
3. Observe the PWM signal at the pin3.

Procedure for PPM:

1. Connect the circuit as per circuit diagram shown in figure.
2. Apply a PWM signal as input to PPM circuit as shown in the figure.
3. Observe the PPM signal at the pin 3.

Expected waveform

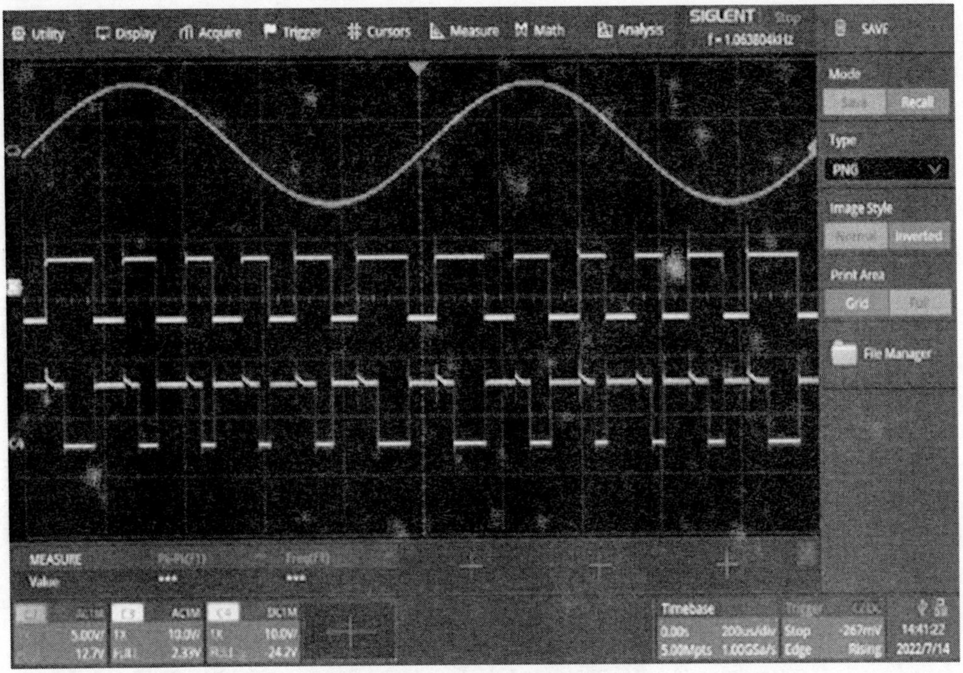

Figure: PWM and PPM outputs

Observations for PWM:

S.No.	Control voltage (VP-P)	Output pulse width(m sec)

Max pulse duration: ______________ Min pulse duration: ________

Observations for PPM:

Modulating signal Amplitude (Vp-p)	Time period(ms)		Total Time period(ms)
	Pulse width ON (ms)	Pulse width OFF (ms)	

Result analysis

Expt. No. 4. Time Division Multiplexing (TDM)

Aim: To design, set up and study the working of a two-channel time division multiplexer.

Components and equipment required: IC $\mu A741$, Transistors SL100 and SK100, resistors, signal generator, CRO, breadboard, power supply and connecting wires.

Theory: The cost of communication line or channel is often very high and therefore it is desired to send many information on the same channel. The scheme for sending several information over a single channel such that signals can be separated at the receiver end without distortion is known as multiplexing. So, the term multiplexing refers to the sharing of communications resource.

In TDM, a set of switches operates at the transmitter in synchronism with another set of switches at the receiver. Switches at the transmitter sample the input signals and send them to the receiver through a channel. Switches at the receiver direct the signals to the corresponding lines.

Circuit Diagram:

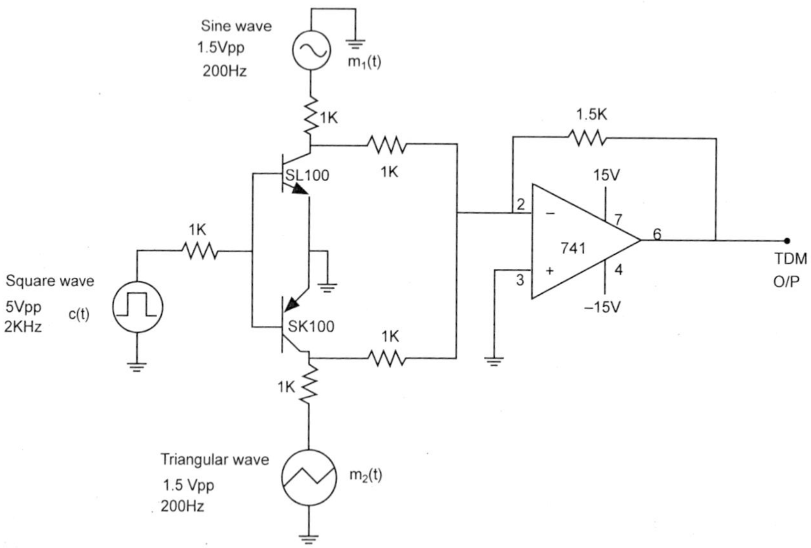

Figure: TDM modulation Circuit

Above figure shows the TDM circuit. It uses complementary transistors SL100 (n-p-n) and SK100 (p-n-p) and an op-amp adder. During positive voltage of c(t), SL100 turns ON and message signal m1(t) gets grounded and message signal m2(t) appears at the input of adder and at the op-amp output. During negative cycle of c(t), SK100 turns ON and message signal m2(t) gets grounded and message signal m1(t) appears at the input of adder and at op-amp output.

Demultiplexer Circuit: Below figure shows the demultiplexer. This circuit works in similar manner.

Circuit Diagram:

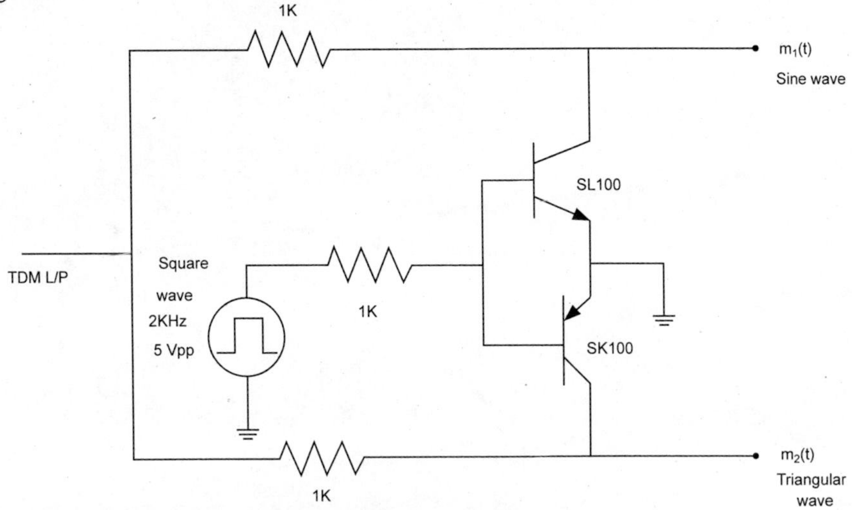

Figure: TDM Demodulation Circuit

Expected Waveforms:

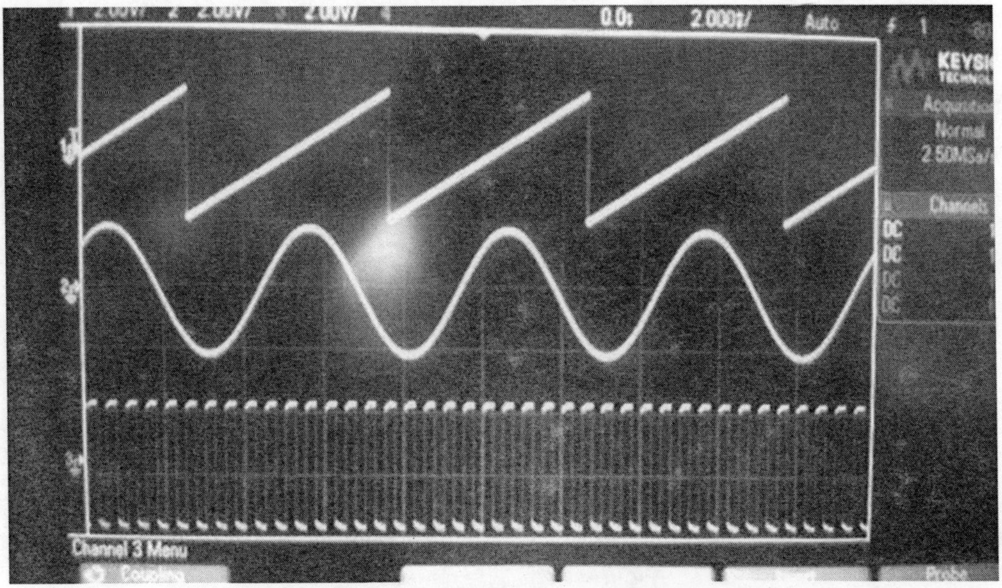

Figure: Three input waveforms m2(t), m1(t) and c(t)

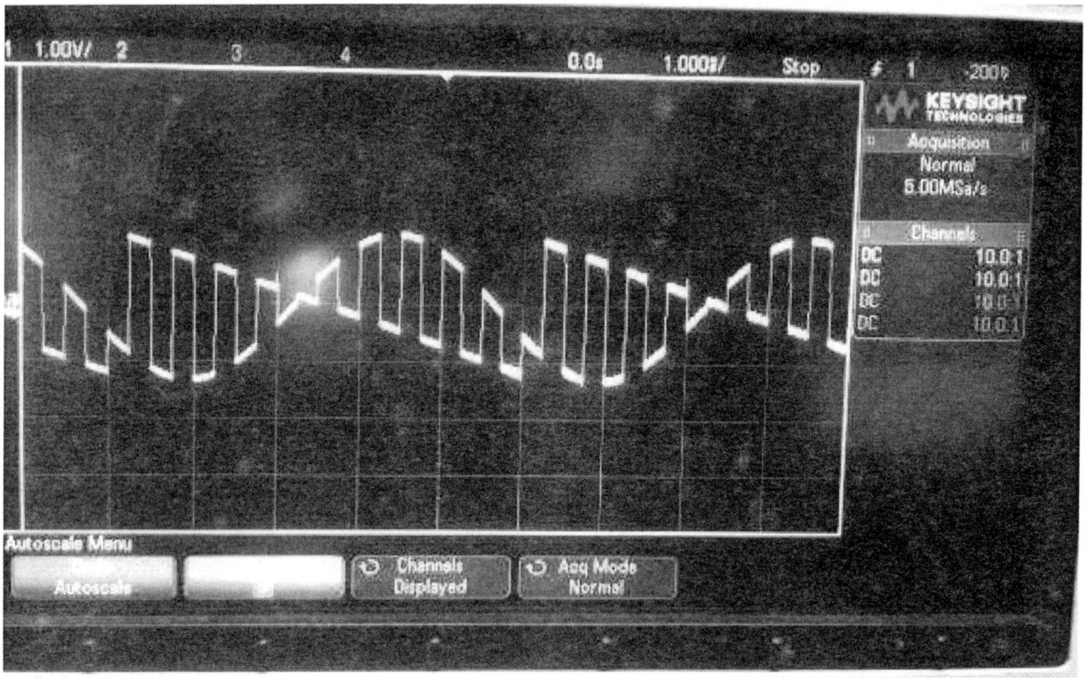

Figure: TDM output

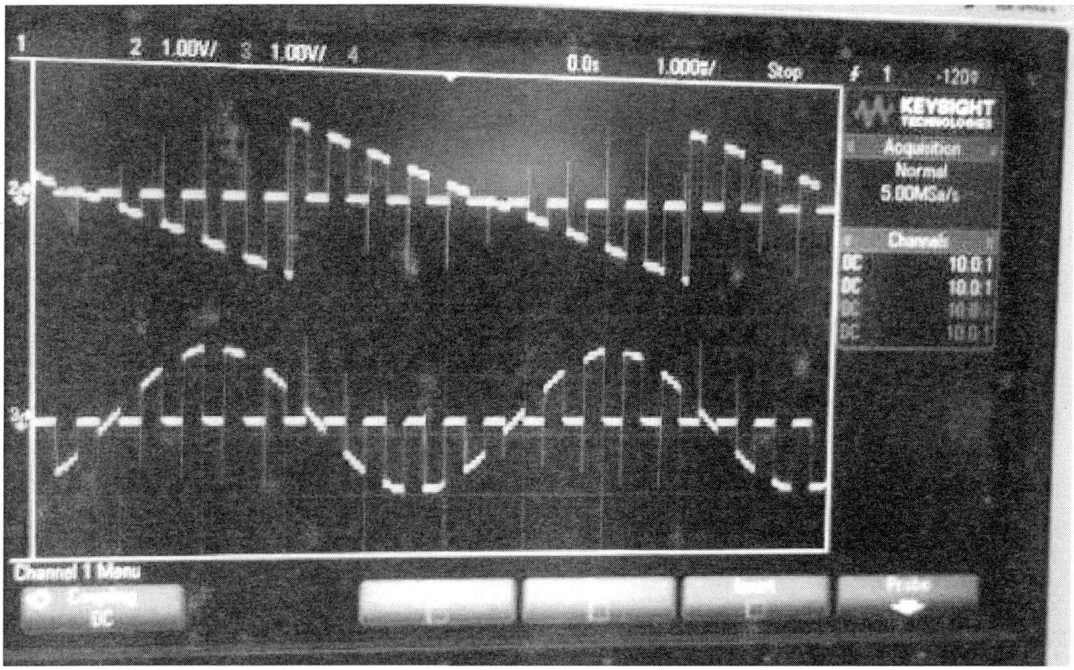

Figure: Demultiplexer output

Procedure:

1. Connections are given as per the circuit diagram 8.1. Both the signals are given as shown in the circuit diagram. (Keep 1.5Vpp for m1(t), m2(t) and 5 Vpp for c(t))
2. The TDM signal is obtained at the output.
3. Connect the TDM output to the demodulator circuit as shown in figure.
4. The TDM demodulated signal is obtained at the output.
5. Observe the outputs and draw the waveform.

Result Analysis

Expt. No. 5. Amplitude Shift Keying (ASK)

Aim: To design, implement and study the working of ASK modulator and demodulator.

Components and equipment required: IC μA741, IC74164, IC7486, Transistor SL100, Diode 1N4001, 10K potentiometer, resistors, capacitor, signal generator, CRO, breadboard, power supply and connecting wires.

Theory: In the binary ASK system, two carriers having different amplitudes are transmitted corresponding to the binary inputs. When the input is at logic 1, a finite number of cycles of a sinusoidal signal are generated and when the input is at logic 0, same number of cycles of sinusoidal signal having different amplitude are generated.

On-Off Keying (OOK) is a special case of binary ASK. As its name implies, there are only two signal states for an OOK signal and one of them is of zero magnitude. The OOK signal appears like that shown in below figure.

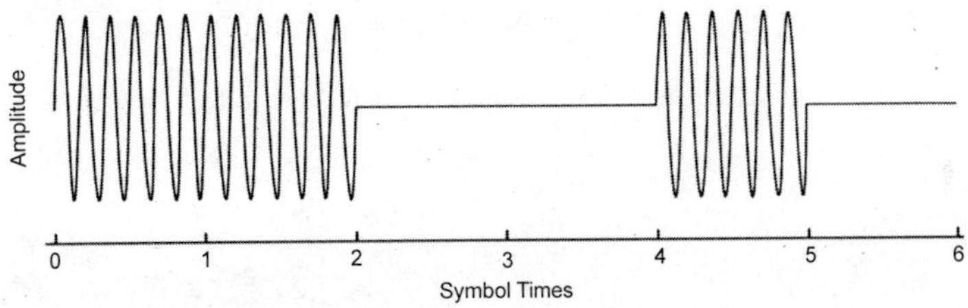

In this experiment you are going to implement OOK modulator and demodulator.

OOK Modulator:

Unipolar binary NRZ data signal (this mimics the sampled and quantized real time analog message signal) is produced using a PN sequence generator. The below shown circuit is used to generate a PN sequence of length 15. Clock frequency is set at 300Hz.

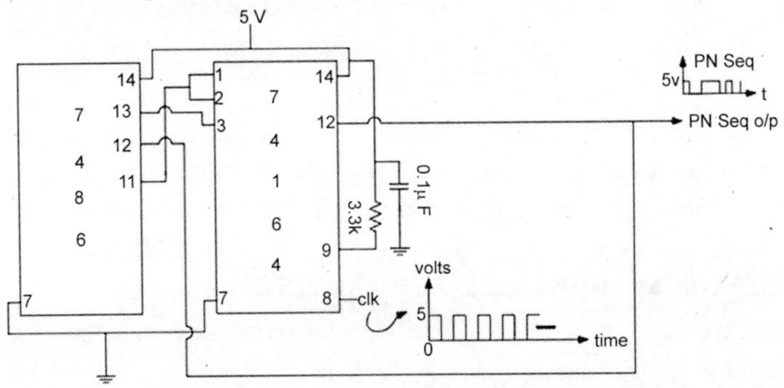

Figure: PN Sequence generator circuit

Transistor SL100 is used as a switch to make on and off a carrier according to binary 1 and 0 input obtained from a PN sequence. For a binary 1 (or logic High), SL100 is ON and you can observe the carrier at output. For a binary 0 (or logic Low), transistor is off and nothing is observed at output. Thus, carrier is made ON and OFF according to input binary data signal. The modulator circuit diagram is shown below.

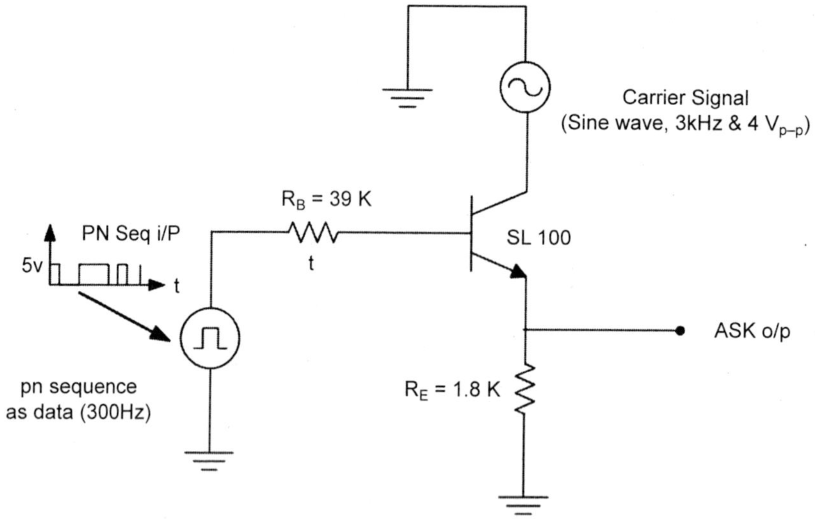

Figure: OOK Modulator

Demodulator Circuit: Consider the circuit diagram for OOK demodulator shown below.

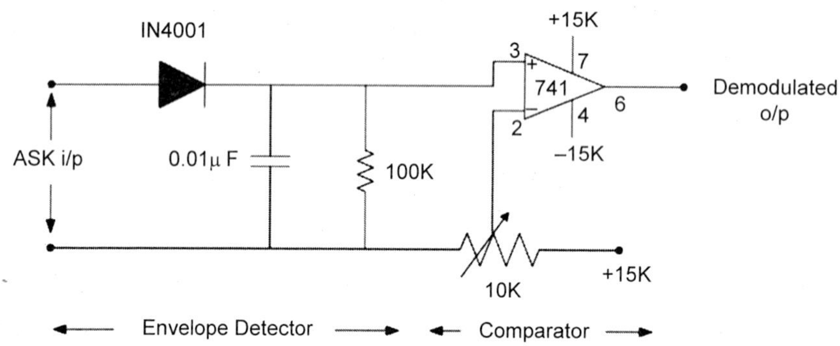

Figure: OOK Demodulator

It is an envelope detector constituted by a resistor and capacitor followed by a comparator employing 741 op-amp. Capacitor charges to the positive peak of sine wave half cycle through diode and discharges through resistor. Before discharging fully, next peak appears and capacitor charges further. The obtained low frequency irregular-shaped square wave is converted to a original data sequence by the comparator using IC 741 op-amp. Potentiometer is used to adjust the reference voltage.

Design: Modulating frequency = fm = 300Hz; Carrier frequency = fc = 3KHz.

The envelope detector should satisfy: $1\ fc < RC < 1\ fm$

In the above circuit RC is taken as one milli second.

Expected Waveforms:

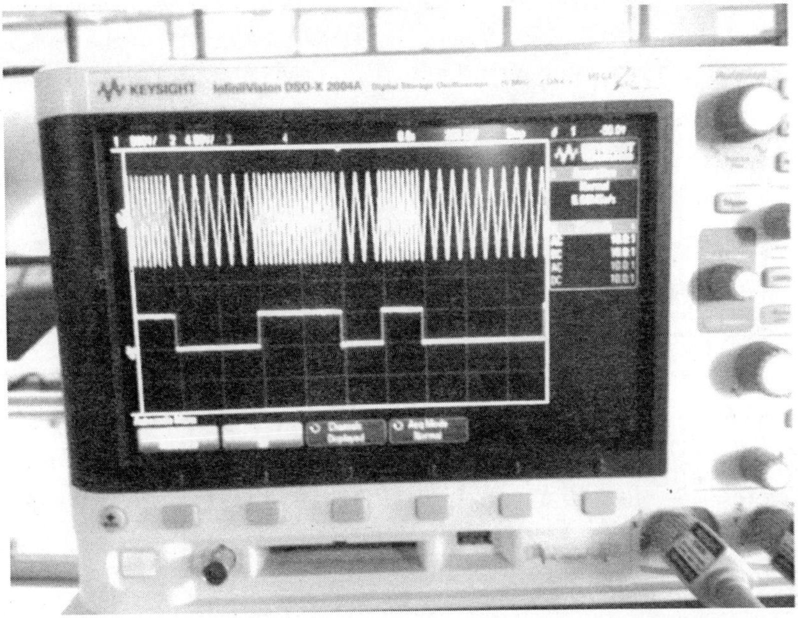

Figure: Modulated, message and demodulated waveforms

Procedure:

1. Design the transistor switching circuit to generate OOK waveform.
2. Apply the sinusoidal carrier signal of 3KHz and 4V peak-to-peak.
3. Apply the data/message/modulating signal (PN sequence) of 300Hz and 5V.
4. Demodulate the OOK signal using envelope detector and comparator. Compare the transmitted message signal and demodulated signal.

Precautions:

1. Switch off the power supply during making connections.
2. Set the proper amplitude and frequency of the signals to get a correct waveform.
3. All the connections should be tight.
4. Supply voltage should not be greater than the required otherwise components might get damaged.
5. All the ground connections should be properly connected to avoid the distortions.

Result: Designed and tested a OOK modulator and demodulator circuit and studied its functioning. Relevant waveforms are sketched.

Expt. No. 6. Binary Phase Shift Keying (BPSK)

Aim: To design, set up and study the working of Binary Phase Shift Keying (BPSK) modulator and demodulator circuits.

Components and equipment required: IC μA741, CD4052, IC74164, IC7486, Diode 1N4007, resistors, capacitor, signal generator, CRO, breadboard, power supply and connecting wires.

Theory: In binary phase shift keying, the binary bits 1 and 0 modulate the phase of the carrier. Let the carrier signal for transmitting the binary bit 1 be $s1(t) = A\sin(2\pi fct)$. For the transmission of bit 0, phase of the carrier is shifted by an amount of 1800. So $s2(t) = A\sin(2\pi fct + \pi) = -A\sin(2\pi fct)$. Since the message is embedded in the phase of the carrier, only coherent detection is applicable for PSK systems.

The BPSK signal appears like that shown in below figure.

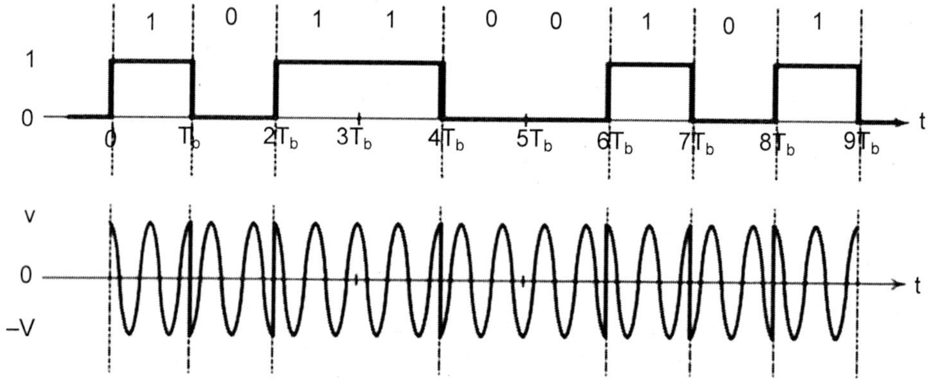

In this experiment you are going to implement BPSK modulator and demodulator.

BPSK Modulator:

Unipolar binary NRZ data signal (this mimics the sampled and quantized real time analog message signal) is produced using a PN sequence generator. The below shown circuit is used to generate a PN sequence of length 15. Clock frequency is set at 200Hz.

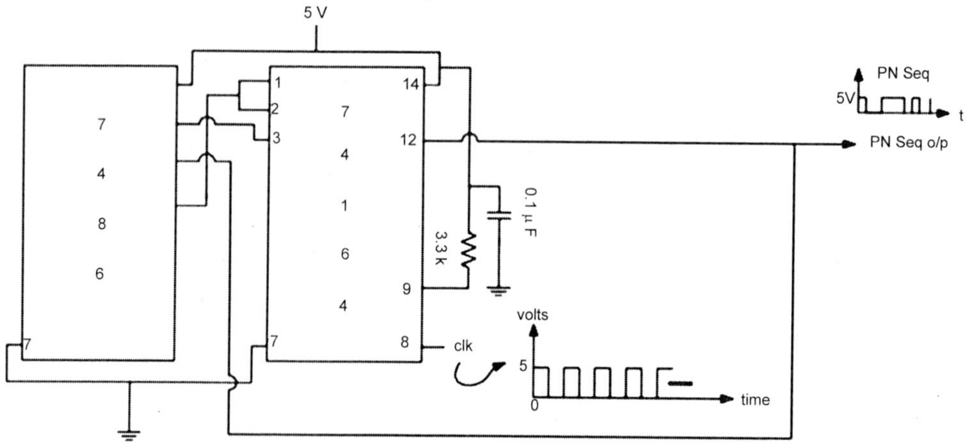

Figure: PN Sequence generator circuit

The modulator circuit mainly consists of a unity gain op-amp inverting amplifier and two analog switches implemented using CD4052. The CD4052 is a dual single-pole 4-channel analog/digital switch suitable for use in analog or digital 4:1 multiplexer/demultiplexer applications. Each switch features four independent inputs/outputs and a common input/output. A digital inhibit input (INH) and two digital select inputs (A and B) are common to both switches. When INH is HIGH, the switches are turned off. These multiplexer chips are ideal for switching serial input/outputs between different sources.

A carrier with 00 phase is obtained from signal generator. Unity gain inverting amplifier provides 1800 phase-shift to the carrier signal. Thus, two carrier signals are applied to the inputs (pin no. 11 & 12) of CD4052. The binary bit stream (i.e., data from PN sequence generator) is applied to the control inputs (also called channel select, pin no. 9 & 10) of CD4052. Thus, one of the carriers is enabled and appears at the output (pin no. 13) in each bit interval according to whether bit 1 or bit 0 occurs at the control input.

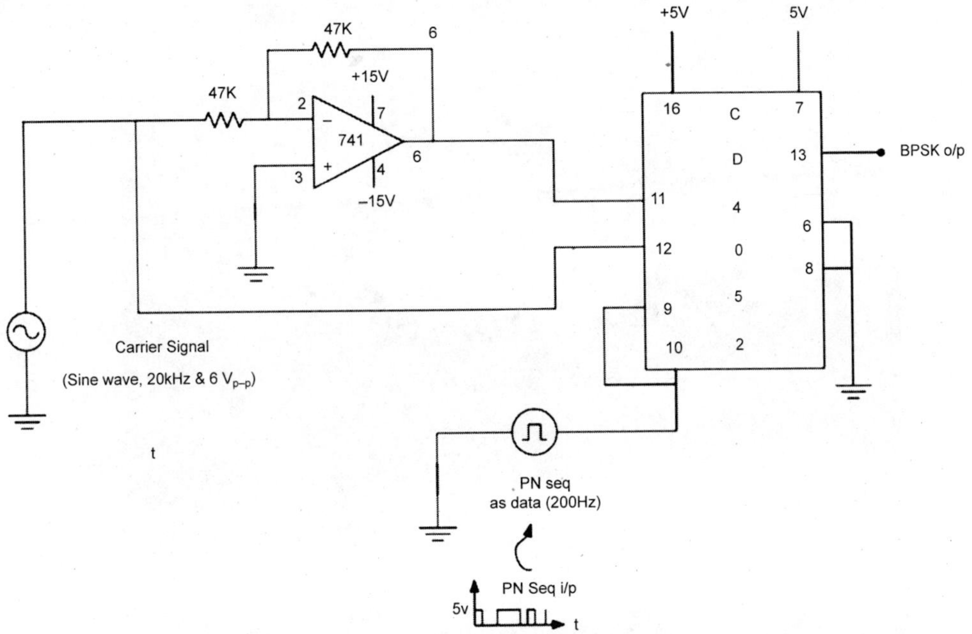

Figure: BPSK Modulator

Demodulator Circuit: Consider the circuit diagram for BPSK demodulator shown below.

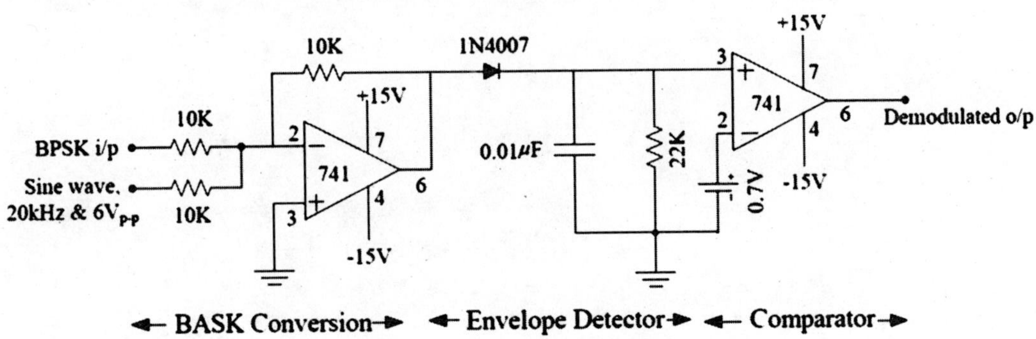

Figure: BPSK Demodulator

BPSK signal can be demodulated by converting it to BASK signal and then by using an envelope detector. The original carrier signal is added with BPSK signal using op-amp summer to obtain BASK signal. BASK signal is further demodulated using an envelope detector. The output of the envelope detector may not be square-shaped pulses. Therefore, the demodulated signal is converted to a square-shaped pulses with the help of a comparator.

Design: Modulating frequency = fm = 200Hz; Carrier frequency = fc = 20KHz.

The envelope detector should satisfy: $1fc < RC < 1fm$

In the above circuit RC is taken as 0.22 milli second.

Expected Waveforms:

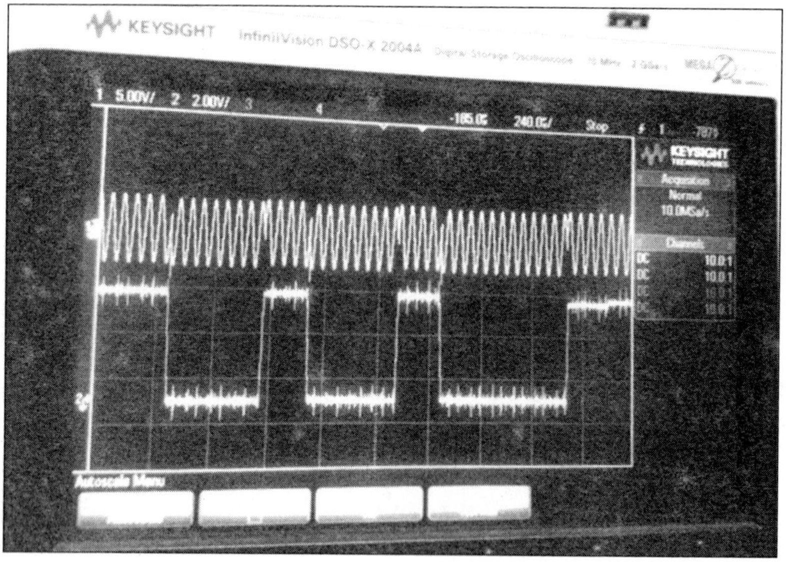

Figure: BPSK modulated waveform.

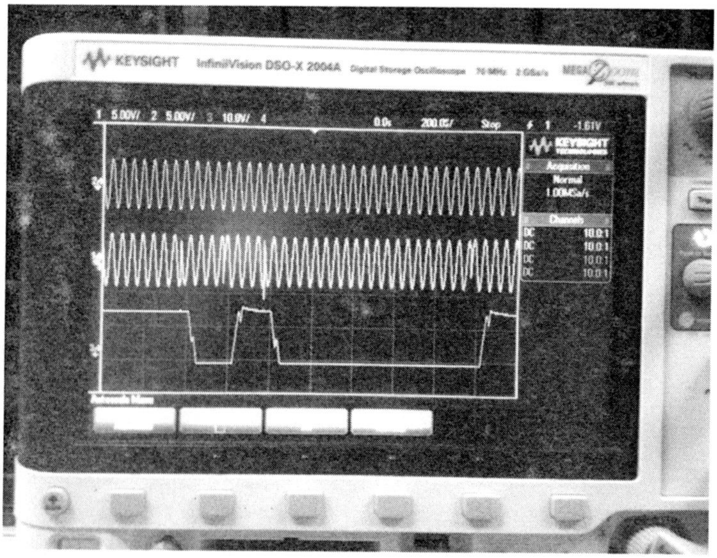

Figure: Demodulated message sequence

Procedure:

1. Set up the circuit after verifying the components.
2. Apply the sinusoidal carrier signal of 20KHz and 6V peak-to-peak.
3. Apply the data/message/modulating signal (PN sequence) of 200Hz and 5V.
4. Observe BPSK waveform on CRO screen.
5. Set up the demodulator circuit and apply BPSK input and observe the output.

Precautions:

1. Switch off the power supply during making connections.
2. Set the proper amplitude and frequency of the signals to get a correct waveform.
3. All the connections should be tight.
4. Supply voltage should not be greater than the required otherwise components might get damaged.
5. All the ground connections should be properly connected to avoid the distortions.

Result: Designed and tested a BPSK modulator and demodulator circuit and studied its functioning. Relevant waveforms are sketched.

Expt. No. 7. Binary Frequency Shift Keying (BFSK)

Aim: To design, set up and study the working of a Binary Frequency Shift Keying (BFSK) modulator and demodulator circuits.

Components and equipment required: IC μA741, IC74164, IC7486, Transistors SL100 & SK100, Diode OA79 (Germanium), potentiometers, resistors, capacitors, signal generator, CRO, breadboard, power supply and connecting wires.

Theory: BFSK is the simplest form of frequency modulation scheme for digital data transmission. This scheme uses a pair of discrete frequencies to transmit binary information. With this scheme, the bit 1 is transmitted by using mark frequency and bit 0 is by space frequency.

The BFSK signal appears like that shown in below figure.

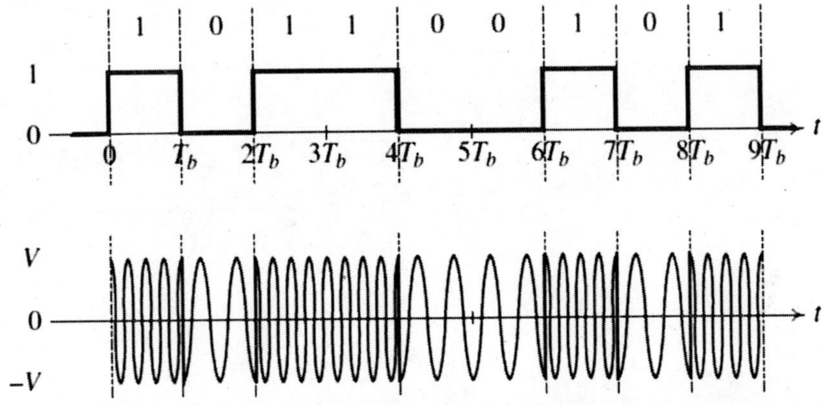

In this experiment you are going to implement BFSK modulator and demodulator.

BFSK Modulator:

The most basic method of generating BFSK is to switch two oscillators with the modulating signal, as illustrated in below figure.

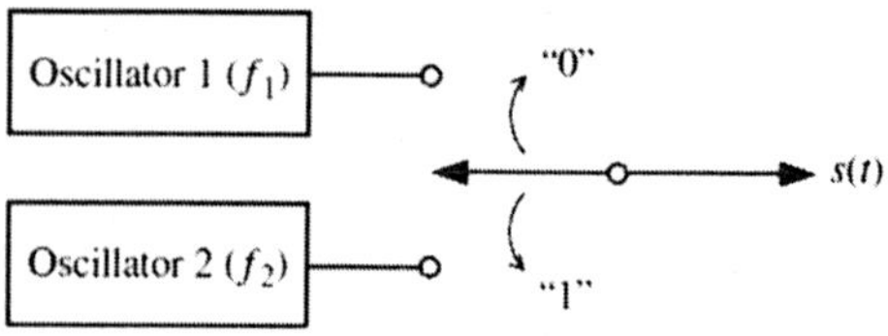

Unipolar binary NRZ data signal (this mimics the sampled and quantized real time analog message signal) is produced using a PN sequence generator. The below shown circuit is used to generate a PN sequence of length 15. Clock frequency is set at 250Hz.

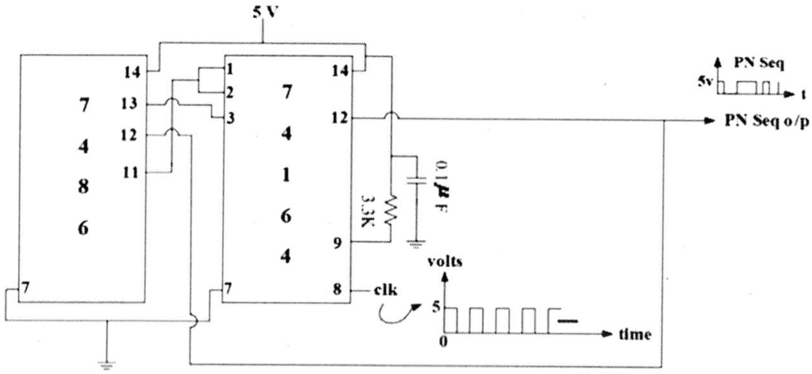

Figure: PN Sequence generator circuit

The circuit diagram for BFSK modulator is shown in below figure.

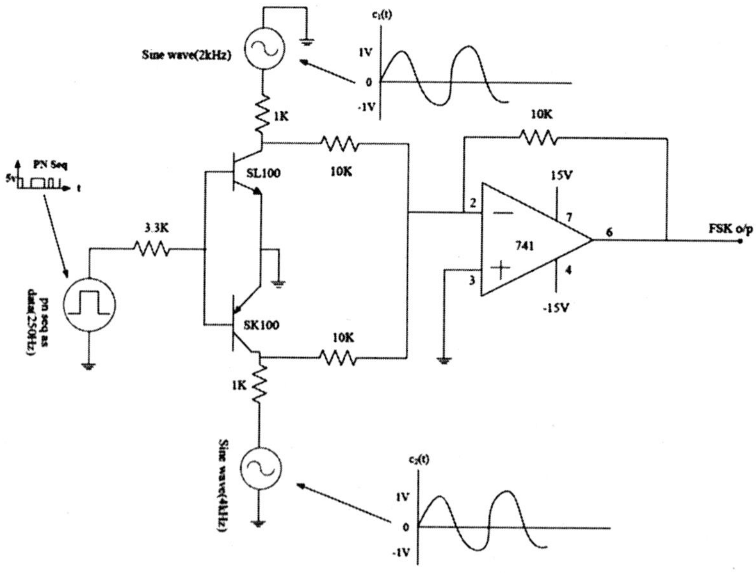

Figure: BFSK modulator

It uses two complementary transistors. When the input binary signal is set at logic 1 state, carrier signal $c1(t)$ is shorted to the ground and signal $c2(t)$ reaches at the input pin of op-amp. Similarly, when the input binary signal is at 0 state, carrier signal $c2(t)$ is shorted to the ground and signal $c1(t)$ reaches at the input of op-amp. Output of the op-amp adder gives you the BFSK signal.

Demodulator Circuit:

Consider the circuit diagram for BFSK demodulator shown below.

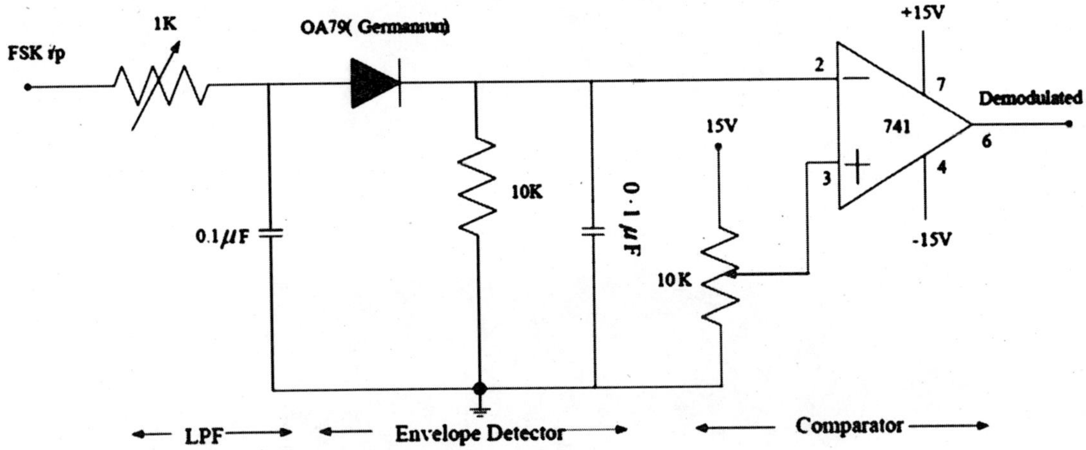

Figure: BFSK Demodulator

Basic idea of demodulator is to retrieve the binary data stream corresponding to distinct frequencies. The above shown circuit consists of three parts: Low pass filter, Envelope detector and Comparator. The low pass filter is tuned to the frequency of either 0 or 1 (here carrier frequency of either 2KHz or 4KHz). The cut-off frequency is given by $fc = 1\ 2\pi RC$. Here, I have fixed the capacitor value to 0.1μF and resistance value can be adjusted using 1K potentiometer. This filter passes the selected frequency and rejects the other. The output is then passed through an Envelope Detector circuit and the output is now above zero volts only.

Here, modulating frequency = fm = 250Hz; Carrier frequency is either 2KHz or 4KHz.

The envelope detector should satisfy: $1fc < RC < 1fm$

In the above circuit RC is taken as one milli second. Next, the waveform reaches at the input of comparator consists of 0 volt corresponding to low frequency signal and a dc voltage corresponding to high frequency signal. Comparator generates a square-shaped pulses with amplitude 0 to 5V. A potentiometer is provided at the noninverting terminal of the op-amp to set the threshold voltage.

Note: The diode OA79 is a Germanium point contact diode. Point contact diodes offer low junction capacitance. Thus, the charge storage at the junction is low. Ordinary rectifier diode fails in the rectification of high frequency signal.

Expected Waveforms:

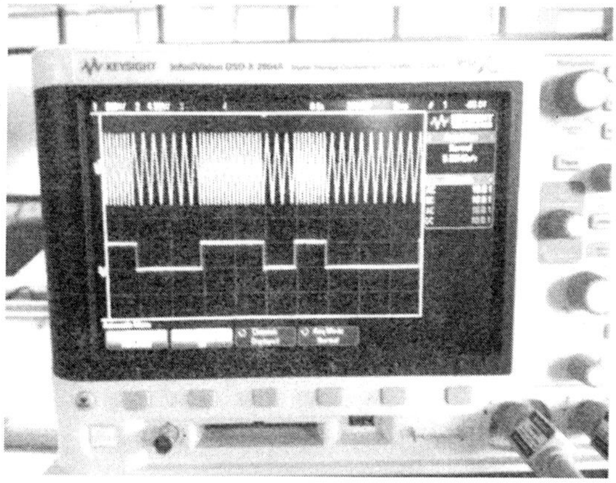

Figure: BFSK modulated waveform.

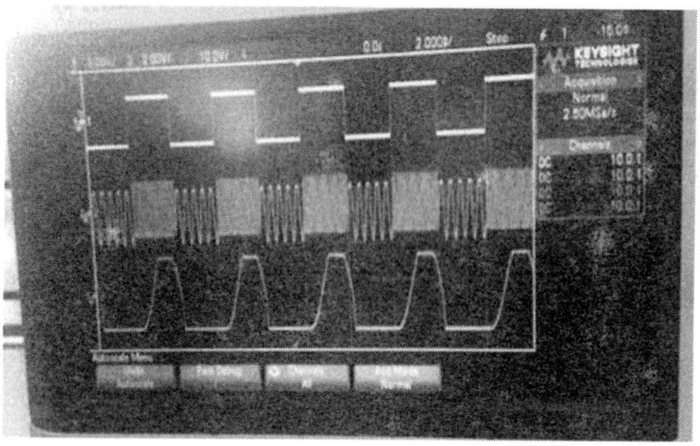

Figure: Demodulated message sequence

Procedure:

1. Set up the circuit after verifying the components.
2. Apply the sinusoidal carrier signal of 2KHz and 4KHz with 2V peak-to-peak.
3. Apply the data/message/modulating signal (PN sequence) of 250Hz and 5V.
4. Observe BFSK waveform on CRO screen.
5. Set up the demodulator circuit and apply BFSK input and observe the output.

Precautions:

1. Switch off the power supply during making connections.
2. Set the proper amplitude and frequency of the signals to get a correct waveform.
3. All the connections should be tight.
4. Supply voltage should not be greater than the required otherwise components might get damaged.
5. All the ground connections should be properly connected to avoid the distortions.

Result: Designed and tested a BFSK modulator and demodulator circuit and studied its functioning. Relevant waveforms are sketched.

Expt. No. 8. Quadrature Phase Shift Keying (QPSK)

Aim: To design, set up and study the working of a Quadrature Phase Shift Keying (QPSK) modulator circuit.

Components and equipment required: IC LM353, CD4052, IC74164, IC7486, resistors, capacitor, signal generator, CRO, breadboard, power supply and connecting wires.

Theory: In BPSK the phase of the carrier is shifted 0 or 180 degrees every bit period, depending on the information bit being a 1 or 0. Thus each modulated carrier pulse transmits 1 bit of information. If, on the other hand, the modulation scheme can use phase shifts of 0, 90, 180, or 270 degrees, each modulated carrier pulse transmits two bits of information. This technique is called quadrature phase shift keying (QPSK). Using QPSK, we can double the data rate when compared to BPSK over a channel of the same bandwidth. QPSK is one of the modulation methods in the family known as quadrature modulation schemes that are popular in satellite, cellular, and telecom modem applications.

The QPSK signal appears like that shown in below figure.

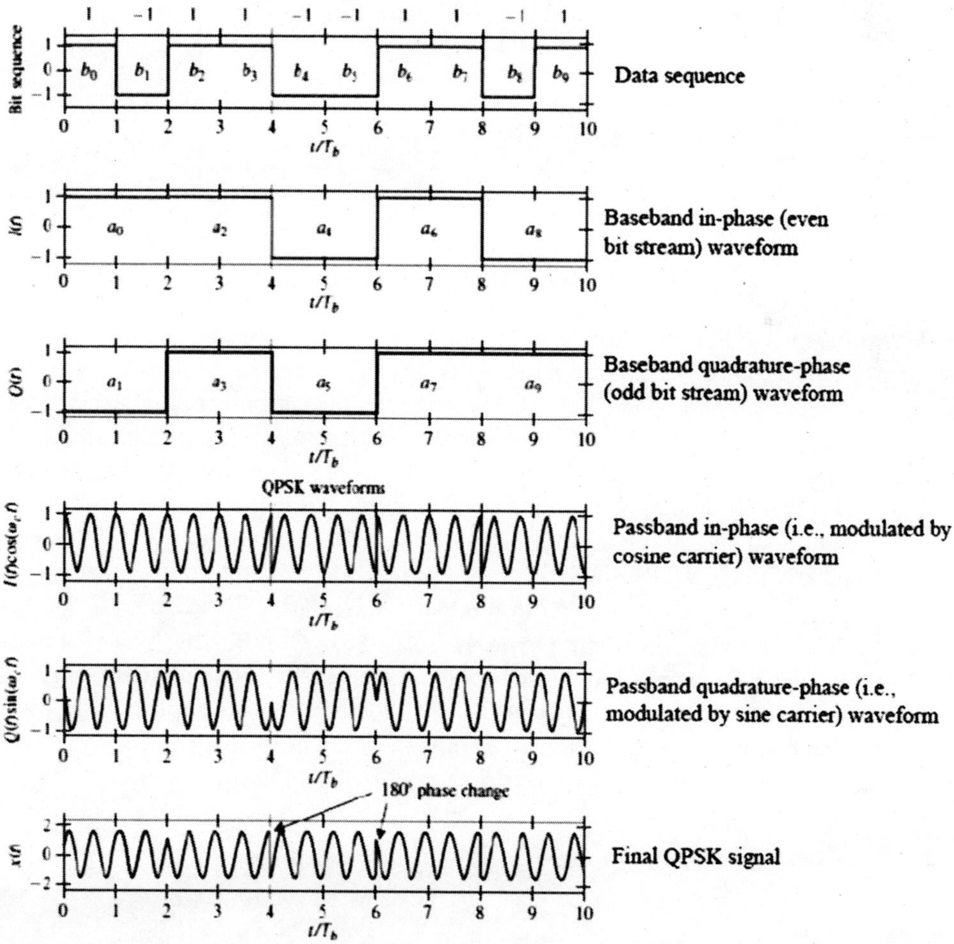

In this experiment you are going to implement QPSK modulator.

QPSK Modulator:

Unipolar binary NRZ data signal (this mimics the sampled and quantized real time analog message signal) is produced using a PN sequence generator. Clock frequency is set at 200Hz. In QPSK, two bits form a symbol (i.e., 00, 01, 10, and 11). Strictly speaking, we have to use two different PN sequence generators of same length to get symbols. But here, in order to reduce the hardware complexity, second PN sequence is obtained as the time shifted version of the first sequence. The below shown circuit is used to generate two PN sequences of length 15.

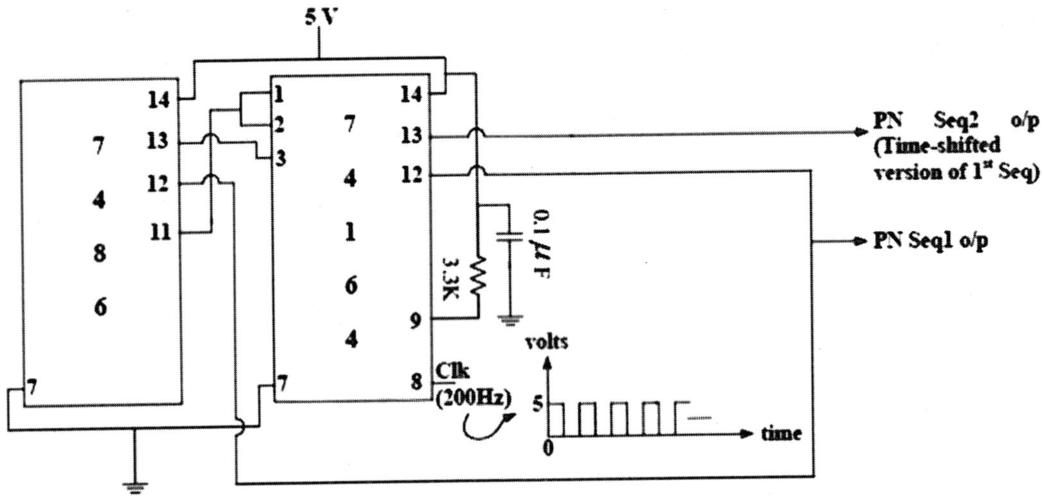

Figure: PN Sequence generator to produce symbols

Next, four different symbols are modulated by four sinusoidal carrier signals with phase shifts of 0, 90, 180, or 270 degrees. This is achieved by dual op-amp IC LM353. This IC is used as unity gain inverting amplifier and 900 phase-shifter (all pass filter) to get the various phase shifts. The switching of these four carriers in accordance with four different data symbols is achieved using CD4052. The CD4052 is a dual single-pole 4- channel analog/digital switch suitable for use in analog or digital 4:1 multiplexer/demultiplexer applications. Each switch features four independent inputs/outputs and a common input/output. A digital inhibit input (INH) and two digital select inputs (A and B) are common to both switches. When INH is HIGH, the switches are turned off. These multiplexer chips are ideal for switching serial input/outputs between different sources.

Four carrier signals are applied to input pin no. 1, 2, 4, and 5 of CD4052. The binary bit stream (i.e., data from two PN sequences) is applied to the control inputs (also called channel select, pin no. 9 & 10) of CD4052. Thus, one of the carriers is enabled at each symbol duration and appears at the output (pin no. 3). The circuit diagram to produce QPSK waveform is shown in below figure.

All-pass filter design: The frequency where the circuit provides 900 lag is

$fc = 12\pi RC$; Here, fc = 10KHz.

Let us fix C = 0.01μF. Then, $R \approx 1.5\text{K}\Omega$.

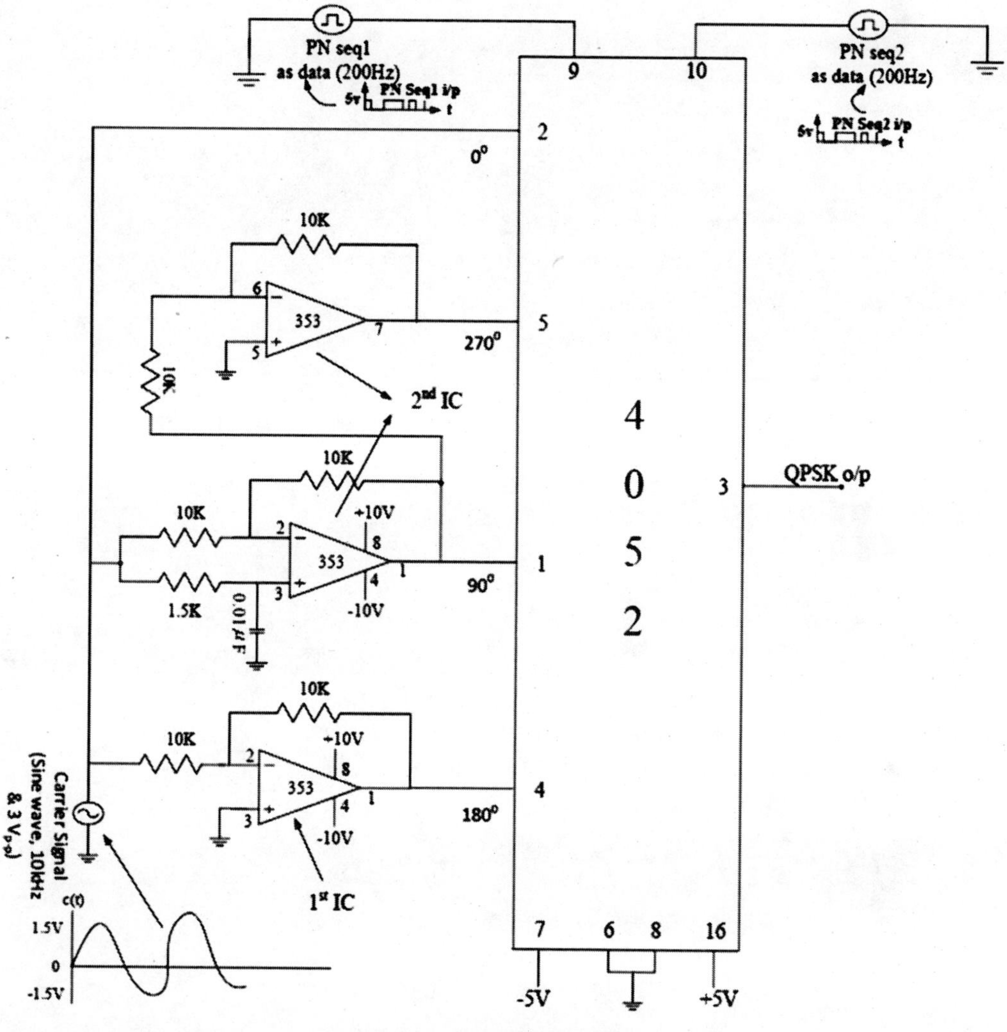

Figure: QPSK Modulator

Expected Waveforms:

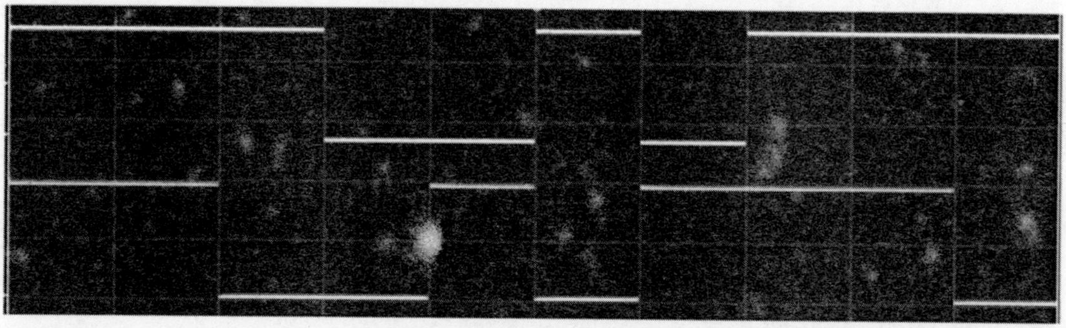

Figure: Two PN sequences

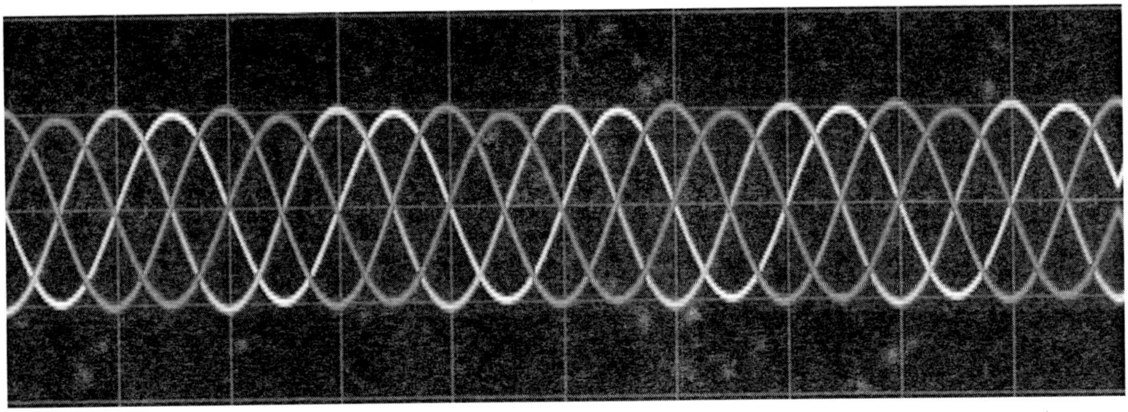

Figure: Four carrier signals with phase shift of 0°, 90°, 180°, and 270°

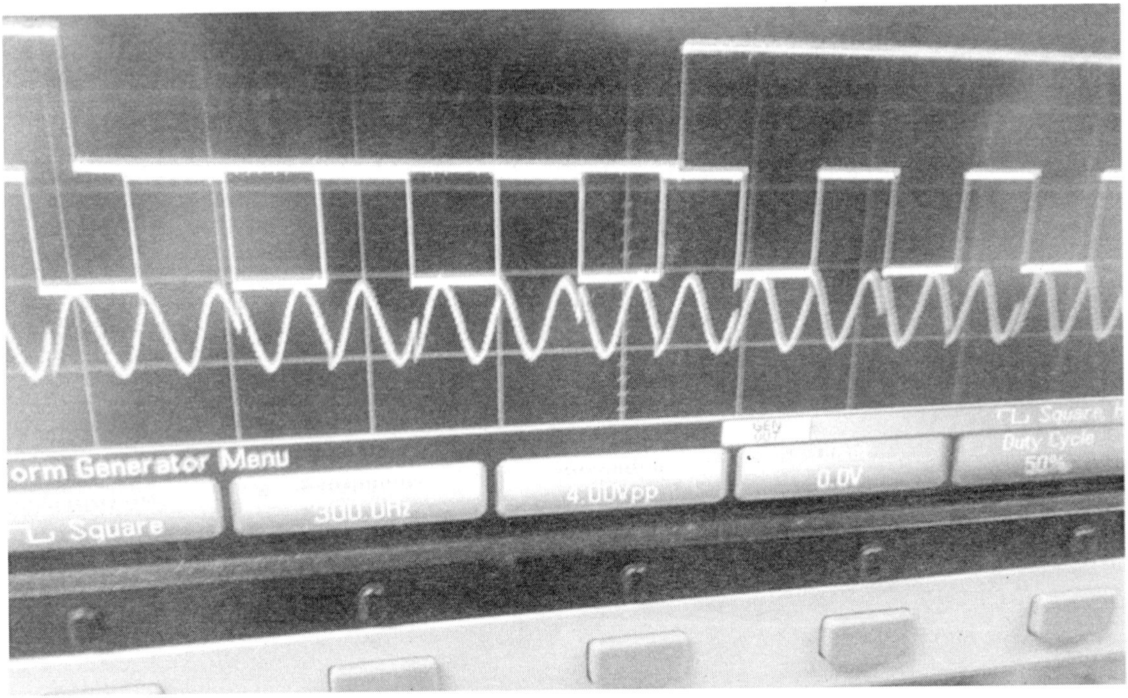

Figure: QPSK waveform

Procedure:

1. Set up the circuit after verifying the components.
2. Apply the sinusoidal carrier signal of 10KHz and 3V peak-to-peak.
3. Apply the data/message/modulating signal (PN sequence) of 200Hz and 5V.
4. Observe and sketch various phase shifted carriers.
5. Observe and sketch the QPSK modulated waveform at pin no. 3 of CD4052.

Precautions:

1. Switch off the power supply during making connections.
2. Set the proper amplitude and frequency of the signals to get a correct waveform.
3. All the connections should be tight.
4. Supply voltage should not be greater than the required otherwise components might get damaged.
5. All the ground connections should be properly connected to avoid the distortions.

Result: Designed and tested a QPSK modulator circuit and studied its functioning. Relevant waveforms are sketched.

REFERENCES FOR FURTHER READING

[1] M. Kulkarni and K. S. Shivaprakasha, "Information Theory and Coding", Wiley (India), 2015.

[2] Ranjan Bose, "Information Theory Coding and Cryptography", Tata McGraw Hill, 2007.

[3] Richerd E Blahut, "Algebraic Codes for Data Transmission", Cambridge University Press; UK, 2003.

[4] W E Ryan and S Lin, "Channel Codes: Classical and Modern", Cambridge University Press; UK, 2009.

[5] T K Moon, "Error Control Coding: Mathematical Methods and Algorithms", John Wiley and Sons, New Jersey, 2005.

[6] Haykin, Simon. "Digital Communications", John Wiley, New York, 2001.

[7] Sklar, Bernad. "Digital Communication: Functions and Applications", Prenice Hall., 1988.

[8] K. Sam Shanmugam , « Digital and Analog Communication Systems», John Wiley, New York, 2006.

[9] M. Kulkarni and Farooq Husain, "Analog and Digital Communication Systems", Umesh Publications, New Delhi, 2005.

INDEX

A- Law Companding, 31, 32, 45
Adaptive Delta Modulation (ADM), 65
Adaptive Differential Pulse Code Modulation (ADPCM), 67, 92
Adaptive Equalization, 90, 93, 95
Average Rate of Information Transmission, 180
Bandwidth, 3, 16, 36
Baseband Transmission, 6, 53, 71
Baseband Transmission Techniques, 6
BASK Receiver, 133
BCJR Decoding, 219
BFSK Modulator, 144, 299, 300
Binary Amplitude Shift Keying (BASK), 130, 136
Binary Communication Channel, 176
Binary Phase Shift Keying (BPSK) 130, 136, 266
Bipolar NRZ, 33, 34, 47
Bipolar RZ, 34, 35, 47
Channel, 2, 4, 5
Channel Capacity, 169, 182, 183
Channel Codes, 193, 221, 227
Channel Entropies, 169, 177, 179
Coherent Detection, 111, 127, 136
Communication Channels, 5, 45, 173
Communication Systems, 2, 3, 24
Concatenated Codes, 191, 206, 220
Continuous Channels, 183
Convolution Codes, 193, 207, 212
Correlation Receiver, 114, 115, 118
Correlative Coding, 53, 85, 93
Decoder, 4, 5, 25
Delta Modulation, 50, 51, 57
Differential Entropy, 172, 184
Differential Manchester, 34, 35, 47
Differential PCM (DPCM), 54
Differential PSK (DPSK), 153
Digital Communication System, 2, 3, 4
Digital Modulation, 2, 5, 126
Digital Subscriber Line, 53, 91, 92
Discrete Communication Channel, 169, 174, 175
DPCM Transmitter/Receiver, 54
Duobinary Signalling, 85
Encoder, 4, 5, 24
Energy of a Signal, 103, 104, 237
Equalization, 4, 90, 93
Error Control Coding, 191, 192, 193
Error Detecting and Correcting Capabilities, 191, 199, 200
Euclidian Distance, 104, 113, 119
Flat-Topped Sampling, 13, 14, 48
Frame Structure, 1, 37, 41
Generator Matrix, 194, 195, 196
Geometric Representation, 98, 99, 119
Gilbert–Varshamov (Gv) Bound, 203
Gram Schmidt Orthogonalization Procedure, 104, 105, 121
Hamming Bound, 203, 204, 282
Hamming Codes, 191, 206, 222
Hard Decision Decoding, 191, 203, 204
Impulse / Ideal Sampling, 8
Information Measures, 170
Inter Symbol Interference (ISI), 53, 71, 77
Likelihood Functions, 98, 110, 113
Line Codes, 4, 5, 33
Linear Block Code, 194, 199, 202
Low Bit Rate Coding, 53, 54, 69
Low Density Parity Check Codes, 221

μ- Law Companding, 45
Manchester, 34, 35, 47
M-Ary PSK (MPSK), 156
Matched Filters, 53, 71, 95
Maximum A Posteriori Probability Decoding, 112, 120
Maximum Likelihood Decoding, 98, 112, 113
Mceliece-Rodemich-Rumsey-Welch (MRRW) Bound, 203
Minimum Mean Square Estimation, 114
Minimum Shift Keying (MSK), 127, 162
Mutual Information, 169, 179, 180
Natural Sampling, 8, 10, 16
Non-Uniform/ Non-Linear Quantizers, 29
Nyquist Criterion, 7, 53, 79
Offset QPSK (OQPSK), 155
Optimum Receivers, 98, 114, 120
Parity Check Matrix (H), 195
Passband Modulation, 125, 126, 129
PCM TDM Hierarchies, 37
Polar RZ, 33, 34, 47
Power Spectral Density (PSD), 133, 134, 140
Probability of Error, 134, 142, 152
Processing Gain, 56, 95
Pulse Code Modulation, 5, 20, 67
Pulse Modulation, 1, 18, 20
Quadrature Amplitude Modulation (QAM), 127, 158, 159
Quadriphase Shift Keying (QPSK), 148
Quantization, 6, 20, 21
Receiver, 4, 5, 6
Reconstruction Circuit, 26
Reed Solomon (RS) Codes, 206
Regenerative Repeaters, 25
Sampling, 2, 6, 7
Sampling Techniques, 1, 8, 16
Sampling Theorem, 1, 7, 16
Shannon Entropy, 171
Shannon Hartley Law, 183
Signal to Noise Ratio, 46, 62, 71
Signal to Quantization Noise Ratio for Uniform Quantizer, 26
Singleton Bound,, 202
Soft Decision Decoding, 204, 205, 206
Squared Length, 103, 104, 119
Synchronisation and Bit Stuffing Mechanisms, 1, 43
Syndrome Calculation, 196, 197
TDM Digital Hierarchy, 39
Time Domain Approach, 208, 210, 211
Transform Domain Approach, 211, 212, 215
Transmitter, 4, 5, 6
Turbo Codes, 191, 220, 221
Types of TDM, 38
Uniform Sampling Theorem, 1, 7, 48
Unipolar RZ, 33, 35, 47
Viterbi Decoding, 216, 217, 224
Zero ISI, 78, 79, 80